# Coaching
# with NLP
## FOR
# DUMMIES®

# Coaching with NLP
## FOR
## DUMMIES®

**by Kate Burton**

**WILEY**

A John Wiley and Sons, Ltd, Publication

Coaching with NLP For Dummies®

Published by
**John Wiley & Sons, Ltd**
The Atrium
Southern Gate
Chichester
West Sussex
PO19 8SQ
England

Email (for orders and customer service enquires): cs-books@wiley.co.uk

Visit our Home Page on www.wileyeurope.com

Wiley also publishes its books in a variety of electronic formats. Some content that appears in print may not be available in electronic books.

British Library Cataloguing in Publication Data: A catalogue record for this book is available from the British Library.

ISBN: 978-0-470-97226-7 (paperback), 978-1-119-99166-3 (ebook), 978-0-470-97303-5 (ebook), 978-0-470-97302-8 (ebook)

Printed and bound in Great Britain by Bell and Bain Ltd

10  9  8  7  6  5  4  3  2  1

WILEY

# About the Author

**Kate Burton** is an international NLP master coach, author and workshop leader whose aim is to give all her clients the space to become consciously aware of how they truly want to live and work, and make the change they desire. She thrives on supporting people in boosting their motivation, self-awareness and confidence.

Kate's business career began in corporate advertising and marketing with Hewlett-Packard. Since then she has worked with varied businesses across industries and cultures on how they can be great communicators. What she loves most is delivering custom-built programmes. Her key corporate workshops and coaching centre on the themes of Leader as Coach, Boosting Confidence through Change, and Energy, Performance and Potential. She also runs private retreats in beautiful locations with amazing views.

*Coaching with NLP For Dummies* is her fifth book. In addition to co-authoring *NLP For Dummies* and *NLP Workbook For Dummies* with Romilla Ready, she co-authored *Building Self-Confidence For Dummies* with Brinley Platts. Her book *Live Life, Love Work* is published by Capstone, an imprint of Wiley. Contact Kate via her website at www.kateburton.co.uk.

# Author's Acknowledgements

When the Dummies team approached me to create *Coaching with NLP For Dummies* I knew I was in good hands once again. My editorial team, led by Rachael and Brian, worked with incredible attention to detail and enthusiasm to refine my chapters: they naturally adopt a coaching style with their powerful questioning and respectful support.

The content of this book is based on more than a decade of learning about and practising the art of coaching and NLP that builds on many more years in business. All my teachers in the personal development arena have my special thanks for their wisdom, including so many coaches I've connected with over the years. To my amazing clients I always appreciate the endless opportunities to do the work I love and learn from every interaction with you. To Bob and the family, your love and support for me in the background makes all the difference. And finally my thanks to the many thousands of readers who have shown their appreciation by buying the books. In the wish that some of the words in this book make their mark, I leave you with a quote from a fellow coach that: 'We never touch people so lightly that we do not leave a trace.'

## Publisher's Acknowledgements

We're proud of this book; please send us your comments through our Dummies online registration form located at www.dummies.com/register/.

Some of the people who helped bring this book to market include the following:

*Acquisitions, Editorial and Media Development*

**Project Editor:** Rachael Chilvers

**Development Editor:** Brian Kramer

**Commissioning Editors:** Nicole Hermitage, Kerry Laundon

**Technical Editor:** Katherine Tulpa, CEO, Association for Coaching and Co-Founder of Wisdom8

**Proofreader:** Kelly Cattermole

**Assistant Editor:** Ben Kemble

**Production Manager:** Daniel Mersey

**Cover Photo:** © Photolibrary

**Cartoons:** Rich Tennant, www.the5thwave.com

*Composition Services*

**Project Coordinator:** Kristie Rees

**Layout and Graphics:** Claudia Bell, Joyce Haughey, Andrea Hornberger, Corrie Socolovitch

**Indexer:** Ty Koontz

---

**Publishing and Editorial for Consumer Dummies**

> **Diane Graves Steele,** Vice President and Publisher, Consumer Dummies

> **Kristin Ferguson-Wagstaffe,** Product Development Director, Consumer Dummies

> **Ensley Eikenburg,** Associate Publisher, Travel

> **Kelly Regan,** Editorial Director, Travel

**Publishing for Technology Dummies**

> **Andy Cummings,** Vice President and Publisher, Dummies Technology/General User

**Composition Services**

> **Debbie Stailey,** Director of Composition Services

# Contents at a Glance

*Introduction* .......................................................................... 1

## Part I: Introducing NLP Coaching ........................... 7
Chapter 1: Combining Coaching and NLP for Great Results .................... 9
Chapter 2: Gathering the Essential NLP Skills .................................... 25
Chapter 3: Developing Your Coaching Alliances .................................. 47

## Part II: Building Core Coaching Skills ..................... 69
Chapter 4: Shaping the Agenda for Change ........................................ 71
Chapter 5: Going for Quick-Win Sessions ......................................... 87
Chapter 6: Getting Greater Clarity ................................................. 103
Chapter 7: Making Goals Come Alive .............................................. 121

## Part III: Deepening Your Awareness ...................... 137
Chapter 8: Tuning into Values ...................................................... 139
Chapter 9: Tapping into Passion and Purpose .................................... 151
Chapter 10: Shedding Light on Patterns .......................................... 171
Chapter 11: Developing Better Strategies ........................................ 185

## Part IV: Working Through Drama, Decisions and Dilemmas ........................................................ 205
Chapter 12: Strengthening Relationships in Tough Times ...................... 207
Chapter 13: Moving through Life's Disappointments ............................ 227
Chapter 14: Coaching through Conflict ........................................... 243
Chapter 15: Smoothing Career Peaks and Troughs .............................. 257

## Part V: Advancing Your NLP Coaching Repertoire ...... 269
Chapter 16: Turning Time to Your Advantage .................................... 271
Chapter 17: Shifting Experiences with Submodalities ........................... 285
Chapter 18: Managing Emotional States .......................................... 301
Chapter 19: Connecting All Parts of a Person .................................... 317

## Part VI: The Part of Tens ..................................... 333
Chapter 20: Ten Powerful Coaching Questions ................................... 335
Chapter 21: Ten Traps to Avoid in Coaching ..................................... 343
Chapter 22: Ten Ways to Enhance Your Coaching Skills ........................ 351

*Index* .............................................................................. 359

# Table of Contents

*Introduction* ................................................................ *1*

About This Book ........................................................... 1
Conventions Used in This Book ..................................... 2
What You're Not to Read ............................................... 2
Foolish Assumptions ..................................................... 2
How This Book Is Organised ......................................... 3
    Part I: Introducing NLP Coaching ........................... 3
    Part II: Building Core Coaching Skills ..................... 3
    Part III: Deepening Your Awareness ........................ 3
    Part IV: Working Through Dramas, Decisions and Dilemmas .......... 4
    Part V: Advancing Your NLP Coaching Repertoire .......... 4
    Part VI: The Part of Tens ......................................... 4
Icons Used in This Book ................................................ 5
Where to Go from Here .................................................. 5

*Part 1: Introducing NLP Coaching* ................................ *7*

## Chapter 1: Combining Coaching and NLP for Great Results ......... 9

Establishing the Differences between Coaching and NLP ...... 10
Pursuing a Coaching Career ........................................ 10
    Defining coaching .................................................. 11
    Surveying opportunities ........................................ 12
    Identifying potential ............................................. 13
    Recognising boundaries with therapy and consultancy ...... 15
Starting with NLP ....................................................... 17
    Appreciating structure .......................................... 18
    Relying on a robust framework that really works .......... 19
    Turning to tools and models for change ..................... 21
Getting into the Dreaming Habit .................................... 22

## Chapter 2: Gathering the Essential NLP Skills ................... 25

Increasing Rapport ..................................................... 26
    Pacing and leading ................................................ 26
    Tuning into non-verbal communication ..................... 27
    Flexing your communication style ........................... 28
    Connecting with the whole person ........................... 30
Working with Some Key NLP Assumptions ..................... 32
    The map is not the territory ................................... 33
    People are more than their behaviour ...................... 34
    Individuals are resourceful .................................... 35

Getting Beneath the Surface ........................................... 36
    Uncovering language's meaning: Two key models ......................... 37
    Playing with the time dimension ........................................ 38
    Separating process from content ....................................... 40
    Capturing the secondary gain ......................................... 40
Modelling Excellence ................................................ 41
    Finding and following exemplars ...................................... 42
    Shifting to unconscious competence ................................... 42
    Moving from confusion to congruence ................................. 44

**Chapter 3: Developing Your Coaching Alliances ................. 47**
Defining the Client-Coach Alliance .................................... 47
Building Trusting Relationships ...................................... 49
    Keeping things confidential ........................................... 49
    Operating with ethics and integrity .................................... 54
    Honouring human reactions and limitations ........................... 55
Contracting Competently with Clients ................................. 55
    Setting the groundwork ............................................... 56
    Picking the right person .............................................. 56
    Arriving with core coaching competencies ............................. 58
    Monitoring motivation ............................................... 62
    Sharing expectations for success ...................................... 62
Thriving on Curiosity and Spaciousness ............................... 63
    Feeling the power of silence ........................................... 64
    Accessing intuition .................................................. 65
    Being okay with not knowing the answers ............................. 65
    Sponsoring clients' natural expertise .................................. 67

**Part II: Building Core Coaching Skills ................. 69**

**Chapter 4: Shaping the Agenda for Change .................. 71**
Opening and Ending Sessions with Elegance ........................... 72
    Being prepared ...................................................... 73
    Setting intents ...................................................... 75
    Taking the learning forward step by step ............................... 75
    Ending things well ................................................... 76
Fine-Tuning the Intake Process ....................................... 77
    Laying the groundwork .............................................. 77
    Capturing the current reality ......................................... 78
Formulating the Desired Agenda ...................................... 83
    Refining agendas .................................................... 83
    Keeping on track .................................................... 85
    Staying in the moment as real life happens ............................ 86

**Chapter 5: Going for Quick-Win Sessions** . . . . . . . . . . . . . . . . . . . . . .**87**

Checking the SCORE . . . . . . . . . . . . . . . . . . . . . . . . . . . . . . . . . . . . . . . . . . . . . 88
 Conversing with SCORE  . . . . . . . . . . . . . . . . . . . . . . . . . . . . . . . . . . . 89
 Symptoms . . . . . . . . . . . . . . . . . . . . . . . . . . . . . . . . . . . . . . . . . . . . . . . . . 91
 Causes . . . . . . . . . . . . . . . . . . . . . . . . . . . . . . . . . . . . . . . . . . . . . . . . . . . . 92
 Outcomes . . . . . . . . . . . . . . . . . . . . . . . . . . . . . . . . . . . . . . . . . . . . . . . . . 93
 Resources . . . . . . . . . . . . . . . . . . . . . . . . . . . . . . . . . . . . . . . . . . . . . . . . 93
 Effects . . . . . . . . . . . . . . . . . . . . . . . . . . . . . . . . . . . . . . . . . . . . . . . . . . . . 94
 Keeping the SCORE . . . . . . . . . . . . . . . . . . . . . . . . . . . . . . . . . . . . . . . 95
Leveraging with Logical Levels . . . . . . . . . . . . . . . . . . . . . . . . . . . . . . . . . . . 96
 Environment . . . . . . . . . . . . . . . . . . . . . . . . . . . . . . . . . . . . . . . . . . . . . . 98
 Behaviour . . . . . . . . . . . . . . . . . . . . . . . . . . . . . . . . . . . . . . . . . . . . . . . . 98
 Capabilities and skills . . . . . . . . . . . . . . . . . . . . . . . . . . . . . . . . . . . . . 99
 Beliefs and values . . . . . . . . . . . . . . . . . . . . . . . . . . . . . . . . . . . . . . . . 99
 Identity . . . . . . . . . . . . . . . . . . . . . . . . . . . . . . . . . . . . . . . . . . . . . . . . . . . 100
 Purpose  . . . . . . . . . . . . . . . . . . . . . . . . . . . . . . . . . . . . . . . . . . . . . . . . . 100
Forwarding Awareness into Action . . . . . . . . . . . . . . . . . . . . . . . . . . . . . . . 101

**Chapter 6: Getting Greater Clarity** . . . . . . . . . . . . . . . . . . . . . . . . . . .**103**

Tackling Blind Spots with Awareness  . . . . . . . . . . . . . . . . . . . . . . . . . . . 104
Creating and Using Mental Maps . . . . . . . . . . . . . . . . . . . . . . . . . . . . . . . 106
 Preferring one sense over another . . . . . . . . . . . . . . . . . . . . . . . . . 107
 Filtering information  . . . . . . . . . . . . . . . . . . . . . . . . . . . . . . . . . . . . . 108
 Allowing the unconscious to get involved . . . . . . . . . . . . . . . . . . 110
Asking Powerful Questions . . . . . . . . . . . . . . . . . . . . . . . . . . . . . . . . . . . . . 112
 Finding the question that lands just right . . . . . . . . . . . . . . . . . . 112
 Posing an inquiry to take away . . . . . . . . . . . . . . . . . . . . . . . . . . . . 115
Listening Intently  . . . . . . . . . . . . . . . . . . . . . . . . . . . . . . . . . . . . . . . . . . . . . . 116
 Listening at four levels . . . . . . . . . . . . . . . . . . . . . . . . . . . . . . . . . . . . 117
 Listening beyond words . . . . . . . . . . . . . . . . . . . . . . . . . . . . . . . . . . . 118

**Chapter 7: Making Goals Come Alive** . . . . . . . . . . . . . . . . . . . . . . . . .**121**

Checking that Goals Are Well-Formed  . . . . . . . . . . . . . . . . . . . . . . . . . . . 121
 Is the goal stated in the positive? . . . . . . . . . . . . . . . . . . . . . . . . . . 122
 Is the goal self-initiated, self-maintained
   and within my control? . . . . . . . . . . . . . . . . . . . . . . . . . . . . . . . . . 123
 Does the goal describe the evidence procedure? . . . . . . . . . . . . 124
 Is the context of the goal clearly defined? . . . . . . . . . . . . . . . . . . 125
 Does the goal identify the necessary resources? . . . . . . . . . . . . 125
 Have I evaluated whether the goal is ecological? . . . . . . . . . . . . 127
 Does the goal identify the first step I need to take? . . . . . . . . . . 128
Balancing Dreams with Reality: The Disney Strategy . . . . . . . . . . . . . 129
 Getting to know the various roles  . . . . . . . . . . . . . . . . . . . . . . . . . 129
 Coaching through the roles . . . . . . . . . . . . . . . . . . . . . . . . . . . . . . . . 131

Generating New Behaviours .................................................. 133
Hearing the soundtrack................................................. 134
Seeing the movie............................................................ 134
Feeling, touching and smelling the result......................... 135

## Part III: Deepening Your Awareness ........................... 137

### Chapter 8: Tuning into Values ................................ 139

Knowing What's Important................................................. 140
Separating must-haves from shoulds............................. 140
Separating means values and end values ....................... 141
Focusing on core values................................................. 142
Setting Priorities ............................................................ 143
Allowing time to refine values ...................................... 144
Assessing values-based decisions ................................. 146
Responding to violated values ...................................... 147
Keeping Values Alive Every Day ........................................ 148
Assessing whether you're walking the talk ..................... 148
Dreaming bigger and better............................................ 148

### Chapter 9: Tapping into Passion and Purpose ................. 151

Waking Up........................................................................ 151
Getting in Tune with Flow States...................................... 152
Finding your flow state ................................................. 154
Accessing the flow state................................................ 156
Maintaining flow in challenging times ........................... 158
Finding the Meaning in Your Work.................................... 159
Seeking value while questing constantly ....................... 159
Making sense of the tough times ................................... 160
Recognising Your Life Purpose ........................................ 161
Noticing what energises you when the going gets tough ............. 161
Finding and using your passion: the DASE model ........................ 162
Defining purpose in your own words .............................. 163
Building a Shared Vision.................................................. 165
Merging different agendas ............................................ 166
Knowing when to bend and when to stay tough ......................... 168

### Chapter 10: Shedding Light on Patterns ...................... 171

Seeing the Metaprograms ................................................ 172
Global/detail................................................................. 173
Options/procedures ...................................................... 174
Toward/away from ........................................................ 175
Internal/external ........................................................... 176
Breaking unhelpful patterns.......................................... 178

Cutting through Collusion ........................................................ 179
    Voicing what you notice ................................................ 179
    Having the courage to hold the space ........................... 181
Establishing New Habits ........................................................ 183

**Chapter 11: Developing Better Strategies . . . . . . . . . . . . . . . . . . . . . .185**
Discovering the Difference that Makes the Difference: Strategies ........ 186
    Setting off strategies ................................................... 186
    Toting around your strategies ...................................... 187
    Tackling unhelpful strategies ...................................... 188
    Sequencing strategies ................................................. 188
    Paying attention to the eyes ........................................ 190
    Redesigning strategies ................................................ 192
    Honouring the intent .................................................. 193
Finding Examples in Others: Models and Mentors ................. 194
    Choosing exemplars .................................................... 195
    Finding new strategies from models of excellence .......... 196
    Imagining mentors ...................................................... 198
Creating New Structures to Be More Effective ...................... 199
    Saying a resounding yes or a definitive no .................... 200
    Counting the days ....................................................... 202
    Colour-coding schedules and diaries ............................ 202
    Checking in ................................................................ 203

## Part IV : Working Through Drama, Decisions and Dilemmas .................................................... 205

**Chapter 12: Strengthening Relationships in Tough Times . . . . . . . . .207**
Identifying the Stakeholders Who Matter ............................ 208
    Mapping out the network ............................................ 209
    Informing – or influencing? ........................................ 210
    Setting priorities for communication ........................... 212
Understanding What Makes Others Tick .............................. 214
    Taking perceptual positions ........................................ 215
    Gazing into the NLP meta-mirror ................................ 216
    Listening for metaprograms ........................................ 218
    Adapting your approach .............................................. 220
Coaching Teams to Bond .................................................... 220
    Forming: Adopting the mindset for success .................. 221
    Storming: Developing a shared future .......................... 222
    Norming and performing: Championing great ways
        of operating ........................................................... 224
    Disbanding: Moving on positively ................................ 225

**Chapter 13: Moving through Life's Disappointments**............**227**

Feeling Okay When Things Are Clearly Not Okay .......................228
    Staying with feelings ..........................................................228
    Increasing self-care.............................................................230
    Breathing out problems ......................................................232
    Finding the good and letting the rest go............................233
Avoiding the Drama Triangle ...............................................234
    Playing the victim ...............................................................235
    Saving the day ....................................................................236
    Bullying others ....................................................................236
Gaining Something from Tough Times ....................................237
    Following the grief and loss process .................................237
    Looking for loss ..................................................................238
    Holding the positive by-products .......................................240

**Chapter 14: Coaching through Conflict.**.......................**243**

Recognising Behaviours under Pressure .................................244
    Checking for patterns..........................................................245
    Holding on to the best outcome .........................................247
Working through Differences ................................................249
    Knowing the enemy well .....................................................249
    Negotiating in the best-sized chunks .................................251
Voicing What Needs to Be Said .............................................252
    Developing the non-violent vocabulary .............................253
    Finessing feedback..............................................................254
    Building the most confident voice......................................255
    Developing appreciative habits ..........................................256

**Chapter 15: Smoothing Career Peaks and Troughs** ..............**257**

Playing to Strengths ............................................................258
    Creating a career recipe......................................................258
    Preparing to lose a job .......................................................261
Owning an Engaging Reputation............................................262
    Gaining insight from others' feedback................................263
    Developing personal stories ...............................................264
    Communicating confidently ................................................266
Recognising the Power of Networks to Support Growth............266
    Connecting online ...............................................................267
    Getting known .....................................................................267

## *Part V: Advancing Your NLP Coaching Repertoire* ....... *269*

**Chapter 16: Turning Time to Your Advantage** ...................**271**

Creating a Personal Time Line...............................................272
    Visualising time...................................................................272
    Working with in-time clients...............................................274
    Working with through-time clients......................................275

Becoming a Time Traveller ........................................................276
    Taking off at will........................................................................278
    Letting go of the negative ......................................................279
Creating the Desired Future ......................................................280
    Touring various aspects, at various points in time.....................280
    Increasing the sparkle dust ..................................................283

**Chapter 17: Shifting Experiences with Submodalities** . . . . . . . . . . .**285**

Understanding the Submodalities ............................................286
    Seeing the distinctions ...........................................................287
    Hearing auditory signals ........................................................288
    Feeling the kinaesthetic differences....................................289
    Mapping across from other resources..................................290
Shifting Positions ......................................................................294
    Associating with the moment..................................................294
    Dissociating from the moment ..............................................294
Changing Beliefs through the Senses ......................................295
    Distinguishing between limiting and empowering beliefs...........295
    Getting beneath the surface and empowering
       the client's potential ......................................................296

**Chapter 18: Managing Emotional States** . . . . . . . . . . . . . . . . . . . . . .**301**

Saying Hello to Emotional States.............................................301
Changing Emotional States ......................................................303
    Checking the baseline state....................................................303
    Anchoring positive states .......................................................304
    Allowing negative states to slide away ................................306
Tackling Interference from Gremlins ........................................307
    Shaking up the peacekeeper gremlin ...................................308
    Messing with the perfectionist gremlin .................................309
    Firing up the procrastinator gremlin.....................................309
    Drawing your gremlins ...........................................................310
Overcoming Fear .......................................................................311
    Championing natural confidence ..........................................312
    Releasing phobias fast............................................................313

**Chapter 19: Connecting All Parts of a Person** . . . . . . . . . . . . . . . . . .**317**

Splitting into Parts.....................................................................317
Keeping Everyone Supported during Change...........................318
    Building on past experiences .................................................319
    Checking for ecology...............................................................320
    Establishing the bale-out position ........................................321
Developing a Unified Identity....................................................323
    Integrating conflicting parts ..................................................324
    Bringing the whole self into play ..........................................326
    Keeping a journal ...................................................................327
Reframing the Situation ............................................................328
    Adopting various frames.........................................................329
    Reframing in six steps............................................................330

## *Part VI: The Part of Tens* ............................................. 333

### Chapter 20: Ten Powerful Coaching Questions ................... .335
What Do You Want? ..........................................................................335
What's Important to You about This?..............................................336
How Will You Know When You've Got What You Want? .......................337
What Is Getting in the Way for You? ...............................................338
What Resources Have You Got that Can Support You? ........................339
When You Accomplish Your Goal and Look Back on
   Your Success, What Will You Experience? ...................................340
What's the Question You Don't Want to Ask Yourself Right Now?........340
What's the Way to Make This Really Easy?......................................341
What's the First Step? .....................................................................341
And What Else? ...............................................................................342

### Chapter 21: Ten Traps to Avoid in Coaching .................... .343
Racing into Detail without Seeing the Bigger Picture .........................343
Getting Caught with Long-Winded Tales .........................................344
Rescuing the Other Person ..............................................................345
Dramatising What You Hear..............................................................346
Being the Know-all...........................................................................346
Slipping into Parent or Child Role ...................................................347
Losing Track of Time........................................................................347
Falling into Love and Friendship .....................................................348
Engaging in Over-Enthusiastic Action-Planning................................348
Being Scared to Say Goodbye ..........................................................349

### Chapter 22: Ten Ways to Enhance Your Coaching Skills ......... .351
Enrol in Diverse Courses and Workshops............................................352
Share Your Knowledge with Others .................................................352
Practise on Willing Guinea Pigs ......................................................353
Model Other Coaches in Action........................................................354
Experiment with New Ideas ............................................................354
Record Yourself and Play It Back .....................................................355
Set a Quality Target .........................................................................356
Work with a Supervisor or Mentor ..................................................356
Join a Coaching Network .................................................................357
Volunteer with a Professional Body..................................................357

## *Index* ...................................................................... 359

# Introduction

· · · · · · · · · · · · · · · · · · · · · · · · · · · · · · · · · · · · · · · · · · · · · · · · · · · · · · · · · ·

**C**oaching and Neuro-linguistic Programming (NLP) are both exceptionally powerful. Bring them together and you have a winning combination. So welcome to *Coaching with NLP For Dummies*, which I trust fires up your enthusiasm to do amazing work.

We live in uncertain times. No one can accurately predict what today's developments in technology, globalisation, demographics and climate change mean for tomorrow, let alone a few years from now. Unsurprisingly, more people than ever are turning to coaches to guide them through life and career transitions as they seek to own their destiny. People need wise, independent sounding boards. They want inspiration and motivation for working lives that are predicted to last longer than ever before. Leaders in organisations are calling on their managers to coach their people, equipping them for a future with more fluid working patterns in which commanding and controlling employees is no longer appropriate.

Whatever your interest in coaching, armed with this practical and fun book, you have a wealth of ideas to get out there and coach at your best.

## About This Book

Coaching is a creative partnership between two people that inspires new thinking and leads to change.

Typically in the coaching world, professional coaches refer to the *coach* and *coachee* as the two key people in the relationship and the *client* as a customer who holds the purse strings in an organisation. In this book, I've deliberately chosen the alternative word *client* for the person being coached to give you a stronger distinction between the two key players involved.

I wrote this book for readers interested in the role of the coach. Yet in every example, the *client* can be you, so play with the exercises to coach yourself as well as others. Whatever made you pick up this book, you're going to discover more about yourself and others. Get ready to open new doors and explore the fascinating world of being human through the coaching relationship.

My aim in every chapter of this book is to cut through any jargon. Top-quality coaching needs to be accessible to all and to that end, I offer practical and relevant tools for you to make your own.

# Conventions Used in This Book

To help you navigate throughout this book, I set up a few conventions:

- ✔ *Italic* text is used for emphasis and to highlight new words or terms that are then defined.
- ✔ **Boldfaced** text is used to indicate the action part of numbered steps.
- ✔ Monofont is used for website addresses.
- ✔ Sometimes I talk about the client and coach as *him* and other times as *her*. I've aimed to vary the gender to give you a fair representation when you read the entire book.

# What You're Not to Read

*For Dummies* books are hugely popular with busy people keen to get to the heart of a subject quickly because you can capture the wisdom between these yellow and black covers fast. To that end, you can easily identify the material you can skip through. This information is the stuff that, although interesting and related to the topic at hand, isn't essential for you to know and includes:

- ✔ **Text in sidebars.** The sidebars are the shaded boxes that appear here and there. They often share personal stories and observations or bits of history and background information.
- ✔ **The stuff on the copyright page.** No kidding. You find nothing here of interest unless you're inexplicably enamoured with legal language and reprint information!

# Foolish Assumptions

I assume, and correct me if I'm wrong, that you:

- ✔ Have a good reason to be reading *Coaching with NLP For Dummies* without the desire to wade through all the possible books and courses on the topic.

✔ Are interested in discovering and applying new coaching and NLP ideas for yourself as well as clients.

✔ Want to enhance your NLP-related skills.

✔ Need to get stuck in with your coaching to tackle real issues immediately.

✔ Want to develop a practical set of coaching tools.

✔ Know that you can benefit from coaching yourself as well as coaching others.

✔ Are committed to being proficient and professional in your coaching activities.

# How This Book Is Organised

I divide this book into six parts, with each part broken into chapters. The Table of Contents gives you more detail on each chapter, and I even throw in a cartoon at the start of each part for your amusement.

## Part 1: Introducing NLP Coaching

In this part, I paint the overall picture for you, demonstrating where coaching and NLP come together to create choice and change for your clients. You get a feel for what is possible as you build greater rapport and get beneath the surface of the initial coaching conversation. You see how to get a coaching partnership off to the finest start by the way you contract competently and sponsor your clients' innate expertise in their own lives.

## Part II: Building Core Coaching Skills

Get ready to allow the magic to begin, opening your coaching elegantly with a clear intake process and shifting step by step forward while knowing how to close a session with equal elegance. In this part, you develop your fundamental skills in questioning, listening and goal setting while holding on to a clear agenda for your clients.

## Part III: Deepening Your Awareness

This part gets even more interesting as you explore coaching at the higher logical levels of values and purpose. You see how to encourage the flow states in your clients in which they can be at their very best with greatest ease. You recognise more about the patterns that drive habitual behaviour and how to break unhelpful ones. In this section I also share the benefits of bringing NLP modelling into coaching to make your clients more effective in any area where they want to develop.

## Part IV: Working Through Dramas, Decisions and Dilemmas

Part IV focuses on the more challenging questions that arise in coaching conversations around living and working with others when the going gets tough. How can you build strong relationships, especially with difficult and demanding people? How do you get teams to work well together? You find out how to support your clients through conflicts and disappointments, including grieving for loss. On the career front, I show you how to ensure your clients can navigate the ups and downs of their working lives with confidence and strong communication skills.

## Part V: Advancing Your NLP Coaching Repertoire

In this part, I encourage you to build more NLP techniques into your sessions, from time lines and submodality work to anchoring and parts integration. All these approaches become crystal clear as you work through the exercises laid out step by step in each chapter. You don't need to be an NLP expert to capture the benefit of these tools to make your client's exceptionally resilient.

## Part VI: The Part of Tens

If you're impatient to get going quickly, start here. This part takes you straight to some powerful coaching questions and ways you can develop as a coach. In addition, I offer warnings of pitfalls you want to avoid. This part of the book is for anyone who, like me, simply can't resist checking out the end of a book before deciding which are the most interesting pages to devour in the middle.

# Icons Used in This Book

A series of icons guide you to the heart of the book.

 This icon indicates real-life experiences of NLP coaching in action. Although based on real clients, the people often have their names changed unless they gave me permission to feature them in the book. Some anecdotes are based on composite characters to portray familiar themes that people raise in coaching.

 This icon highlights NLP terminology that may sound like a foreign language at first yet has a precise meaning to an NLP-qualified coach.

 This icon is a friendly reminder of important points to watch out for.

 Keep your eyes on this target for insightful practical advice.

 This icon suggests ideas and activities to give you tools for coaching and food for thought.

# Where to Go from Here

Jump straight into any chapter that calls to you – the choice is yours. You don't have to work through the book from cover to cover, although you may want to check the table of contents first to see what grabs your interest. For example, if you're keen to get some quick wins, check out the models in Chapter 5. Or if you're working with clients who struggle with relationships, you may want to fast-forward to Chapter 12. Dipping and diving is the name of the game as you build your coaching repertoire based on what you already know and what truly interests you.

# Part I
# Introducing NLP Coaching

The 5th Wave    By Rich Tennant

"Let's see if we can identify some of the stress triggers in your life. You mentioned something about a large wolf that periodically shows up and attempts to blow your house down..."

# In this part . . .

You find out what makes NLP coaching different and why so many people are raving about this approach. From seeing the impact that professional coaching makes, to diving straight into the NLP fundamentals, you'll get ideas about how you can build trusting coaching relationships that get the best from everyone you coach. Very soon, you'll be set up and raring to get beneath the surface issues that clients first talk about.

# Chapter 1

# Combining Coaching and NLP for Great Results

*In This Chapter*

▶ Noticing how coaching and NLP overlap

▶ Looking at a career in coaching

▶ Getting up to speed on NLP

▶ Tapping into the potential for powerful change

> *One isn't necessarily born with courage, but one is born with potential. Without courage, we cannot practice any other virtue with consistency. We can't be kind, true, merciful, generous, or honest.*
>
> –Maya Angelou

Coaching – like living an authentic life to its fullest – involves the courage to be honest and true to yourself in order to reach your potential. Welcome to a journey of exploration that encompasses two exciting, rewarding and fascinating worlds: coaching and NLP!

Coaching and NLP are *not* the same thing, as I explain in this chapter, yet they do make for happy bedfellows. With their common foundation in the service of the client, NLP and coaching naturally complement each other.

Whether you desire a specific type of change, or stability while the world around you is changing, coaching and NLP have much to offer you and your clients. The aim of this chapter – and indeed, the entire book – is to support your development as a person and a coach by sparking new ideas and introducing you to some tried and tested ways of coaching with NLP.

# Establishing the Differences between Coaching and NLP

People often ask me what the difference is between working with a coach and working with an NLP Practitioner or Master Practitioner. Employing a coach is a creative and collaborative relationship that focuses on *incremental and continuous* change. Coaching works with subtle fine-tuning to encourage a different way of thinking, being and doing. Hiring an NLP practitioner is more likely to be for a one-off session to address a particular issue around personal change. An NLP client may experience a dramatic breakthrough at a single intensive session, while coaching tends to have its ups and downs over a period of sessions. Indeed, an individual coaching session may not seem important at the time, yet it contributes to some deeper understanding in the longer term.

Coaches come from very different disciplines and schools of training. What makes the best stand out is that they are not wedded to one approach; they remain hungry for learning. To be a coach requires you to look at yourself, to do the inner work of self-reflection and personal growth. You need to demonstrate the services you offer by 'walking the talk' yourself and investing in your own on-going coaching.

People often hire an NLP-trained coach because they want someone with the steadfastness required to go to hard places, someone able to explore the challenging emotional reasons that drive behaviour. Potential clients may have heard about particular NLP tools and techniques, or they feel that coaching with someone who's undergone a different kind of coach training yields a richer experience.

 Coaching and NLP take different routes to achieve the same end result: to leave clients in a better place physically, emotionally, mentally or spiritually than when they started. Both disciplines address challenges of self-awareness and relationships with others. Bring NLP and coaching together and you have a winning combination to find the unconscious brilliance in each human being.

Both NLP and coaching offer a wealth of practical tools. Neither discipline expects one particular process to be followed to the letter. They offer the flexibility to choose which approach is best for the client at any given time.

# Pursuing a Coaching Career

Coaching is a fast-growing profession, attracting plenty of interest from both the world of personal development and the business world.

Coaching's increasingly popular because it addresses the challenge of living a fulfilling existence in a complex world. It explores an individual or team's experience from two angles – externally and internally – and synergistically combines them:

- The external perspective looks at the context in which someone is operating, their behaviour and communication with others.

- The internal perspective addresses an individual's thoughts, feelings and motivation.

Coaches are naturally curious people who listen and ask questions; even on holiday their eyes and ears are tuned into what's going on with those around them. Like an engineer who likes to find out how machines work, a coach sees another person as a set of intriguing interlocking parts, some running smoothly, others in need of extra oil on the rusty parts. Sound like anyone you know?

Picture the scene. The sun is setting on a white Caribbean beach. A coach walks into a hotel bar with his wife, and they strike up a conversation with a fellow guest who's sipping her pina colada. Over cocktails, the lady explains that she's a landscape architect, staying on the island to redesign a series of gardens for a prestigious hotel group. The coach asks, 'What's important to you about your work here?' That one question and a chance meeting open up an evening of animated conversation that developed into a business-coaching relationship that has lasted for nearly two years.

## Defining coaching

Many people and organisations define coaching. You probably have your working definition of what a coach does. The following are some of my favourites:

- **From the International Coach Federation:** *Coaching is partnering with clients in a thought-provoking and creative process that inspires them to maximise their personal and professional potential.*

- **From Association for Coaching:** *A collaborative solution-focused, results-orientated and systematic process in which the coach facilitates the enhancement of work performance, life experience, self-directed learning and personal growth of the coachee.*

- **From Tim Gallwey, author of *The Inner Game of Tennis*:** *There is always an inner game being played in your mind, no matter what outer game you are playing. How aware you are of this game can make all the difference between success and failure in the outer game.*

Whatever your definition, coaching is a relationship that brings out the very best in both client and coach. During coaching, a special conversation takes place that's completely focused on the client's needs in a way that empowers him to dream bigger dreams, increase performance, articulate what he wants and work out how to get what he most desires.

Being a coach is like working as a sculptor who chips away at a piece of marble to reveal the strength and beauty of the person inside. To reach the desired result calls for skill and sensitivity. Yet in the coaching relationship, the client guides the sculptor as to how to use the chisel and where to tap for the best results, giving permission to poke in some areas and stay away from others. Read more about the design of this coach-client relationship in Chapter 3.

## Surveying opportunities

Professional coaches help clients in various spheres of activity. Some common types of coaches include the following:

- **Life or personal coaches** work with clients on areas where they want their lives to be different. Some clients may have lost their mojo, their zest for living; others just know they have a dream they want to make real. Perhaps they've had one too many challenges from health and relationships, money or family issues and need an independent coach to help them get back on track. Some life coaches specialise in particular fields, such as relationships or finances, while others help groups such as new parents, teenagers or people about to retire.

   Life or personal coaching is the foundation for other areas of coaching because people don't separate career and business issues from the rest of their lives. For example, an executive with health issues or worries about supporting his children is affected by these aspects of his life when he comes to work, even if they aren't the prime agenda.

- **Career coaches** work with clients who want to change jobs or manage their careers. Career coaching shifts clients from waiting to be talent-spotted into a more proactive mode about their careers. While most of the activities in this book apply to career coaches, Chapter 15 focuses on the specific challenges of career coaching with NLP.

- **Business coaches** work with business owners and managers on work-related issues. Although this type of coaching mainly concentrates on the individual or team in the business context rather than the business systems and processes themselves, these coaches still must be comfortable working in the business world.

The overall benefit of this coaching impacts the success of the entire business. For example, a business director may need clarity on vision and direction or face specific challenges with an aspect of the operations. Business coaching is also valuable for raising team performance. See Chapter 12 for more on coaching in a team context.

✔ **Executive coaches** work with leaders and top executives who are often stepping into a larger role and need a trusted space in which to express the pressures they are under, discuss upcoming decisions and develop their leadership approaches. Senior executives have the potential to make vast profits or strides forward for their organisations, but often no one in their organisations can talk honestly with them. The return on investment when executives talk with coaches about their key challenges, hopes, dreams, fears and insecurities and then work towards their full potential can be huge. You may hire an executive coach to prepare for a change of role (like joining a board of directors), to enhance your personal impact or at times of stress, change, conflict or crisis.

In addition to formal coaching contracts, many people take on coaching-type assignments even when the name 'coach' is not in their job descriptions. Developing your coaching skills can enrich many fields of activity. The core coaching competencies I cover in Chapter 3 show you how coaching qualities such as effective communication are beneficial whether you're a parent, business leader or bus driver.

## *Identifying potential*

Coaching involves pushing through the boundaries of potential to ensure that you are the creator of your own positive experiences. The worlds of sport and performing arts assumed long ago that top performers need coaches to raise their game; business has taken longer to catch up with this realisation. In fact, in many organisations, the higher you go, the less training or support you get. Many consider Tim Gallwey, US coach and author of *The Inner Game of Tennis* (Pan Books), to be the father of coaching. In his classic book, Gallwey talks about a person's performance being equal to their potential less interference. He expresses this principle with the equation:

$P = p - i$: Performance is equal to potential less interference

As a coach, you work with clients to identify, honour and transform their points of resistance, closing in on that interference that prevents them performing to their full potential. You also encourages clients to stretch and grow, leapfrogging beyond what they ever considered possible, letting any interference melt away to achieve much more than they may have considered possible.

## Living the dream

What have you achieved in your life that you never believed you could? Take a moment to think back to something you accomplished, something that once seemed impossible for you. Perhaps you recall a job you've done, the home you live in, the family life you've created, some milestone in a hobby or sport that you've reached, an exam you've passed or a setback you've overcome.

As you think about your achievement, notice the spring in your step, the fizz of excitement inside, the smile of contentment and the satisfaction that results when you can validate yourself and your actions, however small.

Now think about this: you are living an earlier dream. You are the creator of your present, already perfect life. See Chapter 16 for more on ideas for envisioning and then living your future goals.

Tim Gallwey brought the principles of the inner mind games from the world of professional tennis and golf coaching into the world of business- and life coaching. Gallwey introduced the concept of Self 1 and Self 2, which he'd spotted in clients' thought patterns when he coached tennis.

- ✔ **Self 1** is the critical voice. It is constantly reminding Self 2 to 'keep it firm, watch that ball, your opponent's about to hit back hard, oh my goodness, turn sideways, racket back, stupid you, you hit it in the net.' Self 1 tells Self 2 what to do as if Self 2 is really stupid and needs to be bullied into action.

- ✔ **Self 2** is the natural, talented, all-watching, unconsciously competent learning machine. Self 2 includes the all-powerful unconscious mind that never forgets, hears everything and is bright and intelligent. NLP recognises that the unconscious mind is incredibly powerful.

The assistance Gallwey gave to his tennis players was to quieten down Self 1 and allow Self 2 freedom to play. He then applied the same principle to the broader field of coach training with the suggestion: get out of the client's way. Coaching is not about telling, but about allowing clients' natural resourcefulness to shine through by inviting them to become curious about their experiences.

In a strong coaching relationship, you find someone who truly believes in you and validates you for who you are, your identity and your contribution to the world in terms of mission and purpose. You enter into a sponsorship relationship with another person.

NLP developer and trainer Robert Dilts talks about *Big C* coaching. Chapter 5 covers the classic Dilts's Logical Levels model, which looks at the client's experience in terms of the six levels:

- ✔ The environment in which the client operates.
- ✔ The behaviours that support excellence.
- ✔ The capabilities and skills developed.
- ✔ The beliefs and values that inspire.
- ✔ The sense of identity that feels authentic.
- ✔ The purpose that guides direction.

Behavioural coaching operates at the three lower levels of environment, behaviour, capabilities and skills – all things that Dilts refers to as *small c* coaching. To achieve potential in the coaching relationship, you need to nurture at all six levels, Dilts's Big C style of coaching. When you support all six levels, you awaken your clients to their purpose in life and help them realise their full potential. Read more about the power of aligning with a strong sense of purpose in Chapter 9.

Every client deserves a coach who truly believes in new possibilities and sponsors him along the way. If you don't have a strong belief in the potential of your client, suggest the client finds another coach to work with.

## Recognising boundaries with therapy and consultancy

Defining something subtle is often easier when you state what it isn't rather than what it is and then notice the distinctions. Coaching is not therapy and not consulting, yet you encounter grey areas around the edges, particularly as more therapists and consultants are moving into offering coaching services.

As a coach, take some time to formulate your own definitions and distinctions regarding the following disciplines, particularly if you come to coaching from a therapeutic or consulting background. Be prepared to explain your definitions to those you work with and recognise where you feel qualified to support your clients.

- ✔ **Therapy** works through troubled emotional experiences, usually taking a slow approach to peeling away the layers of emotion to uncover and then shift persistent discomfort. Often therapy clients don't know what their pain is about and need a very safe space to explore. They may have depressive, addictive, unpredictable, abusive or obsessive behaviours and experiences. They may struggle to form emotional attachments. Therapy provides a healing and remedial approach from qualified and supervised professionals.

The overlap between coaching and therapy tends to occur where clients are stressed, overwhelmed or have suffered a personal setback and require a coach who is comfortable in holding an emotionally-charged space confidently and knows the limits of his abilities. NLP-trained coaches have some tools to resolve certain emotional issues, including fears and phobias, but unless they're separately qualified, they aren't therapists. (See Chapter 18 for more on resolving emotional issues.)

The terminology around counselling, therapy, and psychotherapy varies from country to country, according to different training and qualifications. I use the word *therapy* to indicate any one-to-one work with a qualified professional health worker in the field of mental well-being.

✔ **Consulting** is an advice-giving and problem-solving space where the consultant works with clients' problems and helps them come to appropriate solutions. Good consultants listen and ask insightful questions, and are brought in to give practical answers to problems. Consultants typically have extensive relevant personal experience.

Many independent business consultants refer to themselves as coaches, yet typically they instruct and give information rather than ask questions and allow clients to come up with their own answers. Consultancy can breed a dependency culture in which clients often look to their consultants rather than become experts in their own businesses or lives. Those hiring executive coaches should be mindful of whether they are really looking for a consultant or mentor and hire accordingly.

✔ **Mentoring** involves someone who gives advice, support and guidance based on personal experience and who may make introductions. Boundaries between coaching and mentoring can sometimes become blurred when a coach is hired because he has experience in the issues a client wants to solve.

The ideal mentor works with clients in a coaching style to allow the clients to develop their own skills in line with their natural talents and interests rather than replicating the mentor's approach. Mentors can act as powerful models of excellence and mentoring may happen organically without any formal contracting or exchange of money if you find someone who can be helpful to you.

Coaches often wear both coach and mentor hats. Some people hire me as a coach because I've written books several times before. These individuals are really looking for a mentor who can give practical tips and guidance on writing.

---

## Raising the game through supervision

As you develop as a coach, particularly in business, you'll be asked: 'What about your supervision arrangements?' Supervision began as a requirement in the therapeutic professions and is now applied to the coaching process too. Coaching supervision offers a safe space to reflect on the details of the work you do as a coach. It may take place with a group of coaches or on a one-to-one basis with an experienced supervisor. Coaches can get embroiled in their clients' lives and supervision makes you step back and scrutinise what's happening objectively.

To engage in supervision, you need to be curious, honest and open to learning. In this environment you feel supported without judgement and will look at your coaching interventions: how you operate with your clients; your beliefs and values; and the wider context in which your clients work or live. You gain feedback and insight that leads to greater skill as a coach and the ability to remain ethical and professional, as well as protection for the client.

To find a supervisor, approach the various professional coaching bodies for recommendations.

---

With my coaching hat on, I may say, 'I hear you want to write. Tell me about your energy for this.' My pure coaching questions tap into their motivation, passion and purpose. Switching into mentoring mode, I might say: 'You need to develop a convincing proposal and submit it to a publisher. This is what it must look like.' My mentoring approach directs the client down a particular path based on my personal experiences as an author.

Mentoring and consulting often assume that the answers lie with the external expert; coaching assumes that the client is the expert.

# *Starting with NLP*

*Neuro-linguistic Programming* (NLP) is defined as the study of the structure of subjective experience, or more simply, as an everyday form of psychology. The indication that it's a great fit with coaching begins with the name Neuro-linguistic Programming in which:

- ✔ **Neuro** refers to thought processes.
- ✔ **Linguistic** examines language structure.
- ✔ **Programming** addresses patterns and sequences of actions.

In short, NLP is about thoughts, words and action – all absolutely essential aspects to consider in any coaching session or programme!

When you begin exploring NLP, you acquire new perspectives on everyday experiences. NLP gives you much more than a set of tools; it gives you a whole new way of thinking that shapes your behaviour on a day-to-day basis.

For example, you separate out the *content* of what is happening from the *structure*. This distinction is invaluable as a coach, enabling you to reach beyond and beneath the words in a coaching conversation.

Consider Max. He's been asked to give the best man's speech at his old school friend's wedding and has been putting off working on it. A conventional starting point addresses the *content* of *what* Max is going to say from start to finish, writing the script, creating some visuals and practising his most embarrassing jokes. By contrast, the NLP approach is interested in the *structure* of *how* the best man and wedding party may experience the speech at all the stages from the moment he gets up to speak until he finishes.

An NLP coach invites Max to consider:

- What may be the sights, sounds and feelings of the speaker and audience at different stages?
- How would Max like other key people to experience his speech and what would he like them to tell others after the event?
- How might Max change the emotional state of the people at specific points in his speech – for example, shifting from curiosity though surprise to good-natured fun simply by behaving differently?
- What is Max's own emotional state about giving the speech? At what point is he most confident and where might he struggle?
- What resources will help him perform at his best?
- How does Max prefer to tell stories – conveying the big picture or fine detail?

With NLP, instead of staying in the first person of yourself and your own world, you develop the ability to take different perspectives. You step into a second viewpoint and imagine what it's like to experience the world as another person or group of people. You step into a third viewpoint and observe the world from the perspective of an independent observer. Chapter 12 gives the low-down on the various perceptual positions.

## *Appreciating structure*

By studying the structure of experience with NLP as your guide, you begin to notice that all communication (including a coaching conversation) has a natural structure from beginning to end, and you can deliberately shape that structure to achieve specific outcomes.

Whether you're working with a client in a one-off session or over a period of time, the interaction shifts through three stages from beginning, through the middle to the end:

- **Introduction** is the warm-up where you get to know each other, build rapport, trust, set expectations and define the agenda for the relationship. This is known as the *pre-frame*.

   Rushing through this stage is tempting, yet allowing plenty of time in this early contracting phase pays dividends in the long-run. Chapter 3 looks in more detail at setting clear expectations from the outset. In the wedding speech scenario, Max needs to connect with his audience to get their attention so they're curious and want to hear more.

- **Change work** is the filling in the sandwich, where the work takes place and people are changed by the experience. In an NLP session, the change work may be a particular intervention like a phobia cure or parts integration.

   In coaching, the questioning and listening often leads to new awareness for the client. In the wedding example I mention in the preceding section, the change work is the key speech messages and interaction between best man and wedding guests that effects change.

   Whatever the specific situation, learning takes place at both conscious and unconscious levels though the interpersonal relationship. (Chapter 2 looks at the conscious and unconscious levels some more.)

- **Closure** is the wrap-up: action-planning and ownership are handed back to the client to take the learning away. The closure part of any interaction needs to be planned for so that the client is never left feeling rushed or short-changed. In Chapter 4 you find guidance on ensuring that the ending of any coaching alliance is elegant. Likewise, in the wedding speech, Max needs to plan the final part of his speech, so that his audience remembers the experience after he's finished.

## Relying on a robust framework that really works

NLP has been around since the mid-1970s and continues to gather momentum with thousands of courses on offer worldwide. John Grinder and Richard Bandler, the co-creators of NLP, were interested in the communication skills of leading therapists of their day and developed some key models and ideas through their research at the University of California, Santa Cruz.

## You're not alone

You inevitably face times in life when you're not quite living the life you really want – or perhaps you have an intuitive sense that life could be better if only you knew how. These moments may last just a short while or seem to go on indefinitely.

When you tackle your challenges by yourself, you usually get stuck. You simply don't know where to look for the answers. When you work with a coach, however, your coach can assist you to look for answers in places you hadn't

considered. It's just like looking for your lost door keys alone and going round in circles until someone invites you to retrace your steps and notice what you're overlooking.

Employing a professional guide on any journey allows you to visit new places and take on greater adventures. A professional coach is not there to tell you where to go, only to show you how you create your own journey and give you the power to define for yourself where you might like to travel next.

Their work centred on modelling excellence, paying attention to the unconscious processing as well as the observable qualities of their first models: Fritz Perls, the father of Gestalt; the great family therapist Virginia Satir; and the renowned hypnotherapist Milton Erickson. They were also influenced by, among others, Carol Rogers of person-centred therapy; Eric Berne, founder of Transactional Analysis and Gregory Bateson's work in psychiatry, cybernetics and systems theory.

Today, NLP has spread to diverse industry sectors and nations. You're as likely to find NLP training for IT workers in Mumbai as for teachers in the Far East and the military in the US. NLP is universally applicable in all these situations because it's founded on four key principles to create communication excellence:

- ✔ **Rapport.** Building a relationship with others and with yourself is the fundamental premise of NLP and an important gift for coaching. For example, a key challenge for many clients is how to say 'no' to a request or disagree with another person while holding their attention and maintaining rapport. I look at ways of creating and sustaining rapport in Chapter 2.

- ✔ **Sensory awareness.** As you recognise just how powerful your sensory filters are, you can engage your natural sight, sound, touch, feelings, taste and smell capabilities to your benefit. Chapter 7 guides you through the process of making goals more exciting by including sensory information that engages the unconscious as well as conscious mind. In Chapter 17, you discover the power of engaging the finer aspects of the senses, known as *submodalities,* in creating new beliefs.

✔ **Outcome thinking.** The ultimate question in NLP coaching is 'What do you want?' Coaches guide clients' attention to what they want to be different as a result of coaching. NLP focuses strongly on future outcomes to shift people to make the best decisions and explore new possibilities. In order to shape up goals and make them attainable, NLP offers the well-formed outcome model detailed in Chapter 7.

✔ **Behavioural flexibility.** People's hunger for coaching increases when what they are currently doing isn't working so well for them; they've hit some kind of block or resistance. NLP adopts the working assumption that the person who is most flexible in any system gets the best results – the one who experiments with new ideas and ways of operating. One way to harness NLP tools for greater flexibility is to encourage clients to adopt different perceptual positions, as I discuss in Chapter 12.

## *Turning to tools and models for change*

In addition to a powerful, flexible overall framework, NLP also offers a wealth of key models that you can quickly build into coaching interventions. The following NLP tools and models appear throughout the book:

✔ **NLP presuppositions** are assumptions that establish a powerful mind-set for coaching. Read more about presuppositions in Chapter 2.

✔ **The SCORE model** is one of the quick-win models you can read about in Chapter 5. Have this model in your head to ensure your coaching doesn't drift into storytelling or lose its direction.

✔ **The Logical Levels model** of alignment and change developed by NLP leader Robert Dilts. I explain it more fully in Chapter 5 and this alignment involves finding a sense of purpose in everyday activities.

✔ **Representational systems** explore individuals' ways of representing their sensory experiences. Turn to Chapters 2 and 7 for more.

✔ **The Meta Model,** one of the original NLP language models with its explanation of the filters of distortion, deletion and generalisation, is valuable to gain specific information on a coaching issue. You can explore more about these filters in Chapter 6.

✔ **Well-formed outcomes** are the fundamental tool of NLP goal-setting. Check out Chapter 7 to discover more on goal-setting.

✔ **Metaprograms** are some of the unconscious mental filters that direct what you pay attention to, how you process information and how you then communicate to others. In Chapter 10 you find the nitty-gritty on these powerful patterns.

✔ Effective coaching involves unpacking your client's **strategies,** the sequence of their thought patterns. Turn to Chapter 11 to find out more.

✔ When clients can **model excellence,** they have the opportunity to fast-track change by making the most of others' examples. Chapter 11 details how modelling works.

✔ **Perceptual positions** involve imagining you're in someone else's shoes as well as taking an independent-observer position on an issue. See Chapter 12 for more.

✔ **The grief and loss process** is a useful tool for clients with unresolved grief. Chapter 13 shows how these steps allow clients to retain the positive aspects of a person or experience that is now lost to them.

✔ **Time lines** help you working in the here and now as well as move towards the future and recognise the impact of past experience. Chapter 16 shows how to play with NLP concepts of time.

✔ Shifting an entrenched belief system is a challenging task in coaching. Working with the subtleties of **submodalities** in Chapter 17 show how this is possible.

✔ **Anchors** are a classic NLP technique to manage emotional states. See Chapter 18.

✔ **Parts integration and reframing** is a more advanced technique for resolving issues of internal conflict and tension between different needs and demands. See Chapter 19.

# Getting into the Dreaming Habit

The world today is pragmatic and critical, so much so that time to dream is squeezed. Allow time to get out of the cognitive, logical thought processes and create a sense of spaciousness where you can explore creatively.

Take yourself off to a beautiful space where you can allow your imagination to run freely. If possible, take a walk in the woods or by a lake, sea or river. Climb a hill or find a quiet and comfortable seat in a room you enjoy.

In this quiet moment, begin the habit of self-coaching. Consider the contexts in which you want to develop your coaching skills and services. Ask yourself:

✔ In what industries, organisations or settings do you want to provide coaching? What geographies or types of people come to mind?

✔ What are you curious to learn more about right now?

✔ What is your dream for coaching?

✔ What would be an outstanding outcome for you?

✔ What difference can you make for others if you become the coach you imagine?

Allow yourself to frame one question that you would like to answer for yourself while you read other portions of *Coaching with NLP For Dummies*. Capture this question in one word and keep that word in a safe place to remind you of your dream. And if you prefer, capture an image, a perfume, taste or sound that you can return to as you read other chapters in this book.

---

# Peace and happiness

'Can you make me happy?' asks the potential coaching client as he looks for a coach. No, a coach's role isn't to make a client happy! Taking on responsibility for anyone else's happiness is an impossible task. Yet a sense of peace and happiness inevitably emerges from masterful coaching. In fact, the best news is that coaching is really good fun.

Clients may arrive in the coaching space with a sense of being out of control of their lives, as if life is being done to them by some external power. The more people feel like they're guiding their own direction, the greater their sense of contentment.

Concepts like peace, fulfilment and happiness are often considered to be something desirable for the future and elusive given day-to-day challenges. Clients say, 'Life will be good when . . .' and then go on to list myriad things – when the children grow up, when I have a new job, when my business is successful, when I have more time . . .

Yet everyone can choose peace and happiness in the moment on a daily basis. Ongoing personal exploration and developing a relationship with yourself are key – and fortunately the essential activities in coaching!

Recognising you have choices may increase a sense of comfort with not knowing and ambiguity in life. With every decision you take, whether that's about the exercise you do today, the business calls you'll make, the people you speak to or the ideas you hold in your head, you create the person you are and in turn the experiences you have.

By shining a light on his present life, the one he's created, and answers powerful questions, the client learns to notice his ability to influence his current state of happiness and what he can do right now to give himself the happiness and peace he desires.

# Chapter 2

# Gathering the Essential NLP Skills

. . . . . . . . . . . . . . . . . . . . . . . . . . . . . . . . . . . . . . . . . . . . . . . . . .

*In This Chapter*

▶ Developing rapport quickly

▶ Setting your mind for dynamic coaching

▶ Going beneath the words: two key NLP language models

▶ Modelling others' successes

. . . . . . . . . . . . . . . . . . . . . . . . . . . . . . . . . . . . . . . . . . . . . . . . . .

*W*hen you first hear the term *NLP* or *Neuro-linguistic Programming*, it may sound like a software package or operating system. In some ways, that's true: exploring NLP is like discovering a human operating system. Beneath all the jargon, NLP contributes a common sense approach to understanding how people think, speak and take action – one that applies to all aspects and walks of life.

NLP is based on an experiential point of view rather than a cognitive one, that is, you learn most by *doing*, not by being *told* about how NLP works. So as you read about NLP in this chapter, keep in mind how you can experience the approach and use it as the foundation for coaching relationships.

Coaches the world over use NLP to support clients in getting the outcomes that they want – including in the worlds of business, education, health, government and many more. Most importantly, you can use it to improve any area of your own life, as well as that of others.

In Chapter 1, I cover NLP's core framework of rapport, sensory awareness, outcome thinking and behavioural flexibility. I also introduce the specific NLP models that appear throughout the book.

This chapter examines the fundamental NLP principles (and some key techniques) that can jumpstart and enhance your coaching. With NLP you can become a great coach who creates rapport quickly, adapts your language for greater effectiveness, models excellence and encourage your clients to do the same.

# Increasing Rapport

*Rapport* is a fundamental skill in relationships, and the effectiveness of your coaching depends on the quality of your relationships with clients. Having rapport in place at the outset of a series of coaching sessions sets you on the road to success. Good rapport means you are highly sensitive to your clients' moods and responses, as well as highly challenging, really stretching yourself and your clients to exciting levels.

Yet rapport is tricky. Often you become aware of rapport by its absence rather than its presence. Without rapport you have no spark or connection between two people or within a group; the essential links between you are missing.

I once had a disastrous telephone conversation about some potential work in which the client on the other end of the line said, 'I'm too busy for this. Let's cut the polite talk and assume we have rapport.' Actually, you can't ever assume rapport; you need to build it and earn it.

Building rapport involves paying exquisite attention to the other person, including her style, needs and interests. If you're overly concerned about yourself and how you come across as a coach, you stop noticing the client's reactions, which detracts from rapport building.

Laying the foundation for rapport begins even before the first meeting. Notice how a new client communicates by phone or email and respond by behaving in a similar manner. For example, in a simple email connection, you can match the length and style of messages, including the level of familiarity. Similarly, when conversing by phone, be sensitive to the caller's energy and work to match it. See Chapter 12 for more on how to adjust your communication style to build rapport.

## Pacing and leading

If you want to influence anybody to your point of view, take note of NLP's concept of *pacing and leading*. First you need to pace people by listening and paying attention to where they're coming from before you try to lead them round to your way of thinking. NLP advises you to pace, pace and pace again before you attempt to lead. This advice translates as listen, listen and listen some more before you speak. Remember why everyone has two ears and one mouth!

# *Tuning into non-verbal communication*

When you get into the habit of becoming fully aware of your client's breathing, body language, tone of voice and energy levels, you pick up crucial information that she isn't sharing, such as topics that your client avoids – the very places where the real coaching work occurs.

Elizabeth's coach asked her to get some informal feedback in between coaching sessions from her colleagues on the board of directors. Elizabeth contacted the directors and asked each for an email commenting on where her strengths lay and what she may need to change.

When going through the comments, her coach noticed how Elizabeth became breathless and her neck flushed pink when reading some comments, while her breathing deepened and her colour cooled when receiving others. Her coach pointed out the changes in physiology she'd seen and asked Elizabeth what was going on for her while reviewing the feedback. Eventually Elizabeth admitted that she struggled to connect with certain members of the board and felt very upset by any of their comments that she found challenging. She also struggled with feedback that she perceived as unnecessarily complimentary. Elizabeth owned up to not acknowledging good things about herself because doing so felt wrong to her.

At different points in your coaching sessions, consciously breathe in time with your client and ask yourself what you notice about her breathing patterns. Is your client's breath relaxed or hurried? Does it change when talking about certain topics? Or does her face colour change? Get curious about what is going on for your client right now.

*Matching and mirroring* refers to adopting another person's style to gain rapport. Matching and mirroring happens naturally when you are in rapport because you're highly attuned to the other person. If you look at two people in a conversation who are in rapport, you notice that one is like a mirror image of the other. Their bodies move in unison with similar gestures, speed of movement, volume and tone of voice.

Use the following technique to build rapport quickly.

1. **Observe the other person's behaviour.**

   In particular, pay attention to:

   - The way the person uses her body. How does she sit, walk, stand and use gestures?

- The way the other person breathes. Does she breathe with the whole body, including the abdomen, or is the breath restricted with tightness in the neck and chest area?

- The other person's pace and energy levels. Is the person slow or fast-moving? Fidgeting or relaxed?

- The sound of the other person's voice and speed of speech.

2. **Deliberately match and mirror the other person.**

   Choose one or more of the attributes you note in Step 1 and match and mirror it. Rapport may seem easier for you after you adjust a few attributes.

3. **Check whether you have a sense of rapport.**

   The litmus test for rapport is to mismatch the other person and notice whether she follows your lead, adopting your style of behaviour. For example, if you raise your voice a notch or become more animated, does the other person follow you? If not, go back and continue to match and mirror the other person.

There's a fine line between matching and mimicry. People naturally feel uncomfortable if they sense any lack of sincerity from another person. Practise your matching and mirroring in a no-risk situation with family and friends to hone your skills, so that you can do it with great subtlety and consciously build rapport more quickly when you need to.

## *Flexing your communication style*

Behavioural flexibility, the proposition that the person who is most flexible wins, is one of the four key principles of NLP. NLP assumes that the responsibility for the success in any communication lies with the sender, not the receiver. So you take responsibility for other people receiving your message in the way that you intend. This assumption also fits with a principle that coaches encourage their clients to adopt: for things to change, I must change.

NLP pays attention to the preferred style or *representational system*, of different individuals. Identifying someone else's representational system involves listening to *how* people speak – not just what they say – to connect more easily and allow your message to be heard.

Representational systems describe the different channels through which humans code information internally through their senses. The main channels are visual, auditory and kinaesthetic (known as VAK for short), and refer to sight, sound and feeling or touch. *Predicates* are sensory-specific words that give clues to a person's preferences. Table 2-1 gives some examples of sensory-specific words and phrases that your clients are likely to use. As you become familiar with communicating with sensory-specific language, you can adapt your own style to match that of your clients.

## Sharing wave lengths

Back in the 70s, when John Grinder and Richard Bandler were developing the first NLP models, they ran a series of workshops to share ideas and understand more about language patterns. Those early sessions involved a variety of activities in which the pair listened for and experimented with the participants' representational systems.

For example, Grinder and Bandler gave each participant a coloured card according to the participant's representational system (such as red for visual, blue for auditory and green for kinaesthetic) and then ask the participant to join with others who held the same colour card for an exercise. The researchers found that participants communicated more easily in groups made up of people with the same representational system than in groups with mixed systems.

| Table 2-1 | VAK Words and Phrases | |
|---|---|---|
| *Visual* | *Auditory* | *Kinaesthetic* |
| Bright, blank, clear, colour, dim, focus, graphics, illuminate, insight, luminous, perspective, vision | Argue, ask, deaf, discuss, loud, harmony, melody, outspoken, question, resonate, say, shout, shrill, sing, tell, tone, utter, vocal, yell | Cold, bounce, exciting, feel, firm, flow, grasp, movement, pushy, solid, snap, touch, trample, weight |
| It looks like . . . | It sounds like . . . | It feels like . . . |
| A glimpse of reality | So you say | We reshaped the work |
| We looked after our interests | I heard it from his own lips | Moving through |
| This is a new way of seeing the world | Who's calling the tune? | It hit home |
| Now look here | Clear as a bell | Get a feel for it |
| This is clear cut | Important to ask me | Get to grips with |
| Sight for sore eyes | Word for word | Pain in the neck |
| Show me what you mean | We're on the same wavelength | Solid as a rock |
| Tunnel vision | Tune into this | Take it one step at a time |
| Appears as if . . . | Music to my ears | Driving an organisation |
| What a bright day | That strikes a chord | The pressure's on |

Develop your sense of language with the following activity:

1. **Build your own list of VAK words and phrases that you hear in every-day communication.**

   Start with the examples in Table 2-1 and add others you hear in conversation and notice in written documents.

2. **Listen to key words that your coaching clients use to see whether you can pull out a strong preference for visual, auditory or kinaesthetic language.**

3. **As you become familiar with the representational systems, adapt your own style to match those of different clients.**

   Phrase questions to target clients representational systems. For example, match a visual client:

   > Client: I can't *see* where I'm going.

   > Coach: What would it *look* like?

   Match an auditory client:

   > Client: I don't *hear* anything good coming from my team.

   > Coach: What does 'good' *sound* like?

   Match a kinaesthetic client:

   > Client: I can't *get a handle* on this.

   > Coach: What would it *feel* like?

If you have any doubt about another person's representational system, use a variety of different predicates in order to cover all the senses. Don't be unduly concerned if you find some clients have little sensory-specific language. They think and speak in a highly logical and conceptual way rather than through images, sounds and feelings. NLP calls this mode of representing the world *digital language*.

## Connecting with the whole person

When you first meet clients, you encounter them in a particular context of their life or work.

- ✔ If coaching takes place in a business setting, you may see clients in their offices or workplaces and even observe them with some of their colleagues, although you have no clue how they are with their families.

- ✔ If you're life coaching, you may never see your client in a work environment.

## Bigger picture

Michael was coaching Maria as part of a global leadership programme for a North American company. Maria was bright and a very able communicator, so Michael was struggling to understand how she lacked self-belief. She consistently belittled her achievements, only noticing where her skills were lacking.

One day Maria blurted out that her husband didn't believe that she deserved a promotion that she'd earned. After Michael understood the bigger context in which Maria lived, he worked with her to build her self-belief. He realised that she was mapping across her experiences in her home life to work and applying an unhelpful filter to her experience. (See more on filters in Chapter 6.)

Michael challenged Maria to acknowledge every hurdle that she'd overcome, so that she consistently celebrated her achievements on a daily basis. Michael, suspecting both husband and wife behaved in a similar way, encouraged Maria to acknowledge her husband's successes too and see what happened. As Maria grew more confident, her work *and* her home life blossomed.

Of course, any person is much more than what you observe through coaching sessions. People adapt according to their environments, and part of your challenge as a coach is to build a sense of the whole person in order to bring out your client's greatest potential.

Become curious as to how your clients think, feel and behave in different contexts. When you find out where they are already operating at their best, explore that context and then *map across* specific aspects to help clients be their best elsewhere. Chapter 15 explores how to use NLP submodalities to take the qualities and resources clients have in one context and bring them to another.

Consider a client who you want to understand better and then step into her shoes. Use the following questions to construct your own sense of what it would be like to be this person. Ask yourself:

- ✔ What is a typical daily routine like for this person?
- ✔ What gets this person out of bed in the morning?
- ✔ How does this person spend her time?
- ✔ What are the pressures on this person from other people?
- ✔ Who supports this person?
- ✔ How does this person look after herself physically, through diet and exercise?
- ✔ How does this person relax?
- ✔ What's important to this person?
- ✔ What does this person believe to be true?

## At cause or at effect?

The choices people make in the hubbub of each day affect their experiences. You have only to observe the behaviours of two individuals to notice great differences in several areas:

- How they spend time, money and energy
- What they want to pay attention to
- What they hold onto and let go of physically and emotionally
- The goals they set
- The habits they have
- The way they respond to others
- How they look after their health

All these behaviours result from decisions people make, which create their own worlds. When people are *at cause,* they take ownership for everything that happens. When they are *at effect* they give reasons, excuses and justification for what has happened to them.

NLP and coaching both encourage people to be at cause – empowered and responsible for their own lives. Sharing the at cause/at effect distinction with clients is useful so that they can become more observant of how they behave and what they can do to make changes.

While it's useful to step into your client's world, remember to step out of it too, particularly if the client has a very challenging situation! After a session, imagine yourself taking an energetic shower in which you shake out the client's life situation to save yourself from becoming too caught up in it.

If you find yourself becoming over-involved in a client's situation, something is happening to trigger an issue that you need to work on. Coach supervision enables you to step back from your efforts to ensure that you're working in a way that is healthy for both coach and client. See Chapter 1 for more on coach supervision.

# *Working with Some Key NLP Assumptions*

NLP offers a set of guiding principles or convenient assumptions known as the *presuppositions*. This section examines three that are particularly relevant to get you into a strong mindset for powerful coaching:

- The map is not the territory.
- People are more than their behaviour.
- Individuals are resourceful.

When you take these on board, you change your perspective in a way that makes you a more effective agent of change with your clients. You don't need to share these concepts with clients, but keep them in your mind as guiding principles.

# The map is not the territory

You may have heard the phrase 'the map is not the territory'; this fundamental NLP premise comes from the work of Alfred Korzybski, a Polish-American scientist. People create their own realities based on their life experiences, beliefs, values and memories. The words they use describe their *perception* of reality, not reality itself.

The map is the perception, while the territory is reality. For example, Scott, who'd like to find a new relationship, may have a view that: 'I'm too old to be on the dating scene and anyway, all the decent girls are married by age 35.' This is Scott's map of the world based on his experience. However, that's not necessarily the truth: his map may be a very limited one because he hasn't been to the best places to find his soul mate. The real territory holds many more potential life partners than Scott's limited map of the world.

Clients typically come to coaching because they sense that they need to fine tune their maps. Noticing that your clients' maps of the world are different to yours encourages you to be curious about how the maps differ. Where do their maps serve them? Where are they too small or incomplete? You can also encourage your clients to check out other people's maps in order to develop their own.

Jane coached a psychiatrist working in a mental hospital. Her client was extremely diligent, but his desire to get the best outcome for his patients verged on perfectionism and put his own mental health at risk. As Jane notes:

> *My client came from a world where he expected all his clients to behave irrationally. That was his model of the world. As a coach, I tend to think of my clients as rational. That's my model of the world. I found that in order to work with him, I needed to get further into his world in which other people are irrational. Using the NLP perceptual positions, I put him into an observer position to dissociate from the situation and invited him to listen to himself as the irrational client. Then he got the breakthrough he was seeking – he realised that he was being as irrational as the clients who were mentally ill.*

## *People are more than their behaviour*

Human beings are capable of an amazing range of behaviours. At the extreme, they can be model citizens and criminals at the same time. Most people display a range of behaviours with some that serve them well and others that don't. Coaches need to acknowledge a person's human qualities without judgement.

NLP assumes that behaving badly in a particular context doesn't make someone intrinsically bad. Separating the *behaviour* from the *person* is really important in order to coach well. People may behave badly when they don't have the inner resources or ability to behave differently in that particular instance. Perhaps they find themselves in an environment that has unhelpful role models, yet they don't know that at the time.

Through coaching, you can help people to develop new skills or switch to more conducive environments, which can lead to dramatic changes in behaviour.

As part of a team development coaching programme, Richard was allocated a performance coach. In one of his early sessions, Richard confessed that he was really worried about telling his employer about a criminal drug offence in his youth, and as a result he'd avoided government projects that required security clearance. He wasn't sure if the omission of this information on his CV put his job as a project manager at risk. He also referred to himself disparagingly as a criminal. Richard's coach worked with him on a plan to discuss his history with his manager and his HR representative. The coach also reminded him that he was not a criminal, but someone who had offended in the past.

When somebody talks about themselves in a critical way at an *identity level*, you can defuse that criticism by acknowledging it at a behavioural level. For example:

- ✔ If a client says, 'I'm an alcoholic,' you can say, 'You're someone who has a drink habit.'

- ✔ If a client says, 'I'm a fat slob,' you can respond, 'You're someone carrying excess pounds.'

- ✔ If a client says, 'I'm a useless parent,' you can offer, 'You're someone who hasn't yet found the best way to support this child.'

When clients have behaviours that don't serve them, NLP assists by breaking down the behaviours into small and manageable sequences of strategies. (In Chapter 11, I discuss unpacking and redesigning behaviour.) As a coach, you can work with clients to identify any specific aspect of the strategy that may benefit from being redesigned. For example:

✔ A client who persistently overworks can find the trigger that makes her keep going rather than take a break. When she's aware of the trigger, she notices what's happening and has the opportunity to switch behaviour rather than perpetuating the habit.

✔ A client who never quite makes it to the gym can benefit from adding in an extra sub-routine that triggers the new behaviour she desires.

## *Individuals are resourceful*

NLP assumes that people have all the resources (such as mental resilience or the ability to learn and find role models) that they need to make the changes they want. Furthermore, people aren't unresourceful; they may just be experiencing an unresourceful *state* at a particular time. You don't come to coaching with the aim of fixing anyone. Instead, you assist clients to get out of their own way and to recognise their own brilliance, as Marianne Williamson so aptly puts it in the sidebar 'Brilliant, gorgeous, talented, fabulous?'

In NLP, *state* is the internal emotional condition of an individual: worried, happy, confused, joyful and so on.

A person-specific set of physiological characteristics, behaviours and thought patterns accompany each state. Thus, one person may do 'worry' by pacing the room and fretting about what can go wrong. Another person may do 'worry' by waking in the night and feeling nauseous at the sight of food at mealtimes.

If you have a client who's playing small, shrinking into a smaller version of herself, design a challenge to stretch the client out of her comfort zone. (If you have no client in mind, challenge yourself.) Make the challenge relevant to the context in which you're coaching. Some examples of challenges include:

✔ Going on a holiday or adventure alone.

✔ Submitting a proposal for a project.

✔ Making a phone call to someone you believe doesn't want to speak to you.

✔ Organising an event and leaflet drop the neighbourhood with invitations.

✔ Making ten cold calls each afternoon for the next week.

Your client may reject all your suggestions, yet come up with even better challenges for herself that you couldn't have thought of. The important thing is to get her thinking about how to stretch herself.

## Brilliant, gorgeous, talented, fabulous?

In her best-selling book *A Return to Love: Reflections on the Principles of a Course in Miracles*, (Harper Collins), author Marianne Williamson beautifully summarises the potential that everyone has.

*Our deepest fear is not that we are inadequate. Our deepest fear is that we are powerful beyond measure. It is our light, not our darkness that most frightens us. We ask ourselves, Who am I to be brilliant, gorgeous, talented, fabulous? Actually, who are you not to be? You are a child of God. Your playing small does not serve the world.*

*There is nothing enlightened about shrinking so that other people won't feel insecure around you. We are all meant to shine, as children do. We were born to make manifest the glory of God that is within us. It's not just in some of us; it's in everyone. And as we let our own light shine, we unconsciously give other people permission to do the same. As we are liberated from our own fear, our presence automatically liberates others.*

*(Reproduced with permission of Marianne Williamson.)*

People stretch most readily when they feel resourceful and well supported. Chapter 18 guides you through the NLP process of anchoring in order to get your client into the most resourceful state.

# Getting Beneath the Surface

Coaching involves going beyond superficial discussions to uncover what's really happening for your client. In NLP, change happens when you explore values, beliefs, purpose and identity – and the various tools in this book help you delve into all these.

In his seminars and writing, NLP leader Robert Dilts often quotes the Danish physicist Niels Bohr who identified two types of truth: superficial truth and deep truth. According to Bohr, 'In a superficial truth, the opposite is false. In a deep truth the opposite is also true.'

Is your head spinning yet? Think of the distinction this way: a superficial truth is that 'John is everybody's friend.' A deeper truth is that 'John is also capable of making enemies.'

 People are complex and capable of a complex range of behaviours. NLP aims to get to the deep truth for your clients by acknowledging the shadow side of life as well as the lighter side. The shadow side can involve acting badly at the same time as the lighter side can work miracles. After people are awake to such a deep truth, they can choose where to devote their energies – to the bad or the good, the light or the dark.

In this section, I look at key ways to access your clients' natural creativity by exploring language patterns and establishing behavioural change.

# Uncovering language's meaning: Two key models

In NLP programmes, participants work with two key language models, the Meta and Milton models, that John Grinder and Richard Bandler built through their studies of great therapists. Each model describes specific language patterns that they observed. They were curious as to how some people excelled at effecting change for their clients and found that superb communication skills rely on not one but several models.

As a coach, both models offer lessons in adapting your language to communicate better with your clients. Based on their individual maps of the world, people naturally filter language through three core processes:

- Deleting information.
- Making generalisations.
- Distorting information.

Both models have a range of detailed linguistic patterns that NLP practitioners explore in depth during training. *Neuro-linguistic Programming For Dummies* by yours truly and Romilla Ready (Wiley) devotes a whole chapter to both the Milton and Meta models. I explore the filters of distortion, deletion and generalisation in Chapter 6.

## The Meta Model

The Meta Model seeks to overcome ambiguity. Its value for the coach lies in challenging a client's potential limitations. This model approaches language by asking questions that gather more specific information that is missing in communication.

An example of the Meta Model in practice may be for you to say, 'I've got a tough client right now.' Unless you give me more specifics or I ask you questions to gather information, I have an incomplete map of your experience and may make up the rest of the story. To overcome this lack of detail, the questions to ask can include:

- What specifically is tough about your client?
- Who is this tough client?
- Will this client be tough later or just right now?

The aim of the Meta Model is to ask questions that bring details that have been filtered out to a client's conscious awareness.

### The Milton Model

By contrast with the Meta Model, the Milton Model approaches language from the opposite direction by making specific information deliberately vague. It relies on making broad statements that are hard for a client to disagree with.

An example of the Milton Model in practice may be that you say: 'I've got a client at the ABC company who is driving me mad because they keep re-scheduling appointments and hasn't paid her bills for three months.' A response in the Milton Model would be to shift the specific to a more ambiguous:

- ✔ 'That's right. Sometimes people are challenging.'
- ✔ 'You'll make it work in your own time, you know.'

The aim of the Milton Model is to put clients into a light trance in which they can access their unconscious resources by switching from the particular detail to a larger framework.

John Grinder and Richard Bandler created the Milton model by painstaking analysis of the language patterns of the great hypnotherapist Milton Erickson. As a masterful storyteller, Erickson conveyed therapeutic messages through his words and speech patterns to very sick clients. Storytelling and metaphors can be hugely powerful ways of distracting your clients' conscious minds that may be busily caught up in their own stories. Stories and rich word pictures place clients in a more resourceful state to come up with creative solutions and make new meanings from their experiences. I write more about creating your own stories in the *NLP Workbook For Dummies,* co-authored with Romilla Ready (Wiley).

## Playing with the time dimension

People often come to coaching with struggles around time, particularly business executives or manic parents with busy lives and many demands on them. They may say that they are looking to 'manage time' – clearly an impossible goal!

Time and how people organise time is fundamental to the structure of someone's experience of the world. Clients vary tremendously in how they perceive, structure and react to time. These preferences affect their ability to be punctual, plan, be willing to listen and take action.

## Monochronic or polychronic?

A *monochronic* time system means that things are done in sequence, one thing at a time in precise steps. Time is scheduled, arranged and managed, and people worry about wasting time. Some monochronic cultures, such as the Swiss, Germans and Americans, place a huge emphasis on getting tasks done in a scheduled way. (Notice the generalisation when talking about all the people from one country!)

A *polychronic* time system is one in which several things are done at the same time and a more easy-going approach is taken to time. This kind of time system is more typically found in Southern Europe, Latin America, African and Arabic cultures where people often pay more attention to relationships than watching the clock.

Be aware that your view of time can be different to your neighbours and appreciate the difference.

Time lines (find more in Chapter 16) are great tools for coach and client. By creating and exploring time lines in coaching you sessions, you identify whether your clients operate:

- ✔ **In time.** These people live in and for the moment. Consequently, they may struggle to plan for future events.

- ✔ **Through time.** These people take a detached view of time or they may seem to observe time passing. They may put life on hold until some time in the future and not enjoy the moment.

- ✔ **In combination.** When people can switch between in time and through time, they get the best of different worlds. They enjoy spontaneity in their current reality and they can plan for the future. As a coach, you need to do both: dance in the moment while holding the larger agenda of your client's life.

Working with questions of time changes perspective on an issue. For example, ask the client to imagine a time in the future when things are different with a question such as: 'How will this be six months from now?' Taking the client into the future like this allows her some distance from the topic under discussion and thus yields insight.

Coaching people who struggle with time is not about squeezing more activity into their busy schedules; it's about setting priorities, which begins by exploring values. When you know what's most important for you and your client, you can set off in the right direction. In Chapter 8, you can read more about making choices based on values.

---

## Staying clean

James Lawley and Penny Tompkins, authors of *Metaphors in Mind* (Developing Company Press), are pioneers in developing clean language training, based on their modelling of the work of the late David Grove. Penny and James's approach, known as Symbolic Modelling, allows clients to become more resourceful when faced with challenging topics. Clean language is particularly appealing to coaches who want to preserve their clients' models of the world without imposing their own.

Grove felt that other therapists imposed their own maps on clients, so he created a set of clean questions that explore the client's own metaphorical landscape. While the questions look strange out of context, they can enable a client to work on an issue without ever revealing the content. For example, Penny and James suggest that one way to put a client in a resourceful state is to ask, 'And when you're at your best, that's like what?'

See www.cleanlanguage.co.uk for a wealth of resources on clean language.

---

## *Separating process from content*

One of the strengths of NLP coaching is the ability to work with clients without getting hooked in the details of their stories. In Chapter 17 I discuss submodalities, which offer ways that you can work with clients on topics without knowing the specific content of their issues.

The danger of hearing too much about someone's story is that her story connects with your own stories. You may become distracted and even begin to share your own tales, only realising later that you've been colluding, not coaching. (See Chapter 10 for ideas to cut through collusion.)

## *Capturing the secondary gain*

Clients love change to be easy, which becomes possible when they recognise the *secondary gain* of a behaviour. NLP assumes that all behaviour, even very bad behaviour, has some kind of positive outcome for a client. After you honour this principle, you're on track to get to the deeper truth below the unwanted behaviour, and thus to come up with new strategies. The NLP coach looks to reveal and honour the secondary gain that keeps a client stuck.

Sharon had been a chain smoker all her life. Even though she'd lost a best friend, Sue, to lung cancer, she continued to smoke. When asked what she got out of smoking, at first she could only list the negatives, such as the regular bouts of bronchitis and fear of cancer. When her coach challenged her, she came up with a list of gains that included:

> ✔ Time away from squabbling children
>
> ✔ A break from my desk
>
> ✔ Gossip with colleagues
>
> ✔ Connection with friends at the pub

What surprised her most was that she also recalled the pleasure of time with her late friend and said she'd felt most strongly connected with Sue when the two smoked. Her coach worked with her to find alternative ways that she could meet each and every one of these positive needs without smoking.

The following exercise provides coaching on an unwanted behaviour. Examples to focus on include unhelpful habits such as procrastination, being impatient or staying up too late. Ask and answer the following questions, in order:

1. What are the positive things that this behaviour is doing for you?

2. What else do you get out of doing this? (Keep asking this question until you're sure you have a complete list of all the things you get from the behaviour.)

3. Which of these benefits do you want to keep?

4. In what other ways can you meet each identified positive need?

As you work through the questions, create a list of other possible ways to meet each need. Review the list and select the new behaviours that you can adopt wholeheartedly to replace the unwanted behaviour. (Turn to Chapter 10 for more ideas for establishing new habits.)

# Modelling Excellence

Modelling lies at heart of NLP, and learning about modelling provides a fast track to developing new ways of behaving and being. NLP assumes that people can learn much faster by finding models of excellence. After all, if someone has already successfully done something, why waste time reinventing the wheel? Instead, find someone who has already trodden the path you want to follow.

Modelling is particularly valuable when your clients are enthusiastic about wanting to make change. In Chapter 11, I explore the modelling process in more depth, and you see that modelling can extend from easily observable behaviours to less obvious ones, such as modelling beliefs and thought patterns.

## Finding and following exemplars

Modelling begins when your client has clear outcomes and can identify her *exemplar,* the person she can learn various strategies from. The more specific clients are on a tangible skill, the easier modelling someone becomes. Think about it: modelling someone who can fix the shower or run a charity supper night is probably easier than modelling someone who knows how to be happy.

The ancient philosopher Socrates provides a superb role model for coaches: 'As for me, all I know is that I know nothing'. By staying in the 'know nothing' space, you as a coach remain curious and open to discover rather than to teach.

Sian is a business analyst who knew she wanted to be a better communicator in her work within a local housing association in order to further her career. Based on a performance appraisal and some honest feedback from colleagues, she came to performance coaching with a clear idea of five areas of communications she wanted to work on over a period of months. Her agenda centred on:

- ✔ Making strong first impressions.
- ✔ Building effective working relationships.
- ✔ Negotiating contracts to get the best deal with builders.
- ✔ Presenting confidently to tenants.
- ✔ Participating proactively in team meetings.

Although her coach had a strong background in communications, she wanted Sian to take ownership of her agenda. Her coach suggested that Sian find two or three role models for each of the five qualities of strong communication, so that Sian arrived very well prepared for each coaching session to explore what she'd already discovered.

Begin to feed modelling questions into your coaching conversations when clients are ready to work on the 'how to' of behaviours they're looking to change or skills they want to develop. Ask your clients: 'Who do you already know who's achieved the capability that you want to learn?' 'Who can you model?' Encourage them to choose models from a range of different environments and activities.

## Shifting to unconscious competence

Coaching and personal growth go hand in hand. Your clients can discover more about themselves, how they relate to others and what they truly want out of their lives, so that they take action following each session. Coaching creates responsibility in the client for doing things differently and thus achieving more. And as coach, you can learn something new from every client you work with.

## Unconscious plus conscious mind

NLP loves to tap into the quirks of the uncon- scious mind for its wonderful qualities of creativity, intuition and the ability to work holis- tically. Your conscious mind has awareness of what's happening at a given point in time: it's logical, sensible and may be best-suited to the boring tasks like getting you to file your tax return on time; your unconscious mind can do wondrous things like store a lifetime of memo- ries, come up with creative ideas and take care of your emotional well-being.

Your unconscious mind is a wonderful learn- ing machine. Give it experiences like a walk in nature, meditation, time to write in your journal or watch the stars, a trip to a gallery or concert, and it is in its element. As a coach, encourage your clients to engage in activities that free them from conscious, busy activities and you open up the amazing powers of unconscious thought.

Achievement isn't always about attaining huge goals: it can be changing some- one's approach to life. Often this is about giving her time to think and enjoy the moment in a relaxed way.

When you accompany your clients on their coaching journey, they naturally move through four steps of learning; NLP identifies these steps as:

- ✔ **Unconsciously incompetent.** Clients don't know what they don't know. At this point, they are operating in the dark. You're encouraging them to reduce the blind spot.

- ✔ **Consciously incompetent.** After clients start paying attention, they realise how much they don't know. Clients in this space can feel vulner- able; coaches can add positive reinforcement and encouragement of the client's strengths and commitment to learning.

- ✔ **Consciously competent.** Clients know what they are doing, yet still may refer to notes and checklists. Coaches can support these clients to keep practising until they reach the final stage.

- ✔ **Unconsciously competent.** Clients do the new behaviour naturally with- out consciously thinking about it. Here the client feels empowered and the coach has done her job.

Your own journey as a coach naturally shifts through these stages as well. After you notice that you are unconsciously competent in some way, you suddenly discover a whole new area where you have so much to learn. Such is the joy of coaching! As your skills increase, you become a model of excel- lence for newcomers and you can continue to look for new models from whom you can learn.

# *Moving from confusion to congruence*

Everyone goes through periods of confusion; it's part of the human condition. NLP views confusion as a powerful state of transition. You're suddenly aware that something is amiss and you want an answer. Your search has begun!

The hypnotherapist Milton Erickson developed a technique using confusion to deliberately put clients into a trance. Often he played on the ambiguity of words, using questions and statements that included words that sound the same and have different meanings such as 'write' and 'right'.

Confusion assumes some kind of muddle or blur. It disrupts your normal thinking processes and puts you in a space to change. All of which make confusion an excellent place to inspire coaching.

Matthew moved from a banking job to an accountancy role in the not-for-profit sector working for a small international charity: he assumed that it would be a friendlier organisation to work for than the bank. He'd always had some mild problems with migraines, yet two months into the new job, he was suffering very badly with weekly attacks.

Through working with an NLP coach, he realised that the migraines were exacerbated by the in-fighting within the new organisation. Matthew valued customer service, strong financial management and wanted to make a difference for the charity's beneficiaries. Yet he felt that the charity's director was an insincere character more concerned with getting his staff to work on insignificant activities that furthered his own career. The boss had a reputation for alienating all around him. The clash of personal values was showing up as physical symptoms for Matthew.

With his coach, Matthew worked on challenging the boss around reprioritising projects. Only then did he feel the work he was doing added value for the beneficiaries, and his migraines subsided.

NLP also talks about *congruency*, that sense of personal alignment when you're walking your talk. Another way to consider congruency is as a state of flow, when you have a sense of inner peace and harmony. Think back to a time when another person told you 'I'm fine', but the tone of voice or body language didn't match at all. You knew instinctively that something was wrong that the other person wasn't saying – or perhaps even acknowledging. You recognise the conflict and inconsistency when congruency is absent.

In NLP coaching, you're working to model congruency with yourself in order to encourage it in your clients. Congruency shows up as having presence, integrity, wholeness and being inspiring to others; you're living according to your values. Beware: congruence is infectious!

# Chapter 3

# Developing Your Coaching Alliances

*In This Chapter*

▶ Getting the coach-client relationship off to a great start

▶ Establishing trust and safety in your coaching sessions

▶ Assessing and enhancing your professional competencies

▶ Recognising the qualities that make a great coach

*C*oaches often describe coaching as a *designed alliance*; a dynamic relationship between two people – the coach and the client – who communicate fluently with each other.

This chapter focuses on getting the coach-client relationship off to the best start possible by building trust. I also touch on the four core areas of competency that any professional coach needs to deliver throughout the coaching alliance and then explore further qualities that a coach brings to strengthen the alliance.

## Defining the Client-Coach Alliance

Coaching demands trust, respect and integrity between the players – qualities that underpin all strong alliances. (I examine the process of building trust in the following section.) That said, the coaching relationship has some unique characteristics.

Think of the art of coaching as a dance between two figures on the dance floor. When the partners in the dance are in complete rapport, the dance is smooth and enjoyable. You can almost touch the rapport between them. Similarly, with a strong coaching relationship, the work becomes easy. The client enjoys the finest chance of getting the desired results while the coach revels in the satisfaction of doing work he loves. Without this chemistry in the relationship, both parties suffer disappointment.

Unlike other relationships in life, a coaching alliance may be relatively short-lived, more likely to last months rather than years. While therapy often continues for years, coaching may only take six or eight sessions, spread out over a few weeks. With coaching, two people come together for a defined purpose, and their project is to make some difference in a specific area of the client's work or life.

The success of the coaching comes as much from the client as the coach, yet often the client hasn't had a coach before and is a novice at designing this kind of relationship. Hence the coach takes the lead in the dance, at least initially, until the client gets familiar with the give and take of the alliance.

From the outset, invest time and energy in getting to know each other. Also acknowledge the need for trial and error in which both you and the client are open to discovery. You never know how another person ticks immediately, unless you both give feedback to one another.

The joy of coaching comes from the special qualities of the client/coach relationship. People who choose to spend their lives as coaches are immensely privileged. You accompany clients on journeys of personal discovery in which others trust you with thoughts, ideas, fears and dreams that they may have never voiced to another soul before, not even themselves.

As the coaching progresses, each session builds on the previous one, developing and deepening the relationship. Familiarity also brings its challenges. Coach and client may become too matey or get into a habitual way of working. Like any relationship, coaching can turn stale with unhelpful patterns.

Plan to regularly review your relationships with clients so the coaching alliance can continue to give your clients what they need. Feedback is an essential part of coaching best practice.

At regular intervals, check in with your clients to evolve the alliance. Ask basic questions, such as:

- How is the coaching working?
- What do you need more of?
- What do you need less of?
- What can we do better or differently?

Listen to your clients' responses and work with them to formulate action plans for adjusting the flow of your forthcoming sessions. For example, they may like coaching to be a quiet, reflective time or relate better to a snappier pace. They may want to brainstorm ideas or use the time as thinking aloud space. Some types of questions work better than others to shift their thinking. Time spent developing the client-coach relationship is incredibly valuable to the overall success of the client's experience.

# Building Trusting Relationships

*Trust* is a complex thing to define in any kind of relationship. It involves qualities such as:

- Reliability; being able to depend on the other person to do what he says he will.
- Confidence in the other person's honesty.
- Worthiness – a sense of valuing each other and yourself.

Building trust takes time. In sales situations, for example, common wisdom says that you need to contact a prospect seven times before he buys from you. So unsurprisingly, many coaching connections come from word-of-mouth recommendation; your reputation as a trusted coach goes before you.

During the initial meetings your words and actions need to demonstrate that you are a coach who clients can trust. You don't have long to prove your trustworthiness. A whole coaching contract may only last for six sessions, so you need to get up to speed fast. In every interaction with your client, you must live by the principles of confidentiality, ethics, integrity and respect – which are exactly what I cover in the following sections.

## Keeping things confidential

To say that confidentiality is an essential ingredient in establishing a coaching relationship may be to state the blindingly obvious, but your clients must feel extremely safe in your hands. Reassure them of this fact in the first few minutes of their first sessions and remember that safety is a fundamental human need.

Consider what *confidential* actually means to you by putting yourself in your clients' shoes. As a client, what do you want from your coach? For example, in order to build trust in any relationship:

- Both parties must know the boundaries of the relationship. As coach, you aren't acting as friend or consultant.

- Both parties must agree the contractual terms of the way you work together, including the fee structure, scheduling of meetings and location.

- Clients must feel completely secure to share information honestly with you.

Of course, the specifics of any confidentiality issues or agreement – who is entitled to know what information – vary, so I address confidentiality issues in the following sections. Whatever the specifics of your coaching situation, you, as the coach, need to be clear about what you say about any clients and to whom. Your conversations about confidentiality can cover many facets, including how you keep records and notes, who may know the identity of a specific client, and what type of content may go with permission outside conversations between the two of you.

Some clients are naturally quite open, while others are extremely reserved. I coached a director in his own office, and he has subsequently shared ideas that came out of the coaching about his own strengths with his colleagues. By contrast, I met another client in a quiet hotel area because he was terrified that anybody remotely connected with work would see us together. A client's preferences and concerns at the initial meeting give you useful clues about how the client behaves, what supports and what holds him back. For example, the director who was more open found life much easier than the reserved client who had many issues around self-confidence to work on. One was comfortable with his identity while the other was finding out about himself.

### Private clients

With private clients and business owners, the confidentiality rules can be very straightforward. As Figure 3-1 shows, nobody outside the two of you needs to know anything at all about the coaching. No names or details are shared with the outside world unless the client offers to provide a testimonial or reference to support the coach's marketing to other clients, and even then the content of the sessions remains private.

Be sure to talk with clients about supervision as part of your discussion of confidentiality. For coaches (like myself) who have a coaching supervisor, explain the value of supervision to increase your competency and the possibility that you may want to take a case study into your own coaching session, although in such a way that the identity of the client remains confidential. If one of my clients isn't happy with this explanation, I respect that completely and don't use the client as an example when I'm receiving supervision.

# Researching the coaching bodies

Coaches don't need to be licensed in order to practise, yet those who take their work professionally are members of a professional body to support their continual development. The main international professional coaching bodies that are independent of coach-training providers include:

✔ The International Coach Federation (ICF): www.coachfederation.org

✔ Association for Coaching (AC): www.associationforcoaching.com

✔ European Mentoring and Coaching Council (EMCC): www.emccouncil.org

In addition, you can find a number of smaller, local professional bodies operating in other countries.

**Figure 3-1:**
Coaching a private client creates a closed loop of information.

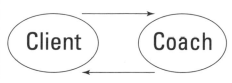

### Executive clients

The client-coach relationship becomes more complex with executive coaching for corporate and organisational clients. Simply put, the person funding the coaching has an interest in the outcomes of the sessions.

In these cases, I recommend starting the coaching with a three-way *contracting session* that includes the coach, the coaching client and their manager or sponsor, as Figure 3-2 shows.

**Figure 3-2:**
Coaching an executive client is often a triangular relationship.

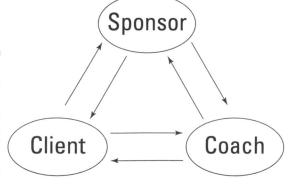

A contracting session enables you to set expectations about what the coaching is about, why the investment is being made and what change the manager is expecting. This session can also provide good insight into how the organisation works and how the coaching client and manager related to each other. As you assess the situation, ask yourself:

- ✔ Has the client chosen to be coached or told he must be coached?

- ✔ Does the manager or sponsor support your client or is there tension between the two?

- ✔ Is coaching a last-ditch effort before firing the client?

- ✔ Is coaching seen as a valuable investment in a valued employee?

At contracting sessions, I invite the manager or sponsor to give some brief input on the qualities and strengths of the client and any behaviours and skills he thinks need to be developed for the client to succeed in his role. I also look for insight into the bigger system that the client works in. What's the culture like? What changes are going on? What are some challenges my client may be up against that are beyond his control?

All this information shapes the big agenda for coaching. For example, suggestions may arise that a client works on leadership style, new business development or skills such as communication or team-building. Perhaps the client has a poor work-life balance and needs to become better at organising and delegating.

In terms of feedback to the organisation, I always explain that I don't supply any detailed content about the sessions to anyone, unless the coaching client has given permission. This boundary preserves confidentiality. Manager and client may want to share details on actions and plans, and they must establish their own agreements. What I do is report back on whether the person turns up for coaching and engages with the sessions. After all, coaching is a significant investment by an organisation, and you, as the coach, have a responsibility to see that the money is well spent.

### *Internal clients*

If you're an internal coach – someone who takes on coaching at work for other employees – you must set very clear boundaries between the different roles you have in an organisation and recognise and declare any conflicts of interest. You may even need to resign as coach if you're asked to evaluate a client for a project or job.

# The ICF Standards of Ethical Conduct

The International Coach Federation presents guidelines for all ICF members providing professional coaching services. Here's a sample:

- ✔ I will not knowingly make any public statement that is untrue or misleading about what I offer as a coach, or make false claims in any written documents relating to the coaching profession or my credentials or the ICF.

- ✔ I will, at all times, strive to recognise personal issues that may impair, conflict, or interfere with my coaching performance or my professional coaching relationships.

- ✔ I will conduct and report research with competence, honesty, and within recognised scientific standards and applicable subject guidelines. My research will be carried out with the necessary consent and approval of those involved, and with an approach that will protect participants from any potential harm.

- ✔ I will maintain, store and dispose of any records created during my coaching business In a manner that promotes confidentiality, security and privacy, and complies with any applicable laws and agreements.

- ✔ I will disclose to my client and his or her sponsor all anticipated compensation from third parties that I may pay or receive for referrals of that client.

- ✔ I will not knowingly take any personal, professional or monetary advantage or benefit of the coach-client relationship, except by a form of compensation as agreed in the agreement.

- ✔ I will not give my prospective clients or sponsors information or advice I know or believe to be misleading or false.

- ✔ I will have clear agreements or contracts with my clients and sponsor(s). I will honour all agreements or contracts made in the context of professional coaching relationships.

- ✔ I will carefully explain and strive to ensure that, prior to or at the initial meeting, my coaching client and sponsor(s) understand the nature of coaching, the nature and limits of confidentiality, financial arrangements and any other terms of the coaching agreement or contract.

(Source: International Coach Federation. www. coachfederation.org)

**ANECDOTE**

Trust between client and coach takes a long time to build and is easily lost, as Jonathan found out. As a young software sales support manager working in a corporate organisation, he was offered coaching to support his career development. His coach was an internal HR specialist, and Jonathan found himself discussing his strengths and career opportunities. In one session, he talked openly about his concerns about his abilities in particular sales situations with a major account customer. Soon afterwards, the company went through major restructuring and downsizing. Jonathan discovered to his horror that some of the information shared in confidence was used by the HR department and Sales Director in making decisions about the allocation of roles in the new organisation, and ultimately Jonathan lost his job. Little wonder that he's now wary about the information he shares and only hires coaches that he assesses thoroughly and pays for himself. Clearly the coach wasn't acting ethically, and Jonathan potentially had a case for unfair dismissal.

## Are you enough?

When new coaches start out, they suddenly become aware of how much they have to learn, which can lead to debilitating self-doubt. I often share with them the story of renowned therapist Carl Rogers, whose work influenced the development of NLP. In a seminar, Rogers analysed what he did as a therapist by demonstrating his positive approach to the client in a therapeutic session. He expressed the following profound insight:

*I realise there's something I do before I start a session. I let myself know that I am enough. Not perfect. Perfect wouldn't be enough. But that I am human, and that is enough. There is nothing this man can say or do or feel that I can't feel in myself. I can be with him. I am enough.*

As a coach, remember that you are not perfect, but you are enough. Often just being with your client is the greatest gift to him.

The Carl Rogers story demonstrates the power of setting your intent before a session (that is, deciding how you want to operate); the trusting relationship between coach and client begins when as coach you have trust in yourself.

## Operating with ethics and integrity

Ethics are the guiding principles of your coaching. Any doubts about them call your integrity into question and link back to the instinctive question in the client's mind: 'Can I trust this person?'

As a professionally qualified coach accredited with the International Coach Federation, I take the ICF code of ethics as my benchmark for the way I work (see the sidebar 'The ICF Standards of Ethical Conduct'). Other coaching organisations and affiliations have similar principles that are worth checking out on their official websites. Reviewing all these codes of conduct gives you a sound basis to develop your own principles regarding how you work with clients.

Some key points include:

- Be honest about your qualifications.
- Keep confidentiality.
- Honour agreements.
- Avoid conflicts of interest.
- Serve your client's best interests.

## *Honouring human reactions and limitations*

In coaching, clients engage in personal change work with great courage; they bring their humanity and their limitations under scrutiny. Although coaching is about becoming the best you can be, the best approach to the process also accepts the fact that no one is perfect. Indeed, perfection would be a miserable and dull state of affairs.

Avoid striving for perfection because it's unattainable and ends up wrecking your confidence. Also, as a coach who shows that you're human and imperfect, you give your clients permission to be human too.

I am often surprised by how little coaching some coaches have had themselves. Hiring your own coach so that you know what it feels like to be on the receiving end of coaching forms an essential part of your skill development. From each different coach, you gain a huge amount of insight into the ways others work. These experiences inform your own development. Coaches who aren't willing to be coached themselves limit their own growth.

# *Contracting Competently with Clients*

These days many people in roles that involve managing or influencing others call themselves coaches, so it's easy to overlook the fact that coaching is a skilled profession with professional training. Some coaches are extremely experienced in their practice, others less so. All come with different experiences and methods that shape how they work.

Professional coaches refer to *contracting* as the verbal contract or agreement between coach and client. Contracting covers all the practical arrangements of the coaching as well as an agreement on the style of coaching – how much the client wants to be challenged, what areas the client is willing to talk about and what, if anything, is out of the scope of the coaching.

A coaching alliance, as opposed to a one-off coaching session, operates within an overall framework that is likely to develop through the following stages:

- ✔ Preliminary discussions and chemistry check.
- ✔ In-take session in which you establish the contract.
- ✔ Ongoing sessions.

✔ Mid-contract review (as part of a session).

✔ More ongoing sessions.

✔ Completion session and feedback.

All coaching relationships have their ups and downs. Clients may very well blame their coaches if the changes they seek are facing setbacks or not happening quickly enough, rather than taking full ownership for their progress. Open communication between coach and client is essential.

## Setting the groundwork

Initial phone calls and chemistry checks in person before the real contract begins enable both parties to decide if they're happy to work together (head to Chapter 4 for more on the intake process). This discussion usually takes about an hour face to face, slightly less by telephone, and is probably free of charge. At these points, you as a coach need to reflect on:

✔ Do I feel comfortable with this person?

✔ Do I believe that we can work well together?

✔ Can I make a difference?

✔ Can I serve this person's agenda?

✔ Would somebody else be a better choice for this person?

✔ Is there any reason why I can't operate honestly and ethically for this person?

Often clients don't really know what they're looking for in a coach and choose on the basis of 'this person has the answers I seek', particularly in executive coaching. The client may be tempted to choose someone who is more of a mentor, able to offer advice and share useful professional connections, rather than act as a coach. See the sidebar 'Coaches and mentors' for more.

## Picking the right person

Finding the best coach can take time, and working with different coaches at different points often yields the best results. However, looking at career experience on a CV is not the only indicator of the quality of the coaching. Clients need to consider coaches' personalities and coaching styles, as well as their credentials and previous work.

# Coaches and mentors

The terms *coaching* and *mentoring* can be confusing, especially for clients who have never experienced either but know they need to make professional changes.

A simple comparison between coaching and mentoring is to consider the difference between *asking* and *telling*.

✔ A *coach* is someone who brings an independent view, often with no specific knowledge, to share. The work of a coaching session is about *asking* questions based on the pure coaching skill set and challenging the client to achieve his goals or greater potential. See the later section 'Arriving with core coaching competencies'.

✔ A *mentor* is someone who teaches and guides based on particular knowledge, experience and skills. The emphasis in mentoring sessions is on *telling*, or giving advice.

A coach needs to make this distinction clear to the client, and if necessary, point him towards a mentor if he needs mentoring rather than coaching.

Some questions for the client to reflect on before engaging a coach include:

✔ Does this person have appropriate coaching qualifications and coaching experience for me and my situation and goals?

✔ Will this person bring out the best in me?

✔ Can I communicate openly with this coach?

✔ Do I feel that this coach listens to me?

✔ How do I want to work? Predominantly face to face or by phone? Can this person accommodate my preferences?

✔ Am I willing to invest in the coaching experience in terms of my time, money and energy?

✔ Does this coach understand and respect the change I'm trying to make?

✔ Has this person coached other people with similar issues and needs?

For the alliance to work, the coach must be able to answer these questions satisfactorily if the client asks. If you as the coach feel that the client hasn't currently got the necessary commitment to coaching, then tell him to come back later when he's ready.

After a client selects a coach and they begin working together, each needs to be aware of their relationship and how to give and receive feedback openly. This giving and receiving is what NLP describes as 'the difference that makes the difference', and is the key to an effective relationship over time. Chapter 14 offers tips for giving feedback that can be applied to the coaching relationship.

# *Arriving with core coaching competencies*

Because you can't attend university and study for a degree in coaching, various professional organisations and affiliations have established core competencies for members.

Most of these groups provide summaries of their core competency expectations, often as handy checklists. Reviewing these summaries allows all coaches, regardless of professional training and affiliations, to check their skill level and decide where they may need to raise their game.

The core coaching competencies that the International Coach Federation uses for its accreditation process are listed below. The ICF groups the core competencies logically into four clusters. However, no cluster is more important than another; they're all critical for any competent coach to demonstrate. For full definitions and descriptions of related behaviours, visit the ICF website at www.coachfederation.org.

- ✔ **Setting the foundation.**
  - Meeting ethical guidelines and professional standards.
  - Establishing the coaching agreement.
- ✔ **Co-creating the relationship.**
  - Establishing trust and intimacy with the client.
  - Creating coaching presence.
- ✔ **Communicating effectively.**
  - Listening actively.
  - Questioning powerfully.
  - Communicating directly.
- ✔ **Facilitating learning and results.**
  - Creating awareness.
  - Designing actions.
  - Planning and setting goals.
  - Managing progress and accountability.

In the following sections, I look in detail at what these four clusters of competencies mean at the start of forming a coach-client alliance.

## *Setting the foundation*

As a coach, you need to operate ethically from the outset and demonstrate that you have a professional code of ethics that shapes the way you work. At the beginning, make clear the distinctions between counselling and therapy. (See Chapter 1 for the distinct characteristics of both.)

Several potential clients have contacted me over the years because they thought they wanted coaching and soon found they had some deeper issues that they wanted to unravel slowly with specialists in longer-term therapeutic relationships. This type of realisation is not a failure on the part of the client or the coach. Clients need to be functioning in their lives and work without serious emotional issues to resolve in order for coaching to be most valuable. Indeed, many clients hire both a coach and a therapist, and some professionals work in parallel.

Coach and client also need to agree about what is being offered, including the number of sessions, in-between communication, fees and the inclusion of any personality or behavioural tests. Create a clearly written letter of agreement that summarises the contract, and then have both parties sign it.

Be especially clear about your cancellation terms and payment if a client can't make a session or wants to reschedule a session at the last minute. Also agree what happens if the client wants to quit the coaching relationship altogether.

### Co-creating the relationship

The ICF defines establishing trust and intimacy with the client as 'the ability to create a safe and supportive environment that produces ongoing mutual respect and trust.' I discuss how to build trust earlier in the section 'Building Trusting Relationships'.

As coach, you must champion new behaviours for the client, including risk-taking, and also be mindful of asking permission when addressing sensitive subjects, such as family arguments or unhealthy eating or drinking habits.

Coaching *presence* is something almost tangible that you can observe when a coach has a spontaneous, open and confident style. You hear presence mentioned frequently in the coaching world as something that is important to have because it demonstrates personal confidence in the coaching role as well as respect for clients.

A similar concept in NLP is *congruence*, which happens when people are clear about their identities, values and beliefs, all of which show up consistently in their behaviour. Congruence combined with presence allows coaches to hold the coaching space open for clients with a light touch and energy that makes experiencing even the strongest emotions possible.

As a partner in a professional services firm, Elaine has hired various coaches over the years during her own career transitions and times when she's been stretched on major client projects. She feels she can pick up on presence when hiring a coach and acts on her own gut feel rather than looking for a proven business track record. She says:

*Presence is definitely something I look for in a coach, and it's hard to put into words, yet you feel the difference when someone has it. For me, it's just a feeling I get that this coach has the confidence in his own ability to work with you on important issues very intuitively. They make it easy for me to explore what I need to see without trying to prove anything about themselves. It's clear that the coaching is going to be about me, and his personality doesn't get in the way.*

### Communicating effectively

Effective communication includes the core skills of active listening, powerful questioning and then clearly articulating what you notice. NLP-trained coaches comes to coaching armed with a strong awareness of communication – from knowing how to build rapport and dissociate from emotional issues to paying fine attention to people's language patterns and non-verbal cues. See *Neuro-linguistic Programming For Dummies* and the *Neuro-linguistic Programming Workbook For Dummies* by myself and Romilla Ready (Wiley) for in-depth content and exercises. You can always refine your listening and questions skills; read more in Chapter 6.

Communication competencies get below the *surface structure* of what clients say to discover what's really happening for them at a *deeper structure*. As a coach, you then share your observations in a way that has the most positive impact on clients, perhaps by being very specific on details or illustrating a point with metaphor and analogies.

### Facilitating learning and results

When you create awareness for your clients, you shine light on their blind spots; the things they do, yet don't recognise or take ownership for doing. By helping clients discover new beliefs and behaviours that galvanise them into action, you assist them to get the results they want.

After clients have this awareness, life is never the same again; the knowledge doesn't go away. You can build on it to discover practical structures and discipline that truly work for your client, who can then develop and learn beyond the coaching session.

Be sensitive that everybody learns in different ways. Actions that work for one person to cement learning almost certainly won't work for another. For example, Brian was struggling with spending time on strategic work to look at the future development of his business. He arrived for coaching with a wonderful assortment of diaries and colour-coded spreadsheets that had been suggested to him by colleagues, none of which he kept to. After we explored how he worked at his best, Brian realised he needed a much simpler approach to his day. He focused on committing to 50 minutes of uninterrupted work with ten-minute breaks to stretch or make quick calls or send email. We looked at how he could break various important activities into a few fixed 50-minute packages each day. This structure was much more sustainable for his work style and realistic for his schedule. Brian achieved more with less time and effort.

The key concepts for helping with learning and results revolve around inviting your clients to:

- ✔ Make a *commitment* to action.
- ✔ Be *accountable* for following through on action.

As coach, you hold a coaching agenda of the areas your client is working on, yet he owns the details of his goals and plans. During the sessions, you invite the client to commit to actions and let you know how he's getting on, the celebrations and challenges that happen between sessions. One of the reasons that coaching is effective is that the client makes a statement about what he truly wants to somebody else, and that supports him to stay on track, knowing that someone else is interested and supportive of his progress and willing him to succeed.

Use the competencies in Table 3-1 as a personal checklist to rate your own performance after each session as well as throughout the overall contract. For example, how good were you at asking powerful questions? Were you fully present or slightly distracted with other thoughts?

Rate your performance using a scale of 0 to 10, with 0 being low and 10 being high. Use this table to make a note of what you did specifically and where you can improve. Identify areas where you'd benefit from more training. Any accreditation process looks for evidence that that you demonstrate all these competencies, and your coaching stays more effective when you raise your own awareness of the competency framework.

| Table 3-1 | Personal Competency Checklist | |
|---|---|---|
| **Personal Competency** | **Score 0–10** | **Notes** |
| Meeting ethical guidelines and professional standards | | |
| Establishing the coaching agreement | | |
| Establishing trust and intimacy with the client | | |
| Creating a coaching presence | | |
| Listening actively | | |
| Questioning powerfully | | |
| Communicating directly | | |
| Creating awareness | | |
| Designing actions | | |
| Planning and setting goals | | |
| Managing progress and accountability | | |

## Monitoring motivation

Coaching is like an iceberg. The actual session between the client and coach shows up as the very tip of the iceberg, while the rest of the client's life is the huge remainder beneath the surface. In general, the coach only sees the client in the session and has to deduce from that brief time together how the client behaves on a day-to-day basis. Sometimes you do get the chance to see clients interact in other places, socially or in business, which gives you more evidence of how they actually behave rather than what they tell you, but many strong coach-client relationships are based solely on interactions in sessions.

In order for your client to make progress on his agenda, you make *requests* of your client to do some things differently and then support and encourage him to make these changes in the easiest ways. Clearly the client doesn't report to the coach, indeed the business transaction is the other way round; the coach is hired by the client.

Ultimately, the motivation for making and committing to change comes from your client – just as the client is responsible for his successes. Coaching is not about nagging! However, given that coaching is a partnership, you must check for motivation and stay curious if things aren't happening. The question for both coach and client to be curious about is: 'What is going on that may be getting in the way?'

*Metaprograms,* the unconscious filters that determine how people think, provide helpful clues about others' motivations, particularly motivations that differ from your own. (See Chapter 10 for more on metaprograms.) Investigate how clients naturally work at their best and then bring this information into the coaching relationship. For example, if a client shows that he likes to follow a process, he'll be confused by too many choices in coaching sessions, so work in a logical sequence. If another client likes lots of details, get him to report back in details rather than summarising.

## Sharing expectations for success

If I asked a dozen coaches 'What makes coaching a success?' I'd get a dozen answers. Success means different things to different people; NLP calls the word *success* a nominalisation.

In NLP-speak, a *nominalisation* is an abstract noun, usually built on a verb. *Love*, *trust*, *honesty* and *relationship* are all nominalisations. These abstract nouns are hard to define in a way that everyone agrees on.

To get more clarity on the meaning of a nominalisation for an individual, turn the noun back to a verb. Rather than the question 'What is success in coaching?', ask something such as 'How specifically will you succeed in the coaching?' Notice that by changing the language in this way, someone is taking ownership for the concept of success.

In the initial stages, coach and client need to agree on what their particular brand of success is like. Set specific, clear definitions, especially when a client's agenda is vague, such as: 'I want to be happy/confident/ successful.' The danger in these situations is that coaches become mind readers, interpreting these concepts in ways that may not match their clients' understanding at all.

To work out specifics or recover information that clients may be omitting (consciously or unconsciously), ask questions such as 'What precisely will you look like when you're happy?' or 'What exactly will you be doing when you're confident?'

At the start of the coaching alliance, establish a shared understanding of what success (and any other abstract concept) looks, sounds and feels like. When you and your client are specific, you're both set up to meet expectations.

The skills and techniques you use in coaching often spill over into other areas of your clients' lives. For example, one client told me that the way we worked in coaching reminded her to negotiate with a commercial supplier for her company with more specificity than her normal style dictates. She spent time setting ground rules and getting to know how the supplier worked best before embarking on a major office refit project. This ripple effect is one of the value-added benefits often overlooked when measuring the return on the investment of coaching.

# Thriving on Curiosity and Spaciousness

Great coaching leaves people feeling curious about their lives and with a sense of space to breathe. Often clients arrive frazzled, anxious and confused and leave feeling light and energised once more. The art of coaching lies more in the way coaches are *being* in the relationship rather than in what coaches are *doing*. Your behaviour acts as a model for your clients to emulate. A coach who is positive, calm, clear and fully concentrating in the moment with rapport (being) is better than one who can demonstrate a specific coaching tool or NLP technique (doing).

In this section I look at some of the extra qualities that coaches bring to the client-coach alliance that make this relationship so special.

## *Feeling the power of silence*

A fast-paced world leaves few opportunities to savour silence; a challenge that contributes to the frazzled experiences of many corporate executives. In the silent spaces of coaching sessions, clients can access their real power, presence and passion. This silence allows them to retrieve what they've lost deep in themselves. Silence takes clients into a space of self-reflection, where different perspectives lay waiting for them to uncover. Here they achieve leaps in awareness, which in turn leads to positive change.

So often organisations measure people's worth by how visible they are and how cleverly they speak. Who dares to stay quiet in a corporate meeting for fear that they aren't projecting their brand profile or being seen to be a valuable contributor? Similarly, coaches may be tempted to prove their worth and fill silences.

Silence is a powerful coaching tool. A prerequisite for silence is to slow yourself down. If as a coach you're racing along, your clients will follow at speed. Take time to consider your questions, deliver them at the right moment and allow them to land. Notice the effect, paying full attention to the details of facial expression, gestures and tone of voice, as well as anything clients actually say. See Chapter 6 for more on questioning and listening.

Consider silence as the white space necessary around the words to highlight them. Prepare for coaching by being silent for a while before you go into a session.

Many coaches talk with great enthusiasm, which can make you appear too eager in clients' eyes, as if you're not inclined to listen to them. One of my favourite master coaches, Jan, tells the delightful tale of a telephone coaching session during which she placed her phone on mute. (Always a good idea if you have a dog barking, child chatting or builder drilling away nearby.) However, she forgot to release the mute button as she asked the next question and made further comments on what she was hearing. The session was going extremely well, with the client getting wonderful insights until eventually she heard him ask: 'Jan, are you still there?' The lesson for Jan was just how powerful that silence had been for her client even though Jan had felt she needed to be asking questions or making reinforcing statements to demonstrate her presence. Less is more.

Find a quiet, comfortable place in your home or office where you won't be interrupted. Sit in silence for 20 minutes, doing absolutely nothing and clearing your head of thoughts. As thoughts come, just tell yourself, 'Interesting' and let them go as if they belong to someone else. Notice what you see around you, the colours and shapes; what you hear in terms of sounds, voices and music. How do you feel emotionally and physically when you are quiet? Is pressure building inside of you to hurry up and do something? Let these pressures go. Simply enjoy being in the silent space.

## *Accessing intuition*

Have you ever noticed how when you go for a walk in the woods, drive up a mountain or look at a lake or the sea, you just feel different? Perhaps you gain a sense of clarity, awe at the universe or a new perspective on something you've been wrangling with in your head. Such connections put you in touch with more of yourself as you connect with the bigger natural world. They enable you to tap into the creative part of yourself and your unconscious – rather than your logical – mind. You are in the home of *intuition*, the place where you make unexpected connections.

Voicing your intuition in coaching is incredibly valuable. You're sharing the intangible; a thought, feeling or idea that seems to come from nowhere and links with curiosity. Intuition comes naturally when you slow down and pay exquisite attention to your energy, noticing where something feels right and where it goes off-balance.

As a coach, trust what you are thinking – that hunch, theory or idea that nudges you to say something, and then share it with your client. Have some language to frame these moments of initiation and ask *permission.* Try something like:

> ✔ I have a theory that may be completely wrong. Can I try it out on you?
>
> ✔ My instinct is telling me something here. Is it okay to look at this?
>
> ✔ There's something I'm feeling about this. Would you like to hear about it?

Intuition is not necessarily right or wrong; it can just shed extra light on a challenging area.

I experiment in some sessions with simply blurting out whatever comes into my mind in the moment. Perhaps a metaphor comes to mind, a feeling in my body like tension in the stomach or something that the situation reminds me of. This technique is a powerful way to let go, be in the moment and make the coaching more intuitive. When I'm more intuitive, the way opens for the client to access his own intuition too.

## *Being okay with not knowing the answers*

Don't fret if at some point in a session – or even at the very start of a session – you don't know the answer to a client's question. The client needs to find his own answers. You can work with clients in a spirit of curiosity to open doors that have been closed or begin exploring some possible solutions (Chapter 6 can help you to frame better questions). Curiosity has an attractive childlike playfulness, as if you're both sharing a delicious secret, while coaching that becomes hard work saps energy from both parties. When you're curious, your clients go looking for the answers themselves. Affirming the value of curiosity in your sessions takes the pressure off you as the 'expert' and serves your clients so much more because they celebrate finding their own answers and taking control of their existence.

When curiosity comes into play, clients can envision themselves as being on a magical quest with their coaches as allies by their side. The client, not the coach, is the hero of the story; the one who finds the treasure.

Incorporate the word *wonder* into your conversation to encourage a client to become more curious. Try beginning sentences with 'I wonder . . .' as in 'I'm wondering what is coming up for you this week?', 'I wonder how this could be fun for you?', 'I wonder what that's about?' Ask the question and then be silent while the client processes it.

Questions that engage curiosity have a different quality to them. They shift beyond seeking logical information into a space of open exploration for the best possible outcome. Exploratory questions are open-ended and require answers beyond 'yes' or 'no'.

Practise your ability to ask different types of questions, including information-gathering questions and exploratory ones that engage someone in a line of inquiry.

1. **Quickly write down a list of questions you'd ask a client who's facing a major decision.**

   For example, perhaps you have a client faced with a decision about his future. He's considering retraining in a new career, which requires three years of study, and is trying to decide how to move forward. What do you ask him at your next coaching session?

2. **Assess your list of questions.**

   Ask yourself which ones are information-gathering questions and which encourage open exploration and staying curious about the future.

   *Information-gathering questions* collect more information. Some examples include:

   - What are your travel options?

   - How will you fix that problem in the system?

   - What are you going to do next and when?

   - What meals will you eat this week?

*Exploratory questions* are broader and encourage thinking outside of the box. Some examples include:

- What becomes true for you if you do *x*?

- What would *x* do for you?

- What other options might be even better?

- What's it like to feel content with all aspects of your life?

- How could this decision/choice/task be easy?

Both information-gathering and exploratory questions have their place at different points in coaching. Sometimes your clients need challenging into action, yet the danger is that they choose one solution too quickly by simply following the information-gathering route.

3. **Develop and revise a few of your information-gathering questions to give them that exploratory edge.**

The following questions shift beyond information-gathering to a deeper level of exploration.

- What are the top skills you need to do this job? (Information-gathering) could be rephrased as: How could the new skills learnt here enhance your life in other ways?

- When will you get your building work done? (Information-gathering) could be reworded as: If completing this work became straightforward, what difference would it make for you?

In your next coaching session, allow yourself time to frame exploratory questions as they come to you in the moment. These types of questions expand and stretch clients' thinking, opening them to more choices.

## *Sponsoring clients' natural expertise*

As you deepen alliances with your clients, hold the thought that they are experts in their own lives. They've lived with their experiences all their lives, and you only see a fraction of who they are. Respect and honour that knowledge without judging the choices they've made.

Some NLP assumptions, also known as *presuppositions*, can inform your coaching sessions. For instance, NLP proposes that:

✔ **Individuals have all the resources they need to achieve their desired outcomes.** Individuals hold amazing potential to develop and grow. They're naturally resourceful and don't need to be fixed by anyone. They can find the necessary resources for change either within themselves or externally, for example, by hiring a coach.

✔ **Every behaviour has a positive intent.** People do what they do for a reason; behaviour gives them a *secondary gain*. For example, a young man may be struggling to get out and meet new people; and the reason he stays sitting on the sofa may be because he fears making conversation with strangers. The secondary gain he receives may be to feel safe and warm staying home with mum and dad, who don't expect small talk. In order to make change, the client needs to be aware of the secondary gain and find other ways to meet that need, such as going out to a new group with a sociable friend until he feels confident enough to go alone.

Sponsoring involves acknowledging and championing someone else without judgement of them. By sponsoring clients' identities – by believing that they are naturally resourceful and not the same as their unhelpful behaviours – you can naturally release their potential and accompany them as a valuable coach on their personal quests. Such sponsorship boosts confidence that permeates all aspects of your clients' lives.

# Part II
# Building Core Coaching Skills

The 5th Wave                    By Rich Tennant

"I sense that you're becoming more defensive and unapproachable lately."

## In this part . . .

Ever wandered around in a foggy haze with no real sense of direction? So much becomes clear when you know where you're going and how to get there. In this part you find out how to shape a precise coaching agenda with your clients so that they're fired up to work in a way that's powerful and compelling. You'll hone the essential skills of questioning and listening.

Also in this section you'll find two core frameworks to get results quickly – the Logical Levels and SCORE models. In addition, you'll bring the power of one of the greatest creative talents, Walt Disney, into the goal-setting space to encourage your clients to dream bigger dreams and make them happen. Here you enable your clients to star in the movies of their own lives.

# Chapter 4

# Shaping the Agenda for Change

. . . . . . . . . . . . . . . . . . . . . . . . . . . . . . . . . . . . . . . . . . . . . . . . . . . . .

## In This Chapter

▶ Beginning and ending sessions effectively

▶ Gathering important personal and background information

▶ Sifting through the client's aims and ideas

▶ Setting the priorities for sessions

. . . . . . . . . . . . . . . . . . . . . . . . . . . . . . . . . . . . . . . . . . . . . . . . . . . . .

C lients come to coaching for a rich variety of reasons: they recognise that something is not working as well as it could; they're hazy or unclear on their direction; they sense that things can be different and they're not sure how to go about making changes; they have a lot on their plates and need support; they want a sensible sounding board; they've hit tough times, transitions or new challenges; or they need to make decisions.

Coaching isn't always about solving problems. It can provide space for people to stretch and grow in their careers, develop leadership abilities or generally maintain a sense of well-being.

When the coaching begins, clients may have a jumble of thoughts and issues racing around in their heads, rather like a wardrobe in which everything has been piled in! Coaching gives this jumble a shape, adding specific entry points and exits for each session as well as the overall contract. In between the clear opening and closing phases (which I discuss in this chapter), you and your clients have a rich period to explore that confusion of ideas. Your role as coach is to provide a supportive platform that gives clarity, structure and process so that clients can explore and shape their agendas.

This chapter looks at how you create shape and focus out of the content that the client wants to work on. I show you how to create efficient, effective openings and endings to individual sessions, how to gather the most useful details during the coaching intake process and hold clients' stated agendas over time while also being flexible enough to dance with them in the moment according to what's happening for them.

# Opening and Ending Sessions with Elegance

The way you open and end any conversation makes a real difference in the value both parties take from the interaction. Have you ever been in mid-conversation with someone when your talk ended too quickly? Perhaps you've been on the phone or in a meeting and the other person suddenly says, 'Got to go, thanks a lot,' and then disappears. You're left feeling short-changed and confused. You may wonder if your presence even mattered to the other person.

Some years ago, a recruiter interviewed me by telephone for an interim role and opened the call with: 'Let's skip the niceties. Your CV looks good. I haven't got much time. Just tell me who's the most senior person you've worked with and how much money they saved by working with you.' Whoa, this comment, before I'd had a chance to say 'Good morning', left me feeling uncomfortable for the whole interview.

---

## First impressions

In *Body Language For Dummies* (Wiley), personal impact coach Elizabeth Kuhnke offers a wealth of advice for engaging with and influencing others. In particular, she reminds readers of the old adage that you never have a second chance to make a first impression. Meeting potential clients for the first time is an interview-type meeting in which they decide if you're the best coach for them.

Elizabeth advocates that in order to go into interviews or meetings feeling good about yourself, you need to consider six things:

✔ **Warm up.** Remind yourself of what you want to achieve and how you want to be perceived. Practise breathing from your abdomen, warming up your voice and letting tension go from your shoulders.

✔ **Claim your space.** You have a right to be in the meeting with a potential client – and you're ready and waiting to greet the client with a smile.

✔ **Make your entrance.** Move confidently, smoothly and purposefully – especially if you're entering your client's office. When the client visits you, ensure you're a welcoming host, making her feel comfortable in your space.

✔ **Shake hands.** Hold your palm straight and return the same amount of pressure.

✔ **Position yourself.** When you and the client take your seats, move your body to be at 45 degrees to the other person rather than directly across a table. Face to face is too intense. Respect the client's personal space by keeping a comfortable distance.

✔ **Make your exit.** When the time comes to leave, move calmly, smile and head towards the door. Turn back and smile again, so the last impression is of your face, not your rear! Likewise, if the client is visiting your office, accompany her to the door and ensure her last impression is a friendly farewell.

Any satisfying communication requires the basic ingredients of rapport and connection. NLP talks about the idea of *pacing* and *leading*. You need to pace people and create rapport before leading them on to what you want to communicate. Without pacing, neither party feels listened to or able to listen to what the other person says. (See Chapter 2 for more on building rapport.)

In this section I look at how to begin and end each coaching interaction, thus wrapping the session with purpose. For special considerations related to initial meetings with potential clients, flip to Chapter 3.

## Being prepared

Preparation for coaching starts in advance of the session, not as you greet your client. As you work with specific clients, you're likely to think about them outside of your sessions and notice ideas to share with them. You certainly want to allow time to prepare for the session immediately beforehand and to capture your thoughts at the end of each session. Without that space, you begin to feel frazzled. Coaches vary on how much time they spend in preparation, but typically this averages out to 30 minutes before and after a face-to-face session and slightly less for shorter telephone coaching.

For the first session, set up your own paperwork with a form for capturing session notes. You typically send an intake pack for the client to prepare for the first session, plus contract and payment details (see the later section 'Capturing the current reality').

Marketing consultants often offer training to self-employed consultants, including coaches, on how to book yourself solid. On the surface, this promise may sound appealing, but be wary. Alex, a fellow coach, put himself forward for a professional coaching accreditation and needed to increase the number of hours he'd coached in order to complete his coaching log. He booked his diary solidly with additional clients and found himself offering one-hour sessions on the hour, every hour, for many hours each day. He quickly realised that he hadn't allowed space to process his thinking and was not serving his clients well by jumping from one session to the next. 'Never again would I do that,' Alex says. 'Having my diary booked back to back was futile. I was not in a good state to coach.'

### Welcoming clients

As you prepare for any coaching interaction, consider how you'll open the conversation. Ask yourself how you want to connect with your client and make them feel welcome, particularly if you're talking by telephone. You can keep your welcome very simple, just a couple of words such as, 'So, this is your time, I'm wondering . . .' or 'Hello, Jo . . .'

Your tone of voice and body language need to convey your welcome. See the sidebar 'First impressions' for more tips. Whatever you choose to say or do, your language and actions must demonstrate that the space is open for your clients and that they have your full attention.

### Generating effective opening questions

The questions that you ask at the beginning of a session send your clients thoughts in a particular direction. Depending on your understanding of your clients' needs, you may take them along a route that reviews what's happened since you last spoke, keeps them in the present moment or directs them to the future.

Notice the impact that your choice of initial questions has for different clients. For example, if you ask: 'Tell me what's going on for you', your client may go straight into a long and detailed story – one that leaves you looking for ways to interrupt. For this type of client, you may want to experiment with a more specific opening, such as 'What's the one thing uppermost on your mind today?'

Or you can lead with some open questions, such as:

- What would you like to work on today?
- What would you like to focus on?
- What's on your agenda?
- What's the most useful thing for you right now?
- What have you noticed since we last spoke?
- What have you appreciated about yourself in the last few weeks?
- What are some things you have to celebrate?
- What are the challenges you're facing?
- What's coming up for you?

---

## What's occurring?

Immaculate dialogue, characterisation and understated humour has won the British TV comedy series *Gavin and Stacey* many awards. This good-natured working-class sitcom takes the viewer across Britain, westwards from Billericay in Essex to Barry in Wales. Nessa, Stacey's larger-than-life best friend, played by actress and series co-writer Ruth Jones, has many of the funniest lines on the show. In her inimitable Welsh accent, Nessa often begins each interaction with her friends with the question, 'What's occurring then?' – a question that's becoming a stock phrase amongst fans. She asks the question with a consistent tone of voice each time and allows it to land beautifully, demonstrating the ability to ask a very open question and giving the recipients their turn in the spotlight to answer thoughtfully.

Avoid very specific questions such as 'What are you doing about your financial plan?' or 'How's your relationship with Fred been?' The client's life has continued in the interval between the coaching sessions, and what was important last week or last month may not be what's really on her mind today.

## Setting intents

A popular story amongst NLPers tells of a group of trainee NLP Master Practitioners who were completing a modelling project and had the opportunity to observe a shaman healer working with a client to heal a leg injury. As I mention in Chapter 2, modelling closely examines the thoughts and actions of an exemplar, in this case, the shaman, and so the enthusiastic students made notes of the great man's movements and words, relishing the opportunity to ask questions of him. One question that landed well was 'When does the healing actually begin?' The students expected to hear an answer such as 'the moment when I shake my hands above the wound' or a similar response. Instead, the shaman answered, 'When I went up the mountain alone yesterday and set my intent.'

An *intent* directs attention to an outcome, a desired result. When you set your intent for a session and invite your clients to do the same, you focus on getting the results you want. You may set your intent to work on a particular competence in a session or just to be more confident or challenging. The intent is focused on serving the client in some way, yet isn't necessarily discussed with the client.

Before any session, consider your intent as coach. How do you want to behave today and what would be a good outcome for you? Perhaps you want to say less, focus on non-verbal messages or be more challenging. Maybe you'd like to improve a skill, such as cutting through your client's long-winded stories?

As you plan for your session, make a short note of your intent for the session.

## Taking the learning forward step by step

By signing up for coaching, clients are taking that first brave step towards making change in their lives. From the intake session right through the contract, clients are on a voyage of self-discovery: figuring out what makes them tick, how they relate to others and what they can shift to get the results they desire.

Much of the learning takes place unconsciously. In order to create greater awareness, bring your observations to your clients' attention and invite them to find places outside the sessions also to practise and make these new insights habitual.

Incremental change – like compound interest on savings – is powerful. Clients who steadily develop new habits and integrate them into their everyday lives stand a better chance of lasting change, compared to over-enthusiastic ones who do something quickly and intensely as a one-time effort. Think of the contrast as the difference between a crash diet and a healthy slow weight-loss scheme based on sound eating and exercise for life. Similarly, cutting back on expenditure by 10 or 15 per cent each month over the course of a year adds up and hurts less than one drastic cut. Less, spread out over a longer time frame, can be more.

As you and your clients start to design actions together, find other areas in their lives where they already get the results they want and apply similar strategies. Notice how they take in information best. Do they prefer time to reflect or just like to have a go? Any action clients take needs to be *ecological*, that is, it must fit with their existing commitments to family, community or work and other things that are important to your clients to sustain. Most clients already have a lot on their plate, so progress steadily rather than over-loading the action list too fast.

As part of the contracting process and ongoing feedback, let your clients know that your aim is to pace them rather than overload them. Check that they feel the pace of coaching is working for them.

## Ending things well

When you close sessions, you have the opportunity to leave clients in a satisfied state, as if they've finished a healthy and enjoyable meal. With the action-planning complete, your clients are on the point of moving on. Now's your chance to ensure that you've acknowledged the work your clients have done and the commitments they've made to coaching. Think of this moment as the stamp of approval that endorses success and keeps them motivated.

A curt 'thank you and goodbye' leaves clients feeling dismissed. By contrast, when you allow concluding space, you encourage clients to become aware of the value of giving themselves this time to think differently and notice how they're becoming different as a result of coaching.

Some possible concluding questions include:

- ✔ What's the most valuable thing you're taking away?
- ✔ What have you really discovered today?
- ✔ How will you be different in future?
- ✔ What's changing in you as a result of thinking differently?
- ✔ What does all this add up to?

The end of a session can also be an appropriate time to follow the concluding questions with a special type of question known as an inquiry. An *inquiry* provokes thought beyond the more tangible subject matter of coaching. These types of questions give your clients something to ponder for a longer time and then bring back their answers to open up the discussion in the next session.

Some example inquiry questions include:

✔ What is a rich and precious life for you?

✔ What is your baseline state as you go through next week?

✔ What could make life easy for you?

✔ What triggers you to be at your best?

✔ Where is your attention going?

You can read more about inquiries in Chapter 6.

On a practical note, wrap up the coaching session with a clear understanding of the next scheduled appointment and tie up any administrative details, including any questions about payment. Ideally, have the payment and diary organisation set up in advance for a series of sessions or handle it separately by email. Then the feel-good factor of the actual coaching isn't diminished by the details of a business discussion.

# Fine-Tuning the Intake Process

Some coaches parachute straight into a coaching relationship to focus on the issues that clients say they want to work on. Others spend time – from a couple of hours up to a couple of sessions or days – laying the foundations for the coaching contract before work on the stated agenda begins. In Chapter 3, you can read about the personal qualities you need to bring to the contracting phase to build trust and provide a safe space for your clients.

In the following sections, I look at how to develop your process for taking in new clients that suits the needs of both coaches and clients.

## Laying the groundwork

The long-term success of any coaching interaction lies in getting off to a good start, and experienced coaches agree that the initial set-up phase is essential to getting results.

The *intake process* is the time you spend with a client, gathering personal and background information and building a relationship. The process allows you to capture a snapshot of what's going on in the whole of the client's life and work.

During the intake, clients often find that what they thought were the key challenges are only part of the picture; in fact, these issues may not be the ideal places to focus their energies in order to get the best results. You need to point this out to the client and encourage her to develop a more rounded agenda. Typically, I work with a client on three main topics or themes. For an executive or business owner, perhaps one topic based around their leadership style or career development, one on a key project or strategy and another more personal aim that supports their general well-being outside of work. Private clients typically are looking at changes in health, relationships or career, and the final agenda shapes up after we've looked at the balance wheels (see the next section for more on balance wheels).

NLP advocates flexibility. For clients who are clearly hungry for instant gratification, the intake process can seem too long-winded, so be prepared to adapt yours if necessary. For example, you can choose to capture pertinent background information over a couple of sessions entwined around coaching on real-time issues.

Consider using the SCORE or NLP Logical Level models that I outline in Chapter 5 to achieve some quick wins and build your clients' confidence in the value of longer coaching engagements.

## Capturing the current reality

The intake process is your opportunity to get a detailed sense of what's happening right now for your client, what NLP calls the *present state*. During intake, you also set expectations of the *desired state*, the specific life experiences that the client truly wants to create.

Ideally, clients have had time to consider what's on their agendas and have some ideas of what they want to get from coaching – that way they're already engaged in the process.

In advance of your first session, you can mail or email a new client a preparation pack that covers some of or all the following topics:

- ✔ Your profile and coaching qualifications.

- ✔ Information about coaching and what to expect in the sessions. Chapter 3 has some useful ideas on this topic.

- ✔ Forms to gather contact details, including key stakeholders if you're coaching a business client and names of friends or family for a private client, and background information. (See Figures 4-1 and 4-2 for sample forms.)

- ✔ A Wheel of Life (see Figure 4-3 for an example).

- ✔ A professional wheel form (as shown in Figure 4-4).

- ✔ Space to record strengths and talents.

- ✔ Space to write about personal values.

- ✔ Outline agenda of the areas the client wants coaching.

- ✔ Space to provide other information, including previous experience of receiving coaching, feedback that she's received at work from peers, staff or managers, or psychometric data that may be relevant.

In addition, the coach needs to draw up a coaching contract with details of session arrangements, payment terms and cancellation conditions (see Chapter 3 for more on the coaching contract). Figures 4-1 through 4-4 provide sample forms to include in your own intake pack.

 Filling out lots of forms can overwhelm clients who don't like paperwork, so consider agreeing the contract in person as part of the initial intake session and then asking clients to work through the various preparation documents between sessions. Doing so gives clients time to consider how committed they are to change and you an opportunity to design the sessions and timing to best suit clients' needs and style.

### Contact details

Ask your client to fill in a basic contact information form, as shown in Figure 4-1.

| Name | |
|---|---|
| Address | |
| Telephone numbers<br><br>Home:<br><br>Business:<br><br>Mobile: | |
| Email work (1): | ——————————— |
| Email home (2): | |

**Figure 4-1:** Contact information form.

## Background information

Ask your client to fill in a form like Figure 4-2 to provide a basic profile.

| | |
|---|---|
| Current job or role | |
| Name of employer of type of business owned | |
| Key members of your family | |
| Key friends | |
| Key colleagues/or stakeholders who you interact with in the organisation _____ | _____ |

**Figure 4-2:**
Background
information
form.

## Wheel of Life

The Wheel of Life, shown in Figure 4-3, is divided into eight sections to represent the relationships between different areas in your life. Score your current level of satisfaction with each life area. Assume that the centre of the wheel is scored at 0 (for low) and the outer edge is scored at 10 (for high). Join your scores on the wheel with a line to create a new outer edge. The new perimeter of the circle represents your current life wheel. How bumpy would the ride be if this were a real wheel?

## Professional wheel

For your professional wheel, shown in Figure 4-4, use the eight segments on the blank wheel to list the key areas that are your work priorities. Label with titles that are meaningful for you. Some examples may include: Delegation, Communication, Strategic Planning, Team Development or Team Working, Business Processes, Decision Making, Professional Development, Managing Change, Customer Service, Risk Taking, Innovation/New Products, Results/ Financial Performance.

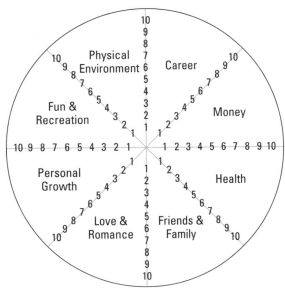

**Figure 4-3:**
Wheel of
Life form.

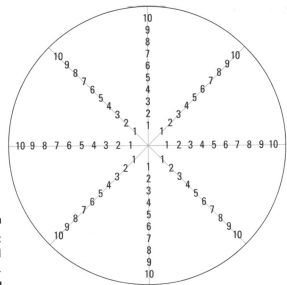

**Figure 4-4:**
Professional
wheel form.

### Key talents and strengths

Take a piece of paper and list all your talents. Be sure to include technical expertise such as DIY projects or an ability to understand the workings of the latest mobile gadget. Include activities that you're especially good at in the home: ordering shopping, looking after pets, creating games for children, helping the older generation. Think of every situation you can – work, community, friends.

List your outstanding personal qualities. Are you patient, ambitious, great on detail? Do you have big dreams? List every skills and quality that comes to mind until the page is packed.

### Values

Your values dictate the choices you make in life. Take a sheet of paper and come up with a list of core values that are central to your identity.

- ✔ What is important to you? (For example, health, honesty, freedom, learning.)
- ✔ What do you care about?
- ✔ What do you want more of in your work? What do you want more of in your life?
- ✔ What do you want less of in your work? In your life?
- ✔ What would make you stay in a situation when everything goes wrong?
- ✔ What would make you leave when everything is going well?
- ✔ Think about your extreme moments. When has life been amazing? When have you felt on top of the world? What was important to you about this time?
- ✔ What makes you angry, fed up or frustrated? What value is being violated that stops you being true to yourself?

### Outline coaching agenda

What areas do you want to focus on during this coaching contract? For each one, give a simple heading, plus a short statement of how you'll know when you've completed it. For example:

**I complete the website.** I've sourced quotes and appointed an external agency. I have created a project plan and managed the steps to go live by 5 October.

**I feel more confident.** I'm able to talk in group situations and feel that I have something valuable to contribute. I can say no to ideas that aren't a good fit for my interests. I pass unsuitable projects on to colleagues.

# Formulating the Desired Agenda

As I discuss earlier in this chapter, the intake session allows both client and coach to get a sense of how they work together and see what's happening in all facets of the client's life. After intake, the actual agenda becomes the focus of work. Coach and client keep coming back to the agenda, usually with a mix of work and home-life content.

## Refining agendas

Some clients want to complete the intake forms in advance of a session, others prefer to work through them in person with the coach. Whichever is the case, go through the forms with your client in person to get a shared understanding of the client's starting point. Then both parties can keep a copy in paper form or an electronic version. You need to keep these documents confidential.

Initially your clients' agendas will state the core aims they want to work on, with simple measures of the present state and desired state at the end of the contract. Early on clients need to articulate to you the changes that they want to experience and express a broad sense of what their lives will be like when changes happen. They are now engaged in creating a new possibility.

Accept that the goals may seem a little vague at the initial meeting. Your focus is to create structure and focus for the goals, so clients aren't overwhelmed by all the possible things they could be doing. The NLP concepts in Chapter 7 help refine your clients' goals.

Encourage your clients to have a mix of professional and personal topics as aims. However, people need to choose things they want to change for their own benefit, not just what they feel they ought to work on to please someone else. Start framing their aims in positive language of what they want rather than what they don't want. Following are some sample aims that clients may include in their outline agendas:

- ✔ Professional aims

  - **Personal effectiveness.** Identify how I spend my time, hire a PA and delegate all the budgeting administration and event logistics.

  - **Team building.** Build a united sales and marketing team that can communicate our product offering.

  - **Leadership development.** Develop my style of leading the team, focusing on my best qualities.

  - **Sales.** Double the revenue from major account customers in the next three years.

  - **Organisation.** Create job specifications for all my team and reorganise people to support the new business structure around the new product areas.

- ✔ Personal aims

  - **Health.** Develop healthy eating habits and an exercise programme that support me to reduce my weight to 65 kilos by next September.

  - **Confidence.** Have the confidence to make a speech at the Rugby Club dinner.

  - **Wealth.** Double my savings in the next three years and have a deposit for a house.

  - **Relationship.** Put myself on an online dating site and attract a minimum of one date per month for six months.

  - **Home.** Refurbish the spare bedroom so I feel happy to invite a guest to stay.

  - **Career.** Polish up my CV, approach three recruitment agencies and ask friends to give me practice interviews.

Most executives who come to coaching are already very hardworking and focused on business success, so developing business aims is often easier than personal aims. Encourage clients to also include a goal or two related to their own well-being, health, home or external hobbies in order to build their personal resilience.

# Keeping on track

Clients hire coaches to enable them to achieve the change they are struggling to achieve on their own. Work with your clients to set challenges that stretch without overwhelming; you want them to push the boundaries and make moves.

As a coach, your role is to hold your clients accountable for action – to remind them of what they say they want to do. Avoid nagging your clients. Simply share with them what you notice and question whether a particular action is taking them forward.

Most often clients forget to notice what is going well and beat themselves up about what hasn't happened fast enough. A key part of keeping clients on track is to celebrate any progress, however small, that takes them in the direction of achieving their agenda.

I always keep records, purely for my own use, of clients' agendas and progress session by session so I can see the journeys they're taking. I also encourage clients to keep their own notes and prepare for the sessions between our meetings by recording their own observations in a notebook. Not everybody likes to keep notes, yet they serve as a reminder to pay attention to all the successes, however small, along the way.

Create a personalised tracking form for your clients to record their experiences in the time between sessions. Include a handful of questions that draw their attention to how they're staying on track with their own agendas. Include space for them to capture the high spots and low spots and the challenges they'd like to bring to their next coaching session.

## *Staying in the moment as real life happens*

NLP holds that the person who has the most flexibility in a system is the winner. A coaching agenda may begin by being focused on one area and then the client decides that she really wants to work with you on something else. That's fine, just so long as you and the client are aware of this shift and that it's not an avoidance strategy.

While coaches work hard with clients to keep them on track and focused on their agendas, bear in mind that the topics they bring to coaching aren't the whole of their lives. Strange things happen when you allow the spontaneity and sense of fun to come alive within and outside coaching sessions, as the sidebar 'Spontaneous comment, big change' notes.

### Spontaneous comment, big change

Nick wanted to leave his teaching job to set up his own internet-based business; he was extremely fed up with the bureaucracy and the personality of his head teacher. He'd also recently come out of a long-term relationship when his girlfriend had left him for her fitness trainer, so he vowed that romance was firmly on hold. His coaching agenda centred on all the work needed to establish his company.

At the same time, he began to date a charming and capable accountant, yet he was slightly dismissive of her support for his ideas. 'She's not the woman of my dreams,' he said. 'Sure,' I replied and left him with the comment that popped into my head: 'I wonder what she'd have to be like to figure as the woman in your dreams for this week?' This slight shift from finding his ideal of a perfect woman to be with for ever and ever to just enjoying one week at a time seemed to make all the difference for Nick.

Real life materialised in the form of a speedy romance, marriage and a move to Australia as he accompanied this lady back to her homeland to set up his new business there. Nick told me that he looked at his girlfriend in different light after our session and that completely changed the direction of his life. Such is the effect of an innocent remark!

# Chapter 5

# Going for Quick-Win Sessions

. . . . . . . . . . . . . . . . . . . . . . . . . . . . . . . . . . . . . . . . . . . .

*In This Chapter*

▶ Getting started on timely issues

▶ Playing with coaching frameworks

▶ Navigating the SCORE and Logical Levels models

▶ Encouraging clients to take action

. . . . . . . . . . . . . . . . . . . . . . . . . . . . . . . . . . . . . . . . . . . .

*I*n an ideal world, you sit down with your client for a prearranged coaching session that lasts a few hours in a quiet space with no interruptions. Yet the need for a coaching conversation may happen in a hurried moment in a busy place – or even over the phone. When your client asks, 'Can I have a quick word?', how do you respond?

When speedy coaching is required, coaching models or structures that you can pull out of your mental repertoire are helpful. And if you're new to coaching, having some easily remembered models is invaluable; you can build your confidence and coach someone without having to refer to notes. These models give you some quick wins – that is, fast results for the client.

In this chapter, you discover two NLP frameworks created by NLP expert Robert Dilts that lend themselves to exploring issues. You can apply the SCORE and Logical Levels models quickly in a coaching context, using them both conversationally or in greater depth while exploring issues during a longer session.

 Both models are also easy to share with clients, so that they can unpack the structure of their experiences. By sharing models, you extend the value of coaching and make your clients more able to solve their own issues in the future or to help others. Thus, the power of coaching ripples way beyond the session that you have together, which is what NLP is all about.

# Checking the SCORE

The *SCORE model* offers a simple framework to shift thinking from problems towards solutions. SCORE addresses five core elements of any situation, and is easy to remember using the following handy acronym:

- ✔ **S**ymptoms are the aspects of a problem that are consciously noticeable.

- ✔ **C**auses are the less obvious reasons that are triggering symptoms.

- ✔ **O**utcomes are the new states, behaviours or goals that replace the symptoms.

- ✔ **R**esources are the elements that can solve the issue by dealing with the symptoms (including specific NLP change techniques such as a parts integration exercise) and which can support the outcome.

- ✔ **E**ffects are the longer term results of achieving outcomes.

Figure 5-1 shows the SCORE model graphically and defines the elements of the model with helpful questions. I describe each element of the SCORE model in the following section.

## Systematically tackling the problem

The original NLP approach to solving problems begins by defining the present state, or *problem state,* then sets a goal or outcome as *the desired state.* Coach and client then work on the steps to closing the gap between problem and outcome.

Robert Dilts and Todd Epstein developed the SCORE model in 1987 when they realised that they systematically approached problems in a different way compared to their students. Key differences in the SCORE model as compared to traditional NLP problem-solving include:

- ✔ Tackling problems by breaking them down into smaller component parts and getting to the deeper root causes.

- ✔ Distinguishing between a problem's *symptoms* (characteristics) and its *causes* (the circumstances that created the problem).

- ✔ Distinguishing between the outcomes that the client desires and the effect of achieving long-term goals.

- ✔ Separating techniques (such as NLP tools) from deeper resources (such as extracting lessons from different personal experiences or mobilising a range of skills) that transform problems into the achieved goals.

To find out about more advanced applications of the SCORE model, see Robert Dilts' Encyclopaedia of NLP available at www.nlpuniversitypress.com.

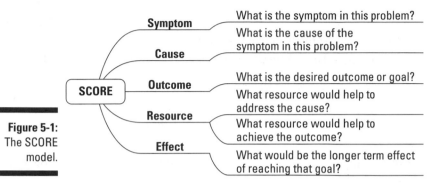

**Figure 5-1:**
The SCORE
model.

# Conversing with SCORE

The SCORE model has five important elements. How can you possibly address them all in a short time frame?

The following very brief telephone conversation between Jeff and his coach gives some insights into the process of incorporating SCORE elements quickly and seamlessly. All the elements of the SCORE model are covered in the space of just a few minutes.

As you read the following conversation, notice the questions that the coach uses and the impact they have on shifting Jeff into taking action about a family situation that's worrying him.

**Coach:** What's going on for you just now? (Symptoms)

**Jeff:** I'm feeling very anxious about my son. He's being completely unrealistic about his exams coming up. He wants to be out all the time and won't settle to his revision.

**Coach:** I can sense that's a concern, and what's that anxiety like for you? (Symptoms)

**Jeff:** I'm waking up at four In the morning and then going back to sleep and waking up late feeling wrecked.

**Coach:** Anything else? (Symptoms)

**Jeff:** I think I'll really lose it with him, and that's just going to make things worse. Then when I come into the office, I can't concentrate on what I'm supposed to be doing. I'm really losing focus on the China project.

**Coach:** Yes, and what's really underneath this anxiety of yours? (Causes)

**Jeff:** I really worry that if he doesn't study, he won't get decent grades and with the job market so tough, he won't be able to get a job.

**Coach:** What's all this worrying doing for you? (Causes)

**Jeff:** Well, I want to be a good dad.

**Coach:** I'm sure, and anything else? (Causes)

**Jeff:** I'm worried about him hanging around with the wrong people.

**Coach:** I can tell that you're a good dad, and I'm hearing various threads here; one is about you – your levels of anxiety and how that's affecting your work, while the other is about your son – his exams and the company he keeps. What would be the most useful outcome or result for you to focus on right now? (Outcomes)

**Jeff:** Actually, I'm so tired. The most important thing is I need to be able to get to sleep at night so I can think straight.

**Coach:** What is that sleep like? (Outcomes)

**Jeff:** Ah, bliss! A nice early night with a good book and no late calls asking for a lift.

**Coach:** What will improve when you get to sleep like that? (Effects)

**Jeff:** I'll come to work in a better state to concentrate.

**Coach:** And what difference will that make? (Effects)

**Jeff:** Oh, it'll be huge. I can get the team working properly on the China project, then the director will be pleased, and I stand a chance of getting the promotion that I've been waiting for these past eighteen months.

**Coach:** So, this sounds really important to fix! What can help you get this sorted? (Resources)

**Jeff:** I could ask my wife Anita to let me sleep while she drives to pick up our son.

**Coach:** What else? (Resources)

**Jeff:** I could give him money for a taxi.

**Coach**: And what else might work? (Resources)

**Jeff:** Actually, it's about tough love. I know how to be firm here at work and tell people what I think and what needs to be done. The same is true at home.

**Coach:** So what happens now? (Here the coach is concluding with a call to *forwarding the action*, explained later in this chapter.)

**Jeff:** I'm just going to say to him that we won't be giving him lifts until the exams are done, that Anita and I'll be going to bed early to get some rest and suggest he does the same.

**Coach:** Is that enough for now?

**Jeff:** Yes, I'll have the conversation with him tonight, and I'll let you know how I get on.

In this quick-win session, Jeff commits to do one thing differently; in subsequent coaching conversations, Jeff and his coach can delve further into what may need to change in Jeff's relationship with his son. Throughout the conversation, the coach concentrates on what Jeff needs to do to get into a better, more rational place. The coach knows that the client can get unstuck in just a few minutes if Jeff commits to doing one specific thing differently. One change can reduce the client's anxiety. After Jeff sleeps better, many other things improve so that when they have a longer session, Jeff may be in a completely different place. Indeed, some of the problems with Jeff's son may appear much less significant by the time the next coaching takes place; this in turn spurs on additional positive changes.

In the following sections, I take a look at the five elements of the model and suggest questions that can help you open up valuable conversations with clients.

 Coaches can dart around the SCORE model, but ensure you get a sense of the symptoms before moving on to underlying causes, and get a sense of the outcome before identifying the resources required. As you work with the model, your intuition develops about the next question to ask.

## *Symptoms*

*Symptoms* are the visible, tangible aspects of a problem. When you go to visit your doctor, you go because you have worrying or painful symptoms that indicate a problem. You're looking for help in making the symptoms go away and restoring your body back to health.

Similarly, clients come to coaching with symptoms of varying degrees of severity. They may be in physical or psychological pain. By contrast, they can be physically fit and well, yet sense that something else is needed for them to be on top form and get where they want to be. The symptoms may materialise as confusion, concern or lack of focus.

Some opening coaching questions and statements to explore symptoms include:

- ✔ What's going on for you right now?
- ✔ What are you experiencing?

- ✔ What is the problem?
- ✔ What's getting in the way of you achieving what you want?
- ✔ What stops you from being the way you want to be?

The client's been living with the symptoms, so don't spend a disproportionate amount of time on them – five to ten minutes should suffice.

## Causes

Imagine you set yourself the task of weeding the garden, but you only skim off the dandelion heads with a hoe. Not surprisingly, the weeds quickly reappear. In coaching as in gardening, you must prod a bit deeper, right down to the root of a problem, if you want to achieve lasting results.

In order to come up with longer term solutions, allow time to explore an issue to the point where you're confident you are getting to the root cause. Be aware that causes often relate to a larger system in which the client operates. Some indicators that you're getting there are when the client tells you how the current situation relates to something bigger they've been struggling with for a while. For example, the manager who's worried about a negotiation coming up may say he's always found it tough to ask for what he wants as that seems too pushy.

Go into a coaching session with an active, objective mind. The presenting issue, or what the client initially believes is the issue, is very likely not the real issue. Don't jump to conclusions or dive in too quickly before you and your client take sufficient time to explore the symptoms and the underlying causes.

Some opening questions and statements to explore causes of a problem include:

- ✔ When did this problem start?
- ✔ What seems to trigger the problem?
- ✔ What else is going on for you that might be causing this problem?
- ✔ What is stopping you getting rid of this problem?

A cause may include what NLP refers to as *secondary gain*, in which clients get some positive benefit from sticking with their symptoms. For example, a person who's trying to lose weight stays in his comfort zone by not going out on a cold morning for a run. Procrastination may protect a person from the stress of taking on a project in which he could fail.

# Outcomes

The *outcome* is the desired state, the place your client wants to get to. An outcome can be many things – getting a new job, having a more harmonious relationship, paying off all credit card bills, developing a skill, finishing a project or gaining a sense of purpose. (See Chapter 9 for more on purpose.)

Without an outcome in mind, your client has nothing to work on in a coaching session, and you as the coach have no real understanding of the problem that needs to be resolved or a current situation that can be changed for the better.

Until the client has some kind of outcome in mind, he's directionless and may behave like young Alice in Lewis Carroll's *Alice in Wonderland* who, when asking the Cheshire Cat for directions, says she doesn't mind where she goes, as long as she gets *somewhere*. The cat replies that it doesn't matter which way she goes 'if you only walk long enough'.

Beware of clients who want you to define their outcomes, because they may not be satisfied with where they end up! I've seen many examples of inappropriately defined outcomes from managers who set objectives for staff without getting true buy-in from them. The motivation to achieve the desired outcome must come from the client. The more clients use all their senses to imagine the specific qualities of the outcome and the effect of achieving it, the more powerful the results (Chapter 7 explains outcomes in more detail).

Some opening questions and statements to explore outcomes include:

- ✔ What specifically is your goal?
- ✔ What do you want?
- ✔ What do you want more of?
- ✔ If you were able to get what you wanted, what would it be?

At this point, just check that the goal is one that the client can state positively and has control over achieving. Remind him that making change begins with those things that he can change in himself.

# Resources

Problems may need various resources to solve them. Resources can include a change in beliefs, some technical skill or help from another individual. In order to find the right resources, you and your client must understand the root cause of a problem.

Some opening questions and statements to explore resources include:

- ✔ What resources – skills, beliefs, tools or techniques – do you have that will help you get what you want?

- ✔ Who else do you know who could help?

- ✔ When have you been in a similar situation before? What did you do then?

- ✔ Do you know other people who have been in similar situations? Can they advise you?

- ✔ Imagine yourself months from now looking back on this situation and you've successfully solved it. What advice would you have for your current self?

Look separately at the resources that can help a client alleviate the immediate symptoms of a problem (for example, resolving sleep issues) as well as longer term goals (changing the nature of a relationship full of conflict and misunderstandings). Given that you're looking for some quick wins, guide the conversation so that the client pays some attention to the short-term goals as a priority that can fit into the larger ones later.

## Effects

One outcome is usually a stepping stone to an *effect*, which NLP sometimes refers to as a *meta outcome*. I call an effect the 'goal beyond the goal'. For example, your outcome may be to refurbish your spare bedroom, yet the effect may be that you can now invite friends and family to stay at your home in comfort.

Looking beyond an outcome to the effect achieved can either increase clients' motivation to achieve their goals or make them realise that the outcomes they're working on need to be re-evaluated. (Read more about the re-evaluation process – ecology checks – as well as well-formed outcomes in Chapter 7.)

A coaching client was struggling with a complex project at work and faced some difficult decisions along the way to finish it. When we explored the end-point of the goal and the effect it would have on him, I anticipated he'd have reason to celebrate. Instead, when exploring the effect, he struggled to restrain himself from crying. With more thought and discussion, he recognised that if he completed this project, the likely effect would be to increase his workload still further – something he just couldn't face because he was already under considerable stress. By getting in touch with these underlying fears, we switched the focus for the session away from project completion to coming up with a strategy to reduce his workload now and in the future.

Some opening questions and statements to explore effects include:

- ✔ What will this outcome do for you?
- ✔ What will be the end result when you've achieved this goal?
- ✔ What is the goal beyond the immediate goal?
- ✔ After you do this, what happens next?

## *Keeping the SCORE*

Working with a simple framework such as SCORE enables you to break a problem into smaller parts and then identify and tackle those aspects that will have most impact. You can use a SCORE form in various ways; initially, use it within a coaching session to capture information to give to the client. If he finds the process useful, invite him to fill it in himself for another challenge and bring it to coaching to review together.

Table 5-1 is an example of the form as filled out by a client, Amy, who wants a new job. Amy works as a hairdresser in a small community where she is well-liked, yet earns little. If she's going to buy her own home with her boyfriend, she needs to earn more money by making some job changes. She decided that she wants to move to working in an office, but she needs to update and improve her CV in order to attract prospective employers. By working with a coach, Amy comes up with a practical plan to create a more polished CV and share it with her network to attract opportunities. However, her coach also notes that Amy has some confidence issues about her identity as a hairdresser and her perceptions about switching to a business environment. Her coach suggests they address these other larger issues in later sessions. Thus, Amy and her coach break down the outcome of getting a new job into several smaller outcomes, including creating a strong CV and building her confidence in an office environment.

Amy had a clear outcome in mind – she desperately wanted a new job – so that was entered in the first column in Table 5-1. If she hadn't had a clear outcome in mind, she would have left that column blank and captured all the symptoms in Column 2. Anticipate that you'll move around the columns adding information in the appropriate column as it comes up. The next step in the discussion was to look at the effect of getting the outcome in order to increase Amy's motivation; the coach didn't want her to dwell too much on the symptoms, which she found depressing. She was uplifted when she thought about the benefits of achieving the outcome.

| Table 5-1 | | Amy's SCORE Chart | | |
|---|---|---|---|---|
| *Outcome* | *Symptoms* | *Cause* | *Effect* | *Resources* |
| I want a well-paid job that gives me job satisfaction. | I'm brain dead, don't earn enough money and am bored. | My CV's not finished.<br><br>I'm scared of not being good enough.<br><br>I'm stuck in my comfort zone.<br><br>I'm worried that if I move jobs, then I'll be the first to be made redundant.<br><br>I'm not very computer-literate.<br><br>I work very close to home and am good friends with the owners of my current shop. | I'll improve the quality of my life and be able to live in my own home with my boyfriend and some kittens – we both love cats. | I know I can take on challenges because I gave up smoking.<br><br>My friend will help me on my CV.<br><br>I've got a strong network of contacts looking out for opportunities for me.<br><br>I know I can do it. In fact, I can be determined when I want something. |

# Leveraging with Logical Levels

When clients are leading full and busy lives, they can discover they're paying attention to one area of life at the expense of another area and seek ways to change that combination. The *Logical Levels model* is a classic NLP framework that helps you work with clients to quickly readjust the mix among aspects of their lives by identifying exactly where change needs to happen. This model illustrates the interplay between feelings, thoughts and actions to create a sense of purpose. The model is a powerful tool that shifts clients' attitudes, helping them feel motivated and inspired.

In the NLP world, the word *congruence* describes the sense of power and ease that comes when you're acting in accordance with what feels right at all the logical levels. You're thinking and acting purposefully, in a state of flow (flip to Chapter 9 for more on flow).

Try sketching out the Logical Levels graphic in Figure 5-2 for your client. The drawing is particularly helpful because it visually breaks down a problem into its component parts, and most people respond to strong visuals. By sharing the model, you give clients a tool they can then use to coach themselves when they're stuck in the future.

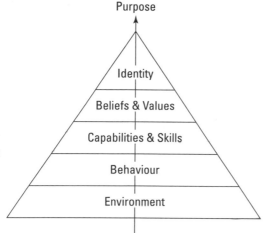

**Figure 5-2:**
The Logical
Levels
pyramid.

The six levels where change may need to happen in order to get back into a sense of alignment are:

- The environment in which you operate.
- Your behaviour.
- Your skills, capabilities and talents.
- Your beliefs and values.
- Your sense of role or identity.
- Your sense of purpose or connection.

I explore ways to make changes at each of these levels in greater detail in the following sections.

Imagine that your client Jim has just been offered a new job and needs to make a decision about whether to take it quickly. As his coach, he's turning to you for support, yet you only have a quick 20-minute call with him before he has to make the decision to accept or not. As you read through the following sections, come up with your own list of questions that you feel are most valuable to ask him and cover all six logical levels. While I offer numerous example questions in the following section, make your questions fit naturally with your style of conversation.

Notice if you have a tendency to concentrate on one level of questioning at the expense of the others and ask yourself whether your focus limits your coaching. Do you, for example, only look at values and not see how values are lived out as tangible behaviours? Or vice versa? Have you ever tapped into the clients' sense of purpose?

## Environment

The *environment level* refers to external opportunities or constraints: people you meet, places you go, the kind of organisations or groups in which you operate.

Some questions to explore environmental factors include the *where*, *when* and *with whom* type of questions, as in:

- ✔ Where do you operate at your best?
- ✔ When are you at your most content?
- ✔ Who do you work best with?

## Behaviour

The *behavioural* level is made up of specific actions within the environment and answers the *what* question.

Some questions to explore the behavioural factors include:

- ✔ What are you doing in this specific situation?
- ✔ What are you not doing?
- ✔ What do you need to do differently?
- ✔ What is the typical behaviour here?

# Capabilities and skills

This level of the model refers to knowledge and skills, the how-to's that guide and give direction to behaviour. Capability and skill questions answer the question *how?* They refer to experience and personal qualities as well as formal technical skills and knowledge.

Some questions to explore the *capabilities and skills* factors include:

- ✔ How are you using your skills and talents?
- ✔ What new skills might you need?
- ✔ Does what you're doing here fit with your skill set?
- ✔ What capabilities do you need to bring to do things differently here?

# Beliefs and values

*Beliefs and values* provide the reinforcement (the underlying drive, motivation and permission) to support or deny your capabilities. This level is potentially more challenging to investigate because doing so delves into the question *why?* Beliefs are the fundamental assumptions people make about themselves, others and the world around them; they're types of generalisations that may or may not be true. Values are the unconscious criteria that guide an individual's choices, and the relative importance of different values to someone can change over time. Like beliefs, they're different for each client. Many people share the same values, for example, honesty or family, yet behave in different ways to honour those values. I delve deeper into values and beliefs in Chapter 8.

Be aware that somebody may never have consciously considered their values before, and discussing values and beliefs may bring up some internal conflict that the client was not consciously aware of. For example, family and work are usually important values, and conflicts arise when a person pursues one at the expense of the other. (You can explore more on values in Chapter 8.)

Some questions to explore the beliefs and values factors include:

- ✔ What's important to you?
- ✔ What do you hold to be true?
- ✔ What beliefs or assumptions support you?
- ✔ What are you assuming that may hold you back?

# *Identity*

You play many roles in life, and these identities or roles are fundamental to your self-awareness. Exploring these aspects answers the question *who?* Often clients have some conflict between different roles (for example, parent versus worker) or a sense of being an impostor in a new role, particularly if they lack experience or specific skills.

Some questions to explore identity factors include:

- ✔ Who are you in this situation?
- ✔ Who will you become?
- ✔ What roles do you play? What roles do you want to play?
- ✔ How does this situation that you find yourself in fit with your sense of who you are?
- ✔ How do you describe yourself?

# *Purpose*

The level of *purpose* goes beyond self-consciousness to relate to the bigger picture of mission or vision. At this level, you're asking the questions *what for?* or *for whom?* Explore clients' sense of purpose, contribution and connection with others – all essential ingredients to feeling that life is worthwhile. You can read a whole chapter on this topic if you turn to Chapter 9.

Some questions to explore the purpose factors include:

- ✔ What meaning do I draw from this experience?
- ✔ How does what is happening here fit with my overall purpose?
- ✔ For what reason am I behaving in this way?
- ✔ How does this situation connect with the bigger picture?
- ✔ How does my experience relate to other areas of my life – or the lives of others?

All too often, coaching conversations never venture beyond the levels of environment, behaviour and capabilities because these levels are generally quite safe and factual. Yet the coaches who are willing to shift the conversation into the higher levels of values, beliefs, identity and purpose witness transformational change for their clients because they're connecting with things that people care about passionately. That said, be sure to handle these conversations sensitively without judgement and with the utmost respect for your client's well-being.

Over time, coaches develop their own judgment as to which logical level of questioning feels most appropriate in a particular coaching situation. If in doubt, then begin at the lower logical levels and work upwards, especially with a new client. As you develop greater experience of working together, you build the rapport and trust to work at the higher levels, going deeper into beliefs and sense of identity. As you listen to the client, pay attention to the type of information he gives you and respond by pacing him at that level before leading him higher up. (Pacing and leading are covered in more detail in Chapter 2.) For example, take a mental note of whether he talks about his sense of identity and his beliefs, and what values come out in the conversation as he tells you what is important to him. You need to use judgment as to whether he only wants to work at a behavioural level or whether he's open to talking about passion and purpose.

# *Forwarding Awareness into Action*

The SCORE and Logical Levels models help you release the creative thinking of your clients, taking them from a stuck place to some awareness of what's holding them back and what they'd like to be different.

Yet awareness of what's happening isn't enough to make change happen. Just knowing what's going on doesn't solve the issue, even though developing this knowledge is an essential part of the coaching cycle. Awareness needs to result in action, which means adopting new habits and behaviours.

Even the shortest coaching session is incomplete without a conclusion that reinforces the need to take action. Some simple questions to develop actions include:

- What happens now for you?
- What will you do now with this awareness?
- How would you like me to hold you accountable?
- What else do you need to take action?
- What is the first step? And when?

While I'm not a great fan of creating long action lists during a coaching session, you still need a safety mechanism so that clients don't revert back to old habits. As you work with people, you learn how much structure they benefit from and what formats works best for them. For many clients, having a coach who can hold them accountable to certain deadlines is a powerful motivator for action. Yet some people are more slippery than others – and often for good reason! The change they seek may be very uncomfortable to achieve; it may challenge the habits of a lifetime.

When clients says they'll do something, stop and check just how motivated they are. You can ask them to give a quick score of how likely a specific action is to happen. Ask 'On a scale of zero to ten, with zero being unlikely and ten being definite, where are you now?' If the response you get is anything less than ten, you may have more issues to discover or other pressures to identify in another round of coaching.

Never be frustrated by an apparent lack of commitment because you may have uncovered a deeper symptom or challenge that your client hasn't discussed before. When clients don't do what they say they'll do, stay curious about the information you're getting. Their reticence may lead to some new discovery.

## The power of a picture

Anything that reminds clients of their end goals – the ultimate outcome or effect of making change in the SCORE model, an enhanced sense of alignment or congruency in the Logical Levels model – can act as a powerful motivator. This reminder may be a picture of a place they'll spend time in, of themselves looking or behaving differently or a note of their aims – any tangible symbol of how things will be different.

Clients can carry this reminder with them in their purses, wallets, briefcases or bags, or they may want to tack up the image near where they work. By focusing on this reminder in spare moments every day, they engage their unconscious minds to get to work to help them achieve what they want.

# Chapter 6

# Getting Greater Clarity

· · · · · · · · · · · · · · · · · · · · · · · · · · · · · · · · · · · · · · ·

## *In This Chapter*

▶ Uncovering blind spots

▶ Discovering mental maps – and how to read them

▶ Posing powerful questions

▶ Developing your listening skills

· · · · · · · · · · · · · · · · · · · · · · · · · · · · · · · · · · · · · · ·

*W*hen your clients arrive for coaching, they bring with them ideas, beliefs and experiences of the world that shape their perceptions of what's possible for them. You too arrive with your own ideas, beliefs and experiences of the world that shape your perception of what is possible for them. Coaching aims to cut through perceptions that limit a person's ability to achieve her full potential.

According to NLP, everyone creates *mental maps* of the world – that is, people make their own interpretations of how the world operates, and each person has a different map. However, in NLP *the map is not the territory*. These mental maps, like a map of your local town, are only constructs; they're not the real thing. Indeed, any map – geographical or mental – is an abstraction that leaves out the richness of detail.

People often come to coaching when life feels confusing or overwhelming in some way. Typically, the question they seek to answer centres on: 'How can life (or an aspect of it) be better for me?' Coaching tackles clients' blind spots, things that they aren't aware they don't know. Their assumptions come under the spotlight so they can choose to create new and better maps. Clients question whether what they are currently doing and thinking serves them well for the future. They start to acknowledge their successes and champion their talents.

As a coach, your mental map grows thanks to the understanding you gain from working with each client. As a result, coaching can be incredibly rewarding for the coach as well as the client.

In this chapter, I examine how you can help your clients gain greater clarity by exploring how they create their maps and using the unconscious mind as a tool to expand these mental maps. You also discover how to ask powerful questions and listen more effectively to the answers you receive.

# Tackling Blind Spots with Awareness

When clients come to coaching, I'm often amazed at how they hide their talents and stay in the shadow of their lives. Only rarely do people come with a 'look at me, I want to be famous' mentality: they are much more likely to be modest and restrained.

While being out there in the spotlight all the time is clearly not appropriate, seeing clients step into their own spotlights on the right stage for them can be very satisfying. As my creative writing teacher David says when encouraging his students to be more adventurous, 'I want you to paint on a larger canvas.'

People have blind spots about their talents – and their weaknesses too. By hiding their light, these talents stay in the dark. Many people fear inviting feedback in case they hear something that's too critical or they fear the vulnerability that comes from revealing information about themselves. Yet when they do, they're amazed at the positive benefits that come out.

Invite clients to get into the habit of asking people whose judgement they trust to give them honest and impartial feedback. By encouraging your clients to invite feedback and take risks around their vulnerabilities, they grow more self-aware and confident, and the blind spots get smaller. Check out Chapter 14 for more on receiving feedback.

Coaching begins with encouraging self-awareness, and the *Johari window* illustrated in Figure 6-1 offers a useful model to share with clients early in a coaching relationship. (This model's name is derived from the first names of its inventors, Joseph Luft and Harry Ingham.)

|  | Known to self | Not known to self |
|---|---|---|
| Known to others | Open | Blind |
| Not known to others | Hidden | Unknown |

**Figure 6-1:** The Johari window.

The Johari window model is a matrix with four key quadrants:

- **The open window** represents what we all know, the details in the public domain. For example, everyone may know that you have blonde hair, what your job is and that you're a trustworthy person. The open window is the space where you feel free to be yourself and allow others to see who you are.

- **The blind spot** is what others know about you that you haven't noticed yourself. For example, people may know that you bend over backwards to help others and are a fantastic expert on spreadsheets, but you may be oblivious to these qualities (after all, you assume that everybody can do these things). The way to expose your blind spot is to invite feedback to see where you shine and what annoying habits you have that get in the way.

- **The hidden information** is what you know about yourself that others don't know. This information only shifts to the open part of the frame if and when you reveal it. For example, you may have things that you choose to keep private or talents you haven't thought to share, like my friend Judy who never thought to tell her colleagues she'd taken Russian A-level until attending a trade fair in Moscow. They were shocked by her ability to read the signs and translate for them; she went up in their estimation that week.

- **The unknown information** contains what you and others don't know about you. You may not know, for example, how calm you can be in a crisis until you're put in that situation, or that you're a natural coach.

Coaching can encourage you to push at the edges of your talents as you venture into unknown territory. At the start of a coaching assignment, invite your clients to draw their own Johari windows that they can revisit regularly at later points in the coaching. They can do this on their own as an assignment outside a coaching session and bring it back to discuss with you. Invite them to make notes in each section prompted by the questions below. Your clients' windows become living records of their self-awareness journey through coaching, so that they can track their growth.

- In the open window: what does everyone know about me, who I am and what I want?

- In the blind window: what do other people know about me? What am I learning through inviting feedback?

- In the hidden window: what I am willing to reveal about myself? What might other like to know?

- Unknown: what I am finding out about myself that nobody knew?

# Creating and Using Mental Maps

NLP offers a commonsense view of human psychology. The NLP Communication model illustrated in Figure 6-2 explains how people create their mental maps.

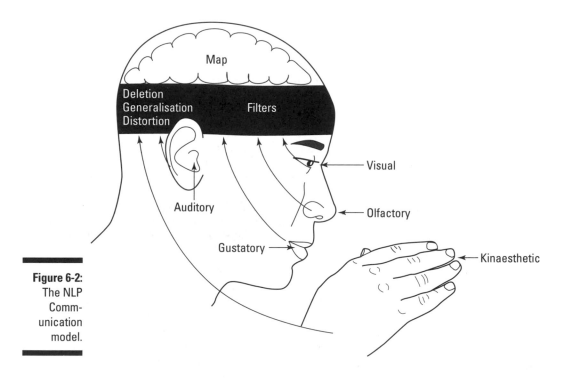

**Figure 6-2:**
The NLP
Comm-
unication
model.

All people, including your clients, go through the process Figure 6-2 illustrates. Specifically, they:

1. **Gather specific types of information about an event through each of five senses.**

   - Visual: sight.

   - Auditory: hearing.

   - Kinaesthetic: touch/feeling.

   - Olfactory: smell.

   - Gustatory: taste.

2. **Filter the information in three ways:**

   - Distortion.

   - Generalisation.

   - Deletion.

   See the later section 'Filtering information' for more on these filters.

3. **Create an internal representation, or *map*, of the world around them.**

   *Internal representation* refers to the pictures you see and sounds you hear in your head or the feelings that are generated within you, in response to the information you take in from the world around you. These sights, sounds and feelings are what's left of the information after passing through the filters.

4. **Create a state of being that is a combination of their mental and physical states.**

5. **Behave in response to their state.**

   For example, if you're feeling anxious, this feeling affects what you observe, the words you say and the sound of your voice.

## Preferring one sense over another

Clients have *lead representational systems* that determine what they pay attention to and how they prefer to think. Look for clues to your clients' preferences in their spoken words and body language, as Table 6-1 highlights.

| Table 6-1 | Spotting Representational Preferences | |
|---|---|---|
| *Preference* | *Language clues* | *Body-language clues* |
| Visual | It looks like . . . | Strong upright posture. |
| | I can see . . . | Looking upwards towards sky or ceiling. |
| | My perspective is . . . | |
| Auditory | It sounds like . . . | Head to one side and a hand on the side of face, as if listening on the telephone. |
| | I can hear . . . | |
| | My question is . . . | Leading with an ear when someone else is speaking. |
| Kinaesthetic | It feels like . . . | More rounded and slouchy posture, with the focus of attention around the stomach. |
| | I can touch that . . . | |
| | My emotional reaction is . . . | Often like to hold on to something, like a pen, when talking. |

As you pay attention to clients' preferred representational systems, frame your questions and suggest actions in ways that fit with their natural styles. However, don't rely on just one representational system. Challenge your clients to go outside their comfort zones. For example, invite an auditory client to draw a picture rather than talking through a topic.

## Filtering information

To cope with the enormous amount of information coming at you through your senses, your brain filters information in three ways: it deletes, distorts and generalises information. To gain greater clarity, you need to recognise what specifically your clients are filtering and how this filtered information interference can affect their potential.

In order to take control of the filtering system, you need to create awareness for your clients, beginning with their language. The words your clients use are of paramount importance, especially the self-talk that goes on internally in selecting what they pay attention to and what they miss.

The following sections examine the core filtering systems your clients use.

Your tone of voice is very important when questioning your clients. Ensure that your questions come out in a tone that expresses genuine curiosity rather than judgement.

### Distortion

A *distortion* is a false representation of the facts or misinterpreting what is being said. A client may tell you that she's been badly treated by her colleagues, yet you may get a completely different point of view if you coach her colleagues.

When you suspect that a client may be distorting a situation, use the following questions to challenge the distortion:

- ✔ Is that true?
- ✔ What's the impartial evidence?
- ✔ How do you know that is the case?

### Generalisation

When you group a range of happenings under one heading, you're making a *generalisation*. Generalisations can relate to things and people, as well as events. This filtering system can offer huge benefits in making sense of information. Imagine if you had to relearn how to type on a keyboard every time you used a different computer. Fortunately, you can apply your generalised typing skills to a variety of situations and achieve useful results.

In coaching, listen out for words like 'everyone', 'always' and 'never'. Pay attention to sweeping statements such as 'I have no confidence', 'I'm useless at talking to groups' or 'Nobody likes me because I'm South African.' In each of these cases, clients are most likely generalising from one or two instances to the whole of their experiences.

Some questions to overcome generalisations include:

- Is that always the case?
- What is an exception to that rule?
- What is an example of a time where you can . . . be confident? Talk to a group? Be liked regardless of your nationality?

# Leaping into future experiences

Planning big changes can seem daunting, but by taking a big step into an imaginary future and engaging all your senses, you can get a sense of how the future can be different.

Some years ago, I developed a fun workshop with the title 'Create Your Own Tomorrow, Today'. The aim was to get people to imagine what they wanted in their lives and make plans with the support of NLP tools. One of the most popular exercises became known as the lily pads experience, and I still use a variation of this activity in one-on-one coaching.

For this activity, you step forward and declare what you want in the future as if you were already there – what NLP calls the *as-if frame*. I had participants step onto a green piece of paper shaped like a lily pad, hence this exercise's name. In this new physical place, you spend time imagining your *desired state,* the place you want to get to at a point in the future. This place can explore many things: a loving relationship, a home in the country, a lighter body or a fun family celebration – anything you can dream of that seems out of reach today.

To increase the intensity of the experience, you need to engage all five senses, identifying the specific sights, sounds and feelings as well as the smells and tastes of this desired state. Describe the state to a partner or coach as specifically as possible, noting what you see, hear, feel, smell and taste in the future when you achieve the goal.

When people experience such a strong sense of future possibilities, they find the motivation to make them reality as long as they like what they've imagined. If not, they can make adjustments until they're happy with their perfect future.

Armed with the vision of a compelling future, people map out a practical route on their time lines to get to where they want to go. The power of the exercise lies in the fact that it engages the unconscious mind to work on the desired future.

After leading this exercise, I frequently received emails about its impact. One client emailed a week after a workshop to say that she'd moved from London to Brighton and was in the process of renegotiating her job and finding a new flat, and many others have told me how they've changed dead-end jobs and relationships.

### Deletion

*Deletion*, allowing the conscious mind to ignore a mass of incoming information, has the benefit of letting you cope with the remaining messages. The downside is that you may ignore important information.

Pay attention to what clients are *not* noticing about themselves or situations. Some questions to recover deleted information are:

- ✔ What is it that you are ignoring here, not noticing?
- ✔ What's missing?
- ✔ Can you tell me more?

## Allowing the unconscious to get involved

In NLP terms, your conscious mind is that part of the mind that is aware of what's happening around you right now; the rest is your unconscious or subconscious mind. Both your conscious and unconscious mind excel at different things, as Table 6-2 shows. NLP enables clients to use all their minds, not just the conscious mind, to create useful mental maps.

| Table 6-2 | Comparing the Conscious and Unconscious Mind |
|---|---|
| *The Conscious Mind Excels at:* | *The Unconscious Mind Is Better at:* |
| Working linearly | Working holistically |
| Processing sequentially | Intuition |
| Logic | Creativity |
| Verbal language | Running your bodily functions (such as breathing) |
| Mathematics | Taking care of your emotions |
| Analysis | Storing memories |

An area of the brain called the Reticular Activating System (RAS) arouses the brain into conscious action. It acts as an antenna, noticing stimuli and alerting your brain to pay attention to data that is relevant to your goals. It also works as a filter, preventing the conscious mind from becoming overburdened by incoming information. It sorts information, deciding what to let through to the conscious mind and what to store at a subconscious level.

In coaching, as you get your clients to decide where they want to get to and support them in imagining what that can be like, the unconscious mind is free to get to work in supporting them in achieving what they want.

The following exercise engages the creativity of the unconscious mind by creating a representation of the future that your client stores as a memory. After she creates the memory, the RAS goes to work to filter information through to other parts of the brain that support her in achieving the goal.

1. **Invite your client to state her goal or desire positively.**

   An example goal may be 'I want to feel relaxed when I go home at night' or ' I want to teach my best lesson ever'.

2. **Ask your client to lay a piece of paper on the floor and then step onto the paper.**

   The paper represents a point in the future when your client has achieved the goal.

3. **While standing on the paper, ask your client to imagine being in the future when the goal is accomplished.**

4. **Ask your client to describe in detail the various elements of the future.**

   Ask your client to describe each of the following:

   • The visual elements: what can you see? What are the images around you?

   • The auditory: what are the sounds? What do you hear?

   • The kinaesthetic: what do you feel? What are the textures that you touch?

   • The olfactory: how does it smell?

   • The gustatory: how does it taste?

Don't get caught in the practical content of *how* anything will happen. Simply keep with the sensory information and encourage your client to enjoy creating the perfect future experience for herself. Some clients find it easier to access some senses than others. You may need to offer clues, such as: 'If it had a soundtrack, would that be loud or soft?' or 'If you could taste something, would it be spicy or bland?' If one sense isn't present, then let it go.

5. **Invite your client to capture the experience as if she were in a movie of her life and having fun.** Your client will naturally hold the memory unconsciously. Ask your client what will help them to keep hold of the experience consciously for the future. She may decide simply to file it away mentally, make a written note of it, draw a picture, or find a small object or tune that reminds her of it.

People get what they want in life according to their existing patterns of thinking and belief systems. By deliberately showing the unconscious mind the change that you consciously seek, the unconscious mind enables the RAS to filter for data that's useful in making the change happen. The process comes down to the old adage: 'Whether you think you can or think you can't, you're right!'

# Asking Powerful Questions

Powerful questions cut through clients' hesitation and confusion to reveal necessary information that benefits both the client and the coaching relationship.

Evaluate the power of your questions by asking yourself whether they:

- ✔ Demonstrate that you're listening and understand your client's perspective
- ✔ Challenge your client's assumptions
- ✔ Create clarity, new possibilities and learning for your client
- ✔ Move your client closer towards what she wants

This section explores how to ask effective questions during sessions as well as some bigger questions to give clients to reflect on between sessions.

## Finding the question that lands just right

One of the NLP assumptions or *presuppositions* is that 'the meaning of any communication is the response that you get'. You know whether the question you ask lands just right by the response you get; clients tell you directly, as in 'That's a tough one to answer!', or indicate with their body language that a powerful question has stopped them in their tracks.

Finding ways to phrase powerful questions is a process of trial and error. The perfect question for one client may have no effect on another, which means you can't just work from a checklist of perfect powerful questions. You need to test the response, see what effect it has and then frame your next question or statement accordingly.

Allow your questions time to land. Try the eight-second rule, and wait eight seconds after asking a question before you consider saying anything else. Count the seconds in your head; you may be surprised by how long eight seconds really is. Nothing is more confusing for a client than being asked multiple questions without having time to think and respond.

Coaches build a repertoire of good questions that they find useful. In Chapter 20, I offer you ten particularly powerful questions, with the rationale behind each one, and in Chapter 4, I share specific suggestions on questions to open and close sessions.

As you start out in coaching, compile a written list of questions to build your confidence. With experience, you can trust yourself to frame the question in your head in the moment without the need to refer to any notes. Get to this point of trusting yourself to spontaneously find the right question and you tap into your skill of being fully present with the client. In this way you become a more powerful coach.

Take a notebook and start to collect questions that you use yourself, hear from other coaches or come across in books and training. Group them in useful categories for yourself. Table 6-3 lists some useful categories and questions. Find other categories that mean something for you.

| Table 6-3 | Examples of Powerful Questions |
|---|---|
| *Type of Question* | *Example* |
| Action | What's next? |
| | What's the first step? |
| | What will you do? When do you do it? |
| As if ... | If this had already happened and you look back, what do you notice? |
| | Fast forward a year. What do you notice when it's all forgotten? |
| Beliefs | What do you believe – or need to believe? |
| | How are other people's beliefs supporting or detracting here? |
| | What is it like to believe in yourself 120 per cent? |
| Brainstorming | What would be ten ways to shift this? |
| | What are all the possibilities here? |
| | What are the wild options? |
| | What would you do if there were no limits? |

*(continued)*

### Table 6–3 *(continued)*

| Type of Question | Example |
| --- | --- |
| Fun | If you made this so much fun you couldn't resist, what would you be doing? |
| | How can you have this be fun? |
| | Who can you make laugh? |
| Summarising | How would you summarise where you are? |
| | What's your conclusion? |
| Outcomes | What do you want? |
| | What would be a good result for you? |

Questioning is a fundamental skill in coaching. So while I'm on the question of questions, here's a reminder of the way that NLP adds some extra tools to the coach's repertoire of questions. The Cartesian questions are particularly useful when a client is faced with an important decision, while the Logical Levels framework helps you choose the most appropriate question to ask.

### Cartesian questions

Clients bring their major decisions and dilemmas to coaching:

- Should I leave my job? My partner? My home town?
- Should I invest in this training? This business? This new super mobile phone?

These and others big questions have deeply personal answers. How can you support your clients to make the decisions that are best for them, regardless of what you would do in the same situation?

NLP offers four key questions, known as the Cartesian questions, to guide your client in making a decision, whether the decision is life-changing or something smaller.

- What will happen if you do?
- What will happen if you don't?
- What won't happen if you do?
- What won't happen if you don't?

The four questions are based on Cartesian logic. All you need to remember is that they offer powerful linguistic patterns that enable you to examine a subject from different angles.

Asking these questions focuses clients' attention and challenges their thinking. As you get to the last question, clients are likely to say: 'That's confusing'. Good. You're arriving at a breakthrough point. Confusion is the pathway to understanding.

These questions encourage people to check out decisions based on the impact on the whole of their lives, in a healthy way – what is called an *ecology check*. When clients change one area of their lives at the expense of another area, chances are that change isn't going to last. For example, a career shift that jeopardises family life may cause problems for a client in the long term. Splashing out on expensive gadgets and treats that leaves the cash-stretched client unable to pay her rent may get her into serious debt. As a coach, you can hold a mirror to your clients' behaviour for them to see how their behaviour impacts the results they get.

### Logical levels and questioning

The NLP Logical Levels model (which I describe more fully in Chapter 5) is a valuable framework for asking questions at six different levels with clients in order to gain clarity.

Each level invites a particular type of question that leads clients' thinking in different directions.

- **Their environment:** Where, when and with whom do you spend time?
- **How they behave:** What are you doing?
- **Their skills, capabilities and talents:** How do you do that?
- **Their beliefs and values:** What's most important to you? What do you believe?
- **Their sense of role or identity:** Who are you?
- **Their sense of purpose or connection:** Why are you here?

As you develop your questions, notice which logical level you're working with. (Flip to Chapter 5 for more examples of questions.) As you mature as a coach, you find yourself wanting to move beyond coaching that only addresses the lower levels of environment, behaviour and skills issues. Great clarity emerges for clients as they question the beliefs and values that drive them and recognise their sense of identity and purpose in life.

## Posing an inquiry to take away

An *inquiry* is a particularly powerful question to close a session with and to invite the client to consider issues from a larger view of life. Inquiries offer the potential to shift focus from *doing* at the behavioural level of the NLP Logical Levels model to *being* at the identity level.

Compile a list of inquiries that you can give to a client as an exploration exercise. Choose ones that address your client's sense of identity and purpose, such as:

> **Identity:** What kind of a leader am I in my own life? Who would I like to be?

> **Purpose:** What motivates me to be passionate? How do I know when I am acting purposefully?

Inquiries are big life questions to expect someone to answer, so only ask one at a time and leave it with your client to ponder for a week or month between your sessions. If your client chooses, she can capture her answers in a journal for sharing in a future session or reflecting on for herself. Some coaches always end a session with the same inquiry that clients come to expect such as 'And what is it to lead a rich and precious life?' The late and much loved American coach Laura Whitworth was famed for concluding sessions with such an inquiry.

# Listening Intently

Listening is potentially the most difficult skill in life, let alone in coaching. How often do you think you're listening carefully to someone only to realise that your mind has wandered off? Inevitably, a word or phrase from another person makes a connection in your brain, setting a trail of memories or possibilities in motion.

The International Coach Federation defines *active listening* as 'the ability to focus *completely* on what the client is saying and not saying to understand the meaning of what is said in the context of the client's desires and to support the client's self expression.' What a tall order to listen for – what isn't being expressed, as well as what is!

Listening requires you to know when to be silent and when to intrude with a question or comment that moves the client forward. Listening is an important skill so that you create the space to pick up on your client's:

- Concerns
- Goals
- Values and beliefs
- Non-verbal clues

## Listening with empathy

People listen with different degrees of expertise. In his book *Solving Tough Problems* (Berrett-Koehler), Adam Kahane talks about the way he developed the ability to listen from the point of view of a *whole system* in order to be part of international peace situations. Specifically he says:

> It is not sufficient to listen rationally to inert facts and ideas: we have to listen to people in a way that encourages them to realise their own potential and the potential in their situation. This kind of listening

is not sympathy [...] it is empathy, participating from within them [...] I needed to open up and to sense subjectively from the inside phenomena that were real but could not be seen objectively from the outside.

Kahane's passion for listening led him to become involved in some of the most traumatic situations of modern times, including post-apartheid South Africa and reconciliation amongst factions in Columbia, Argentina, the Middle East and Northern Ireland.

And you must do all of this without judgement to cut to the heart of your clients' challenges and growth.

## Listening at four levels

In my coaching skills workshops, I teach the following model of listening that combines NLP perceptual positions with the work of Adam Kahane (see the earlier sidebar 'Listening with empathy').

One of the ways that NLP encourages you to build rapport with people is by distinguishing three points of view, known as *perceptual positions*. First position is your own viewpoint; second position is about shifting into someone else's shoes and third position is taking an independent position.

In workshops, we practise the following four types of listening in small groups so people can really feel the way they normally operate and what it might take to raise their level of listening. Ultimately coaches need to find the creativity of the highest level of listening – meta position listening – for powerful coaching.

> ✔ **Downloading.** When you download, you say what you always say. You're stuck in what NLP calls first position, where you just state your viewpoint without noticing the other person. At this level you're basically dumping data.
>
> ✔ **Debating.** When you debate, you begin to recognise another person in the interaction, listening openly to the other (you're aware of this

second position). You allow time for the other to talk and wait your turn, listening with your rational mind.

✔ **Empathy listening.** At this level, you open your heart to listen from the position of the person telling the story. The quality of dialogue improves as you empathise and truly get into second position, able to understand others' issues and reflect them back in your dialogue.

✔ **Meta position listening.** At this level, you take on the third NLP perceptual position where you listen from an independent fly-on-the-wall position, yet you stay connected with the other person. You're witnessing the whole picture from all points of view and listening with your full heart and soul to all elements of the system in which your client operates. This level of listening is where you can generate the most creative solutions.

Think back to conversations and meetings that you've had in the last week with people and consider at what level you listened to others. Were you really listening, or merely waiting for your turn to talk. Over the next week, aim to raise the quality of your listening to the Meta Position level. Notice how you're likely to say less at this level, yet what you say is more incisive and interesting.

## Listening beyond words

Research suggests that only a very small proportion of communication is affected by the actual words said – maybe as little as 7 per cent. The implication is that you can listen even better when you concentrate on your non-verbal skills of matching and mirroring the body language and tone of voice of your client (see Chapter 2 for more on matching and mirroring).

In a coaching master class, I had the opportunity to coach a client who's language I couldn't understand. Although he understood English, the exercise involved him responding in his native language. This experience proved to be wonderfully informative and proof that the quality of listening is an important part of coaching. I couldn't comprehend his actual words, yet I picked up on the rhythm of the conversation, his physiology and emotion, and responded intuitively.

I never knew what the client's specific challenge was, only that this content-free coaching made a huge shift for my client because I concentrated on listening at the deepest possible level. If you'd been a fly on the wall documenting the session, you'd note that my questions for a 20-minute session were minimal, while the client's answers were extensive.

Following is a summary of coaching questions and statements made by the coach in a typical content-free session. (The responses are omitted because they're in a language that the coach doesn't understand.)

*You have something you'd like to be coached on?*

*And is it OK for me to coach you in English and you respond in your native language knowing that I don't understand the words?*

*Would you like to give me some sense of what's happening for you?*

*And is there anything more about this?*

*I can tell this is very significant.*

*Ah, interesting.*

*OK, I can feel that too.*

*And what's truly possible for you in all this?*

*Something's blocking your way?*

*What do you need most of all right now?*

*And you know where to access that?*

*Who do you become when this is resolved?*

*And anything else?*

*It feels purposeful and complete. Are we done?*

*Thank you.*

To pace this kind of content-free coaching frees the coach to say very little and hold the space for the client to express her thoughts and feelings. The coach needs to tune in and decide when the client has said what she wants to say and when to respond. The session is like a dance in which you feel your partner move and you respond only when you're invited to move. Learn the dance by getting out there and experimenting!

If you have a client who speaks a language that you don't understand, invite her to respond in her own language. You can also use it with the client giving responses in gobbledegook, which is a useful technique for sensitive subjects that a client doesn't feel comfortable talking about.

# Chapter 7

# Making Goals Come Alive

## In This Chapter

▶ Confirming the well-formed conditions of a goal

▶ Increasing creativity with the help of Disney

▶ Developing new, compelling behaviours

Some people know what they want in life from an early age; they feel compelled to climb summits, step on to the stage or fly high to achieve an ambition. So tools and methods to envision the future, create strategies and follow through on plans may come naturally for them. Other people prefer to allow life to unfold in an organic way, and they never want to let goal-setting get in the way of their spontaneity.

NLP suggests that dreaming is a good thing. Coaching encourages people to shift towards their dreams by taking actions in appropriate ways. Goal-setting in some form is at the heart of coaching, even if the goal is to change the client's approach to each day rather than the fast achievement of specific plans. In fact, a reasonable goal for a client can be to allow himself more spontaneity and letting go of always having to be in control of life.

This chapter introduces three specific NLP tools that support goal-setting. You see how to take your clients competently through the classic NLP well-formed outcome process, the Disney strategy and the New Behaviour Generator. All three tools engage the creative processes by working with the senses rather than concentrating on logical problem-solving.

# Checking that Goals Are Well-Formed

Coaches understand the value of setting goals with clients. Clients' goals must be motivating and realistic, while taking clients towards the changes they most desire.

You may already be familiar with SMART principles. According to the SMART model, goals need to be Specific, Measurable, Achievable, Realistic, and Timed (hence the acronym). This approach instils valuable focus and discipline to the goal-setting process, which NLP builds on. By including sensory-specific information, as well as taking clients through a proven process, you support them to create meaningful change.

The NLP approach to making SMART goals smarter is known as the *well-formed outcome process*. This process requires you to answer a series of questions that really help you explore the hows, whys and wherefores of your desired outcome. By following this process you begin to understand your true motives for wanting your goals, and you can weigh up the pros and cons of success versus failure.

When your desired outcome meets the following criteria, it satisfies the *well-formed conditions*. For every goal or result you want to achieve, ask yourself the following seven questions:

1. **Is the goal stated in the positive?**

2. **Is the goal self-initiated, self-maintained and within my control?**

3. **Does the goal describe the evidence procedure (in other words, when will you know that you've achieved your goal)?**

4. **Is the context of the goal clearly defined?**

5. **Does the goal identify the necessary resources?**

6. **Have I evaluated whether the goal is ecological?**

7. **Does the goal identify the first step I need to take?**

The following sections explore each condition of the well-formed outcome process in detail so that you can coach anyone through these steps, including yourself.

Take the first two steps in order and then you can jump around the stages a little. You don't need to share the questions with your client, although if you do, you're giving them a checklist that they can follow again for themselves. Always make sure that you conclude with clarity on the action needed, as in Step 7.

## Is the goal stated in the positive?

Creating positively worded goals is a critical foundation for the goal-setting process. Having negative goals like 'I don't want to do this warehouse work any more' can adversely affect your client's chance of success because he ends up focusing on what he doesn't want. Instead, keep the language framed in positive terms or reframe negative goals into positive ones. How much more liberating when the client declares for the first time: 'I want a job that connects with my interest in motor racing.'

The questions to ask your client are:

- ✔ What do you want?
- ✔ What would you rather have?

In addition to being positive, a goal also needs to be specific. Vague goals such as 'I want to be happy' or 'I want a successful career' are hard to quantify. People with these types of goals often lose focus. More specific goals such as: 'I want to establish a group of local friends who I can call up and invite to go to the movies with me.' or 'I want to work in an organisation that pays me £50,000 per annum and gives me professional training' are more specific and helpful.

Often people haven't ever considered what they want. Clients may come to you initially feeling the pressure of what they want to give up or get away from. With these clients, you may need to persist to get them to explore what can be better. Try words to the effect: 'Knowing that you don't want X, what's one small change you'd love – just for starters?'

# Is the goal self-initiated, self-maintained and within my control?

In coaching sessions (and in life in general), you often hear someone talk about an issue that someone else wants solved, such as 'My wife wants me to lose weight as she's worried about my health.' Your client has a far better chance of succeeding if the motivation to attain a particular outcome comes from within. For example: 'I want to feel fit and energetic so I have more bounce – for me.'

Similarly, if the goal is 'I want the directors to promote me next spring', your client needs to accept that the directors may have a different agenda and this goal isn't under your client's control at all. Instead, the client needs to set goals to put himself in the best possible situation to be promoted, knowing that the ultimate desired result is in the hands of others.

The following two questions put the client back in the driving seat:

- ✔ Am I doing this for myself or for someone else?
- ✔ Does the outcome rely solely on me?

When Anna came to coaching, she was extremely stressed by her work in a government department experiencing cutbacks and the fact that she was filing for divorce. Her anger centred on her ex-husband who kept visiting her elderly mother, doing jobs around the mother's house and generally playing the sympathy card. She felt that her mother and ex-husband were ganging up on her and increasing the pressure on her to return home. She felt extremely guilty, tired and confused.

Through the coaching, she recognised that her coaching agenda could focus on how to hold brave conversations with her mother and her ex-husband as well as her boss. These conversations set the record straight about her needs and decisions. She also worked on managing her emotional state when she met her ex and allowing herself to grieve for the loss of the marriage and family home.

Over the course of several coaching sessions, she broke her problems into several well-formed outcomes that put her back in control of her future. Anna said:

- ✔ 'I want to let go gracefully of my attachment to the house.'

- ✔ 'I want to have conversations with my ex-husband, during which I stay calm and focus on facts and decisions.'

- ✔ 'I want to honour the good times and fun we've had as a couple and family.'

- ✔ 'I want to tell my mother that I am 100 per cent committed to ending the marriage amicably and moving on; and I'll request that she accepts that with love and respect for me.'

- ✔ 'I want to work regular hours, leaving the office by 6 p.m.'

Read through Anna's goals a second time and notice that she can initiate her own actions for each goal, regardless of how others behave around her.

## Does the goal describe the evidence procedure?

*Evidence procedure* is another way of asking: 'When do you know that you've achieved your goal?' Most road trips have a specific destination in mind, even if the path between Points A and B is unknown.

The following sensory-specific questions invite your clients to ponder on goals that are too vague or goals with unclear outcomes:

✔ How do you know that you're getting the desired outcome?

✔ What will you be doing when you get it?

✔ What will you see, hear and feel when you have it?

In the last question, you're inviting clients to step into the experience by imagining the visual, auditory and kinaesthetic aspects of the achieved goal. With this sensory experience embedded in the memory, the unconscious mind gets to work to support the goal. (You can read more about sensory details and the unconscious mind in Chapter 6.)

## Is the context of the goal clearly defined?

Defining the context in which you want to achieve a goal enables greater specificity. Context refers to timing, places and people. Ask your client, 'Where, when and with whom do you want to achieve your goal?' This question helps to fine-tune what you want by eliminating what you don't want.

For instance, if the goal is simply to move house, you're likely to find estate agents bombarding you with unsuitable properties in dozens of locations. You must get more specific about where you want to settle. Do you want to move together with your favourite sister? Do you need to find new house-mates or live alone? Do you want to live in a specific geographical location?

By defining *when* you want something, you may identify steps that you need to take before you can have it. For instance, the goal 'I want to move house when I can afford to move into a swish new townhouse in London' may make you realise that you need to raise your income before you can contemplate moving house. Thus, your more pressing goal may be to polish your CV and contact some agencies to find a better-paid job before touring any potential new homes.

## Does the goal identify the necessary resources?

The four following questions about resources help clients identify what resources will enable them to achieve their outcomes. The questions help clients to draw on past experiences when they made use of resources that may prove useful this time around.

Resources cover a broad range of items including:

- Time, money, energy
- Skills
- Information sources
- Supportive people
- Equipment such as computers or machinery
- Positive mindset and good health

The answers to the following four questions are from Nick, a young man who wants to set up a hairdressing salon.

- **What resources do you have now?**

  Nick: I'm very resilient. I come from a working class background, so I didn't have anything handed to me on a plate. I know that to get what I want, I can work all the hours it takes. I'm prepared to take a minimum salary myself for the first three years and top that up with my savings. I have the support of my Mum and Dad who've taken early retirement and are keen to help get me started.

- **What resources do you need to acquire?**

  Nick: I definitely need some help on the tax and accounting side. I've never had to manage a payroll system for employees before, work with accountants or file tax documents. I'm also going to need a reliable handyman and plumber that I can call on if there are problems with the building or sinks.

- **Have you evidence of achieving this type of goal before?**

  Nick: Well, I've worked in other people's salons for ten years, so I've seen what they've done and how it all works. I've also taken on big projects like buying and renovating my flat; that was really old-fashioned when I found it and now it's stylish and attractive – the same kind of look and feel I want for the salon.

- **What happens if you act as if you have the resources?**

  Nick: Then I just go for it. I know I'll make some mistakes, but hopefully not major ones. I'll learn as I go along.

The final resource question – acting 'as if' the resources are available now – helps the client to recognise and shift any beliefs that may be holding him back. He can also try the outcome on for size. He may change his mind at this point, which saves him investing in a goal that doesn't fit just right.

If a client really struggles to find resources, you can try other angles. Here are some suggestions:

✔ Coach him to find another time in his life when he was resourceful and take the lessons from that.

✔ Ask him to identify someone he knows who is resourceful and what he notices about that person.

✔ Identify the resources that he definitely doesn't have, as this can lead to setting other goals to get them. For example, the person who doesn't have the necessary experience for his project may decide to get some work experience or go on a training course.

# *Have I evaluated whether the goal is ecological?*

When NLP coaches talk about *ecology checks*, they're simply asking questions to make sure that the outcome fits within all aspects of a client's life. If a client sets up a new business, what will be the effect on his health or family? What does another client stand to lose or gain by signing up for a two-year Master's degree?

Ecology checks shine a strong beam of light on any hidden agenda or *secondary gain* that the client may not have considered when setting the outcomes. A *secondary gain* or *positive by-product* refers to a behaviour that appears to be negative or problem-causing, when in fact it serves a positive function at some level.

For example, the secondary gain that a smoker obtains from their cigarettes may include finding peace, time to think or relaxation. These secondary gains need to be met through an alternative activity for the smoker to sustain a new behaviour of not smoking. He may need to enlist in some mindfulness training, meditation classes or sports activity to get the relaxation or build in a ten-minute break away from noisy children to get the peace and quiet he craves at home.

The following questions get to the heart of your clients' desires. As you ask your clients these questions, invite them to be aware of any pictures, sounds, and particularly feelings that their unconscious minds raise. Encourage them to listen sympathetically to the responses they get as their unconscious minds naturally want to protect them.

---

## Sharing the goal of losing weight

The essential motivation for weight loss can be very personal to each client. Vera wanted to lose two stone in weight and her real purpose for this was to stay healthy as she got older: she wanted to run around energetically with her young grandchildren. Logically, she knew that she'd gain energy and look good in her clothes. However, she also recognised that she'd lose the spontaneity of making supper according to what she fancied and eating out easily. She'd also lose out on munching pizzas with the grandchildren.

To lose weight, she needed to track her eating habits, make more nutritious meals and get into the routine of planning meals for several days ahead. She knew that her husband, who was naturally lean, wasn't motivated to cook but would help her by taking on the internet grocery shopping. In addition, she found a female buddy to make meal-planning fun and to cook a batch of healthy meals together to freeze for days when they were busy. By sharing her goal, she gained support from those around her for the longer term.

---

> ✔ What is the *real* purpose why you want this?
>
> ✔ What will you lose or gain if you get it?

After considering these questions and allowing the unconscious mind to come into play, clients may need to fine-tune their goals accordingly.

If a client comes with a goal that doesn't appear to serve him well, challenge him as to what he'll lose or gain. For example, if he's making a life-changing decision like leaving a well-paid job, then coaching provides the space to talk that through and see it from different perspectives, which he may have missed in the emotion of the moment. Ultimately, the client makes his own choices and as coach you can only put these under the spotlight.

## Does the goal identify the first step I need to take?

Deciding to do something and actually doing it are not the same thing. You may decide that in order to be a proficient coach you need to study with the world's best, clock up your coaching hours and become accredited. So what happens if every time you think of booking onto a formal programme, you discover something else in your schedule that takes precedence? Your goal is likely to remain just a dream.

To turn a dream into a concrete reality, you have to take that first vital step because without it, you don't build up sufficient momentum to take the next step . . . and then the next. The first step may not actually be booking a training course, but an even smaller step like checking out the scheduled dates and pencilling them into your schedule.

As a coach, you travel with your clients as they make these steps, encouraging and supporting them to act on their beliefs and desires, to stretch beyond their comfort zone.

# Balancing Dreams with Reality: The Disney Strategy

From his study of the late, great Walt Disney, NLP trainer and developer Robert Dilts created a model of creative success known in NLP as the Disney strategy, which is based on Disney's amazing ability to turn dreams into real projects. The Disney strategy enhances the goal-setting aspect of coaching to bring goals alive and ensure their viability. The Disney strategy's particularly useful with large and challenging projects for individuals and teams.

## Getting to know the various roles

*Imagineering* is the term Walt Disney coined to describe the way that he formed dreams and turned them into reality. This unique way of working created the enduring appeal of characters like Mickey and Minnie Mouse and the legacy of the film-making and theme park empire enjoyed by millions of people worldwide today.

Successful imagineering brings together three key strategies: the Dreamer, Realist and Critic roles, all of which are needed for innovation and problem-solving to ultimately reach goals. Indeed, Disney's co-workers said that three different Walts actually came to work, and they were never sure who was going to come into a meeting. Would the Dreamer, the Realist or the Critic pitch up today? No doubt this uncertainty kept everyone on their toes!

In NLP anything is achievable as long as you tackle it in small enough parts. *Chunking* refers to the level of detail or size of an information nugget. *Chunking up* means going for a larger view, while *chunking down* breaks the issue into smaller elements.

As a coach, you take your clients into each of the three ways of thinking in turn, including demonstrating the body language that suits each role.

- ✔ **The Dreamer.** In this role, you're looking to the future and thinking of the bigger picture. You want to see every piece of the story or project. To think like a Dreamer, sitting in a symmetrical and relaxed posture with your eyes looking up helps. The question being explored here is what you *want*. Table 7-1 offers questions concerning what you want to do.

- ✔ **The Realist.** The next role shifts the idea to a workable plan by chunking down a level. To think like a Realist, sit symmetrically and with head and eyes looking straight ahead and slightly forward. At this stage, you focus on the questions of *how* the plan will work. Table 7-1 offers questions concerning how to make the plan work.

- ✔ **The Critic.** The Critic's job is to check for flaws in the plan, looking for what's been overlooked by asking 'What would happen if . . .' type questions. To think like a Critic, your head and eyes look down and slightly tilted, with one of your hands touching your chin. The critic evaluates the *chances* of this really happening. Table 7-1 offers questions concerning the chance to make the plan work.

Typically you begin with the Dreamer, shift to Realist and then Critic. Sometimes you find that a client arrives with a plan he's already working on, so he's already familiar with the Realist role, yet the Dreamer and Critic roles are missing. In this situation, a team effort can often take a plan and make it much stronger and more inspirational.

| Table 7-1 | Working through the Disney Strategy Roles |
|---|---|
| **My Goal Is:** | **Answers:** |
| **Dreamer 'Want to'** | |
| What do you want? | |
| What is the purpose? Why do you want this? | |
| What will you see, hear and feel when you have this? | |
| What are the benefits? | |
| When can you expect this to happen? | |
| Where do you want this to take you in future? | |
| Who do you want to be or be like as a result? | |

| My Goal Is: | Answers: |
|---|---|
| **Realist 'How to'** | |
| When will this goal be completed? | |
| Who are the key people involved? | |
| What are the steps in the plan? First step? Second step? Third step? | |
| What's the evidence that you're on track? | |
| How will you know when you reach the goal? | |
| **Critic 'Chance to'** | |
| Who will be affected? | |
| Who can make or break this idea? | |
| What would make them object? | |
| What are their needs? | |
| What are the payoffs of keeping things the same? | |
| How can you preserve those benefits when you implement the new idea? | |
| Where and when would you not want this? | |
| What's missing or needed? | |

# Coaching through the roles

You can use the Disney strategy and roles in many ways to make goals more real and achievable. You may mention one role in a quick conversation to get a client to think differently, or you may guide clients through a facilitated process lasting several hours. I use the Disney strategy with teams to set a vision for the organisation, and I use it with individuals on a range of goals.

One Scandinavian advertising agency that I've worked with recognises that its creative work must deliver business results and relies on a variation of the Disney strategy to make this happen. The Managing Director organised three different rooms in the agency for the different processes. The Dreamer space operates with standing-room only for meetings, and ideas are captured on an electronic whiteboard. The comfy chairs are allocated to the Realist space, while the Critic space features more formal hard seats and tables.

I find going through the Disney roles works best when you put out three different chairs or allocate parts of a room to explore each role in turn. As Figure 7-1 shows, chairs work very well when you're coaching in a public space because you can easily sit at a table with four seats – one for you, three for your client to take in turn.

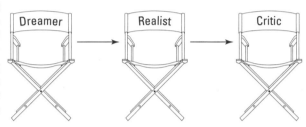

**Figure 7-1:**
An arrange-
ment of
chairs for
assuming
the three
Disney
strategy
roles.

Dreamer → Realist → Critic

The following exercise encourages clients to experience the different perspectives of the three Disney roles.

1. **Invite your client to a session to work on something truly important.**

   You may want to work on the client's personal vision of life, a life-changing project or other significant goal. Of course, you can use this process for yourself too.

2. **Place three chairs in a triangular position.**

   Sit alongside the client yourself in a fourth chair as you talk through the process. Figure 7-1 suggests a possible layout. However you arrange the space, keep out of the client's creative space!

3. **For each step in the creative cycle, guide the client to sit in a specific chair and change body language for each role.** Start with the Dreamer, then shift to the Realist and finally the Critic.

   I describe the body language for the three Disney roles in the earlier section 'Getting to know the various roles'.

4. **Ask the client questions relevant to a specific role and capture the client's answers.**

   Use the questions and form in Table 7-1 as a guide.

5. **Have the client move to the next position and assume the next role.**

   Ask the appropriate questions and record relevant answers.

6. **After the client assumes all three roles, quickly revisit each role and ask what's missing.**

   For example, I was working with an entrepreneur on a new property development. Through the Disney strategy, he realised that he was missing out by not working with other investors who had different technical backgrounds. By involving other business partners, he could build a more innovative eco-friendly scheme than he'd originally considered.

7. **When you're confident that your client has covered all the positions, review the answers you've collected together to co-create a meaningful goal with a realistic plan of action.**

# *Generating New Behaviours*

Change requires people to *do* things differently – things they may find difficult as they seek to achieve their goals. The *New Behaviour Generator* allows your clients to mentally rehearse new behaviours by harnessing all their senses. In this exercise, they talk it through internally, picturing it and checking their reactions until it feels right.

In the New Behaviour Generator exercise, the coach sits or stands alongside the client and directs him to change the way he sits and moves his gaze. The eye-movement patterns tie in with the idea of *eye accessing cues.* The original co-creators of NLP, Richard Bandler and John Grinder, noticed that people naturally move their eyes around according to whether they're thinking in terms of images, sounds or feelings. (See Chapter 11 for more on eye accessing cues.)

In this exercise, like many in NLP, you can work content-free, which means clients don't need to tell you specifically what they want to do differently, nor even actually speak. Working content-free enables clients to stay involved with their own experiences, without any unintended distraction from the coach.

In the following sections, you can see how each round of the exercise works in turn. You may need to cycle two or three times round the steps until the client feels he's got it. In the first cycle, clients' responses can be quite vague, yet they typically become more precise with the second and third rounds.

After you become familiar with the exercise and have a sense of your client's preferred representational system, try using one part of the exercise as a quick check in with him during a coaching conversation or to reinforce an action. For example, inviting a visual client to look up and picture himself doing a particular action that he's committed to do can support him in creating new habits for success.

# Hearing the soundtrack

The first position of the New Behaviour Generator is the auditory one. Have the client sit and look down to his left-hand side to enable him to connect with his internal dialogues. After the client assumes this posture, ask the questions given in the example below.

In this example, Tim's been procrastinating about getting some articles written and published to promote his chiropractic business. His coach is aiming to engage Tim in what the new behaviour (writing and publishing the articles) will sound like when he's actually doing it. The coach is aiming to get Tim to identify internal sounds, such as what he's saying to himself, as well as the everyday sounds around him.

> **Coach:** Look down and to your left. Notice what you hear as you ask yourself: 'What do you want to do?'
>
> **Tim:** I want to *focus on writing an article that will be published in the professional magazines.*
>
> **Coach:** And what does that sound like?
>
> **Tim:** I hear various phone conversations with the publishers, my fingers tapping away on the keyboard, a call to an artist friend of mine who says she'll create some illustrations for me. I also hear myself saying 'On no, I have a deadline for this!' and probably lots of drafts getting ripped up.

# Seeing the movie

The second position of the New Behaviour Generator is the visual one. Ask the client to shift his gaze to his upper right-hand side and imagine what the achieved goal will look like.

In the following example conversation, the coach is aiming to engage Tim in what the new behaviour will look like when he is actually writing his article in full and glorious Technicolor – as if he's starring in the movie of his life!

**Coach:** Listen to those sounds and look up and to your right. What does that look like, *when you are focusing on writing an article that will be published?*

**Tim:** I see myself on the day I work at home, setting the timer on my watch and really concentrating, then taking a tea break, then coming back to it. I can see myself sitting in my office at the computer screen and sending the article off to another colleague who says he'll take a look. I'm looking quite scruffy in my old jeans and a warm sweater because my office can get cold.

# Feeling, touching and smelling the result

The third position of the New Behaviour Generator is the kinaesthetic one that refers to touch and feelings as well as smell and taste. Invite the client to sit comfortably, looking down and to the right to access feelings.

**Coach:** Keeping those sounds and images in your mind, look down and to your right. What does that feel like, *when you're focusing on writing an article that will be published?*

**Tim:** It feels pretty good, although a bit chilly in my office. So, I want to switch some extra heat on. I have the feeling that it's really going to happen. I can anticipate the smell of the magazine when it's published, taking it out of its plastic wrapper when it arrives through my letterbox. I feel excited to have my name in print at last and satisfied that it will promote the good name of the practice too.

Now that you've been through one cycle of the exercise, invite the client to repeat it more quickly for two more cycles, capturing any more information he notices on the way. The client now has his own sense of the new behaviour he wants. Ask him to summarise what has emerged for him that's now different and to commit to what action he'll take as a result of the exercise.

# Part III
# Deepening Your Awareness

The 5th Wave          By Rich Tennant

"I don't know if we have irreconcilable differences or not. We never talk."

## In this part . . .

You're now ready to stretch further and deeper in your coaching as you focus on values to enable your clients to follow their real priorities. From getting clients in touch with their passion and purpose through to understanding their style of behaving, you enable them to become more effective.

Stay in this part to re-engineer unhelpful strategies and model what works from those who excel. You'll capture the keys to creating new habits that serve long-term success.

# Chapter 8

# Tuning into Values

*In This Chapter*

▶ Identifying what drives you to act

▶ Overcoming the *oughts* and *shoulds*

▶ Making decisions you truly believe in

▶ Going further with your values as guides

Some of the biggest questions you can ask yourself in life centre on values. What do you stand for? What's most important to you? What keeps you awake at night? What enables you to sleep peacefully? What do you really want?

Values bring energy and direction; they're at the core of what makes an individual tick. When people deeply understand their values, they can create a way of operating in the world that leads them to purpose and meaning. When people live according to their innermost values, they feel satisfied that they are being true to their identities, genuinely being who they are. By contrast, when people's values are not being met, for whatever reason, they feel uneasy.

Values can change over time, depending on your experiences. People often come to coaching at moments of transition, perhaps from one job to another, as well as from one cluster of values to a revised cluster.

In this chapter, you look at how you can enable your clients to clarify their core values. They then can make whatever adjustments are necessary to honour those values in their daily lives. Acting based on values is a hugely significant piece of personal development work that you can do with a client. Together you're finding a compass for the future direction of someone's life and happiness.

# Knowing What's Important

The act of identifying your core values acts as the catalyst to shift beyond what you think you *ought to do* towards operating on the basis of what you truly *want to do*. Core values are the fundamental drivers behind your decisions and actions, which I refer to as *end values* in this chapter.

## Separating must-haves from shoulds

Most people live more in their heads than in the outside world of events. The human mind is a tricky place, filled with thoughts, gremlins and assorted voices that buzz around.

The way you interpret an event and give it meaning results in pleasure or pain. For example, when a person you care for doesn't call, you can choose how to react. Are you happy because he may be busy and enjoying himself – or sad because he's probably forgotten you? Do you think a person should or ought to behave in a particular way?

The NLP Meta Model of language states that you are continually filtering information and making assumptions using the patterns of distortion, generalisation and deletion (refer to Chapter 6 for more about the Meta Model).

In coaching, you're likely to hear clients say, 'My boss says I *should do* X' or 'My boyfriend thinks I *ought to* do Y.' The Meta Model calls these types of generalisation patterns *the modal operators of necessity*. The clients' lives seem dictated by other forces rather than the clients' own free will.

While the boss or a dear one may well have your client's best interests at heart, clients become disempowered when they always act from the position of doing what they think they ought to or should do, rather than what they really want to. Similarly, they are disempowering others by continually pushing their own interpretation of shoulds and oughts rather than giving other people freedom to decide for themselves.

As an NLP coach, tune your ears to listen for modal operators and counter the statements, for example, with 'What would happen if you didn't do this?' or 'What other choices exist here?' Push your clients to make reasoned choices.

Values work enables people to make better decisions based on what is most important to them – based on must-haves rather than shoulds. When clients call the tune themselves, they shift to a place of new possibilities. After you have clarity on values, you understand why you want to act in a certain way. The *should* and *ought to* switches to *want* and *choose*. You may still do what someone else requests of you, but when you do it from a place of choice, the internal battle ceases. See the sidebar 'Working hard – for the right reasons' for a great example of this type of shift.

ANECDOTE

# Working hard – for the right reasons

Joe took on a big mortgage that put him under huge pressure to earn money and forced him into a corner professionally. When he encountered jobs that he didn't want to do as a self-employed builder, he made statements such as 'I have to do this because I must pay the mortgage' or 'I have to be the main breadwinner.' As a result, resentment built at home with angry outbursts from Joe when he was working long hours. His wife, Sam, and the family learnt to tiptoe around Joe's moods.

By working with a coach, Joe realised that his top values were around his family and security. He wanted to make a commitment to providing a beautiful home in which he could relax with Sam and their two daughters. He felt that he was failing to be a good husband and dad if he didn't take on every job that paid the mortgage and showed his commitment to the value of 'Love for Family'.

His coach encouraged him to find other ways in which he honoured the value of Love for Family as well as being the main breadwinner. While the girls liked the fact that their dad provided a lovely home and plenty of material possessions,

given a choice they wanted a more relaxed dad who'd play with them.

Together with his coach, Joe also looked at practical strategies to ease Joe's financial pressure and create the kind of work that he wanted to take on. Joe said, 'Actually, with interest rates low, the real pressure wasn't the mortgage, but the fear I might not be able to support the family if I got injured.'

With this realisation in mind, Joe and Sam made several adjustments:

- ✔ Both Joe and Sam were spending money on credit before he'd earned it. Together they agreed that Joe would feel more secure if they built up a buffer fund so that he could pay the bills even if he had to take a year out.

- ✔ Sam volunteered to develop her interior design skills to take on projects for others.

- ✔ Joe realised he could create income through his excellent skills at project managing more complex building jobs and having self-employed tradesman working for him. Additionally, this type of work could continue if he were injured.

# *Separating means values and end values*

In working with clients to identify values, aim to distinguish between *means values*, the things that are important, yet are a means to an end, and *end values*, which are the absolute core bedrock things that need to be in place.

The following list illustrates the difference between means and end values:

- ✔ Money, home and work are all examples of means values.
- ✔ Money can create end values of security, freedom, peace and fun.
- ✔ Home can provide end values of safety, space and joy.
- ✔ Work can give end values of purpose, energy and freedom.

You generally experience end values as feelings: love, peace, freedom, self-worth, confidence, power, honesty, knowledge and joy. All are concepts that you can't touch, but you know intuitively when you have them and when you don't.

# Focusing on core values

The following exercise takes you through the process of establishing your initial values list. This exercise can be eye-opening for both coaches and clients.

1. **On a blank piece of paper, write down a list of your values.**

   Your answers to the following questions can help reveal values:

   • What is important to you?

   • What do you need in your life?

   • What's so critical to who you are that you'd almost forget to mention it?

   Table 8-1 gives you a selection of words to start the values conversation, but feel free to find the words that are most meaningful to you. Invite your clients to add key words to this list.

2. **After you have a list of about 12 to 15 values, see how they group and overlap; refine the values list to no more than nine items.**

   Some words may have a similar enough meaning that you can count them as one value, such as integrity/ honesty or purpose/direction.

3. **Take each word in turn and ask 'What does this value give me?'**

   Keep asking the question until you're convinced you've arrived at an *end value* – that point at which you know you (or your client) have reached a fundamental need.

   A client, Tony, first answered that his motorbike was very important to him. When his coach asked, 'What does that motorbike give you?', he replied, 'Access to the open road.' When his coach drilled further by asking, 'And when you have access to the open road, what does that give you?' Tony answered, 'It's all about *freedom*.' Freedom is Tony's end value and his prized motorbike delivers it.

4. **Capture this fully revised values list as the important building block for future planning, goal-setting and decision-making activities.**

Some people like to keep the list on the wall, others in their diaries or mobile phones. Find somewhere easily accessible to keep it so you can refer to it often.

| Table 8-1 | Values Words | |
|---|---|---|
| Achievement | Adventure | Affection |
| Authenticity | Balance | Change |
| Closeness | Community | Connection |
| Contribution | Creativity | Discipline |
| Energy | Family | Freedom |
| Friendship | Fun | Growth |
| Harmony | Helpfulness | Honesty |
| Independence | Innovation | Integrity |
| Learning | Love | Loyalty |
| Order | Peace | Pleasure |
| Power | Purpose | Recognition |
| Relationship | Respect | Security |
| Service | Spirituality | Success |
| Teamwork | Trust | Wealth |
| Wisdom | | |

# Setting Priorities

After you identify your core values (see the earlier section 'Focusing on core values'), you have a blueprint to guide the process of setting priorities and taking action.

Although this chapter's focus is an individual's values, the principles of identifying values and living them also applies to a team or larger organisation in the same way. See Chapter 12 for more on coaching teams.

## *Allowing time to refine values*

Two people may have the same set of values, yet behave in very different ways. For this reason, you need to understand how the values translate into behaviour in everyday life and where your priorities lie.

Ollie talked about a disagreement within his family when his son and daughter-in-law were having financial problems. The daughter-in-law accused Ollie of not loving his son because he wouldn't pay his debts. Ollie argued that it was *because* he loved his son that he didn't bail him out financially. Ollie believed he was demonstrating tough love by showing his son that he needed to take responsibility for his spending. Both Ollie and the daughter-in-law were acting from positions of love, yet behaving in different ways.

### *Establishing evidence of a value*

You and your colleague may both say that learning is important to you. Yet when questioned, one of you may say that learning is about getting a formal qualification, while the other says that learning is about putting knowledge into practice. So who's right? Actually both of you are! Interpreting a value has no right or wrong answer.

Do the following exercise to become more specific as to *how* you know that you are honouring a value in your own way. Take each value that you identified in the earlier section 'Focusing on core values' and ask your client the following questions:

- ✔ What specifically does [this value] mean to you?
- ✔ How will you know when you've got it?
- ✔ What will you see, hear and feel?
- ✔ How will you behave?

After your clients know how they live specific values personally, you can also explore with them how the key people they connect with may have the same value, yet express it in a different way. Invite them to consider their key stakeholders (see Chapter 12) and the values that are important to each of them.

### Working towards a hierarchy

Not all values are equally important, and often something must be missing in life before you sit up and pay attention to its importance. For instance, if your health takes a tumble, getting well moves up your priority list. If carving out a career is most important to you, wooing a partner may go on the back burner.

A natural tension exists between some values. Furthermore, a person's hierarchy of values changes according to current circumstances. The poet David Whyte has a useful way of thinking about these tensions and changes. Whyte suggests that three core relationships you engage in are with yourself, with a significant other and with work (or purposeful activity). Maintaining all three relationships is like having three marriages simultaneously (hence the title of his book *The Three Marriages*). Each relationship is dear, and you don't want to be forced into either/or decisions placing one ahead of another. Ideally, you want strong relationships in each of the three spheres.

Invite your client to place each value in order of importance and create a hierarchy of values. Write each value on a card or sticky note and then move the values around on a flat surface. Creating linear lists proves challenging to more options-oriented clients! Use a form like Table 8-2 to list your hierarchy of values.

| Table 8-2 | Prioritised List of Values |
|---|---|
| *Order of Priority* | *Value* |
| 1 | |
| 2 | |
| 3 | |
| 4 | |
| 5 | |
| 6 | |
| 7 | |
| 8 | |
| 9 | |

## When the unthinkable happens

'The hardest thing to me was burying my mother and my sister with my own hands in the ice,' says Fernando Parrado, co-author of *Miracle in the Andes* (Orion) and successful Uruguayan businessman. Nando, as he is generally known, is one of 16 survivors of the 1972 plane crash in the Andes mountain range between Argentina and Chile. The flight was taking a rugby team from a Montevideo school to play in Santiago de Chile. Only age 21 at the time of the crash, Nando had invited his mother and little sister along for support.

Over a period of 72 days, the survivors became true comrades who worked in teams to innovate, to make heart-rending decisions in high-pressure conditions and to endure amazing hardships with optimism and patience. Besieged by death for two months, nevertheless 16 of 45 crew members and passengers survived. Their tale has been the subject of films, books and countless talks, and the survivors continue to tell their tales today and share the lessons that shaped their lives forever.

In an inspirational talk, Nando spoke about his values in terms of the most important lesson:

*Today I can define which things are important and which ones are not. I like business and I want to be successful, but only if the other aspects of my life are okay. We can't deny that today our families are the most important thing for us. A hundred per cent of the people who were at the Andes wanted to came back to their families, not to their contracts, studies or money. We burnt all the money on the plane; we burnt it to obtain warmth. That means that money is important only if the other things are on its right place. I'd rather a successful family than a successful business.*

## *Assessing values-based decisions*

Values need to be lived every day, so small decisions and bigger ones must fit with values, otherwise the client feels a sense of unease. After clients have articulated a list of values, ask them to score themselves as to how they're living their values from Table 8-2. Take each in turn and invite them to give a score from 0 (low) to 10 (high) to determine how well they're doing. When they are facing a major decision such as a job change, home move or investment of time or money, ask them to look at their list of values and how this decision fits – or doesn't – with the list.

Chantal runs a marketing consultancy that includes several coaching organisations amongst its clients. She recounts how quite early in her business set-up she met someone running a coaching business who was looking for copywriting services. When explaining his products, the man said that he had no real belief in the work; his clients served as the route for him to create wealth. This statement didn't sit well with Chantal, and she realised the vital role values play in how she attracts clients.

*For me, this man had no integrity, and I knew I couldn't work with him. Since then, I decided only to work with clients when our values are a good fit, and that's meant that during the ten years running this business I've attracted like-minded clients who are fun to work with.*

Trust is another core value that influences the way Chantal manages her staff and suppliers. She gives a clear brief with support and then trusts people to get on with the work. 'I assume people are trustworthy, and guess what? People seldom let me down. I'm honest with people, and they are honest with me.'

## Responding to violated values

Not meeting values to your standards can cause huge emotional conflicts, both internally and with other people. For example, not everybody you come across interprets honesty in the same way. Invite your client to tell you about her most uncomfortable moments, the depths of despair, and you can be sure that her values will have been violated. Ask her to tell you briefly about a bad situation and what she learnt from that about what is most important to her. In this way, you get greater clarity on her most important values and how they may get violated unless your client takes action for change.

Andrew came for coaching feeling stressed out by his role in a recruitment agency. He'd taken the job knowing that it would be unsocial hours and hard work, yet he was keen to develop new skills and to carve out a good living for himself. As he explored his values, he found that two essentials for him to feel happy were missing.

The first was fun. Andrew's colleagues were deadly serious and unsociable, and he'd come from an office where he enjoyed camaraderie and banter. Andrew realised he may not get his fix of fun in the same way at work any more, so he had to adapt to make his own fun. He began compiling funny tales based on his colleagues' quirks to amuse himself.

However, the biggest conflict of values came when Andrew realised his boss Malcolm was dishonest and had no remorse about his bad behaviour. Andrew's value for honesty amongst colleagues felt violated. Andrew felt increasingly uncomfortable about the complete lies his boss happily told about progress on clients' projects. Crunch-time came when Andrew heard his boss dishonestly promising performance bonuses for the whole team and then setting up targets that were impossible to meet. Malcolm's bullying tactics began to take their toll, depressing the work atmosphere even further.

By planning out some difficult and challenging conversations with his boss in coaching, Andrew decided his future lay in finding a more honest organisation to work with. He realised that Malcolm's bosses wouldn't act against him, so Andrew negotiated a fair severance package.

# Keeping Values Alive Every Day

An exercise in revealing values isn't a one-off activity. To feel happy means remaining alert to all the factors that are important to you and noticing what's changing.

When something just doesn't feel right, go back to your list of core values and check whether something's slipped out of alignment or if a hidden value is coming to the fore.

## Assessing whether you're walking the talk

Most coaching programmes with a client include work on values at the intake phase (refer to Chapter 4). As a coach, you're in a position to uphold a client's values, just as you uphold a client's overall goals and agenda.

When a client is struggling with a problem, simply ask, 'What would happen if you brought more X to the situation?' The X could be any value that the client has expressed, from joy to simplicity to energy. Another question to explore is: 'How does what you're saying here fit with your values?'

As an exercise in self-awareness, create structures to remind your clients to pay attention to their values from day to day and week to week. An example may be to get them to review how they lived their values during the day each evening, and decide what they'd like to have happen tomorrow. By developing these reflective habits, your clients take new understandings forward from coaching and let this information permeate their everyday lives.

## Dreaming bigger and better

Most of this chapter looks at values as general guiding principles to help direction. What about situations where things are already working pretty smoothly? You can also use values to explore bigger dreams and shift from what my own coach calls the 'present perfect to future perfect'.

NLP offers the as-if way of thinking to encourage bigger dreams. Step into an imaginary future as if you're already there. Explore your dream job, dream life, dream relationship or dream living environment.

The following exercise encourages clients to dream as if anything were possible. Try it on for yourself, too.

1. **Step into the future.**

   Choose a specific timeframe – six months from now, five years or what-ever seems most appropriate. Place a marker on the floor and physically step into the space.

2. **Pick a context for your vision of the future.**

   Your context can be the whole of your life, or a specific aspect, such as your work or your leisure pursuits.

3. **Reassure the client that she can always honour her values and invite her to creatively explore what might make the future even more perfect than today.**

   Allow plenty of time and space for this exploration. Gently gather answers to the following questions:

   - What would you like more of?

   - What do you want less of?

   - What would you like to be best known for?

   - In an ideal world, what does your typical week look like?

   - What is most gratifying to you about the choices you've made?

   - To what do you attribute your success in achieving exactly what you want?

   - What's absolutely essential that you retain?

   - In your wildest dream, what would you really like to happen?

4. **The final step is to take action based on what the client's discovered.**

   Invite her to consider:

   - Now that you've had time to explore, what is one first step for today that will impact on the future?

   - What will you do that leads you to your dream?

# Chapter 9

# Tapping into Passion and Purpose

● ● ● ● ● ● ● ● ● ● ● ● ● ● ● ● ● ● ● ● ● ● ● ● ● ● ● ● ● ● ● ● ● ● ● ● ● ● ● ● ● ● ● ● ● ● ● ● ●

*In This Chapter*

▶ Getting motivated with flow states

▶ Paying attention to sources of passion

▶ Discovering personal purpose

▶ Coming together with passion and purpose

● ● ● ● ● ● ● ● ● ● ● ● ● ● ● ● ● ● ● ● ● ● ● ● ● ● ● ● ● ● ● ● ● ● ● ● ● ● ● ● ● ● ● ● ● ● ● ● ●

*H*ave you ever come across people who strike you as the living dead? They seem to lack passion and connection with the world. They're going through the motions of everyday existence with no destination in mind, simply plodding around as if life is just too much effort.

In NLP-speak, these individuals are *dissociated* from the richness of life. They operate *at effect* rather than *at cause*, which means they respond passively to events rather than proactively engaging in the experience of creating the lives they want to lead. (See Chapter 2 for more on at effect and at cause.) The aim in coaching is to empower the client to be at cause. When at effect, people wait for others to give them opportunities or solve their problems. When at cause, people go out and find opportunities and solutions to their problems.

This chapter concentrates on ways to help your clients reconnect to their essential sense of purpose, which shifts them from that living-dead space to being fully alive within their own lives. I also explore the state of flow as a source of passion and purpose, and then explore coaching techniques and tools you can use to connect clients with their true sense of purpose.

## *Waking Up*

Any process of growth or transformation is usually accompanied by an awakening; just as in spring when nature comes alive after the winter dormancy. NLP developer Robert Dilts talks about *Coaching with a capital C*, in which

NLP coaches operate as *awakeners*, bringing people alive to their natural spirits and opening them to connections that go beyond their own identities.

Wake up clients from that disconnected zombie state by shifting focus from an individual's sense of personal identity in the here-and-now to thinking about the larger landscape of his life: invite him to ask himself what he really cares about, how does he want to connect with others, what's going to be most meaningful to him to lead life in a way that makes him happy?

As a coach, you need to be wide awake in order to awaken others. You can't expect to fire up others with passion and purpose unless you're clear about your own sense of direction. As a coach, you need to be working on your own development and not just fixing other people. In addition to the exercises in this book, *Personal Development All-in-One For Dummies* edited by Gillian Burn (Wiley) offers a wealth of ideas.

# Getting in Tune with Flow States

The most productive coaching sessions happen when client and coach can access the client's *flow state,* where the client recognises how he can operate at his best. Until you tap into that flow state, your time with a client is purely task-focused and logical, lacking the creative dialogue between coach and client essential for real transformation to begin for the client.

In a flow state, people connect with what they really care about – their passions and ultimately their purpose (see the following section 'Recognising Your Life Purpose'). Being in a flow state is as if your body is on auto-pilot, unconsciously knowing exactly where it's going and not having to think or worry about anything; you just take off and get on with life in the moment. Think of Tom Hanks in the film *Forrest Gump* when he begins to run and then keeps on running right across America with grace and ease. Just as long-distance runners gets into a state of flow, the experience of flow brings a sense of easy movement right through your body and mind. You feel engaged, supple, quick and flexible.

Often you can detect a client's flow state by its absence rather than its presence. When a client isn't in a flow state, something is interfering. This interference may be linked to skills; when some people face challenges that that they don't feel competent to handle, they experience anxiety, and the flow state can't happen. By contrast, when people's skill levels exceed the challenge, they may feel bored and disconnected. Think of the flow state as the space in which your clients thrive.

# Going with the flow

Perhaps the only way to relax enough to pronounce the Hungarian name of psychologist Mihaly Csikszentmihalyi is to be in the state of heightened productivity, happiness and focus. In his book *Flow: The Psychology of Optimal Experience* (Harper Perennial), he came up with the notion of *flow* to describe the way that people experience life when they're operating at their mental best.

In the state of flow, you aren't fazed by huge challenges; instead, you take them on with the greatest sense of well-being. No wonder organisations around the world have become enamoured with Csikszentmihalyi's research. Who wouldn't want to find the essence of what motivates employees to get involved with tough tasks and work at their best?

While much of psychology focuses exclusively on human dysfunction, Csikszentmihalyi is more curious about the positive states, the moments when human beings are on top form. Years before publishing his seminal work, he noticed just how good he felt when he was doing something arduous like rock climbing or studying.

His research lead him to interview and observe exceptionally creative people at work, a vast array of people including chess players, musical composers and ordinary people going about their business. In one of his studies, subjects carried pagers that bleeped at random for one week. When the pagers bleeped, the subjects wrote down what they were doing and feeling at that moment. Csikszentmihalyi and his subjects were surprised by the results: people were happiest when engaged in an absorbing task, often work, or a hobby rather than passively relaxing in front of the TV or a movie.

In addition to skill-related issues, your clients may lose the flow state if they're:

- ✓ Constantly weary or experiencing low energy
- ✓ Over-anxious about everyday situations
- ✓ Unfocused in their activities – dabbling in different activities without sticking to anything

By contrast, when clients experience the flow state, they're:

- ✓ Fully absorbed in their activities and extremely focused
- ✓ Ready to carry on with the job in hand because they're having such a good time
- ✓ Alert, content and unselfconscious

## Finding your flow state

Passion is purposeful. You can experience passion as a noisy outward demonstration of what you believe in as well as a quiet internal feeling.

To see passion in action, tune into your own flow state and that of others around you. Notice that people in flow states aren't sitting back and basking passively in the sunshine; they're actively engaged in ways that create the quality of their daily lives. While these people may be working intently, they are also likely to:

- Feel thankful for the simple pleasures in life
- Quit the need to try hard at every task in order to impress others or achieve perfect results
- Make space to think and relax about non-work topics
- Enjoy what's happening in the moment

When Jeff hired me as his career coach, he was working as the head of marketing for a hospitality company. His job involved covering a lot of weekend sporting events and travelling all around the UK, but his heart was no longer in the job. His wife had recently given birth prematurely to twins, which hastened his desire to find a new role that allowed him evenings and weekends with his family. While Jeff's coaching agenda focused on the practicalities of how to attract the kind of work he wanted (such as polishing his CV and talking to the right people), the subtext of our coaching was to keep him in a state of flow so that he could make the best career choices. We looked at the parts of his current job that were effortless for him. By focusing on these activities during his work day, Jeff was better able to conserve his energy for his family. Essentially, he re-engineered his existing role in the organisation to fit with his own talents and gained the necessary experience to make him more attractive to his next employer. Parts of the job Jeff didn't enjoy so much remained, yet he concentrated on the ones where he wanted to improve his skills and delegated the mundane tasks.

Much of coaching involves working on the ways clients go about their everyday lives rather than assigning specific tasks. Think of this as working on clients' ways of being rather than doing. As clients become more tuned into how they operate at their best, most confident self more of the time, the details of what and when they do things fall into place more easily outside of the coaching sessions.

Following are four ways to access the flow state by tuning into the place of being.

### Feeling thankful

When you pay attention to what you're thankful for in life, you can't help but filter out the bad stuff more of the time. This principle is the basis of solutions-focused coaching approaches, or *appreciative enquiry practices,* which identify what's going well and then build on that. Deliberately paying attention to what you have to be thankful for is also the basis for many general meditative practices.

A useful exercise to encourage thankfulness and your awareness of what you're thankful for is to complete a gratitude journal at the end of a day. Make a quick note of what you feel thankful for and review it periodically, especially when you're feeling down. Another good habit is to make a note of what you appreciate about others and share that with them.

### Letting go of trying hard

My colleague Elizabeth Kuhnke, author of *Body Language For Dummies* (Wiley), coaches senior executives on their personal impact and presentations at meetings. To encourage better performance, she recommends that her clients ban the word *try* from their vocabularies. But trying hard is a good thing, right? Not really.

When you try hard to do anything, your face usually forms a grimace and tension builds in your shoulders. Holding this effort in your body prevents your unconscious mind from doing its job of just allowing you to perform at your best because your conscious mind gets tangled up in all those must-try-hard pressures.

When you find yourself trying very hard at something, remember the *Pareto principle,* which states that 80 per cent of results come from 20 per cent of the effort, and that it takes four times the effort to shift the remaining 20 per cent to reach 100 per cent. A good lesson in the cost of perfection!

As a coach, when you try hard to make a session excellent, you can lose touch with staying focused on your client in the moment and thus diminish the quality of the experience for your client.

### Allowing space

The coaching session itself is a fantastic space for a client to think in a relaxed, non-judgemental way – an hour or two of pure peace and indulgence. Indeed, meeting with a coach may be the only time clients get to consider what they want for themselves between other pressures in their lives. Shifting away from the urgent pressing activities to have quiet thinking time is essential to be more effective in any role, whether as mother or chief executive.

Encourage your clients to take time for themselves outside coaching. Clients may say that feels selfish, yet by creating space they refresh and re-energise themselves, which in turn enables them to support others better.

### Enjoying the experience in the moment

You may have heard the saying, 'The past is history. The future's a mystery. The present is a gift – that's why it's called the present.' Being present to your experience in the here and now is a gift to yourself, and a great way to wake up to life.

Strange as it sounds, something good can always be found in any experience, even if it's the anticipation of the end point. Try finding the good in some experience you're really not loving (perhaps the next time you're in the dentist's chair). Decide you can choose to enjoy the experience right now, even if it's just the chance to lie back and have a little snooze and listen to the radio in the background.

Even better, take a five-minute break in the fresh air right now and look at the sky above you. Notice the sounds, sights and feelings of connecting with nature that are always around you, whatever your environment.

## Accessing the flow state

Use the following exercise to access your own flow state or help your clients to access theirs. A client can take away this exercise to work on, although you may ask some of the questions as part of a coaching session. Make copies of the questions, sit with them for a week or two and come back to make a note of whatever comes to mind for you.

No answers are right or wrong. You may like to consider these questions as an extended coaching inquiry over a period of time. (See Chapter 6 on posing inquiries.)

1. **What are you really thankful for in your life?** Some examples may include healthy children, kind colleagues, a reliable car, no major debts, the chance to travel to different parts of the country or world, a comfortable and warm bed, light bulbs and running water. List your examples below:

   ......................................................................................................
   ......................................................................................................
   ......................................................................................................
   ......................................................................................................
   ......................................................................................................
   ......................................................................................................

2. **When and where do you drive yourself hard?** For example, do you set very high standards of tidiness, cleanliness, target achievement or attention to details at work? List your examples below.

   ......................................................................................................................
   ......................................................................................................................
   ......................................................................................................................
   ......................................................................................................................
   ......................................................................................................................
   ......................................................................................................................

   Look over the examples you list above and make a note of where you can let go of trying so hard.

3. **What enables you to feel the greatest sense of spaciousness in your life?** For example, do you have any space to call your own – a spot where you can sit at home or work quietly? Do you walk in the park, woods or by the river? List your examples below:

   ......................................................................................................................
   ......................................................................................................................
   ......................................................................................................................
   ......................................................................................................................
   ......................................................................................................................
   ......................................................................................................................

4. **What stops you being present?** For example, are you worrying about what happened yesterday or what will happen tomorrow? Are you connected to your email when you could be talking to your family? Contrast this with where you really experience being in the moment.

   ......................................................................................................................
   ......................................................................................................................
   ......................................................................................................................
   ......................................................................................................................
   ......................................................................................................................
   ......................................................................................................................

5. **When or where do you really experience being in the moment?** For example, are you able to stop and notice the leaves on the trees, the smell of freshly baked bread, the taste of an orange, the laughter in a colleague's voice, the face of the bus driver, the feel of the ground as you run? List your examples below:

   ......................................................................................................................
   ......................................................................................................................
   ......................................................................................................................
   ......................................................................................................................
   ......................................................................................................................
   ......................................................................................................................

By regularly asking yourself these kinds of questions, you can begin to shift into a flow state more of the time. When you find yourself anxious or over-whelmed, come back to your answers and decide what you need to do to get back into being thankful and enjoying the moment rather than trying too hard.

## Maintaining flow in challenging times

When clients are going though challenging times, they lose their state of flow. They may not want or even be able to talk about what's happening directly, yet a coach with good sensory acuity can notice clues in the client's physiology. Look out for tension in the neck and shoulders, colour change in the neck and face and tightening of the fingers.

NLP recognises that the mind and body are connected (the *mind-body connection*). Indeed, the body is one of the best sources of information about what's going on with a client. For example, a physical health issue may be a symptom of some underlying issue that the client hasn't yet articulated.

James was coaching Clive, the owner of a family-owned construction business, and noticed that Clive had a nervous eye twitch that worsened each time Clive talked about projects that involved his brother. James made an observation to Clive: 'I've seen that your eye twitches a little more when you talk about your brother, and wondered if that's significant?' This gentle comment highlighted the coach's observation and also left the client free to explore that subject or not if it was too painful to talk about. Clive then voiced some worries he had about his brother's capability with financial matters, which in turn opened up Clive's real issues and beliefs that coach and client hadn't addressed in earlier coaching sessions.

Of course, as an NLP coach, James is equipped to work on a topic in a coaching session content-free – that is, without talking about the specific details of a problem (refer to Chapter 2 for a more detailed look at content-free coaching). So if Clive has an issue that he doesn't want to talk about, he can just name it 'Problem X' or something similar. James can work with Clive to imagine the outcome for Problem X that he wants and encourage his client to pay extra attention to his body and how it feels when the issue is resolved. James could then invite Clive to consider what needs to happen for his eye to feel relaxed once more and let James know when he has the answer.

As a coach, you can train clients to pay more attention to their physiology, so that they recognise the subtle signals that all is well – or not well. This process encourages a client's unconscious mind to support him.

If a client consistently seems low and unable to shift from this state with coaching, he may be suffering from a physical illness or depression, in which case suggest seeing a doctor or therapist and put coaching on hold until the client feels stronger. Never push a client to override physical symptoms where the body is offering valuable information.

# Finding the Meaning in Your Work

Perhaps you've heard the story of the three stonemasons.

A man comes along to a building site and asks the stonemasons what they're up to. The first stonemason barely looks up and answers: 'I'm chipping away at the stone with my chisel. I do it all day, every day, and it's been going on for years.'

The second stonemason invites the man to hold the stone figures he's carved and answers: 'I'm making the gargoyles that will go over the main door.'

The third stonemason stands up, smiles and gestures expansively before answering: 'I'm building a cathedral for the glorification of God and for people to enjoy for generations to come. It's going to be truly magnificent.'

Which of the three has found meaning in his work?

In any job, stronger motivation comes when you have a sense of doing something worthwhile, something that adds value for others and makes good use of your time and talents. The third stonemason has connected with a sense of meaning.

## Seeking value while questing constantly

The job that engages someone today may not feel fulfilling tomorrow or satisfy an individual's desire to grow and develop. As a coach, your role involves enabling your clients to get clarity about their desires; the more you connect them to find the value in what they do, the happier they'll be jumping out of bed on a Monday morning, yelling 'Yippee, it's Monday!'.

Elements of any job can become tedious and repetitive, yet like the stonemasons I mention at the start of this section, one question to consider about any job is: 'How does the work I do make a difference to other people, or connect with what matters most to me?'

The hairdresser cutting the tenth customer's hair in one day can realise she's not just cutting hair, but also boosting her client's confidence. The accountant checking yet another tax return can realise that she provides security for a business client, who in turn provides vital services to others. The financial services salesman filling in more regulatory papers eases the retirement worries of an aging couple when he finds the best pension product for them.

As you work with your clients, hold on to the thread that links one person in the system to another in order to see the benefits. As your clients make adjustments in their daily habits, they can focus their efforts where they have the greatest impact, choosing to do more of one thing and less of another.

## Making sense of the tough times

Any work has its ups and downs. You experience times when you don't feel like getting out of bed to face difficult tasks. Some days, major upsets strike – when you have to accept the death of a colleague, lose a major client, face a complete computer meltdown, lose inventory in a flood or fire, lay off staff or say goodbye to your dream job or business.

In such circumstances, staying connected with the passion that originally brought you to your work becomes paramount.

 When husband and wife team Andrea and Jonathan realised their mail-order clothing business needed to be wound up, they worked with an NLP coach with an agenda to minimise their financial losses, find new jobs and keep their marriage supportive through the sale. The coach encouraged Andrea and Jonathan to come up with a list of all their positive achievements to take forward in the next chapters of their lives. These achievements included recognising:

- All the skills they'd developed and gained
- How they stuck to their core values
- Benefits they provided to all their employees, suppliers and customers
- The strength of their commitment to each other

Their coach also encouraged them to take time to mourn the things they were going to miss and to have a celebration party to thank those who worked with them as acts of closure. Photographs from the party later acted as an *anchor* or trigger to remember all the goodwill and fun they'd enjoyed during the years in business.

Through the closure process, Andrea and Jonathan came to realise that the strength of their passion for the business created a sense of meaning for other people's lives as well as their own. They were determined to keep the same energy alive in their next career moves. They also experienced a sense of relief when they acknowledged that their business had been a huge drain on their resources; they chose to revel in their new freedom from financial worries.

# Recognising Your Life Purpose

As a coach, you owe it to your clients to invite them to ask the big questions of life, including 'Why am I here?', 'What's my life about?' and 'What's my legacy?' as well as the more immediate and practical ones such as 'What shall I work on today?' and 'Is this exhibition worth attending?'

Larger self questions like 'What are you?' or 'Who are you becoming?' take your clients into the realm of questioning their identities and exploring how identity in turn relates to life purpose. You're asking clients to figure out how identity relates to the larger systems and communities in which they live. You're inviting clients to grow stronger and more powerful – just as an oak tree that extends deeper roots while reaching for the sky. These questions stretch your clients to the highest level of psychologist Abraham Maslow's famous hierarchy of human needs – the level of *self-actualisation*, where you realise your true potential in life.

## Noticing what energises you when the going gets tough

Life events have an uncanny way of making you re-evaluate your direction and connecting you with a stronger sense of purpose. Having a strong sense of purpose can support you through the toughest times in life, enabling you to shift beyond the anxiety or discomfort of your current situation and take a longer term view.

Madeline, a doctor whose husband died unexpectedly of a viral infection, told me about the lack of direction she was experiencing: 'I've lost my sense of purpose. My whole life was tied into being his wife. Now I'm a widow and I don't know how to behave any more.' Notice in Madeline's language that she has a new unwanted *identity* as a widow rather than her familiar role as a wife. (See Chapter 5 for more on identity.) As a wife, she knew how husband, family and colleagues expected her to behave, what was important to her and how her work fitted with the rest of her life. As a widow, she suddenly found herself in new territory, unskilled and unsure of herself, and wanted to re-establish her sense of being on the right track.

Clearly Madeline needed time and space to mourn the loss of her beloved husband, yet as a bright and determined woman, she also wanted to carve out a clear route for herself rather than dwell on her grief. We looked at the identity she wanted and how that might take shape over a period of time, without putting her under unnecessary pressure to find her new identify quickly.

Madeline eventually realised that she wanted to be a healer for less privileged communities. She decided that she'd gone into medicine originally to make a significant difference in the world. That dream had been realised only partially through her work, and she'd found her purpose more satisfying as wife and mother. Now that her children were grown, she decided to shift her work away from the general practice that no longer fired her with enthusiasm and move towards international relief programmes that filled her deeper need to connect with poorer communities.

Her first step on this journey was to contact one of her patients and volunteer her services in a local programme that supported an orphanage in India. Focusing on a short-term commitment was a safe stepping-stone, an opportunity to see how she fared as she put her new identity to the test.

## Finding and using your passion: the DASE model

You can access your passion – or help clients access theirs – by looking at the peaks or troughs of experience. In my DASE model (explored more fully in my book *Live Life, Love Work*, also published by Wiley), you explore passion from the extremes of what pleases you and what makes you mad by tapping into strong emotional states of delight (D), anger (A), sadness (S) and ecstasy (E). I use this tool to coach people to get back in touch with emotive issues that really fire up their passion. In person, the client can talk you through experiences from the past, yet he can also use the DASE model for personal reflection in preparation for a coaching session.

1. **Divide a piece of paper into four quadrants with pen or pencil.** Label the four areas Delighted, Ecstatic, Sad and Angry.

2. **Consider each quadrant on the page.** Ask yourself the following questions and make note of specific situations and experiences where your emotions were so heightened that you can still recall them.

   • **Delighted:** When were you delighted, experiencing a gentle sense of joy and feeling blessed with life? Consider times when you noticed kindness and gratitude that stopped you in your tracks.

   • **Angry:** When have you been angry or disgusted? Consider times when you were ready to fight for your rights or a cause dear to your heart.

- **Sad:** When have you been sad, disappointed and low? What moves you to gloom and that sense of wanting to give up and hide under the duvet away from the world?

- **Ecstatic:** When have you been *ecstatic*, experiencing the peak of exuberance and well-being? What really brings you alive and makes you jump up and down with excitement and sing from the rooftops?

3. **Review everything you wrote on your page.** Which experiences and episodes do you consider the best of times? The worst of times? Which moments stand out as really firing up your passion?

4. **Look for themes in your experiences.** For example, notice what you do when you stand up for what you care about, which in turn makes a difference for others. What happens when you get emotional? What impact does it have on your behaviour and that of those around you?

5. **Consider your sense of who you are during your most passionate and satisfying moments.** If you were to identify yourself with a role or animal, what would it be? Are you naturally a hunter or tiger, a nest builder or squirrel? Allow this role to inform your answers to activities in the following section, which focuses on defining purpose.

After you know what fires your passion, you can turn that inner drive into practical, well-formed outcomes. (See Chapter 7 for the well-formed approach to turning your passion into action.)

## Defining purpose in your own words

Successful organisations define their business purpose, their rationale for existing, as part of business planning. They often create and share great statements about their vision such as:

- ✔ 'To be the world's best quick service restaurant experience ... so that we make every customer in every restaurant smile.' *McDonald's.*

- ✔ 'To create happiness by providing the finest in entertainment for people of all ages, everywhere.' *Disney.*

- ✔ 'Bringing the best to everyone we touch.' *Estée Lauder.*

Yet if you turn to a friend and say: 'What's your purpose?' or 'Why do you exist?', you're most likely to be met by a blank stare and offered a cup of tea and the chance to sit down. You can almost see the thought bubble emerge: 'Is my friend going mad?'

Not many people give much consideration to their purpose beyond saying they'd like to make a difference or help others. But you can define your personal purpose, and, in doing so, create a greater sense of meaning and direction for your life. Such meaning serves you on the days when life feels tough because you have a reason to get out of bed in the morning knowing that you can do something worthwhile.

As I explore in Chapter 8, your values unconsciously drive you in a purposeful way to make an impact in the world, whether that's in bringing up healthy and happy children or taking on global peace negotiations. In the coaching context, invite clients to explore the question of their personal purpose.

A great question to begin exploring personal purpose is: what are the words that you use to describe your life purpose? Of course, this question may be the most difficult question to answer, so allow clients to sit with it for a period of weeks – even months, if necessary. Return to the question occasionally. Add words to the definition, take out a few or replace some words with more specific ones.

The following exercise can also help you or your clients with the process of exploring and defining personal purpose.

1.  **Write a statement of life purpose.** Capture your thoughts in a simple sentence that begins by focusing on your *identity*, for example:

    - *I am someone who . . .*

    - *I am a healer . . .*

    - *I am a light . . .*

    - *I'm a mum . . .*

    - *I'm a carer . . .*

    Notice that your identity may be metaphorical (as in a light or a healer) as well as real (mum, carer or other role).

    You may find working with a specific role or identity easier to start off. Later, you can shift to the more abstract metaphorical approach that may encompass who you are in more than one area of life. If you have a number of roles (as is most likely), start with one or two that are very important to you. Later you can refine these into one statement.

2.  **Add a verb and an object to your sentence that further describe what you do.** For example:

    - *I'm a polisher who shapes human gems . . .*

    - *I'm an IT whiz who designs technology . . .*

- *I'm a waste-disposal expert who protects the environment . . .*

- *I'm a healer of animals who helps them recover from illness and injury . . .*

3. **Add a few words to connect your identity and actions with people, places or situations.** Choose words that extend beyond yourself and the present time. Here are examples of *connection statements.*

- *I'm a conductor who creates harmony and understanding in schools.*

- *I'm a marketer who designs phone services that enable non-technical people to communicate with anyone they want.*

- *I'm a homemaker who creates a welcoming environment where family and guests can recharge their batteries.*

When you're happy with your statement, put it in a place where you can see it each day – on your desk, your bathroom mirror, your personal organiser or the fridge door. You may want to add it to your business card or email signature.

# Building a Shared Vision

One person's passion creates momentum in a project or a career. Multiply that passion up into a family, team, group, organisation or nation, and it can become extraordinarily infectious and a powerful agent for change. Great organisations, whatever their size, combine and harness individuals talents in ways that acknowledge individual contribution as part of greater successes.

You can guide clients to build visions and mission statements, strategies and plans that:

✔ State core beliefs and values

✔ Recognise the organisation's contribution to employees, customers, clients, the public and other stakeholders

✔ Share the strategic direction that the organisation is heading in

✔ Present a plan of action for how to implement the vision, using the organisation's talents and resources

Why do some visions remain just a loose, intangible concept while others create enthusiastic followers who make them happen? Although many factors affect business success, great visions engage and motivate people when they incorporate a sense of passion and purpose that enables everyone to access their own passion and purpose. (Great vision statements are also likely to engage people by adopting sensory-specific language. You can read more in Chapters 2 and 6.)

Vision statements aren't limited to the business world. What would it be like to have a family vision statement or one for your school or club that included a sense of passion, values and purpose? Consider the following vision statements:

- ✔ **For a family:** To truly look out for each other in this family, listen and feel a depth of love and kindness in everything we think, do and say, whether we are physically together or far apart.

- ✔ **For a school:** To come to school to share knowledge with a passion that can be seen and heard in all our activities every single day, and which ultimately makes a difference in the world.

- ✔ **For a club:** To create an environment where everyone has a valuable part to play and feels better every time each member visits, gaining new energy to further inspire others.

Such vision statements provide a foundation of shared commitment to all the members of the group; an implicit message of what you stand for and what makes you come together.

## *Merging different agendas*

Ultimately, dreams and visions without coordinated actions remain just charming notions or frustrating ideals that no one ever succeeds in attaining. (See Chapter 7 for the NLP Disney strategy to coach a dream into reality.) The following section explores ways to assemble visions that are inspiring and achievable.

### *Getting bigger, getting smaller: Chunking*

As a coach, you need to work with your clients at different levels at different times to make grand abstract visions achievable on an everyday basis.

NLP took the idea of *chunking* from the world of IT, in which complex programs are broken into sequences, sub-sequences, lines and ultimately bits and bytes. NLP coaches talk about *chunking up* to consider big-picture information at a conceptual level and *chunking down* to tackle the details of implementing any decision.

The concept of chunking is particularly useful when people come together to implement any programme and arrive with different skills, needs and agendas. In agreeing direction and priorities for any collaborative activity or business endeavour, people need to be able to connect with the shared vision as well as recognise the detailed work beneath it.

Coaches working with teams encourage and support the natural diversity that exists within these groups to harness a mix of abilities and needs to create outcomes that the teams are looking for.

In order to steer diverse people into action, spend time building relationships and recognising each other's talents. Being able to coach others to acknowledge and listen to one another can be extremely useful. After individuals recognise their own and others' talents, they can work together to build a shared agenda by formulating their goals as well-formed outcomes. (See Chapter 7 for more on goal-setting and Chapter 14 for more on chunking.)

### Confessing your strengths

The following activity encourages individuals to acknowledge their strengths – and for others in the group to acknowledge them as well. This activity is well-suited to teams, committees, small businesses and departments where people have little knowledge of each other and want to bond more closely. Try the following exercise to get a group sharing, listening and acknowledging each other.

1. **Divide the group into trios, each with a Person A, Person B and Person C.**

2. **Ask Person A to answer the question 'In what ways am I amazing?'**

3. **Person A confesses his talents and skills to Persons B and C.**

   Give Person A ample time to talk about his capabilities and share specific examples and stories.

4. **Persons B and C listen to Person A and encourage him not to be modest.**

   Persons B and C may even want to extol Person A's virtues confidently if he's naturally reticent.

5. **Person B and C make suggestions as to how Person A's talents can be used to good effect in the current group and area of focus.**

6. **The members of the trio switch positions, until each has had a turn confessing their strengths to the group.**

7. **After each member confesses his talents, the trio captures their ideas in writing.**

In the end, each team member should have at least three areas of excellence and an outline of how to use these areas of excellence in practice to further the team agenda.

8. **Finally, bring each trio together with the rest of the group to look at the overall talents, acknowledge them and see how they can be put to good use in a practical way on the work ahead.**

## *Knowing when to bend and when to stay tough*

Passion and purpose are wonderful things, but they can bring with them a mental toughness that can verge on rigidity, stubbornness and even blinkered obsession at times. If you're too focused on what you want for yourself, you can lose touch with what other people want along the way. An inability to see others' views and needs can lead to a loss of other things that are important to you. (Try perceptual positions exercise in Chapter 12 if this is the case.)

During some executive coaching, Ray told me he couldn't understand why his wife of 30 years left him until their marriage was well and truly over. In his wife's view, his passion for classic cars had overtaken his passion for her, and Ray was definitely passionate about cars, bringing up the topic frequently during our sessions. With additional coaching, Ray became aware that when he's passionate about something – whether his consulting work or his cars – he filters out information he doesn't want to listen to. While he came to terms with the fact that his wife wasn't returning, he was able to take some lessons from the experience of his failed marriage and begin a new relationship on a stronger footing with a clear sense of what other people need from a relationship with him. In particular, they need his time and attention, to share activities and feel acknowledged and valued.

Fortunately some fundamental NLP principles can assist passionate people like Ray to navigate differences of opinion and overcome blind spots. As a coach, you can help passionate clients to develop greater rapport with other people by working on their interpersonal skills in terms of:

- **Behavioural flexibility.** NLP asserts that the person with the most flexibility in a system is the most effective. *Flexibility* means being able to do something different when what you're currently doing isn't working. As a coach, brainstorm some alternatives with your clients to come at problems more creatively. Invite them to take different *perceptual positions* with others. (I explore perceptual positions in Chapter 12.)

✔ **Pacing and leading others.** NLP advises us to pace, pace and pace again *before* you lead. Pacing is about increasing your listening skills. You can only lead someone to your agenda when you first meet them in their map of the world. The power of listening to others' passions as well as your own can never be overrated. I cover pacing in more depth in Chapter 2.

Often people come to coaching after they realise that life shouldn't be so tough and that they want to make life easier. Finding the antidote to the living-dead state in which people are detached and exhausted isn't necessarily about getting more sleep; it's about becoming wholehearted about life. By enabling your clients to reconnect with a sense of passion and purpose, you can help them get back on track to the rich and rewarding lives they deserve – and make sure that they have lots of fun on the way.

# Chapter 10

# Shedding Light on Patterns

*In This Chapter*

▶ Identifying what makes you tick

▶ Listening for the vocal messages

▶ Breaking through blockages

▶ Making change last longer

*H*ave you noticed how easily you connect with some clients while you struggle to connect with others? A client's language patterns can play a major role in forming connections.

NLP offers insights into the structure of language for clues into how people think and how these thought patterns in turn affect behaviour. The *structure* of language is the *way* your clients use language rather than the *content* of what they're saying.

This chapter helps you become aware of how listening for patterns of communication in your clients' spoken words enhances your skills as a coach. In addition, you find out how to more closely examine the unspoken messages conveyed by the individual characteristics of a voice.

Of course, communication is two-way. The way that you use language and your voice has an effect on your clients just as much as what you notice about theirs. As you read this chapter, ask yourself what lessons you can apply to your own communication style.

Patterns of thinking and behaviour stay entrenched when we work to keep them in place. These entrenched ways of thinking and acting may be from fear of expressing something that others may not like to hear, or perhaps a negative pattern hasn't been identified yet. Whatever the case, this chapter also inspires you to have courageous coaching conversations in the coaching space. For old patterns to change, new ones need to become embedded to take their place, so the chapter concludes with ways to establish new, more empowering habits that serve your clients.

# Seeing the Metaprograms

In order to handle the wealth of information that bombards your five main senses at any one time, you naturally filter information, paying attention to some things and letting go of others. *Metaprograms* are some of the unconscious mental filters that direct what you pay attention to, how you process information and how you then communicate with others.

In the NLP literature (including *Neuro-linguistic Programming For Dummies* and *Neuro-linguistic Programming Workbook For Dummies*, both by Romilla Ready and yours truly and published by Wiley), you can read about several types of metaprograms that people run without conscious awareness. This section introduces you to four useful ones within coaching that can inform the quality of your conversations and observations.

I explore four metaprograms in the following sections:

- ✔ **Global/Detail:** Watching the big picture versus the specifics.
- ✔ **Options/Procedures:** Working with choices versus step-by-step methods.
- ✔ **Toward/Away From:** Shifting towards pleasure or away from pain.
- ✔ **Internal/External:** Paying attention to one's own experience or what is happening for other people.

Begin to pay attention to spot these patterns, noticing clues in language and behaviour. For example, when a client talks about an issue, is she more likely to give you the big picture (global) or flood you with information (detail)?

Other metaprograms that I don't examine in detail in this chapter but that you can look for in people's communication and behaviour include:

- ✔ **Sameness/difference:** Noticing what's the same as what they already know versus sorting information for what's new and different.

Gemma often bemoaned how difficult she found getting along with her mother-in-law Joan. Joan seemed to constantly pick holes in the way Gemma ran her home and brought up her children. After Gemma realised that Joan sorted for *difference* while Gemma sorted by *sameness*, Gemma relaxed and stopped taking Joan's comments as personal criticism. Their relationship improved dramatically.

- ✔ **Time perspective:** Seeing the short term versus paying attention to the longer term outlook.
- ✔ **Proactive/reactive.** Working in advance of potential situations versus responding to situations.

Metaprograms aren't either/or. A person isn't only proactive and never reactive, for example. Metaprograms relate to specific *contexts,* so people's behaviour is different in each situation, just as the child who is noisy, boisterous and attention-seeking at home can be quiet and private at school. Try to work with your clients to explore different contexts (for example, how do they operate when going shopping compared to parenting their children or working with colleagues) to see how they behave differently. You may discover that they have skills in one area that you can bring into another context.

Metaprograms offer three key benefits for both coaches and clients:

- ✔ Insight into your own patterns.
- ✔ Insight into others' patterns.
- ✔ Insight into how to create new patterns.

As you understand how clients work at their best, you can support them in ways that are going to be most effective. For example, the client who only sees the details and micro-manages her staff may need to work on stepping back to plan strategically if she wants promotion. The person who's hugely internally focused isn't motivated by what others think of her and may not pay attention to important relationships. Another client with a strong options orientation may value coaching as time for creative brainstorming and not respond to forms, processes or psychometric tests.

## Global/detail

People running a *global* metaprogram pay more attention to the big picture at a conceptual level while those running a *detail* metaprogram dive straight into tasks.

You hear the *global* pattern in phrases such as:

- ✔ *Taking a broader view . . .*
- ✔ *Give me the headlines.*
- ✔ *This is the outline concept.*
- ✔ *Let's just agree in principle and fill in the gaps another time.*

You hear the *detail* pattern in phrases such as:

- ✔ *What I mean specifically is . . .*
- ✔ *If we can itemise the tasks here . . .*

> ✔ *Zooming in a level . . .*
>
> ✔ *Exactly what's the breakdown?*

All people need to realise is that not everybody wants – or needs – the same level of information and adjust their style accordingly. Business-coaching clients often express frustration with colleagues who are pernickety about details or not detail-conscious enough.

As a coach, you can provide the space for clients to talk in detail and also step back and see the bigger picture, thus spanning the global/detail spectrum.

One style of coaching does not fit all. During sessions, you need to pace your clients as a fundamental part of gaining rapport. For example, a coach who likes to take a holistic view may well want to see the bigger picture before delving into specific coaching, but this approach can frustrate a client who wants to get into details straight away. You may find it useful to share these concepts with your clients so that they can experiment with another pattern if they want to get different results.

## Options/procedures

People running an *options* pattern love to explore choices and may seem all over the place in discussions, while people running *procedures* patterns are good at doing things in a logical sequence.

You hear the *options* pattern in phrases such as:

> ✔ *Give me some choices.*
>
> ✔ *I like to fix what isn't broken!*
>
> ✔ *I find it hard to stick with the plan.*
>
> ✔ *I like to keep changing and keep my options open.*

You hear the *procedures* pattern in phrases such as:

> ✔ *Let's go through the requirements.*
>
> ✔ *I need to read the manual first.*
>
> ✔ *What are the rules?*
>
> ✔ *First we do this, second this and third this.*

You can recognise highly options-oriented clients as they frequently go off at tangents and change tack. They are likely to design processes and not stick to them. They may cancel coaching unexpectedly. The challenge is to pin them down while allowing choice! One way to do this is to invite them to make their commitments more public and choose who else to share their goals with, apart from you; someone who reminds them of what they say they want to do.

Individuals who are high on procedure are likely to want to tell you stories from start to finish and tend to feel reassured if they understand the coaching process. The challenge is to expand their comfort with ambiguity and loss of control. One challenge can be to stop wearing a watch for a day, let go of being fully prepared for a meeting or visitors, and just to go with the flow to see what happens.

## *Toward/away from*

According to Freud, your *id,* which represents your natural urge, moves you towards pleasure or away from pain. Think of this as the classic carrot-or-stick motivation pattern. People with a *toward* tendency look ahead to a goal that's calling them and drawing them forward, while those with an *away from* tendency look back to what they want to get away from because they fear the pain of it.

The emphasis in NLP is on outcomes, yet some people are actually highly motivated to change by what they don't want. Studies of top-performing sales people show that many are more motivated by the fear of not having enough money to pay their mortgages than by the enticement of hitting their targets or earning bonuses. Reaching the goal gets them away from what they fear.

When I worked in computer marketing earlier in my career, the company changed the style of language in which it sold key support services for computer maintenance. Originally we sold Disaster Recovery (away from) and later Business Continuity (toward) when market research suggested this terminology was more appealing to our customer base.

You hear the *toward* pattern in words and phrases such as:

- *Let's go for it, look ahead, keep your eye on the ball.*
- *Pleasure, fun.*
- *Outcome, hit the target.*
- *Achieve, attain.*

You hear the *away from* pattern in words and phrases such as:

> ✔ *Let's get away from this, get rid of this.*
>
> ✔ *Pain, problems, difficulties.*
>
> ✔ *We don't want that to happen.*

In order to really hear if someone runs a *towards* or an *away from* pattern, ask them 'What's important to you about [the topic in question]?' Drill down with three levels of questioning because at first you may notice clients respond with something positive, which can hide their away-from patterns. In the following example, the initial answer is *towards* money, although subsequent answers reveal an *away-from* preference.

**Coach:** What's important to you about your singing? (level one)

**Client:** I like the extra income.

**Coach:** So what's important to you about the extra income?' (level two)

**Client:** I don't have to worry about paying my credit card bill.

**Coach:** And what's important to you about paying your credit card bill? (level three)

**Client:** It means I don't have to ask my husband for extra cash for treats.

Clients who have an *away from* tendency can come across as negative or critical. They know what they don't want as compared to people with a *toward* motivation. Don't be put off by this. Many jobs need people who can pay attention to what will go wrong and have a critical eye, particularly in manufacturing, health and safety, customer service or airline work.

You may need to work to balance out the critical voice associated with away-from tendencies with the ability to dream so that your client doesn't turn into a miserable character like Eeyore in *Winnie the Pooh*, who's always looking on the dark side of life.

By contrast, people with strong toward tendencies are always looking to the future and what can be better. Sometimes they get overwhelmed because they take on more and more without acknowledging their successes and giving themselves time to celebrate and enjoy the journey. They may also overlook risks and make snap decisions that they regret later.

## Internal/external

People with a high *internal* focus make assessments based on their own feelings and interpretation of events. People with a strong *external* focus are highly sensitive to others' opinions and needs.

You hear the *internal* pattern in phrases such as:

- ✔ In my view . . .
- ✔ I'm not concerned with others' opinions.
- ✔ I know I'm right.
- ✔ It's my decision.

You hear the *external* pattern in phrases such as:

- ✔ Tell me what you think.
- ✔ They say this will work.
- ✔ My wife thinks I should.
- ✔ I don't want to upset anyone.

Clients who are highly internally focused may be strong and self-sufficient, or self-obsessed and self-critical. They may stride out on their own and lack the ability to listen to others, receive feedback, delegate or ask for help.

The client who is externally focused may be great at listening to others, yet is always trying to get consensus and team buy-in. Taken to an extreme, they want to please everybody and put their own needs on the back burner. In doing so, they end up not pleasing anyone.

In the coaching relationship, internally focused clients make their own assessments of what they should be doing. They're more comfortable coming up with their own answers and suggestions, which may be what they've always done. However, they may not be open to exploring new possibilities. Externally focused clients are more likely to want to please the coach and get the coach to come up with suggestions and ideas for them: 'Can you tell me what I should do?'

In terms of giving and receiving feedback, each has different needs and styles.

- ✔ Internally focused people tend to set their own standards and don't often see the need for input from others. They know for themselves whether they're doing OK.
- ✔ Externally focused people want reassurance that they're on track.

Having one of each type in a relationship, business or domestic, can prove challenging. In a business team, the internally focused employee may not be interested in customer feedback while the externally focused one wants to listen to customers, so this tension can cause conflicting views on levels of service. When people understand their natural preferences, they can learn to adapt their behaviours.

# Breaking unhelpful patterns

Great coaches find ways of unlocking exciting goals and possibilities in the minds of their clients to break through stalemated situations. Often patterns of behaviour have become entrenched and no longer serve the client. Dreams remain dreams unless they're translated into action, and procrastination is a key driver in hiring a coach.

The first step of getting started on any job is often the worst, so here's a brief exercise to break through procrastination and kick-start motivation. Try it for yourself and then with others.

1. **Pick one small and annoying area that you are procrastinating about in your life.**

   You don't need to choose anything major. Perhaps something that you estimate will take no more than an hour or two: gathering the papers together for your tax return, dealing with an untidy cupboard, finishing overdue language homework from your Italian evening class, chasing down a supplier, making an awkward call, putting your profile on a dating website or writing your blog posting or diary.

2. **Notice what it's like to feel distracted and come up against your own resistance.**

   Allow yourself to sit quietly for 20 minutes to consider the situation. What inner talk do you hear? How does the resistance feel in your body? What are the images that come to mind? How does this experience of resistance affect your overall motivation?

3. **Replace the inner distracted voice with a firm 'let's crack on with it' voice.**

   Imagine how you'll feel when your project is done. What will you say to yourself?

4. **Just do the task.**

   Stay completely focused on the end result you want until you achieve what you set out to do. It may take longer than you first imagined or surprise you that it's faster. If it really is longer than a couple of hours, break the job into a series of smaller ones to tackle one by one.

5. **With the job complete, pat yourself on the back and then reflect on your experience.**

   What do you need to say to yourself in future when you're stuck? What positive feelings from this experience can you connect to later? What images delighted and motivated you? What resources have you got that can accelerate you to your potential?

Congratulations! You already know how to coach yourself on small things. The bigger challenges are simply a set of small steps all joined together!

# Cutting through Collusion

The dictionary defines collusion as 'secret cooperation between people in order to do something illegal or underhand'. Collusion in coaching is bit less sneaky, but it does involve some kind of avoidance when you sense an area that's uncomfortable. As coach, you may be hesitant or fearful to say what you're thinking because of the potential impact on the client. Or you may pick up on your client's hesitance to break a pattern.

By listening carefully to a client's voice, you can glean lots of useful information, particularly about topics that you and your client may be avoiding. After you identify the collusion, you can courageously intrude and break a pattern.

## Voicing what you notice

The voice has a powerful and often overlooked role to play in coaching. Richard Bandler, the co-creator of NLP, has suggested that everyone should have a voice coach. The history of NLP is rich with great teachers who use their voices with masterful flexibility, notably Milton Erickson, the late hypnotherapist and more recently one of Erickson's students, Stephen Gilligan.

As a coach, you can develop and use your own voice as an invitation to communicate at different levels – with lightness, warmth, humour and all manner of appealing qualities. When listening well, you also gain a huge amount of information from the client's voice.

In her excellent book *Voice of Influence* (Crown House Publishing), NLP trainer and voice coach Judy Apps explores the relationship between people's voices and their inner world of thoughts and beliefs and suggests that the voice tells a story about the speaker's personal history. She distinguishes between those people you hear who have voices that don't change at all and those who change their voices in different situations. Often when people's voices are stuck at some point, it can shed light on times in their lives when they've repressed certain emotions.

Judy's discussion of different voices reminds me of one coaching client who switched to a little girl's voice when talking about her health and then lowered her voice considerably when talking about her work in a charity that she was passionate about. The contrast in the two voices was really marked. We discovered that the child's voice went back to some childhood embarrassment centred on not being good at sport and feeling foolish. The deep adult voice was congruent with her true personality.

Perhaps you've had clients where the voice doesn't match the person. Or those clients who clear their throats and switch tone of voice when talking about a particular topic. The voice reveals much information about areas where people are not fully congruent.

NLP refers to congruence as a state in which all aspects of the person are aligned and authentic. You could also say that someone was walking their talk.

Judy Apps' work highlights four types of voice. Recognising and being able to activate each one can be useful during coaching sessions. For each type of voice, an underlying message (given here in brackets) is conveyed from speaker to the listener:

- **The head voice ('I'm excited').** The head voice rings full of enthusiasm and carries the listener along with its energy and excitement. The downside of this voice comes when it sounds childish or over-strident, like a child whooping and shrieking in the garden.

- **The chest voice ('I mean what I say').** The chest voice gives weight to what you say. Imagine you're Tarzan speaking as you beat your chest. This is the voice of a person who makes decisions firmly and moves things forward. Yet even this strong voice needs to be varied at times to prevent it from becoming monotonous.

- **The heart voice ('I speak as I feel').** To speak from your heart, you need to get in touch with real feelings. The resulting voice comes out with warmth and caring: it's usually quite low with a soft edge and natural vibration to it to draw others into the emotion. Access to this voice gets lost when you push down feelings, and it may only come out again when you find the confidence to express anger. Clients who aren't in touch with their feelings have often lost this aspect of their voices.

- **The gut voice ('I say it how it is').** This voice sounds as if it comes from the whole person and has the deepest resonance. It is slow, uses fewer words and has gravitas. The gut voice is associated with wisdom, leadership and maturity. The client who speaks with the gut voice does so from a place of passion and purpose that is inspirational to others.

The following activity helps you assess a client's various voices and inspire further growth activities.

1. **With your client's permission, use a small tape recorder or recording device to record a short segment of your coaching session.**

Invite the client to talk about something that is very important to them for three to four minutes. If they find this difficult at first, you can prompt with questions such as 'What really matters to you?' or 'Tell me, what's been your best or worst experience?'

2. **Share the description of the four types of voice that I outline earlier in this section.**

3. **Play back the recording and listen together, identifying any moments where the client speaks with one of the four types of voice.**

   Pay attention to the client's vocal range. Which voice is most comfortable for the client? Which voice or voices are absent? Which voices might she want to develop?

4. **Together, examine whether the voice and messages are in alignment.**

   For example, do you hear enthusiasm in the voice about things the client says she's enthusiastic about? Do you hear the quiet certainty of the gut voice when she speaks about meaningful issues? Is there decisiveness and warmth – or is her voice stuck in her throat?

The quality of your client's voice offers you valuable clues as to what's really going on. This exercise pinpoints limiting beliefs, lack of confidence in certain areas or the fact she's doing what she feels she ought to do rather than what she wants to do. She may also benefit from some specific voice coaching or communication training outside the coaching sessions too.

As a coach, the way you speak can affect the results you get. You can record sessions (with the client's permission) to listen to your own voice and see what impact your voice has on your client's responses. Does your voice have variety and range from the head to gut, or do you notice points in the conversation where it gets stuck in your throat? If you can hear the need to develop your range, enlist the support of a voice coach to work with you to free your voice and explore breathing techniques to relax the voice. Tentativeness in your voice may also reveal places in coaching where you need to work on a specific competence. (Chapter 3 lists core competencies so that you can develop your skills.)

## *Having the courage to hold the space*

As you grow as a coach and raise your skill level, coaching presents you with dilemmas where you may question yourself. At times you find yourself treading a fine line between honouring your clients' privacy and blurting out what you think. When you reach this kind of dilemma, you're venturing into territory where you can create transformational results for your clients. You may voice something that they know unconsciously and haven't been able to hear from anyone else. Tread cautiously so that you don't scare your client away, and pay extra attention to any discomfort your client may be experiencing.

Trust is central to the coaching relationship, and you can build on trust in order to explore sensitive ground with courage and eventually break unhelpful patterns. The following sections focus on two skills that come to the fore when helping to break patterns: asking permission and intruding/saying it as it is.

### Asking permission

When you sense that you've hit a difficult area – a topic or issue that a client is avoiding, perhaps – then you can ask permission to explore it. Use simple questions such as, 'Is it OK that we talk about this?' or 'I've noticed something here that I think may be significant. Is it OK to share that with you?'

With permission, you can delve further because the implicit message you send is that the client remains in charge of the conversation. However, if the client says 'no', then you need to respect that wish or risk the entire coaching relationship falling apart. Simply by highlighting what you're noticing, the client can't fail to be aware that she's blocking something and may well be willing to go there at a later date.

Cliff hired his coach to explore business development, yet his coach realised that Cliff had very troubled relationships with his two sisters stemming from an inheritance issue. By asking permission to open up this line of enquiry, Cliff identified various limiting beliefs he held regarding money that he was able to resolve in coaching. Dealing with his family-related money issues enabled him to think about his business model and financial targets with a greater sense of freedom and creativity.

### Intruding

Intruding is the skill of cutting to the chase and saying things that you spot. Consider this skill the spinach-in-the-teeth moment. If you see someone with spinach stuck in her teeth, it's in her best interests to blurt out what you notice rather than ignore it!

As a coach, develop the courage to say what your intuition whispers to you and blurt it out confidently in the moment. 'What's coming to me right now is this . . .' Be aware that the client may not be ready to receive your words and may well bat them away. However, now that you've said what you perceived, the client can take those thoughts of yours away and process them anyway.

How do you intrude effectively? Develop some phrases that can soften the impact and speak with your heart and gut voices (see the preceding section 'Voicing what you notice').

## Bringing concerns to the surface

Marriage, like all relationships, requires sensitivity to each other's needs. Louise has always loved birthdays, Christmas and parties. Even though she's a project manager in her mid-thirties, she gets as excited as a six-year-old as a big day approaches.

On the first Christmas after her wedding to Andrew, she thought she'd get in the festive spirit and surprise her new husband by decorating the house from top to bottom with tinsel and organising a 'Come as Santa' party for friends. Andrew arrived home from work to see all the decorations and all he could do was fret about the damage to the new paintwork, how he was supposed to dress up and whether the party would be any fun. They had an argument and Louise ended up taking down all the decorations and vowing to never have a Christmas party again.

As she learnt more about metaprograms though coaching at work, Louise realised that Andrew had both an *away from* tendency in the context of entertaining and an attention to *detail* tendency, even though he actually enjoyed social occasions very much. She realised that she had to give Andrew space to air all the things he didn't want to happen before he felt comfortable to go ahead.

In subsequent months, Louise changed her language to ask Andrew to share with her what he didn't want before pushing for what she wanted. After that discussion, Andrew was happy to get involved in detailed planning and support for her ideas for celebrations as well as many other shared activities in their new life together.

> ✔ I may be completely off beam here, yet I have a sense that this could be about . . .
>
> ✔ Here's something I've heard from other clients that I think could be valuable for you just now . . .

Timing is critical. Intrusion needs to be *immediate* on hearing something that doesn't sound right rather than brought up later. If you maintain rapport and keep a lightness of touch and respect, your clients recognise your deep concern for their best interests.

# *Establishing New Habits*

Coaching provides the context for people to establish new habits and report back on their progress over a period of time. As a coach, you can give specific feedback on habits or behaviours you've noticed that don't seem to serve them and invite them to choose better ones. Experts say it takes 21 days to change a habit. Change can be instant, yet some entrenched patterns take longer to change, which is why longer-term coaching assignments, of say six months, provide an environment that supports behavioural change compared to a one-off NLP session to fix an issue.

Ultimately clients are accountable for their new behaviours, and as a coach you support them to hold on to these new behaviours to make lasting change because you work with them on a regular basis, through the real ups and downs of life. As clients recognise their own patterns, they become curious about themselves in different contexts and spread their learning from one situation to another (see the sidebar 'Bringing concerns to the surface' for a great example of this dynamic).

In order to change patterns in the long term, challenge your clients to experiment with new patterns in a variety of contexts. Make the challenge interesting and fun and adapt it according to what you discover about their metaprograms based on the activities earlier in this chapter.

More procedural clients may enjoy a system to follow that tracks their progress. Encourage them to report their success stories back to you. Allow option-oriented clients to come up with their own creative methods and be aware that they may find sticking to their plans quite difficult! Those with an external focus are more naturally inclined to celebrate successes with you than those who are internally focused. See Chapter 11 for ideas on initiating new habits by finding better strategies.

# Chapter 11

# Developing Better Strategies

· · · · · · · · · · · · · · · · · · · · · · · · · · · · · · · · · · · · · · · · · · · · · · · · ·

## In This Chapter

▶ Seeing where change can happen

▶ Following the example of people who excel

▶ Initiating new ways of getting things done

· · · · · · · · · · · · · · · · · · · · · · · · · · · · · · · · · · · · · · · · · · · · · · · · ·

**D**o you like to take a shower or a bath? Do you enjoy a quick refreshing deluge of water with zingy shower gel or a luxurious soak in bubbles and oils? Whatever you choose becomes habitual, and before you know it you're a shower person or a bath person. Your behaviour gets wrapped into your identity.

Habits build over a period of time. Sometimes they give you the results you want, and at other times, they serve you less well. For example, I developed a habit of working towards my writing deadlines late at night because I had small children. The upside of this habit is that I wrote five books and hundreds of articles over the years and consistently delivered on commitments to clients. The downside is that I tend to burn the midnight oil rather than feel I'm letting someone down by missing a delivery date. Behind my behaviour lies an honourable intent to be of service to my clients and readers. However, a habit that serves you well can have adverse consequences if taken to the extreme.

Coaching enables people to get the results they want by examining habitual behaviours and deciding how they serve clients. NLP supports the process by looking at the strategies, or *models,* that people run and redesigning them to be more effective. A *strategy* is a pattern of behaviour that someone else can copy or reproduce. Strategies aren't good or bad, simply effective or ineffective. Overall, the coaching process involves understanding how clients operate their models of the world through their sensory experiences or representational systems. (Flip to Chapter 6 for more.)

This chapter look at how strategies work and how to change them to be more effective. Developing effective strategies can make the difference between a client perpetually procrastinating or getting things done, becoming an accomplished speaker or stumbling over his words. You also discover the usefulness of modelling experts, mentors and structures that reinforce new habits.

# Discovering the Difference that Makes the Difference: Strategies

Clients often want a magic solution handed to them. 'Tell me how to make myself thin/rich/attractive/employable,' goes the unspoken plea. Coaches, for their parts, often find wonder in the 'Aha!' moments when clients say, '*Now* I see what I can do here.'

The real magic happens when clients identify for themselves the key that enables them to achieve the results they want. They observe exactly how they've been getting in their own ways and see what they can do differently. They find the difference that makes the difference.

## Setting off strategies

Strategies are like a bead necklace that strings together individual components that create a behaviour pattern. They begin with an external or internal *trigger*. For example, your alarm going off acts as an external trigger to run your getting-dressed strategy. The trigger sets you off on a series of processes that may include brushing your teeth, taking a shower, examining your appearance in a mirror and saying, 'My goodness, I look better with my make-up on.' Your getting-dressed strategy ends and may trigger the eat-breakfast strategy. Or you may skip that one and go right to the drive-to-work strategy.

Alternatively, a *sub-strategy* may run within a strategy. Perhaps you reach a decision point within the getting-dressed strategy where you realise that today is Wednesday, your day for a mid-week run, so you jump out of bed, put on your running gear, head out for a three-mile jog, come back and shower, and then go through your getting-dressed and breakfast routine. Ultimately you achieve your getting-dressed strategy, but you may vary parts of it on different days.

NLP coaches analyse clients' strategies with them by breaking down the structure of the strategy into its component parts and noting what happens step by step. Some strategies clearly don't work effectively. If you spend half an hour trying on different outfits, you're late every day. So you may need a separate strategy that helps you develop a list of five work outfits you can put on quickly.

As you break down strategies with clients, you're interested not only in the actual external behaviours, but also what the clients see, hear and feel at each step.

## *Toting around your strategies*

NLP offers a simple model to explain how strategies run called the *TOTE model*, which stands for Test, Operate, Test and Exit. As Figure 11-1 shows, this model suggests that when you know that you want something to happen, you run strategies until you achieve your goal. Specifically:

- ✔ You check (Test) to see whether a strategy works.
- ✔ If the strategy works, you move on to the next strategy (Exit).
- ✔ If the strategy doesn't work, you refine your behaviour (Operate) until your test shows that you've achieved the goal.
- ✔ You keep looping around the model until each goal is realised.

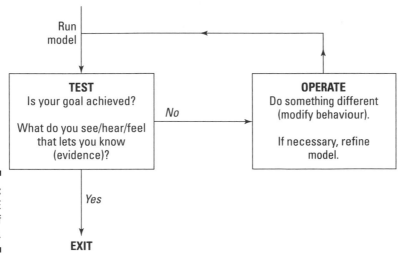

**Figure 11-1:**
The TOTE model of behaviour.

An example of the TOTE in action occurs when you're cooking supper and your goal is to cook the vegetables. You run your cook-vegetables strategy; your various tests to check if the veggies are ready involve looking at them, smelling them and prodding them with a fork. After the goal is achieved, you stop running the cook-vegetables strategy and switch to the dishing-up-supper strategy. However, if the vegetables are still raw after your various tests, you may need to do something different, such as turning up the heat and then running your test again five minutes later.

## Tackling unhelpful strategies

When clients aren't getting the results they want, it's time to create new strategies. You can do this in several ways:

- ✔ **Unpack the unhelpful strategy, noticing what's missing or not working.** The notation technique I describe in the following section 'Sequencing strategies' can be a helpful tool. After you sequence a strategy, adjust the steps or add extra ones, as necessary.

- ✔ **Take a strategy that works well already in another context and apply it to the problem area.** For example, if a client has a helpful strategy to motivate himself to complete his department's monthly budget report and is in need of motivation to do something different, such as cooking supper or weeding the garden, you can help him apply the same structure to a different situation. See the later section 'Redesigning strategies'.

- ✔ **Find somebody else's strategy, copy it and try it out yourself.** You can read more on this in the later section 'Finding Examples in Others: Models and Mentors'.

## Sequencing strategies

In order to understand a strategy, you need to *unpack* it, break it down and describe its smallest components. When you unpack clients' strategies during coaching sessions, you bring clients' unconscious processes to their conscious awareness.

You're looking to uncover the structure of your clients' subjective experience rather than offer an alternative. The questions to ask yourself during the unpacking process include:

- ✔ What's going on inside the client's mind?
- ✔ What's the client thinking as he goes through this strategy?
- ✔ What's the client experiencing as he runs the strategy?

Understanding strategies is beneficial because if you can find times when your client is motivated, energised, excited, making good decisions and really flowing, you can use the same structure in other situations where the client struggles. You're modelling your client's natural excellence.

Unpacking a strategy involves starting with your client in a positive frame of mind and asking questions that explore the *how* of the current excellent state. A good opener is 'You do that beautifully. Teach me how you do it.' In order to make him feel positive, you need to demonstrate a positive frame of mind yourself without any judgement. You may want to anchor a resourceful state using the tools on managing emotional states in Chapter 18.

You can also note down a person's sensory strategies on a piece of paper or flip chart using NLP symbols such as:

- ✔ V = Visual
- ✔ A = Auditory
- ✔ $A^d$ = Internal dialogue or self talk
- ✔ K = Kinaesthetic
- ✔ O = Olfactory
- ✔ G = Gustatory

Make your notation more precise by indicating if a dialogue or feeling is negative or positive, for example, $K^-$ or $K^+$. The client generally knows if the experience is negative or positive, yet with some self-talk, the coach may need to ask if that self-talk is supportive or not. You can also look at whether the source of the data is internal or external, and if it's remembered information stored in the memory or constructed information created in the imagination. Capture these finer details with the following symbols:

- ✔ + = positive
- ✔ - = negative
- ✔ i = internal
- ✔ e = external
- ✔ r = remembered
- ✔ c = constructed

To understand how to capture a typical strategy, consider the following. My friend and co-author of *Neuro-linguistic Programming For Dummies* Romilla Ready loves to speak to groups. She and I discussed her motivation strategy for preparing to give her talks. In unpacking her strategy, I'm paying attention to what's going on in her mental processing. I'm particularly curious about identifying what triggers her to run her motivation strategy and when she knows that the strategy is complete.

Here's Romilla's explanation of her strategy, along with my notes in parentheses:

> As the day gets closer in my calendar, I **get myself into** a little bit of **a panic** (K⁻) and **tell myself** (Aᵈ) that I need to get organised. So I begin to draft a handful of slides, then I go out to talk to people about what they'd like to hear. I gather my information together until I feel like my message **is all coming together** (K⁺). I then start developing and practising the script until **I picture myself** (Vᶜ) being very well rehearsed on the day, really being connected (K⁺) with the audience. Then I **tell myself** that I'm ready (Aᵈ) **and know in my bones** it's going to great **fun (K⁺)**.'

Notice in Romilla's description, I highlight the *structure* of her experience rather than itemise what she actually does in terms of behaviour. Then I can focus on her successful strategy for motivating herself instead of getting caught up in the detailed content.

The steps in her experience look a little bit like algebra as I note them down on paper for her:

$$K^- \rightarrow A^d \rightarrow K^+ \rightarrow V^c \rightarrow K^+ \rightarrow A^d \rightarrow K^+$$

Capturing this strategy is a joint exercise with the client. The client can detach himself from a situation to review what he does and sees where he can make changes to be more effective. Armed with one new strategy, he has a process to change other strategies.

## *Paying attention to the eyes*

The previous section 'Sequencing strategies' introduces a notation system for strategies based on the representational systems. NLP also offers the tool of *eye accessing cues* to give additional subtle clues about what someone is thinking, feeling or remembering. Noticing eye movements can be particularly valuable when you're unpacking strategies that exemplars can't fully explain.

Figure 11-2 shows how the eyes move when accessing a particular representational system. These eye movements give you clues as to what's really happening for another person. For example, if a client frequently looks upwards, he's likely to be accessing images and you may want to use questions that rely on visual language, such as: 'I notice that you looked up when you talked about that, and I'm wondering what you saw at that point?'

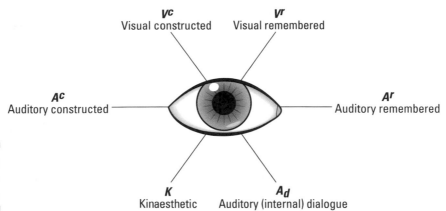

$V^c$
Visual constructed

$V^r$
Visual remembered

$A^c$
Auditory constructed

$A^r$
Auditory remembered

$K$
Kinaesthetic

$A_d$
Auditory (internal) dialogue

**Figure 11-2:**
Eye accessing cues.

The eye accessing cues in Figure 11-2 show what you see when looking at someone's face. The figure assumes that the person is right-handed. Left-handed individuals may access their representational systems the opposite way. You can check if clients are left- or right-handed by inviting them to write something down or observing how they wear wristwatches.

Table 11-1 summarises common activities and the corresponding eye movements. The table includes notation symbols in parentheses (see the preceding section 'Sequencing strategies' for details).

| Table 11-1 | Activities and Eye Movement |
| --- | --- |
| *When a Client is Doing This . . .* | *The Eyes are Doing This . . .* |
| Remembering a picture ($V^r$) | Moving to client's top left |
| Creating a picture ($V^c$) | Moving to client's top right |
| Remembering a sound or conversation ($A^r$) | Moving horizontally to client's left |
| Imagining what a sound will sound like ($A^c$) | Moving horizontally to client's right |
| Accessing emotions (K) | Dropping down and to client's right |
| Having a conversation with himself ($A_d$) | Dropping down and to client's left |

Capturing a model of a simple process or strategy provides wonderful insights for your clients into how they do what they do. By focusing on a simple and non-threatening process, you teach your clients to self-model and give them a tool to compare their strategies to others' and make improvements.

Use eye accessing cues to discover more about a client's strategy. Invite your client to take you step by step through a simple process, such as selecting food from the fridge.

1. **Sit opposite the client so you can see his face.**

   Tell him that you're watching and noting his eye movements. You can show him the images in Figure 11-2.

2. **Ask the client, 'What's the first thing you do or think when you begin this task/action?'**

   As he replies, pay attention to where his eyes move to and make a note of the movement. (You may have more than one movement to capture.)

3. **Ask the client, 'What's the *next* thing you do or think?'**

   Record the client's eye movements.

4. **Continue asking this question until the client takes you step by step through the entire process.**

   Observe and record the client's eye movements at each point.

5. **Help your client go back and forwards through the strategy, seeking any missing steps until you both feel the process is completely described.**

6. **Create a model of the strategy and sequence.**

   Capture the notation on paper as with the examples in the 'Sequencing strategies' section. After you've captured a simple, non-threatening strategy, you can work together on redesigning an unhelpful strategy.

## *Redesigning strategies*

Clients are pretty well-versed at their unhelpful behaviours, so tackle your exploration with a light and humorous touch. Ask them to teach you the unhelpful behaviour. 'You seem to be pretty good at this. How about taking me though it step by step, so that I can be as good as you,' you might ask.

Your clients already feel fed up with the results they're getting. Go easy on them and leave any of your own prejudices or judgements behind. Stay curious and become their willing partner in creating new, more valuable strategies.

Martin told his coach that he was lazy and always procrastinated. His coach was surprised, considering that Martin got up very early each day and worked hard as a dentist.

**Coach:** Mmm, really? What would I have to do to procrastinate as well as you, Martin? Teach me how you do that . . .

**Martin:** I feel really cross with myself, and I know that there's something I want to get on with, but I look and look at what needs to be done. I just ignore it until I feel really bad and the pressure is piling on my neck, then I finally get going. But I don't want to feel like this – under pressure – all the time.

**Coach:** So your strategy to get into action seems to be going like this:

You feel bad, you look and you look and feel really bad.

$$K^- \rightarrow V^e \rightarrow V^e \rightarrow K^-$$

**Martin:** Exactly, and I'm fed up with the fact I'm not doing anything.

**Coach:** OK and I'm wondering what's missing – or not working – here?

**Martin:** I'm looking at what needs to be done for far too long. I need to think of what my mum used to say: 'No time like the present' and imagine what it'll look like when I finish. Then I'll be happy to get going.

**Coach:** So let me check my understanding of your new strategy. You feel bad, you look at what needs to be done, you hear your mother's voice, imagine the finished job, and then feel good enough to get going? Is that right?

$$K^- \rightarrow V^e \rightarrow A^r \rightarrow V^c \rightarrow K^+$$

**Martin:** Yes, that's it!

**Coach:** What's coming up where you can try this new strategy out?

**Martin:** I've been putting off my tax return, and now I'm worried about the deadline that's coming up.

**Coach:** What needs to happen if you apply the same strategy to completing your tax return?

**Martin:** What I can do is get all the papers out to have a quick look at them, then run a little audio in my head with my mum's voice reminding me: 'No time like the present!' The next step is to picture the papers coming back from the accountant in a neat folder with the top sheet typed up and summarised, and then I'm feeling so good that I have a little celebratory glass of wine.

**Coach:** Ah, so you can add a touch of the gustatory too at the end! Let me know how your new strategy works out.

# Honouring the intent

The western world values looking good, success and winning in all areas of life. To call someone a loser may be the worst insult you can inflict. Measures of success tend to be external ones – how you look or what you own. Some people seek white teeth, slim bodies, six-figure incomes, flash cars, smart partners and high-status jobs to hold their heads up high amongst their peers and neighbours.

As a coach, you need to reach beyond the external trappings to connect with and accept your clients, while recognising what the external measures of success give them in terms of personal satisfaction. NLP assumes that people do the best they can do at any one time with the resources they have. NLP seeks to understand the positive intent in any behaviour, however bad it appears at first glance.

People are tempted to beat up themselves when they get things wrong. Your job is to remind your clients that they chose a less helpful strategy for a very sound reason. They can adjust that strategy with some subtle changes and move off in a better direction with new habits in place.

Clients who've developed strategies that aren't working may resist changing them. Work with them to identify the positive intention beneath the behaviours. Ask a simple question such as, 'What does that do for you?' Keep asking the question until the client expresses a fundamental value such as security, freedom or love (see Chapter 8 for more on values).

When Anna married Ralph and stayed home to look after their young baby, she found herself becoming unreasonably jealous when her husband went to work. Frequent tears and tantrums accompanied Ralph's attempts to leave the flat, and then she felt guilty at making his life so difficult and spoiling their marriage. Through a personal development workshop, Anna saw that her emotional outbursts were tied into fears of abandonment going back to her childhood experiences. After she acknowledged the intention of self-protection that lay beneath the behaviour, she was prepared to move forward without judging herself to be stupid. Her coach pointed that there was much more to Anna's identity than this one kind of behaviour – she had a vast repertoire of experiences to draw on. Together they redesigned her strategies about feeling secure when her loved one was out of sight.

# Finding Examples in Others: Models and Mentors

People create their own mental maps of the world, running strategies that sometimes work and at other times do not. The foundation of NLP lies in the work of John Grinder and Richard Bandler, who started modelling the processes of great therapists, including Milton Erickson, Fritz Perls and Virginia

Satir, who were getting great results with their clients. From their modelling work, Grinder and Bandler created linguistic models, notably the Milton model and the Meta Model (see Chapter 2 more on these models).

*NLP modelling* is the ability to fully replicate another person's desirable competence. Modelling works by getting to the unconscious behaviours beneath a particular skill and coding the behaviours in such a way as to teach them to others.

Modelling is taught as part of Master Practitioner training, and it's a useful NLP skill to explore and bring into your coaching practice (see Chapter 22 for more on NLP training). Many excellent books and online sources cover modelling, including a chapter in *Neuro-linguistic Programming For Dummies* (Wiley) by Romilla Ready and yours truly.

In order to develop your own coaching skills, model a variety of different coaches you admire to figure out their successes and see what you can transfer from their experiences to your own.

Mentoring can be a valuable complement to coaching for a client, allowing him to build skills and get practical advice or moral support. Even if your client doesn't have a mentor, in this section you find a practical exercise to imagine the advice a mentor would give. The following sections show you how to apply some of the fundamental principles of modelling to support your coaching work as well as the value of finding mentors as guides.

## *Choosing exemplars*

Modelling involves finding someone who excels in a particular behaviour – an *exemplar* – and then studying him. Through careful observation, you create a *model*, an explanatory framework of how the exemplar functions. You then try out the model and see if you get the same results.

Creating a robust model that can be replicated by other people is painstaking work. In order to make your first modelling attempts easier:

- ✔ Choose an exemplar who's accessible and willing to be modelled.
- ✔ Identify a precise strategy to model instead of attempting to model all aspects of the exemplar's behaviour.

So, if your client wants to be healthier, you can first invite him to define what *more healthy* means in terms of desirable habits and then find exemplars of those habits. Your work together may reveal that *more healthy* involves the taking-exercise strategy or the going-to-sleep-earlier strategy.

## Digging for the inside story

Imagine that you're coaching a client who wants to improve his golf swing. You can find many examples of great players, collect DVDs of their games and analyse how they drive the shot down the fairway or get in place for the final putt – those are all external observable behaviours.

However, NLP is more curious about a person's thought strategies. What's the structure of this great player's subjective experience? What's really going on in his mind when he hits that winning shot?

I once asked a professional golfer to tell me what was going on inside his head when he played his winning shot in a tournament. He said:

> I'm looking at the course and as I think about the next shot, my internal dialogue is completely silent. I feel so relaxed – just as I do when I'm spending a day fishing with nothing to think about. I'm just in a flow state.

Most winning strategies involve quieting down the internal chatter and allowing the outcome to take care of itself. (See Chapter 9 for more on the flow state.)

Modelling involves looking at two aspects of the exemplar's strategies:

- ✔ **The external behaviour:** What the person does, step by step.
- ✔ **The internal processing:** How the person thinks in sensory terms when engaged in the behaviour.

NLP modelling is particularly interested in *how* the exemplar thinks because these insights are the more subtle clues to excellence – the difference that makes the difference. See the sidebar 'Digging for the inside story'.

## *Finding new strategies from models of excellence*

Sometimes you simply don't have examples of some types of helpful strategies in your own life experience. If your clients have considered their own experiences and come up empty, they can look beyond themselves at others' successful strategies to model.

Many people hire a coach with a particular technical or professional background, and Sheila was no exception. She hired me as a coach because she wanted to improve her communication skills at work. As a leader in a public sector role, Sheila wanted to raise her game in order to craft policy documents that were persuasive, attend senior meetings with more confidence and present her ideas clearly. She knew that written and verbal communication was one of my skill areas.

While I'm knowledgeable on all the topics Sheila sought help on and could easily have moved into tell mode, I didn't. Coaches want their clients to learn in ways that suit them.

Sheila and I together created an agenda for a coaching programme where I'd facilitate her learning, offering just a few ideas and observations along the way. Sheila would be responsible for her own learning by identifying and modelling excellence to find strategies that worked for her. Our agreed-to programme of sessions included several defined topics, such as writing persuasive documents, chairing meetings, planning presentations and delivering difficult messages with confidence.

Sheila's task for each session was to identify three people whose work she admired and spend time modelling them. In particular, she needed to come to our sessions prepared with two pieces of information:

- ✔ How each person demonstrated the external behaviour.
- ✔ How the person thought about this work – what were their thoughts at different points?

Clearly the first task is easier. Anyone can observe others from a distance and note their behaviours. The second, however, is more challenging, and this aspect of modelling encourages clients to engage with their models personally and really learn from them.

Ultimately, connecting with others had a huge impact on Sheila's career. She extended her network of contacts into different fields by getting in touch with people she admired in various areas of her organisation as well as some senior women's networks. After she demonstrated interest in other people, they became interested in supporting her progress.

For each of our sessions together, Sheila took the lead by presenting her models of excellence and unpacking what she'd noticed about their strategies. We then compared her own strategies with her role models so that she could identify which strategies she wanted to take on board to excel. She built up her own models of useful habits that she then shared with her team too.

Like so many coaching agendas, the scope of our sessions expanded beyond the original aims, particularly after Sheila realised that she could model excellence in any field. For example, when we first began working together, she mentioned that she had some financial difficulties. As the months progressed, she began modelling a friend who was a financial advisor to work out how to better budget her spending and remortgage her flat to get a better interest rate.

## Imagining mentors

In modelling, clients are drawing on the excellence that they admire in other people to improve their own strategies. You can also encourage your clients to become more resourceful in creating new strategies by imagining what others would advise them to do.

Many successful people are fortunate that they have or have had strong real-world mentors in their lives. Mentors look out for opportunities for others and guide them well. Others haven't had the benefit of these models of excellence.

The following Wisdom of Mentors exercise invites clients to imagine the mentors they'd really like to have now. An imagined mentor can be a friend or a colleague who your client already knows. It may be a family member (alive or long passed) or a complete stranger. I've done this exercise many times, and people choose all kinds of mentors from deceased loved ones to famous business gurus, Mother Teresa to the President of the United States.

1. **Ask the client to select a situation where he'd like guidance.**

   For example, your client may be deliberating on a major decision such as change of home, job or relationship.

2. **Have the client identify three people who have some wisdom about the situation that they can offer.**

3. **Ask the client to visualise the three mentors in three different places in the room.**

   To help the client imagine the three mentors, you can position three empty chairs in the room, or write 'Mentor one', 'Mentor two' and 'Mentor three' on three pieces of paper and place them on the floor around the room. Position a fourth chair or sheet of paper with the client's name in the centre of the room.

   Ask the client whether he'd like you to take notes for him.

4. **Have the client stand or sit in the Mentor one position and have the client answer a question as the mentor.**

   Ask a simple question of the client as mentor, such as 'What advice or strategy can you offer [the client] on this issue?' Have the client as mentor direct the advice towards the client's empty chair.

   If he struggles to get the advice, give him time and reword the question slightly, for example, 'What would you do if you were faced with a similar situation yourself?'

5. **Repeat Step 4 for all the mentors.**

6. **Have the client return to his own chair and take on the advice or wisdom that the client feels is valuable.**

ANECDOTE

## Only do what only you can do

A hugely rewarding benefit of coaching is how much you gain from the excellence of your clients. When you're struggling with an issue yourself, clients may bring gifts to your coaching sessions by working on issues very similar to your own. You can model your clients' strategies too.

My client Liz, an investment banker, came to a session and talked about her enormous workload at just the same time that I was feeling under pressure too. Liz was looking at areas of her leadership where she excelled and compared them with areas that she found more challenging.

Her *aha!* moment in the session came as she noticed that she excelled when she concentrated her efforts on doing the things that no one else in the organisation could do. Liz's realisation may sound obvious, yet people miss the

blindingly obvious at times because something gets in the way.

Liz realised that she'd spent too much effort in areas where she could hire experts who had far more knowledge than herself. Unconsciously, she'd been reluctant to hire people who could be better than her and ultimately succeed to her position. She decided this habit of not hiring brilliant strategists wasn't working any longer and found that changing her internal dialogue made all the difference in her effectiveness and well-being.

As she unpacked her own strategies for successfully leading her team, she developed the mantra, 'Only do what only you can do'. I pay attention to this statement myself when I find I'm struggling with too many things to do – and invite you to do the same!

If you've taken notes for the client, at this point you can remind him of the mentors' advice. Encourage the client to let go of any advice that doesn't seem useful or appropriate.

7. **Invite the client to identify new habits or behaviours that he can take on board from the mentors.**

   Help the client identify situations where he can practise the newly identified behaviours.

# Creating New Structures to Be More Effective

People who crave freedom and flexibility may cringe at the very mention of discipline and structure. The image of a scowling task master or drill sergeant with a pointy stick may leap to mind.

However, appropriate structures or processes to follow can create self-discipline and create freedom from habits and strategies that don't serve you. These structures remind you to notice your impulses and gut reactions; they loosen the power of such reactions over you. Instead of giving in to something out of habit, the new structures remind you to find other choices. Structures provide the support to make change and achieve your dreams by channelling your impulsive reactions where they can be most effective.

In this section, I introduce several types of structure that can support clients to get the results they desire.

## *Saying a resounding yes or a definitive no*

To say yes to one thing means saying no to another. How you spend your time, money and effort is a simple equation. If you spend it on $x$, you can't spend it on $y$.

Susan runs an HR consultancy and like many working mums excels at multi-tasking. She told me how she was decorating the house in between interviewing candidates for a friend's business and periods of long commutes for her own consultancy work. She had a light-bulb moment when I questioned whether one reason she was struggling to find quality time to spend with her sons and husband might be linked to the fact that she was spending so much of her working day giving free consultancy to friends and spending her weekends on domestic chores that she didn't enjoy.

Yes/No lists provide a practical structure to look at the behaviours that have become habitual. By writing them out on paper, you can see what the ideal situation would be and then work towards it.

1. **Take a blank sheet of paper and draw a vertical line down the middle, dividing it into two columns.**

   At the top of the left column, write the heading YES! and at the top of the right column NO!

2. **Decide on an area of your life where you'd like to change something.**

   Some examples of things you may want to change include home activities, a business task or project, a relationship or your health and diet.

3. **Explore the current situation and compile an itemised list of:**

   - The specific things that you're saying 'yes' to.
   - The specific things that you're saying 'no' to.

When Susan drew up her Yes/No list, she realised that she was simply saying yes to – and consequently doing – too much. Table 11-2 shows Susan's Yes/No list on the domestic front.

4. **Review your lists and decide what you want to be different.**

    Ask yourself:

    - What would I prefer to say 'yes' to?

    - What would I prefer to say 'no' to?

5. **Shift items across the columns until you feel satisfied that the list reflects what you want to achieve.**

6. **With a revised list in place, work with your client to focus on what needs to happen to achieve the desired list.**

    As Susan evaluated her list, she realised she needed help. She negotiated the division of labour in the house with her husband so that they each took ownership for particular activities they enjoyed and hired help with the ones they didn't. She similarly reviewed her business approach to see where she could be more generous to herself.

| Table 11-2 | Susan's Domestic Yes/No List |
|---|---|
| **YES!** | **NO!** |
| Cooking supper on Tuesday and Thursday | Doing family laundry and ironing |
| Reading to Ben at bedtime | Shopping for food online |
| Help Tom with maths | Decorating the house |
| Buying the boys' clothes and shoes with them in the school holidays | Arranging car maintenance |
| Shopping locally for basic food supplies if we run out, like milk or bread | Having guests stay when I'm busy with work |
| Taking Tom to tennis on Saturday | Cooking on Friday and Saturday |
| Having guests stay for three weekends in the year | Booking holidays |
| Making family meal on Sunday evening | Putting out the rubbish bins |

Inevitably busy people place more on their lists than they actually have time to complete. As a reality check, invite your clients to allocate a time-estimate to all the activities, indicating how many minutes or hours per week they plan to spend doing each. Then invite your clients to add up the time and see how it fits with their actual schedule. Something else may need to shift from one side of the page to another.

## *Counting the days*

Habits develop over time. A good amount of time to embed a new daily habit so that it becomes a ritual is 21 days. Do the following exercise to ingrain a new habit:

1. **Take an A4 piece of paper, turn it to landscape orientation and draw a chart with days across the top, numbered 1 to 21.**

2. **List activities down the left-hand side of the chart.**

   Activities may be as diverse as spending 50 minutes each morning on strategy, doing 30 minutes of exercise, completing your journal, drinking 8 glasses of water, limiting your coffee to one cup, spending one hour on filing and throwing paper, taking vitamins with breakfast, getting 8 hours sleep, stroking the family pet, checking in with each person in the team or turning off your work phone at 6.15 p.m.

3. **Each day, tick off the list when you complete the ritual.**

   At future coaching sessions, client and coach can share progress.

## *Colour-coding schedules and diaries*

When I was coaching Gerard, the owner of a small manufacturing business, he told me how he liked to go into work each morning, greet all the staff and ask them what problems they had. Little wonder then that he spent all his days sorting panics and problems with no time for strategic activities. He prioritised the problems.

In a typical working day, you need to be aware of how time is allocated. I encourage clients to keep a record of their days for a couple of weeks and then identify tasks and activities as:

- **Panics and problems** are the important deadline-driven jobs that need to be done, but if planned they don't end up as panics, merely problems you deal with.

- **Plans and opportunities** are the important longer-term activities. People are most effective if they spend time doing important activities before they become urgent.

- **Pressing items** are the things other people are pushing for, but which are not top of your personal to-do list. These items are ones to question whether you should be involved at all and delegate wherever possible.

- **Pootling issues** include things such as the chats with friends and more trivial activities. These activities can provide a little refresh space, but they can also become habitual time-wasters.

A simple colour-coding system in a diary can help people to notice where time is going and whether they're spending it on the important and urgent activities or if it's just drifting away ineffectively. Using different-coloured highlighter pens is easy in a paper diary and colour highlights work well on-screen for electronic diaries.

After identifying and labelling various tasks and activities, ask yourself:

- How much time are you spending in each of these areas?
- Is the ratio working for you?
- What might be a better ratio?
- When is the best time of the day/week to spend on this type of activity?

# Checking in

When you're accountable to somebody else in the shape of a coach, your attention becomes amazingly focused.

At times when I'm under pressure, I book in frequent short phone calls with my coach in order to hold myself accountable for sticking with the most important things on my agenda rather than getting sidetracked. Just 30 minutes coaching a week can make a huge difference in my effectiveness.

Coaching works because you know you're accountable to an external person in a way that slips when you try to be accountable to yourself. For clients, the mere act of knowing they're going to tell somebody else whether they did what they said they wanted to do provides a powerful structure and supports the building of new habits. This commitment doesn't have to happen in a coaching session. With email and text messaging, clients can easily send quick notes on progress.

# Part IV
# Working Through Drama, Decisions and Dilemmas

## The 5th Wave
By Rich Tennant

"The reason I think stress might be a factor in your life is because of research, statistics, and the fact that you've straightened out an entire box of paper-clips during our conversation."

# In this part . . .

You explore the real-life issues that arrive in the coaching space including troublesome relationships and tough life and work dilemmas. You discover you can support your clients to adapt their approach and have courageous conversations as they tune into those around them with greater awareness. Here you'll also find ways to coach teams of people to bond and perform at their best.

With the world of work changing, you'll find practical ways that build confident careers – ones that keep people inspired, able to reinvent themselves and feel energetic about their working lives.

# Chapter 12

# Strengthening Relationships in Tough Times

. . . . . . . . . . . . . . . . . . . . . . . . . . . . . . . . . . . . . . . .

*In This Chapter*

▶ Connecting with the right people

▶ Adapting your style with different people

▶ Building cohesive teams

. . . . . . . . . . . . . . . . . . . . . . . . . . . . . . . . . . . . . . . .

*W*hen you go through tough times in life, the pressure builds and inevitably impacts others around you. Under pressure you may revert to unhelpful behaviours, such as focusing on the task in hand at the expense of the relationships around you. Perhaps the hurry-up driver kicks in or the need to look for someone to blame as things go wrong. Emotions can escalate as confidence drops.

Additionally, your perceptions change under pressure because you're not firing on all cylinders. Some senses are heightened at the expense of others. You may increasingly filter information using the patterns of distortion, generalisation and deletion that I introduce in Chapter 6.

In this chapter I look at planning relationships with *stakeholders* – those people who you want or need to communicate with. Then I look at NLP tools to support better understanding between people. This chapter also explores ways to coach teams and build strong relationships that help take groups through tough times.

ANECDOTE

## You're not alone

Employing you as a coach during tough times means your clients don't navigate alone through troubled waters.

Geoff was coaching Dan, a senior psychiatrist. One of Dan's patients had recently committed suicide, even though he was under almost constant observation in a secure hospital. Quite naturally Dan was extremely distressed by this event, and coaching sessions centred on supporting Dan to recognise how he'd done everything possible in his professional capacity to protect his patient.

Geoff said:

*Dan was feeling so guilty, even though he'd taken all the safety measures he could. He's a man with incredible integrity and professionalism: his job is core to his identity. So I saw my role as coach as enabling him to place this sad event in the larger context* of his work for thousands of other patients rather than as personal failure. Dan needed to be able to manage his personal state and find support in order to face the relatives and inquiries that took place and work collaboratively with his colleagues rather than isolating himself.

Over a period of several months, Geoff coached Dan to anchor strong emotional states and to explore different perceptual positions, especially stepping into the third position of an impartial observer in which he mentally distanced himself from the situation. Geoff reminded Dan to keep out of the blame frame of thinking and keep rapport with the family. Dan used some time-line work to let go of negative emotions along the time line. Through coaching, Dan was able to get back his natural professional perspective to work effectively with other patients.

# Identifying the Stakeholders Who Matter

In any community in which you live or work, you connect with different people – friends, family, colleagues and others. Having strong relationships with others acts as a tremendous resource in tough times.

In the business world, *stakeholders* are those people who have a *stake* in the business or project. Business stakeholders may include:

- ✔ Customers – both internal (if you provide support services such as IT, finance, human resources or facilities) and external (where you deliver products or services).
- ✔ Employees, bosses, peers, business partners, colleagues.
- ✔ Suppliers of services and products.
- ✔ Investors and shareholders with a financial interest.

- Members of the media, including journalists and industry analysts.
- External agencies and officials, such as regulatory bodies or non-executive directors.
- Members of professional groups.

Stakeholders extend beyond an organisational context to include all areas of your clients' lives, including personal connections. Clients may not have considered friends and family as stakeholders before, but you can encourage them to consider their personal relationships, such as:

- Spouse or life partner.
- Family members.
- Friends.
- Professional supporters, such as a doctor, solicitor, financial adviser and personal coach.
- Community groups focused on specific hobbies, sports, schools, political affiliations, or volunteer and church activities.

## *Mapping out the network*

When coaching senior leaders in business, I encourage them to build a relationship map of their key stakeholders. This process is particularly helpful when they're running complicated or challenging programmes or hold responsibility for restructuring or merging businesses with multiple stakeholder groups. The same mapping exercise works well for other clients in a personal context.

Your clients need to identify the individuals they need to be in touch with, as well as remember people they may have overlooked who can support them. Too often relationship-building gets seen as a nice-to-have activity. Yet without strong relationships in place, people suffer from a lack of support when they most need it.

The following relationship-mapping exercise also highlights where clients are spending their time and whether they're paying enough attention to building strong relationships.

To create a relationship map, take a large sheet of paper – a flip chart is ideal – and a few pads of sticky notes and follow these steps:

1. **Establish a context for identifying relationships – work/professional, home/personal or both areas of life.**

2. **Ask your client, 'Who is important to you in this context?'**

   Write names of people on sticky notes.

3. **Sort the sticky notes into groups that you can place on a wall or sheet of paper.**

   Groups may naturally form based on roles or activity areas. Example groups can include friends, colleagues, suppliers and so on.

4. **Examine the names in each group and check whether the group is complete or if people are missing.**

   Create additional sticky notes as necessary.

5. **Review each name in a group and assess the strength of the relationship.**

   Score the relationship on a scale of 1 to 10 with 10 being the strongest; the most satisfying and effective.

   To help determine a relationship's strength, ask your client, 'Looking at these names and thinking about these people, who can you count on to respond if you asked for help?' The names that come to mind first are among the client's strongest.

6. **After reviewing all the groups, invite the client to consider who the client needs to spend more time with – and who to spend less time with.**

   Are any relationships failing to serve your client well? Ask her what else she notices about the various groups and individuals.

7. **Encourage the client to come back to the map at regular intervals and review it.**

   Maps develop and change over time, but clients need to actively keep stakeholders on their radars.

This exercise engages the core visual, auditory and kinaesthetic senses (flip to Chapter 6 to read more about the senses in NLP). Your client is looking at the names of the people, talking through the relationships and writing on notes and shifting notes to various groups.

## Informing – or influencing?

You communicate differently with people in order to deepen the relationships or achieve the results that matter most to you.

Not all relationships are equal. Clearly some people nurture your soul while others are mere passing acquaintances. Yet the interesting thing about relationships is that they don't exist in isolation; one connects with another.

Spend any time on a social networking site such as LinkedIn or Facebook, and you soon realise that if you link with one person, you also link with everyone who knows that person in their network, so you form a batch of new, random relationships.

One of the major distinctions in building relationships is realising who you want to impart information to without a close involvement and who you really want to influence in order to meet a need. Table 12-1 offers my four-step Communication model. The four steps are:

✔ **Informing.** Supplying people with factual information.

✔ **Involving.** Creating a dialogue in which you invite others' opinions.

✔ **Influencing.** Where you seeking to persuade other people to your viewpoint.

✔ **Inspiring.** Raising levels of motivation in others.

| Table 12-1 | The Four-I Levels Communication Model | |
|---|---|---|
| *Level of Communication* | *Behaviour* | *Question to Ask Yourself* |
| **Inform** | Telling instructions; giving the facts | Who do I need to give information to? |
| **Involve** | Asking questions; gathering information, feedback and viewpoints | Who do I want to get information from or invite to give feedback? |
| **Influence** | Persuading; appealing to emotions | Who do I need to connect to at an emotional level in order for them to act? |
| **Inspire** | Motivating | What is the broader group that I could impact through my communication and behaviour? |
| | | Who might choose me as a role model? |

Invite your clients to look at the people in their networks to determine the appropriate level of communication for each person or group of people. (See the earlier section 'Mapping out the network'.) Are your clients interacting with people who just need information or do they need to increase their activities to inspire or influence key people?

ANECDOTE

## Shifting communication levels

When Maria's sister Jane married and moved to California, the reality of keeping in touch over the long distance meant the sisters saw each other less than they liked. As their parents grew older, Maria took on a supporting role, helping them through many hospital visits and illnesses that culminated in the death of her mother. Maria kept Jane loosely *informed* of what was happening until she began to realise that she couldn't cope alone with the responsibility of organising care for her elderly father, Peter.

Maria's coach asked whether it might help to strengthen her relationship with her sister and *involve* her more in the decision-making. Maria decided to experiment with the web cam on her laptop.

In her academic work at a university, Maria was good at building teams and delegating work to researchers. She decided to work on building a stronger support team within her family. She invited her American nephews as well as her sister and brother-in-law to regular family pow-wows over the web cam with Peter included too when he was over for meals. She also booked regular Internet-based calls with her sister to share her concerns and ask her opinion. Her level of *influence* increased.

Jane appreciated her sister's efforts and volunteered to research sheltered accommodation options online for her father. Then the whole family came across from the US to support Peter when he moved to warden-assisted care, making the trip a holiday.

Maria felt that applying lessons from her job made a difference at home too. She said: 'At work, my motto with the team is "You cannot over-communicate". I got so wrapped up in the practicalities of supporting Dad that I forgot how my communication motto is so true with the whole family as well.'

In terms of the Communication model, Maria shifted from informing to involving and thus influenced her family by increasing their emotional connections. She wasn't aware that her kindness and commitment to her family also *inspired* her work colleagues until they gave her some feedback in a peer-review process that she was a very positive role model because they saw just how much she cared for her family in addition to her high commitment to work.

## *Setting priorities for communication*

Effective communication involves planning what you want to communicate to whom and the outcomes you seek. Specifically:

- ✔ **Audience.** Who do you need to connect with? One person, several people or a group?

- ✔ **Outcome.** What do you want to achieve? Remember *you* need to initiate and lead the outcome, based on the well-formed outcome process (see Chapter 7 for more).

✔ **Message.** What do you want to communicate in terms of the headline message as well as the key points?

✔ **Method.** What's the best way to communicate your message? Text, phone call, personal or group meeting, professional network, email, web and social media are each potentially appropriate options.

Table 12-2 summarises this simple structure and provides a worked example for you to work out your communication plans.

Fred has an introverted preference and hadn't paid much attention to developing a network of contacts, other than people at his badminton club. However, when he resigned from his role as a charity worker due to stress and wanted to build up local work as a decorator and handyman, he knew he needed to talk to people to attract customers. His coach encouraged him out of hibernation and into strengthening his connections. With the help of a chart like the example in Table 12-2, he developed a communication plan to actively reconnect with friends, neighbours and ex-colleagues. As a result, Fred arranged to meet with friends at his club, did a leaflet drop in his neighbourhood and sent a flyer by email to let people know that he was available for work. In each instance, he provided specific examples of wonderful projects he'd done in his own house and garden.

| Table 12-2 | Effective Communication Plan | | | |
|---|---|---|---|---|
| *Who do I need to communicate with?* | *What is the desired outcome?* | *What is the headline message?* | *What are three key points I want to get across?* | *What is the best way to communicate?* |
| Friends and neighbours. | Create a list of potential clients for decorating and maintenance jobs. | Contact me if you need any decorating or household maintenance done so you can enjoy your weekends without doing jobs. | 1. You can trust me as a friend in your house while you work. 2. Fixed-price quotes. 3. Speedy and clean decorating and garden work. | Word of mouth. Email. Facebook. Leaflet drop. |

*continued*

| Table 12-2 *(continued)* | | | | |
|---|---|---|---|---|
| **Who do I need to communicate with?** | **What is the desired outcome?** | **What is the headline message?** | **What are three key points I want to get across?** | **What is the best way to communicate?** |
| Colleagues at work. | Inform colleagues of the new services I'm offering. | I'm available to support office moves as well as private decorating and household maintenance. | 1. Let me sort office handyman jobs when you relocate desks or sites.<br><br>2. Available for moves at weekends.<br><br>3. I can do essential home maintenance jobs while you're busy at work. | Targeted email.<br><br>Meeting with facilities team.<br><br>Internal company website.<br><br>Notice boards. |

# *Understanding What Makes Others Tick*

In coaching you encourage your clients to understand how they relate to other people, not just themselves. As Stephen Covey, author of *The 7 Habits of Highly Effective People* (Simon and Schuster) put it: 'Seek first to understand, then to be understood.' In this section I explore the value of stepping into other people's shoes, as well as some NLP techniques for doing so.

As you read through the following sections, think of a person you'd like to get to know better; perhaps a client, colleague, friend or family member. Having a specific person in mind helps the activities come to life.

## Scarcity rules

In Mark Twain's classic story *The Adventures of Tom Sawyer* the mischievous Tom finds himself whitewashing the fence as his punishment from Aunt Polly for his naughty behaviour. Yet he's constantly distracted by other boys who are going off to enjoy their freedom and consistently fails to bribe them to swap jobs in return for his small supply of toys and marbles.

Then Tom develops a new influencing strategy: he pretends to another lad, Ben, that he actually likes whitewashing the fence to the point where Ben is taken in by Tom's ruse and asks if he can take over. Tom pretends reluctance as Aunt Polly is so particular about the fence. Soon Ben is bribing Tom with an apple to let him whitewash. Tom eventually agrees, taking care not to show his delight.

Seeing Ben enjoy his privileged position as fence painter, several boys arrive and hand over their treasures to Tom in order to be allowed to have a turn at whitewashing the fence. Tom ends up with a pile of treasures, a perfectly whitewashed fence, and the company of other boys instead of doing the job alone. In addition to a humorous communication lesson, Tom's actions show how the *scarcity principle* influences others: 'In order to make a man or boy covet a thing, it is only necessary to make the thing difficult to obtain.'

# *Taking perceptual positions*

The *NLP perceptual positions* help you imagine what difficult situations look like when viewed with others' fresh eyes. The term refers to the ability to imagine what others are perceiving by pretending that you are that other person. In NLP this links with the assumption that the map is not the territory, and offers a way to enrich an individual's map of the world, which may be limiting her experience.

- **First position** is your natural perspective, where you're fully aware of what you think and feel, regardless of those around you. Clients find this place the most familiar. They've come to coaching because they already have an awareness of their own perspective and the problems they face.

- **Second position** is about imagining what it's like to be another person. Some people are very good at considering others' needs and concerns; for more self-focused clients, imagining second position is a completely alien notion.

- **Third position** is an independent position where you act as a detached observer, noticing what's happening in the relationship between two other people. Good coaches naturally step into this impartial role. In coaching, encourage the client to take this position in order to gain an impartial insight into a situation, particularly to view a relationship the client has with another person.

Introduce perceptual positions to clients by having them physically move to different chairs or places in a room as you describe and discuss the three positions, asking them to notice what they experience while standing or sitting in each position.

NLP offers a number of exercises where coaches ask clients to move into various perceptual positions, including several of my favourites in the following sections. After clients master assuming the preceding three positions, they have the flexibility to imagine stepping into the shoes of any other stakeholder in the system. When doing these exercises, I might ask, 'Who else could give you insight here?' Examples of another perspective could be a family member, business guru, TV personality or spiritual leader. They can be people that the client doesn't know, as well as familiar figures.

## Gazing into the NLP meta-mirror

The *meta-mirror* is an exercise that brings together a number of different perspectives or perceptual positions. The aim is to hold up a mirror to the problem the client is confronting. Clients find answers as they realise their problems are reflections of themselves rather than about someone else. This technique allows the client to step back and see the issue in a new light – hence the idea of the mirror.

The meta-mirror helps clients to prepare for, or review, challenging situations, conversations and negotiations. When people are under pressure, this technique enables them to detach from their emotions and gain new insights as to how they can handle a situation.

The meta-mirror exercise takes four perceptual positions. As coach, invite your client to choose a relationship or situation she wants to explore and then lay out four pieces of paper on the floor to denote four positions (see Figure 12-1).

Be sure to have your client break state between each position by physically moving between each. You don't want her to get stuck in one perspective! Invite the client to shake her body a little or look out of a window and tell you what the weather's like.

Talk your client through the four positions as follows:

1. **Have your client in *first position*.**

   Ask her to assume her own point of view and then look at the other person in second position.

   *Ask the client: 'What are you experiencing, thinking and feeling as you look at this person?'*

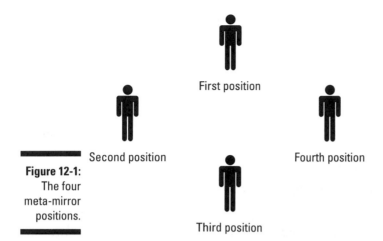

First position

Second position

**Figure 12-1:**
The four
meta-mirror
positions.

Third position

Fourth position

Give the client a few minutes to talk through what's happening for her until you feel she's had a chance to express her feelings without dwelling on any negative emotion for too long.

2. **After your client shakes off first position, have the client move to** *second position.*

   Ask the client to imagine that she's that person looking back at the client in first position.

   *Ask the client: 'What are you experiencing, thinking and feeling as your look at this person?'*

   The client will find this tougher than being in first position, so give her longer in this space. The exercise is for the client to imagine being in the shoes and mindset of the person she wants to connect with. Make sure that she's really taking on the idea of *being* the other person, not just being herself talking about that person. If necessary call her by the other person's name, and say: 'Okay, really being Freda now, what are you experiencing as Freda looking back at Kelly?' Expect to hear her say things like: 'She looks at me as if she's not sure how I'll react' or 'She's a decent person, just hard to talk to.' Or 'I really don't know what she wants from me.'

3. **Have the client move to** *third position***, that of the independent observer looking at both people in this relationship impartially.**

   *Ask the client: 'Looking at yourself in first position, how do you respond to that "you" there?'*

   By now, the client will have got the idea of stepping out of being herself. She's in the space where she can get some insight. Give her time to observe here, and you can add questions such as: 'What are the insights about Freda and Kelly from an independent perspective?' Expect to hear answers such as: 'These people haven't given each other time to get to know each other.' 'They need to go out for a coffee and just talk it through.' 'It would be a pity if things fell apart between them for no real reason.' 'They both really want this to succeed, they just have different styles.'

4. **Have the client move to the *fourth position*.**

   Ask the client to think about how her thoughts in third position compared to her reactions in the first position and switch them around. Whatever reactions the client had in the third position, have her switch them around into her first position in her mind's eye. Don't offer any logical explanation at this point.

5. **Have the client revisit *second position*.**

   *Ask the client: 'How is this position different now? What has changed?'*

   At this point, you can expect that the situation has changed with a sense that the relationship has improved.

6. **Invite the client to come home to first position.**

   *Ask the client: 'How is this position different now? What has changed?'*

   At this point, you can expect that any stuck thoughts and feelings from the original discussion in first position have been replaced with more creative ideas to improve the relationship, and a greater understanding of the other person.

Executive coach Deborah recognised that she was physically exhausted from working with one particular client who was going through marital difficulties and had an impending legal battle. When Deborah realised that she was becoming over-involved with the client's story and absorbing her client's angst, she took the situation to her coaching supervision session. Her coaching supervisor walked her through the four meta-mirror positions to get a sense of the bigger system in which the coaching was taking place and how she could best serve her client. Deborah realised that as her client talked about the details of an unhappy marriage, it brought up memories of her own first abusive marriage. She was so empathetic that she was unwittingly encouraging an outpouring of emotion from her client – emotions that Deborah herself then took away and worried about between sessions. Instead of over-empathising, she needed to stay rational and impartial in order to coach effectively.

## Listening for metaprograms

When people are under pressure, communicating in ways that raise the chances of your words being understood and acted upon is particularly valuable. That means using similar language patterns to deepen rapport.

In Chapter 10, you can read much more about *metaprograms*, the NLP explanation for how to make predictions about people's behaviour from the way they use language.

In order to deepen rapport, you must step back and listen not just to what someone is saying, but also *how* she's saying it. Table 12-3 summarises the most common metaprograms and provides a structure to help you pay attention to how your stakeholder uses language.

The third column of Table 12-3 is particularly useful if you can initiate a phone call with someone and mark in the third column as you hear similar phrases. By figuring out another person's metaprogram patterns, you can then formulate how to respond.

As a coach, pay attention to your clients' metaprograms. You can discover many clues about how to best present new or difficult information to help them achieve greater results.

| Table 12-3 | Capturing Metaprograms | |
|---|---|---|
| **Pattern** | **Sample Phrases** | **Stakeholder's Typical Phrases** |
| Proactive | Let's go for it. | |
| Reactive | I'd like to wait and see. | |
| Options | What are the choices? | |
| Procedures | Take me through things, step by step. | |
| Toward | This is what I want. | |
| Away from | I wouldn't do that if I were you. | |
| Internal | In my opinion . . . | |
| External | Let's find out what the market wants. | |
| Global | The headline story is . . . | |
| Detail | Give me all the information. | |
| Sameness | This is just like what we did last time. | |
| Difference | Let's see what we can change. | |

Metaprograms are highly *contextual*, by which I mean you may stay at the global level of information in one context (while discussing business strategy, for example) yet wallow in detail in another (proudly extolling the virtues of your child). In order to accurately listen for metaprograms, you want to listen to your stakeholder talking about the kind of topic that is relevant to your communication need.

Also, most people have a mix of patterns, aim to listen for the style that a person leans towards most typically.

## Adapting your approach

How tempting to go through life hoping and expecting other people to adapt to your style and needs! Alas, life doesn't work that way. One thought to offer your clients is: 'For things to change, I must change,' or as Gandhi said: 'Be the change you want to see in the world.'

NLP assumes that the person with the most flexibility in the system is the one who wins. This assumption doesn't mean you need to be a pushover who bends to others' needs. Rather, you need to find creative ways to come at situations with fresh eyes and stop perpetuating behaviours that aren't working.

Situations that require people to negotiate with others demonstrate the need for flexibility. Michael is a coach who specialises in negotiating complex contracts and guides his clients to mismatch others' style of words in order to negotiate. For example, when one party is arguing logically, he recommends taking an emotional tack. When the other party comes in with an emotional argument, counter it with a rational approach. 'Flexing the style in this way proves the winning hand,' he says.

# Coaching Teams to Bond

The preceding sections of this chapter look at one-to-one coaching situations. However, all the principles of coaching individuals apply to coaching teams and groups too – including in business, sport, family or other settings.

Teams often come together to tackle tough issues, and a team that doesn't have strong relationships and communication falls over fast under pressure (see the sidebar 'Extreme teams'). Conversely, the team that shows its strength in tough times creates powerful relationships to take forward into other situations.

In this section, I show how you support teams throughout all the classic stages of development including forming, storming, norming, performing and finally disbanding.

## Extreme teams

In August 2010, the task to free 33 miners trapped one kilometre below ground in a Chilean mine set off the most complicated rescue mission in mining history. The miners faced months underground in an area the size of a small apartment. Initially the only access was via two 8-cm-wide boreholes through which communication and supplies were channelled.

Chile's Health Minister Jaime Manalich said: 'If they lose their mental balance, it could create panic and violence and that would be a huge catastrophe.' A diverse team of professionals assembled to assist the miners:

✔ Emergency workers and doctors concentrated on keeping the miners physically and mentally well during their ordeal. Many of the men were huge soccer fans and watched matches on a live feed using a small projector while waiting to be rescued in the depths of the mine.

✔ A team of psychologists encouraged the miners to develop a daily routine that included singing and playing card games to keep mentally alert. The miners were also instructed to follow a daily routine with lights off during night hours.

✔ Speaking to loved ones by phone proved a huge morale boost. The miners felt connected to the people who they knew cared most about them and hearing news from home kept up their spirits.

The whole world watched the rescue operation with bated breath and cheered as, one by one, the miners came to the surface safely in October 2010, 69 days after being trapped. Subsequently, the miners' story of survival is inspiring other teams in many fields. The miners were invited to the UK as guests of Sir Alex Ferguson, manager of Manchester United football team. The miners watched Manchester United play Arsenal and win the match. One of the miners told reporters: 'I am very proud to know that Sir Alex used our story to motivate his players.'

Teams in less extreme conditions can take some cues from the miners and their supporting teams by paying attention to physical and emotional well-being and encouraging individuals to have supportive relationships beyond the team. Good physical and emotional health can sustain a group under pressure.

## *Forming: Adopting the mindset for success*

At the *forming* stage, the team needs to have a mindset that focuses on success.

The following NLP presuppositions offer a great starting point for any team. In any team set-up, the coach can encourage team members to try on the following presuppositions for size and debate what they mean for the team if they're adopted as core principles from the beginning.

✔ **The map is not the territory.** People respond according to their own maps of the world, and everyone in the team has a different map. Refer to Chapter 2 to discover more.

- **There is no failure, only feedback**. This presupposition gives permission for the team members to risk making mistakes.

- **The meaning of the communication is the response you get.** Each team member must adapt his or her communication style in order for others in the team to understand.

- **If what you're doing isn't working, do something different.** The classic sign of insanity in teams is inflexibility! Head to Chapter 14 for more on working with teams.

- **You cannot not communicate.** Even if you say nothing, people assign meaning to your silence and non-verbal clues.

- **Individuals have all the resources they need to achieve their desired outcomes.** No one needs to fix someone else.

- **Every behaviour has a positive intent.** Each person acts in a particular way for a good reason. So strive to get to the intent of an action in order to change behaviours.

- **People are much more than their behaviours.** Separate the person from his or her role and what he or she does. Then you release the natural creativity innate in the whole person.

- **The mind and body are interlinked and affect each other.** Pay attention to physical and mental well-being. I cover this in Chapter 18.

- **Having choice is better than not having choice.** Give people choice if you want them to be motivated and interested.

- **Modelling successful performance leads to excellence.** Find others who have trodden a similar path and learn from them. See Chapter 11 for more on modelling.

## Storming: Developing a shared future

In her early career, GP Hannah covered a maternity-leave vacancy in a busy city practice that turned out to be an unhappy experience for her. She discovered that the relationships between the GPs were at best cool and at worst full of blame and negativity. She told her coach:

> *It's the most distressed and dysfunctional practice I've ever seen. There was no sense of any kind of direction amongst the partners other than to make money and retire early. When I arrived, they made it clear to me that there was no socialising amongst the other doctors, so don't expect to be invited to dinner. Unfortunately, they wouldn't invest in any support to turn the situation around, which was a real shame. The impact on the GPs health was heavy, and morale was very low amongst the nursing teams and admin staff too. The only good thing that came out of the experience was that I vowed*

*to pay full attention to the teamwork aspect of a medical practice when I became a partner myself.*

Through coaching, Hannah learned that tough experiences are exceptionally valuable as long as you take the lessons from them to apply in the future.

As a team enters the *storming* stage, different ideas come to the fore and the team need to agree on the problems they need to solve and the theories and models they'll follow. This stage can be fraught with conflict, testing the team relationships. Here the team coach can concentrate the team's energy on three core activities:

- ✔ **Establish clear, shared goals.** The well-formed outcome process in Chapter 7 encourages teams to build goals that are specific, inspiring and achievable – ones that give the team choices and put the members of the team firmly in the driving seat. From these types of goals, people then develop clarity in what they need to do.

- ✔ **Articulate and honour a common set of values.** Strong teams know what is important to members within the team and identify and live the behaviours that reflect the shared values on a daily basis. The principle of understanding individual values also applies to teams, and simplifies decision-making.

- ✔ **Uncover limiting beliefs and develop empowering ones.** When everyone believes in the capability of the team to achieve its goals, the team can storm ahead. (See Chapter 17 for more on empowering beliefs.)

The following exercise enables teams (and individuals) to be curious about their beliefs. Create a list of about ten statements and invite the team to split into pairs to explore the statements.

Use statements such as the following to get conversations started:

- ✔ *This team is like . . . because it . . .*

- ✔ *We'll be most successful if we . . .*

- ✔ *The three things that will get in our way are . . .*

- ✔ *The top issue we must consider is . . .*

- ✔ *A high-performing team can . . .*

As each pair looks at the statements, ask members to say the first thing that comes into their heads. After the paired exercise, invite the whole team to convene and ask the group:

- ✔ What beliefs might limit this team?

- ✔ What beliefs might empower this team?

Get someone in the group to capture the most empowering beliefs and circulate them to the team members for referencing later.

## Norming and performing: Championing great ways of operating

Through the *norming* and into the high *performing* stages of development, the team coach encourages a team to create processes and ways of behaving with each other that enable the team to stay on track for performance. Norming is the stage when people have bought into shared plans and let go of their own in order to make the team function. If the team survives long enough to get to the performing stage, it has found ways to get things done smoothly without the need for constant supervision; the team makes decisions easily, although may find itself reverting back to the storming stage, especially if new people join the team with different ideas.

The influential coach Tim Gallwey's coaching principle $P = p - I$ signifies that performance is equal to potential less interference (see Chapter 1 for a more in-depth explanation). Team coaching sessions provide the space in which team members address the issues that interfere with performance.

High-performing teams develop deep trust, safety, openness and respect for each other. Team members demonstrate behaviours that:

- **Resolve conflict** by depersonalising issues and express shared willingness to constructively disagree in order to find the best solutions.

- **Celebrate successes** in small as well as big ways, such as a go-home-early day or lunch out together to signify a milestone reached.

- **Sustain momentum** by holding on to the goals and remembering the effect when they're achieved.

- **Avoid complacency** by regularly reflecting on what the team members are doing and inviting feedback from each other and the key external stakeholders.

By modelling the core coaching skills of active listening and asking powerful questions, the team coach shows the value of the preceding activities to the team.

When Ben came to work in the UK from South Africa, he noticed how much time his new team spent building relationships. Working with a coach, he changed his approach to leading team meetings to a more collaborative manner. He spent more time listening to each team member, acknowledging their successes and then asking questions to move forward rather than laying out what he believed needed to happen.

## Disbanding: Moving on positively

Ultimately even the best teams experience the *disbanding* stage as the individuals go their separate ways. The project that the team got together for may be complete or the organisation is restructured.

When coaching a team through its final stages of existence, build in space for them to acknowledge and celebrate their successes, and to capture the lessons they want to take forward to their next teams.

# Chapter 13

# Moving through Life's Disappointments

## In This Chapter

▶ Staying confident regardless of external events

▶ Building personal resilience through tough times

▶ Detaching from the drama

▶ Extracting the good from loss

**D**isappointment is a fact of life. Disappointment has two parts: your subjective perceptions of an event where the outcome you wished for doesn't come true, and how you resolve it. Controlling events is impossible; managing your expectations and how you respond to events is more achievable.

If you look back over the last couple of months, you probably faced some disappointments, some minor, others more challenging. While writing this chapter, I was fortunate that the disappointments in my life were minor ones: the end of a lovely holiday, some lost documents, a bid for work that wasn't successful and a filling that came out of my tooth. (Warning: soft mints aren't soft at all.) All were easily repairable, and I moved on quickly.

Other situations that you face in life cause more trauma. Whether you encounter illness, divorce, financial problems, violence or death, you're very likely to experience strong feelings of loss or failure when things don't go as you planned or desired. How do you pick yourself up, take the lesson and move on? The obvious answer is to hire a coach to accompany you on the way!

In this chapter, you find out more about pacing clients through feelings of loss and failure without getting caught up in the drama of the situation yourself. You also look at the roles in the Drama Triangle and the NLP grief and loss process.

## Coaching through the storms

The coach's role is to support clients through the tough times, not to solve their problems. You encourage your clients to stay resourceful, helping them find tools and strategies that make a difference to them. You respectfully challenge them to find lessons for difficult situations, avoid repeat performances and cope more easily with similar future situations.

In particular, you can increase your clients' awareness that:

✔ Change is a process with ups and downs.

✔ Failure is information and part of experimenting with new approaches. (NLP suggests there's no such thing as failure, only feedback.)

✔ Individual self-worth is separate from a particular situation.

✔ Confidence builds when you stretch yourself.

Many tools in the NLP coach's toolkit can support clients to increase self-awareness as they encounter tough situations, including the NLP presuppositions, metaprograms related to motivation and working style, anchoring techniques to manage emotional states, phobia cures and much more.

# Feeling Okay When Things Are Clearly Not Okay

When things go badly awry, people often go into a state of denial or shock, or feel overwhelmed. Emotions can fly. Understandably, people feel out of control because the situations they find themselves in are not welcome; they are hugely disappointed by the outcome. In this section, I look at how to move at an appropriate speed instead of pretending that everything's fine, when it clearly it's not.

When disappointments come along, not only are they painful in their own right, but also they can connect with other tough situations in the client's past, setting up a chain reaction. Some seemingly minor incident can trigger an unexpectedly strong response. When a business client loses a customer, the experience may unconsciously connect with a deeper, unresolved loss. Similarly, when a private client fails a job interview, the experience can trigger feelings associated with situations of failure and rejection in other non-work areas.

## Staying with feelings

Coaches work with clients through lows as well as highs – when they're under huge pressure, not coping too well, on the point of burn-out, highly stressed or when their confidence has taken a knock.

Ideally, you get the chance to work with clients before disappointments happen. That way, you can support them to build up the safety mechanisms and structures to manage challenging situations before they occur rather than when they've crashed.

Regardless of whether you and your clients have previously developed safety strategies, the key is to stay with less-than-great feelings and accept them as normal. After the feelings are normalised, you can then enable clients to set realistic goals and tackle their situations in stages instead of expecting all to be resolved overnight.

You'll find that people are good at suppressing negative emotions that they don't feel comfortable airing, such as fear, anger, guilt, dislike, envy or sadness. Your body knows instinctively what you're feeling and often produces physical symptoms to slow down and support you.

Donna become comfortable enough during a series of coaching sessions to recount her feelings of suppressed anger with her husband, feelings that she believed were unacceptable to voice over her long marriage. She talked about a time in her thirties when she wanted to set up a downstairs study as a playroom for her young children. Her husband insisted that the room be kept pristine for the occasional times when he wanted to work at home. Each time she suggested making changes, he refused to have the conversation. Eventually she stopped questioning any of his ideas or offering suggestions of her own. As she related:

> *Over the years, I just decided that he was much more important than me; after all, he was the bigger breadwinner. Drop by drop, I found my self-confidence seeping out of me, not just at home but in social and work situations too; I generally felt unequal to friends and colleagues alike, and I'm sure this triggered my recurring eczema.*

## Going deeper

Clients who continually suppress negative emotions around disappointments frequently experience physical symptoms.

Psychotherapist and yoga teacher, Stephen Cope of the Kripalu Centre in Massachusetts tells the story of a client whose elderly husband went into a nursing home. The client began experiencing panic attacks when she was due to go and visit her spouse. Through their therapeutic work together, Stephen uncovered that his client was ashamed by her feelings that her husband had abandoned her, even though clearly he hadn't done so intentionally. The physical symptoms of the client's panic attacks covered her deeper feelings of frustration at the situation that she didn't feel she was allowed to complain about.

Cope's work points to the importance of getting in touch with all aspects of yourself, including the parts that you don't like or aren't particularly proud of. Only after you recognise all parts of your personality can you become whole and well. (Head to Chapter 19 for more.)

# Dear Diary

Simply pressing the emotional override button when you're feeling down doesn't work long-term. Before clients can move on, they need outlets to acknowledge their feelings. One way to take ownership of emotions is to write out these thoughts on paper.

Encourage clients to take a few blank sheets of paper and just write about how they're feeling – totally uncensored – for 10 to 20 minutes. Don't worry about spelling and grammar and being appropriate. Just write what you're feeling.

For example, Madhuri wrote the following diary entry after losing a job opportunity:

> *Today I got an email to say that I haven't got the job. I'm feeling frustrated at the huge amount of time and effort that I've put into this application, polishing my CV, attending three interviews including a telephone one when I was on holiday. And there's all that polishing of shoes and pressing my interview clothes. Talk about tiredness! I'm actually exhausted that I'm back at square*

one. *I could have been doing some really interesting things. It's okay for others to say there are plenty more jobs out there, but how do I get back the time I've put in? I'm concerned about how long this is taking, and my bank balance is very low. I must admit there's tinge of relief because all that commuting wasn't going to be much fun. Yet it's mixed with self-doubt. I keep looking at other people on the street and asking if they are much brighter than me because they have jobs and I don't. Everyone in the world seems to be working instead of me. This is a blow and I'd really like to hide under the sheets. I know I'll get up today, but it feels tough.*

After clients get these thoughts and feelings out of their heads and written on paper, they have rich material to engage with during later coaching session. They can review their writing with detached awareness and come up with ways of handling the current reality, bringing the themes to a coaching session if not the specific details of what they write.

As a coach, you serve your clients by giving them permission, space and tools to air their true feelings. Coaching may be the only space where they feel they can reveal their true identities. Find creative outlets and activities in which clients can connect with their feelings. Making music, dance, drama, writing or drawing can tap into the creative unconscious mind to unlock buried feelings. The sidebar 'Dear Diary' offers a great first step to begin releasing pent-up emotions.

## Increasing self-care

The idea of self-care may sound indulgent, yet nothing is farther from the truth. Self-care builds confidence to take action. Clients need to be healthy and strong for themselves, especially when the pressure builds. *Self-care* involves paying attention to your personal energy in four ways:

- ✔ **Physically,** through a healthy diet and exercise.
- ✔ **Mentally,** through activities that stretch, stimulate and fit your talents.
- ✔ **Emotionally,** through supportive relationships with yourself and others.
- ✔ **Purposefully,** through establishing a sense of meaning in your life.

In each of these areas, develop habits that nurture your energy every day – clients and coaches alike. Here are just a few examples of habits:

- ✔ **Physical energy**
  - Plan and cook a healthy supper.
  - Drink eight glasses of water or herbal tea daily.
  - Exercise for 15 minutes.
  - Keep a food diary to track eating.

- ✔ **Mental energy**
  - Focus on a project mindfully for 50 minutes then allow 10 minutes rest.
  - Read an inspirational piece of writing or play inspirational music each day.
  - Set a time-limit on working hours.

- ✔ **Emotional energy**
  - Say 'no' to requests that don't fit your personal needs.
  - Spend time with people who nurture you.
  - Find something positive in each person you connect with in the day.
  - Meditate for ten minutes before bed.

- ✔ **Purposeful energy**
  - Steer your work or activity to benefit another person or the community.
  - Spend time enjoying nature or experiencing the outdoors.
  - Choose one value to focus on and live today.

What habits and routine need to be in place to ensure you care for yourself? Create a list of four or five daily rituals that can help you stay energetic under pressure. Try to come up with a mix of rituals that connect to all four energies. Keep your list at hand.

## Breathing out problems

When you need to raise your energy levels, having an understanding of breathing techniques is valuable. *Conscious breathing* enables energy to flow freely in and out, allowing you to let go of the tension you hold in all parts of your body. You literally breathe in the atoms and molecules of the universe as you take in fresh air and release the pressure from the back of your neck to the tip of your toes.

John Grinder, the co-creator of NLP, notes that breathing changes how your body feels and reacts, which then changes your emotional state, which then affects your performance in any activity, as Figure 13-1 illustrates. This interconnectedness is why remembering to breathe is crucial. Breathing affects how you shift your thinking and behaviour, especially under pressure.

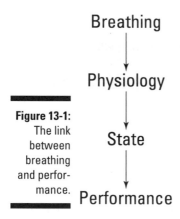

**Breathing**

↓

**Physiology**

↓

**State**

↓

**Performance**

**Figure 13-1:** The link between breathing and performance.

Breathing happens unconsciously while you sleep, yet you can consciously change the way you breathe, and in doing so, switch between highly alert and relaxed states.

Many people don't know how to breathe consciously. When they take deep breaths, they tense their bodies unnecessarily, contracting their abdomens and straining their upper chests. Watch contented babies for visual examples of good deep breathing. Note how they naturally expand their bellies and diaphragms on the *in* breaths while contracting them back towards the spine on the *out* breaths.

I once shared the simple link between breathing and performance with a coaching client who was preparing for an important meeting. My intention was that he'd get his voice loud and clear by breathing well. As he looked at my words on the notebook, he put hands to throat and said: 'Oh my goodness, that's why I need to stop smoking. I simply can't breathe.' To my knowledge, he hasn't touched a cigarette since – the fastest stop-smoking cure I've done!

To change your breathing instantly, you merely have to take it under conscious control. One friendly way to do so is to count monkeys:

1. **Exhale all your breath.** Really squeeze the breath out as if you were pushing the air out of a beach ball. You can put your hands on your diaphragm to notice how it retracts.

2. **Breathe in slowly, to the count of four monkeys ('one monkey, two monkeys, three monkeys, four monkeys').** This time your abdomen extends out, your diaphragm moves up and your chest expands without lifting. Keep your shoulders and neck fully relaxed.

3. **Hold your breath for four monkeys.**

4. **Exhale for four monkeys.**

5. **Hold your breath with your lungs empty for four monkeys.**

   If this final step makes you feel dizzy, reduce the count to two monkeys until you become more used to the exercise and can comfortably hold your lungs empty for the four-monkey count.

6. **Repeat this breathing pattern for five minutes, initially.**

   Feel free to come back to the monkeys whenever you find tension building.

You may find this conscious way of breathing strange at first. Like any exercise, you improve with practice. Stick with it as you'll find it settles you down as your body is actually eliminating the neurochemicals that keep you excited.

## Finding the good and letting the rest go

One benefit of breathing well (see the preceding section) is that it helps you remain calm and relaxed, putting you in the best possible position to stay positive and then let go of negativity. See the later section 'Gaining Something from Tough Times' for more on finding the positive in a difficult situation.

As you breathe, allow yourself to ask: 'What's really good about this situation right now?' This question is also useful both to conclude sessions and to reflect on following sessions. Finding the good in a situation is often easier when you go outside in the fresh air and look at the sky, take a walk or do some exercise that raises your energy level. Chapter 19 goes into reframing situations to get another perspective.

You may challenge yourself to have perfect coaching sessions with every client, every time. Although admirable, this goal isn't realistic. Instead of dwelling on the disappointments and what you or your client could have done better, notice the good learning that emerged and allow the rest to slide away.

---

## Bad weather tops British disappointments

According to a recent survey, the thing that sends the British into deepest despair is surprisingly – wait for it – poor weather on holiday.

Here's the full top ten:

1. Experiencing bad weather on holiday.

2. Waking up and thinking it's a Sunday when it's really a Monday.

3. Having your partner forget your birthday or anniversary.

4. Having your favourite TV series end.

5. Forgetting your passport.

6. Losing your luggage.

7. Finishing a good book.

8. Putting on an old pair of jeans that don't fit.

9. Dyeing a whole load of washing red.

10. Making a cup of tea or coffee to discover the milk is off.

---

# *Avoiding the Drama Triangle*

One of the most useful and simple models that I've found in supporting clients in highly charged situations is Stephen Karpman's Drama Triangle, which fits neatly with NLP exercises involving perceptual positions (flip to Chapter 12 for more on perceptual positions.) (My thanks to my colleague Barbara who first shared it with me as the way she undertook some challenging mediation work in law firms.)

When you enter a client's world, or *system*, you too can be drawn into the client's unconscious psychological games. Indeed, on some level, clients want their coaches to play too.

Karpman's work builds on the ideas of Eric Berne and his famous Transactional Analysis ideas in the 1950s. Berne talked about the games all people play unconsciously that motivate how they interact with others. A *game* in this case is an unconscious belief that directs action in a particular way, which in turn runs the *script* that's going on in your mind.

The Drama Triangle is a game with three playing positions around the dynamics of power, responsibility and vulnerability. Often the game is played out unconsciously between just two people regularly switching positions. Larger numbers of people in family groups, teams and large organisations can also get caught up in the drama games. The Triangle is a good reminder that anyone – coaches included – can get enmeshed in the drama of a situation and that just leads to more problems.

The key point is to stay out of the drama by taking a *meta position* – staying in a place where you observe what is happening in a detached way and offer insights from that impartial space. Clients who are caught in the drama need support to see the roles they're playing and then to come up with solutions to shift out of *all* these roles rather than continually moving from one position to another.

The three positions the Drama Triangle are:

- ✔ Victim
- ✔ Rescuer
- ✔ Persecutor

Figure 13-2 shows the three roles that a client can play and the following sections examine each in greater detail. In order for the client to get out of the triangle, focus on the role taken by someone else he's in conflict with. For example, if someone else is playing victim, the coach can ask the client to check if he's rescuing or persecuting the victim, and if so, what he needs to do differently to stop the game.

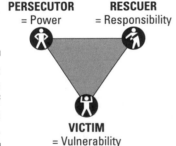

**Figure 13-2:**
The three
roles of
the Drama
Triangle.

## Playing the victim

The *victim* is the position in the game where you feel vulnerable, powerless and don't take responsibility. The script for this role is 'Can you help me?' However, when victims can't be rescued any longer and have to be responsible, they switch to persecuting their rescuers (see the following section 'Saving the day'). If you as coach find yourself being victim, you need to let go of being over-involved in the client's issues, and supervision is a good place to find strategies to help you (see Chapter 1 for more on supervision).

Clients who (unintentionally) play victim want their coaches to rescue them from difficult situations. In sessions, the client desperately seeks solutions from you: 'Tell me what I should do because I can't help myself.' You can stay out of the game by keeping the client focused on his own behaviour by asking powerful questions such as 'What do you need to do differently for this situation to change?' (Chapter 6 explores powerful questions.)

## Saving the day

The *rescuer* role describes people who often seek to valiantly save those they see as vulnerable. Their script is 'I'll help you'. They often do more than their share of the work and switch to Victim or Persecutor mode when they have had enough.

Coaches who seek to rescue others are well advised to do some personal development work on their own needs. Ask yourself what it is in you that makes you want to rescue others.

Clients who are rescuing may want to be in control of a situation; typically in business these individuals micro-manage and are unable to delegate responsibilities. Yet after a while, rescuing gets tiring, and the rescuer stops being nice and helpful, frustrated at the lack of responsibility taken by the other party. You can point out a pattern of rescuing you observe in the client which may be linked to some underlying fears worth resolving. The surface structure of the behaviour indicates a deeper structure of need.

## Bullying others

The *persecutor* role is the most unpleasant and unwelcome one. For the role of persecutor you can also read bully. Persecutors don't realise their own power and actually feel like victims or rescuers who are being persecuted by others. Interestingly, the persecutor script comes out as 'You're not getting this right' while inside they're feeling 'I've had enough of this.'

Some clues as coach that you may be slipping into persecutor role show up when things aren't moving and you're increasingly frustrated by a client's lack of commitment to change. You may push a client faster and harder than he wants to shift, nagging him to make changes and showing disappointment if he doesn't cooperate. You may get into this behaviour with good intentions in order to feel that you're doing the best job and getting results.

A question for the coach is 'Who is the most motivated person in the room?' If the answer is the coach, some serious redesigning of the relationship is called for by going back and renegotiating the terms of how to work together.

Clients who are persecutors are often individuals sent to coaching for bad behaviour in their organisations. They're notoriously challenging if they aren't open to feedback about their behaviour. Bully managers blame everyone else before looking at themselves. You can point out the behaviour you observe and ask questions about what impact this ultimately has for the client (for example, getting fired, losing an important relationship, damaging his health). Ultimately, you need to be willing to walk away from the bullying client who's not interested in changing because he'll blame the coach for lack of results.

# Gaining Something from Tough Times

Remember the old saying: 'What doesn't kill you makes you stronger'? When you hit tough times in life, the experience is intense and affects things that are important: your health, wealth and happiness. As you come through the experience and extract some new wisdom, you build resilience for when tough things happen again. Next time round, you react differently. However, the journey through the tough times may be extremely challenging.

In this section, I explore classic NLP work on resolving grief, which offers insight into what is happening for your coaching clients as they experience significant loss.

## Following the grief and loss process

Back in the mid-1980s, two outstanding leaders in the field of NLP Steve and Connirae Andreas began teaching the *grief resolution process*. They based it on modelling the experiences of people who were particularly resourceful in the ways they handled significant loss in their lives. Other NLP trainers subsequently adapted this process and teach it as part of NLP Master Practitioner training; you hear it referred to as the *loss pattern* or the *grief and loss process*.

The *grief response* describes a feeling of sadness and emptiness and can refer to *perceived* as well as an *actual* loss. I've coached several senior business women who put career before marriage and family. Later in life they experienced a deep sense of loss when they realised that they no longer have the potential to have a family. Other people reach a crossroads when the dream they were pursuing is clearly not going to happen. They're losing something that they perceived as a possibility rather than actually losing children or jobs.

The grief and loss process also incorporates Richard Bandler's work on *submodalities*, the fine qualities that define the structure of a subjective experience. (See Chapter 17 for more on submodalities.) Submodalities are the distinct qualities you note within the main visual, auditory and kinaesthetic representational systems. (I discuss representational systems in Chapter 6.)

The NLP grief and loss process is a powerful tool suitable for experienced NLP Master Practitioners and NLP-qualified coaches according to the contracts they set with their clients. NLP Master Practitioner programmes teach the grief and loss process. Always gain permission and do an ecology check before an NLP intervention of this type.

NLP processes that work with submodalities change the way clients experience memories and thus the effects of the memories on them. For example, if I think of my father who is no longer alive, I could feel very sad. However, thanks to my NLP experience, I can bring him closer to me in my thoughts by considering the colour of his hair, the sound of his voice, his arms hugging me. In this way, I feel his presence more than the loss. By contrast, if I think of someone I don't much care for – an old boss who was unpleasant at work – I prefer to think of him as a dim and distant memory, like a faded black and white photograph in an old album. In this way I stay detached from the negative emotional connection with that relationship.

## *Looking for loss*

Why is it useful for coaches to understand about grief and loss when they're not offering bereavement therapy? Two reasons come to mind:

- ✔ Your clients will experience the loss of a loved one at some point in their lives, with the natural accompanying grief, and some will be unfortunate enough to experience multiple losses.
- ✔ Your clients will face other losses in life that create similar reactions, such as the loss of a job or possessions, the ending of a love affair or a wonderful trip, or moving to a new country.

You might expect that deep grief can cause illness and depression, conditions that cry out for medical or therapeutic interventions. However, Steve and Connirae Andreas also noticed that *unresolved grief* shows up as a lack of motivation or can precipitate a mid-life crisis – typical scenarios raised in coaching.

When clients demonstrate a lack of motivation, procrastination or obsessive behaviour such as micro-attention to details or overwork, explore whether they are grieving. Be curious as to whether they've lost something or somebody important. Be aware that the loss may go back a long way; it's not always a recent loss. You may need to support them on topics seemingly unrelated to work in order to get closure, move on and return their behaviour to normal.

People respond to loss in one of two contrasting ways:

- **Unresolved loss,** where they get caught up in the negative emotions around the absence of their loved one or experience – the loss.

- **Resolved loss,** where they become aware of the positive aspects of being with their loved one or experience – the presence.

The NLP grief and loss process works by restoring the sense of presence to the loss, as the following sections examine.

### Running on empty

People who have *unresolved grief* are unable to access the positive aspects of the person or experience that is now lost. Clients with unresolved grief may:

- Express strong feelings of emptiness and sadness and be unable to get on with their lives as a result.

- Ruminate on the difficult events around actually ending the relationship rather than experiencing the loving connection that characterised the relationship.

- Recall the relationship with a sense of separation or absence. For example, they may only be able to access the person or memory as a fuzzy image or may not be able to hear the person's voice.

- Show controlled resignation. For example, they may say that it's okay, when clearly their body language is down and their tone of voice is flat, thus conveying the opposite message.

- Lose self-identity and perhaps gain a new identity. For example, a retired worker may now call himself a pensioner rather than a business leader or bus driver. People question who they are when they no longer have a role that gave their life meaning.

### Accessing the good feelings

People who have *resolved their grief* are able to access the positive aspects of the person or experience that is now lost. Clients with resolved grief may:

- Express strong feelings of warmth and love and see the loss as part of the bigger picture of their life journey.

- Focus on the positive qualities of the relationship rather than the loving connection that characterised their experience.

- Recall the relationship with a sense of presence. For example, they may feel in contact with the person as they go about their meal preparation, gardening or daily activities.

✔ Show acceptance. For example, when they say it's okay, their body language is relaxed and their tone of voice has movement.

✔ Demonstrate a strong sense of identity. They are positive about themselves regardless of the roles that they've taken on.

## Holding the positive by-products

When people are grieving, they are thinking about their loss, as if the grief and loss are separate and distinct experiences – what NLP calls *dissociated*. In order to resolve the grief, the NLP grief and loss process has two parts:

✔ **Part one** aims to retrieve the sense of the presence in the loss. This part reassociates the client with the positive memories of the person or thing lost and dissociates from the loss experience (such as the moment of death).

✔ **Part two** aims to preserve the positive qualities of the loss. This part enables the client to access all the positive qualities of what they lost, not just right now but also for the longer term.

During the grief and loss process, NLP Master coaches take clients step by step through a detailed process that may take an hour or two. They do submodality work while checking for ecology – that is, checking for anything that doesn't feel right or land well with the client. In this way, the client captures all the positive by-products of the loss and lets go of the pain. The sidebar 'Loving, growing – and moving on' illustrates the key steps of the process, which you could adapt in a coaching conversation to find out what clients really cherished in what they lost.

For the non-NLP-qualified coach who wants to create awareness for their clients through conversation rather than a formal NLP process, here are some areas of exploration to cover in the session to resolve grief:

✔ Allow clients to describe their losses and acknowledge their feelings.

✔ Encourage clients to access another context where they are well-resourced and then notice the difference, so that they know how it's possible to be.

✔ Find out what benefit they are gaining by not letting go of the loss.

✔ Extract the positive qualities from the experience or person who is no longer with them.

✔ Imagine how the future can be with these positive qualities in place.

✔ Explore what empowering beliefs will support them to move on.

ANECDOTE

# Loving, growing – and moving on

During a long summer of working in the US, Greg had an affair with Jo-Ann, a married colleague, who made it clear at the outset that she had no intention of leaving her husband. She craved affection with a very attractive man, but didn't want to disrupt her family set-up. While Greg understood this contract in theory, on his return to the UK, he felt a great sense of sadness and found it hard to settle back into his business life. He also didn't believe he'd meet anyone else he could care for in future. As part of our coaching relationship, he invited me to take him through the grief and loss process, which we did at a structural level. As coach, I didn't need any detailed content about their time together.

The process involved first accessing his memory of the loss of Jo-Ann. Their final meeting was strongest in Greg's memory. I then invited him to access someone else who felt present and accessible to him, even though this person wasn't with him currently. Greg chose his brother, Jason, who lives 100 miles away.

We changed the loss experience into one of presence by switching the submodalities. This means that we worked with qualities, such as a location, moving or still pictures, or a sense of association and dissociation (see Chapter 17 for more on working with submodalities). This activity enabled Greg to think about Jo-Ann and capture a positive sense of her presence in full colour. He could feel her close to him with a loud clear voice and warm skin.

From this first step of regaining a sense of presence, he was able to talk about the value he'd had from the experience of their short affair. For him the relationship was about 'fun, laughter, common sense and connection'. He decided to represent the entire experience and all its qualities with an image of a sunset.

The process concluded by placing this representation on the time line in the future. Greg found that he could look forward to future relationships and access the positive qualities of the relationship without the sense of loss getting in the way.

# Chapter 14

# Coaching through Conflict

· · · · · · · · · · · · · · · · · · · · · · · · · · · · · · · · · · · · · · · · · · · · ·

## In This Chapter

▶ Resolving disagreements while avoiding violence

▶ Shifting away from blame

▶ Increasing team cohesion

▶ Giving and receiving feedback effectively

· · · · · · · · · · · · · · · · · · · · · · · · · · · · · · · · · · · · · · · · · · · · ·

onflict – the state of opposition of ideas and interests – is an everyday fact of life that shows up in different ways. On the positive side, the energy of bouncing differing ideas back and forward allows creative solutions to emerge; the collaboration between two different styles generates wonderful results. On the negative side, conflicts lead to dramatic showdowns, physical violence and even devastatingly destructive wars.

Life would be bland without any creative tension, and expecting peace, joy and harmony at all times is unnatural. In fact, that sounds like some kind of la-la land occupied by children's toys like the Teletubbies. Yet when the battles arising from opposing views and interests escalate out of control, they not only put the parties concerned in danger, but also bring innocent bystanders into the fray.

Clients bring tales of conflict into their coaching sessions from all aspects of their lives: power struggles, money issues, relationship challenges, intellectual differences, cross-cultural misunderstandings and battles with suppliers or customers. Coaching provides a safe space to explore the creative solutions that can emerge through conflict. The battles you assist your clients in solving may be:

✔ **Internal,** involving contradictory thoughts, decisions and dilemmas going on within the client's own mind.

✔ **External,** involving the tension between the client's needs, interests and concerns and those of others the client interacts with.

In this chapter, I concentrate on ways to resolve external conflict. At the same time, each conflict situation raises questions about the client's internal conflict. (Chapter 19 offers ways to address internal conflicts.)

# Recognising Behaviours under Pressure

The first step in coaching clients through conflict is to support them in becoming aware of their own patterns and their typical reactions to conflict situations before exploring ways to work through differences and emerge with more creativity and resourcefulness for the future.

Invite your clients to be curious as to how they naturally react under pressure when emotions are heightened. What is their innate approach to conflicts with others? How do they deal with any conflict's underlying frustrations and the inevitable shifts of power and control? Do they naturally want to run away and hide, or do they want to fight their corner?

## A tale of road rage

I was sitting in the window of a café in North London when the driver of a Range Rover parked clumsily outside, shunted into the back of a Mercedes saloon car, jumped out and walked up the road seemingly oblivious to the damage she'd inflicted.

She returned to her car at the same exact moment as the male driver of the Mercedes. At this point, a potentially murderous scene of confrontation and denial unfolded between two respectable-looking adults. He deftly captured her number plate and picture on his mobile phone. She began shouting and screaming at him. He stood bear-like in front of her vehicle. She started up the engine and began to drive off with him lying on the bonnet clutching her windscreen wipers. She wanted to flee, and he wanted to fight.

'My god, he's going to get run over,' I thought, still watching from inside the café. People ran out to the scene, traffic came to a standstill and a crowd of pedestrians gathered. Various bystanders began remonstrating with the pair to stay calm as the anger escalated, and some barred their possible escape routes. Still more shouting ensued as neither party backed down, and it was clearly not safe for me to intervene personally.

My final view of the conflict was the Range Rover driver shooting up the road at high speed with the Mercedes driver hanging through the passenger window.

How much better it would have been for the two drivers to work through the conflict with a civilised conversation. With some insight into the structure of non-violent conversations, which I cover later in this chapter, they could have avoided putting themselves at great personal risk. They even could have conducted the conversation over a cup of good-quality coffee in the warmth of the café.

NLP affirms that the mind and body are inextricably linked. Stressful situations place the human body on high alert. This natural response to threat invokes what is known as the *fight or flight response*. In this aroused state, the hormone adrenalin is released into the bloodstream, and a person experiences natural physiological changes designed to increase the capacity to fight the enemy or run away.

Your clients may mention any or all the following physiological changes in conflict situations, regardless of whether they want to flee or fight:

- Heartbeat increases
- Rate of breathing speeds up
- Sweating
- Increased sensitivity to sights and sounds
- Butterflies in the stomach
- Hyperventilation leading to dizziness and tingling in fingers
- Feelings of exhaustion after prolonged anxiety

A panic attack isn't just an outburst of nerves or anger. In a panic attack, a person may exhibit any of the above symptoms and more besides, including sensations of choking, tingling and loss of reality as the sympathetic nervous system kicks into action. In particular, the shortness of breath and heart palpitations increase anxiety as sufferers fear they're suffering heart failure and thus the anxiety extends the attack.

Coaching shines a light on people's blind spots, a process that isn't always comfortable. Don't be surprised if clients facing conflict situations abandon coaching or become confrontational with you. Clients may choose to run or fight because they find the issues under discussion too challenging to work through. Just consider: by giving them the space in which they can criticise you as their coach, you're doing them the service of allowing them to express anger and anxiety that they haven't voiced elsewhere!

## Checking for patterns

After clients become aware of how they deal with conflict through coaching conversations, they can develop new strategies to work through it. If conflict is a particular issue, suggest to your clients that they keep a log of difficult relationships and what triggers conflict for them.

# Panic attacks addressed

Adrian, the deputy CEO of an international charity, was given an NLP coach to support him when he began suffering from panic attacks at work. At first, he experienced alarming chest pains and thought he must be having a heart attack. Yet when his doctor and a specialist checked him out, they both pronounced him fit and healthy.

His coach encouraged him to keep a diary of times of day and days of the week when he felt most or least anxious. The aim was to highlight any activities triggering the attacks. They also did some time-line work (explained in Chapter 16) to identify any root causes of the attacks.

The year before his attacks began, Adrian had gone through a divorce and now joined the single dads taking his children to the local amusements and fast-food outlets on Sundays.

He hated being separated from his children and only seeing them at weekends.

Through coaching, a pattern of avoiding conflict through his career and his private life emerged. His marriage had ended in divorce because he didn't want to challenge his wife's constant insistence on upgrading their home, and he retreated to his study and immersed himself in work demands. Eventually, he just stopped talking to her for fear of conflict. Yet this lack of communication led to the marriage falling apart.

Through the coaching programme, Adrian worked on his skills at talking through issues with people where he had differences of opinion. Developing this skill enhanced his credentials at work, improved relations with his ex-wife and eliminated his panic attacks.

While clients are experiencing the intense physical symptoms of panic during conflict, clear thinking can be difficult. The following simple steps enable them to sit with the conflict, without fighting or running away.

- **Stop.** Don't fight the conflict or the feelings – and don't run away from either. Just observe the feelings of panic, noticing the images, sounds and feelings you're experiencing in the moment.

- **Trust.** Know that feelings of panic are simply an extreme case of the normal fight-or-flight response.

- **Accept the gift.** Each experience is a chance to practise moving through conflict and develop new, useful coping mechanisms.

- **Focus on now.** Stay present in the moment, knowing that you are safe and your feelings of panic will pass.

- **Celebrate.** After the feelings pass, take a bow for staying with the situation.

Share these steps with your client. Some people like to keep a small card with the steps written on as a reminder. Others prefer a small object or a peaceful natural image like a beautiful sunset to help them stop panicking.

Conflict with others often arises by thoughts alone; the conflict may not have any basis in reality. For example, you may assume that a colleague isn't willing to work with you or just wants to cause trouble. NLP offers specific techniques to shift that thinking. You can help clients switch submodalities, which are the way clients represents their experiences in images, sounds and feelings, to defuse negative emotion. (I cover these techniques in Chapter 17.) You can also help them gain new perspectives by having them take the perspective of the person with whom they're experiencing conflict, as I discuss in the later section 'Knowing the enemy well'.

# Holding on to the best outcome

In relationships with others, the ideal scenario is a win-win, where both parties get what they want. However, in a conflict, one party always loses, and most likely both parties become the losers. In conflict, you get stuck in a blame frame in which you criticise someone else and hope she changes.

In order to coach your clients to the best outcomes, check whether your questions keep them exploring the problems or shift them to seek positive outcomes. The following sections deal with specific clusters of questions you may ask during coaching sessions.

## Noticing blame-frame questions

When people are caught up in blaming others, the wrong kind of questions keep clients stuck and feeling bad about themselves.

In the following dialogue, notice how the coach's blame questions keep the client stuck in the client's own thoughts.

> **Coach:** What is your problem?
>
> **Client:** The staff are threatening a walk-out over cuts.
>
> **Coach:** How long have you had it?
>
> **Client:** It's been looming for some months now, but people have been ignoring it.
>
> **Coach:** Where does the fault lie?
>
> **Client:** It's the union rep who's been whipping up resentment amongst the staff here.
>
> **Coach:** Who is to blame?
>
> **Client:** Well, it's partly the Chancellor, who's forcing our hand with massive cuts in funding, and partly the last government for over-spending.
>
> **Coach:** What's your worst experience with this problem?

**Client:** I've been having sleepless nights worrying about what's going to happen.

**Coach:** Why haven't you solved it yet?

**Client:** I don't know what I can do. What do you think I should do?

### Shifting to outcome-frame questions

When people concentrate on outcomes rather than problems, their thinking becomes constructive. If the coach switches to outcome-frame questions, new thinking opens up and encourages the client to begin to resolve the problem.

In the following dialogue, notice the shift in the client's thinking to take responsibility for moving forward.

> **Coach:** What do you want?
>
> **Client:** I want us to resolve this labour dispute amicably.

Check that your clients state what they want in positive terms. Using positive language harnesses the power of the unconscious mind.

> **Coach:** How will you know when you've got it? What's the evidence?
>
> **Client:** I'll see us having sensible discussions rather than being held to ransom. We'll have a series of consultations and communications, offering practical help to those we make redundant and feel that we've done the best we can with the budget.
>
> **Coach:** What else will improve when you get it?
>
> **Client:** I'll be able to sleep again at night. I'll have more energy and be better tempered at work – and at home.
>
> **Coach:** What resources do you have already that can help you achieve this outcome?
>
> **Client:** I have access to a lot of expertise in my network, and I'm generally a very calm and rational thinker, someone who's empathetic to other people.
>
> **Coach:** What is something similar that you've succeeded in doing?
>
> **Client:** I once worked on a hostile takeover project, and I planned out a whole series of consultations and communications, including outplacement support.
>
> **Coach:** What's the next step?
>
> **Client:** I'll invite the union rep to have a coffee and an informal chat with me to set up some consultations.

## More flexibility can serve everyone

NLP asserts that the person or team with the most flexibility under pressure ultimately has the winning card. People fighting to get their own ways regardless – as well as people who constantly state that situations aren't fair – ultimately lose out.

Thomas works in a global consulting organisation and is the only member of his team based in the UK. He recounted how last year he had two colleagues, Nigel and Ian working alongside him. There was an international meeting in India to which all three had been invited, yet they needed travel approval from the UK Managing Director in order to go. The travel forms weren't approved in time, and all three missed out on the trip.

Nigel and Ian put in a formal complaint. Thomas stood back and decided that attending the team meeting wasn't a big issue for him. 'The whole of the business was under pressure to keep costs down,' Thomas said. 'I felt the expense wasn't really necessary, even though I wanted to be there.'

Out of the trio, Thomas is the only one remaining with the organisation; the other two lost their jobs in a down-sizing exercise. Thomas said, 'I pick my battles; that one wasn't worth getting upset about.'

# Working through Differences

Conflict arises when two parties become entrenched in their own ideologies. In this section, I explore some practical NLP approaches that offer ways to shift through conflict with greater ease.

## Knowing the enemy well

The famous British military commander Field Marshal 'Monty' Montgomery kept a picture of his German opponent Rommel, The Desert Fox, on the wall of his desert campaign headquarters during the Second World War. In planning the strategy for war, he wanted to focus on his enemy in order to analyse tactics in battle through his opponent's eyes.

When negotiating through conflict, the NLP concept of *perceptual positions* can provide insight into opposing viewpoints and help you separate from your emotions in order to achieve an independent perspective. The three most useful NLP positions are as follows:

✔ **First position** is your natural perspective, where you are fully aware of what you think and feel, but not the thoughts and feelings of others around you.

✔ **Second position** is about imagining what it's like to be another person. (Monty was adopting the NLP *second position* with his enemy, Rommel.)

✔ **Third position** is an independent position where you act as a detached observer noticing what's happening in the relationship between two other people.

Turn to Chapter 12 for more on perceptual positions.

# Team conflicts – and solutions

Teams and other groups can fall apart under pressure. Fortunately, team coaching can bring conflict under control before it skyrockets. Some common sources of conflict within groups are:

✔ **Lack of goals.** Teams with no goals – or confused or contradictory goals – typically experience disagreements and dissatisfaction. As coach, you can help to bring clarity by helping to set goals as well-formed outcomes or SMART goals using a shared methodology. Turn to Chapter 7 for tools and ideas.

✔ **Role confusion.** When people don't know who's doing what and why, group members assume that somebody else is doing something that doesn't happen! As coach, you can work to ensure that all team members understand each other's roles, have clear job definitions and identify any grey areas where two roles overlap and cause potential misunderstandings.

✔ **Unclear or vague expectations.** Teams need a clear communication process so that members can express their expectations and alert the team when something isn't meeting expectations. Teams can rely on formal meetings or reporting systems to keep each other informed and share

expectations. As coach, you can examine the processes in place and work with the team to set up or improve processes in order to encourage better-quality communications. (See Chapter 12 for ideas to support teams shifting through the classic stages of development.) Consider sitting in on meetings and giving feedback about how the team members interact with each other.

✔ **Different styles.** Conflicts arise when different personality types and ways of working come together. (Chapter 10 sheds light on how people work in different ways.) They may be a mix of extrovert or introverts, commanding or collaborative tendencies, as well as containing different talents and knowledge within the group. Administering psychometric tools such as Myers-Briggs and LAB profiles offers insights into how different styles can honour each other's differences and harness these distinctions to achieve positive results.

✔ **Disagreement on methods.** Conflicts arise when the team can achieve the same result in more than one way. The team coach can remind the team that everyone is heading towards the same goal and that these differences add resilience.

Take your client through the following exercise to better work with anyone with whom the client is in conflict. She needs to identify someone that she'd like to understand better, perhaps even someone she's struggled with in the past if she'd like to get a greater understanding.

1. **Lay out three pieces of paper on the floor to denote the three perceptual positions of self, opponent and independent observer.**

2. **Have the client take each position in turn.**

   When your client steps onto a piece of paper, ask the client, 'What are you thinking and feeling in this position?'

   Make sure the client breaks state between stepping into each position. You could distract the client with an everyday question, such as 'What's the weather like outside today?'

3. **As the client steps through the three positions, capture any thoughts and ideas on paper.** Be careful not to interpret the information by paraphrasing it: just capture what is said.

4. **Have the client step back to first position and relay to the client what you heard from second and third position.** Feed back what you heard and invite the client to make sense of it.

5. **Ask the client what ideas the client now has about his or her opponent.**

   Help your client identify some first steps for improving the relationship with this person.

## *Negotiating in the best-sized chunks*

Matching someone else at the right chunk-size of information eases communication. If you give an appropriate level of information, the other person can process it easily. Give too large a chunk – that is, very big-picture or general information – and she's left in the dark. Break it into too many specific details and she's swamped.

Suzanne was bemoaning the poor admin support from the office personal assistant to her coach. When asked specifically how her PA didn't support her, Suzanne kept replying in generalities: she didn't sort things, she didn't take responsibility for the financials. Suzanne is a speedy executive who doesn't like to get involved in the details of paperwork and payments. Her coach quickly realised that, in this specific context of delegating work, Suzanne operated at a global rather than detail level in terms of her NLP metaprograms (see Chapter 10 for more on metaprograms). Suzanne and her coach worked on how Suzanne could slow down and patiently give very precise requests to the PA regarding the details of the admin work.

NLP takes the concept of chunking from the field of computing. *Chunking* refers to taking information and breaking it into smaller *bytes*. NLP also talks about:

- ✔ **Chunking up.** Going from detail to a more general concept.
- ✔ **Chunking across.** Taking an idea from one context to another, normally by using metaphors and stories at a similar level of detail.
- ✔ **Chunking down.** Getting more specific details.

When negotiating through opposing positions, chunking ideas can be very useful. Chunking up enables people to agree on certain principles even if they differ on how they're implemented.

Consider the following example of two manufacturing company directors, Clive and Sara, who are arguing about business strategy. Clive argues that they should be investing in China, and Sara is championing investment in India.

- ✔ **When they chunk up,** they both agree their common ground. In this case, they both see the need for overseas investment. At this level, they can also explore what other main principles they agree on.
- ✔ **If they chunk across,** Clive or Sara might win the other over by telling stories of other successful businesses that have invested in the respective territories.
- ✔ **If they chunk down into specifics** and listen to each other's plans in turn, they might explore the relative benefits and disadvantages of the different investment areas instead of dismissing the area outright.

Chunking up and down between two people isn't easy without a determined effort by both parties. People tend to get caught up in their own specific detail and find it hard to get to the common ground, which is where an independent coach can facilitate the negotiation.

# Voicing What Needs to Be Said

One of the underlying benefits of conflict is that things come into the open and each party can grow based on the new information. Conversations may finally air thoughts and feelings that have been festering beneath the surface for years.

The Johari window is a tool that illustrates that everyone has blind spots (see Chapter 6 for more on the Johari window). Conflict can cut through a history of collusion and hidden information. Yet messages need to be conveyed with respect and appreciation of differences so that people can hear them.

The following sections explore techniques for getting out difficult information in useful, non-incendiary ways.

# Developing the non-violent vocabulary

To shift through conflict, your clients need to be able to communicate without fighting or running away. In order to do so, they must be persistent and stay calm when others may not be.

Practising a simple structure such as the following four-step model in a coaching session gives clients an easy tool to replicate in other conflict situations. Use this activity to rehearse a difficult conversation where your client needs to give challenging feedback.

The following four steps are based on Marshall Rosenberg's model of non-violent communication.

1. **When I saw/heard you . . .**

   Describe the specific, observable behaviour or actions that you've noticed.

   *For example, 'When I heard you raise your voice and swear at me.'*

2. **I felt/the impact on me was . . .**

   Describe your feelings objectively, including the impact the other person's behaviour or words had on you.

   *For example, 'I felt anxious,' or 'The impact on me was to want to cover my ears.'*

   Don't attribute blame to the other person. Avoid language such as 'I felt belittled/accused/suffocated', which implies a negative action on the other person's part. Instead, encourage your clients to own their feelings.

   *For example, 'I felt worried,' or 'I felt I needed more time to explain.'*

3. **I need . . .**

   Describe your underlying need in this situation. In the case of a work-related conflict, your need may be the specific requirements of the job.

   *For example, 'I need to provide good customer service.'*

4. **Can I ask you to . . .**

   Finish by making a specific request of the person and/or give guidance on how the other person can approach the situation differently in order to meet the need.

   *For example, 'If you have a complaint, please can you give me the facts quietly.'*

# *Finessing feedback*

NLP says there's no such thing as failure, only feedback, and places great value on feedback for learning. Those who've suffered with poor managers at work may associate feedback with getting told off and shy away from inviting it. Yet feedback is information that highlights both strengths and areas for improvement. Feedback is critical at home as well as in work environments, and is an essential part of the coach-client relationship. How do you know how you're doing unless you invite the other person to tell you?

In order to give feedback with respect:

- ✔ Give positive as well as critical feedback – the more positive, the better because people tend to focus on the negatives.

- ✔ Bring a constructive spirit. Avoid giving feedback when you're angry or tired, for example.

- ✔ Stick to the facts. Deal only with what you've observed and what others have recognised.

- ✔ Talk about clear, specific behaviours and be prepared to give specific examples.

- ✔ Avoid making assumptions about the person's motives or feelings.

- ✔ Don't blame the other person. You're responsible for your reactions to other people; recognise your reactions and accept your responsibility.

In order to receive feedback graciously:

- ✔ Don't argue or try to convince the feedback givers that they didn't see what they said they saw.

- ✔ Don't attempt to explain your behaviour to the giver, just acknowledge the feedback. Discussing the feedback *later* may be appropriate if you feel you want to learn more from it.

- ✔ Invite the feedback giver to provide specific examples of clear, observable behaviours. For example, ask the feedback giver something like, '*What did I do that told you I was angry?*'

- ✔ If the giver can't state the feedback in clear behavioural terms with specific examples, thank the giver but make your own judgement on the validity of the feedback.

- ✔ Listen carefully to what others have to say and thank them for their input. Your job is to determine what the feedback means to you and how you intend to use it.

- ✔ Stop when you've had enough. Tell the givers that you understand what they're saying or that you want some time to think about it.

If the feedback comes as part of a complaint or disciplinary process, you're right to question and challenge anything you consider unfair and exert your legal rights.

# Building the most confident voice

When people are willing to stay in the space where conflict is happening, they build the self-confidence to express what really matters to them instead of running away. With a constructive approach that looks for both parties to win, participants can increase passion, purpose and release positive energy.

Like many solopreneurs (individual entrepreneurs) selling over the Internet to global markets, Rachel's business is based from her home office. Over a period of months, she became increasingly frustrated by her poor Internet speeds, complaining that although she lived in the equivalent of Silicon Valley, she could get better Internet access in remote areas of the developing world.

After complaining for six months to her service provider and making no progress, Rachel felt that her core values – integrity, professionalism and freedom – weren't showing up in this business relationship. Instead of burying her head in the sand or turning angry, she decided to take action. She drew on her innate resources to ask: 'What can I do?' and 'What can I learn from this?'

Thus began a positive Internet campaign to get action on broadband speeds. From taking the first step of setting up a blog and dedicated website, interest in her campaign snowballed, taking on its own momentum for change. She became the local spokesperson, harnessing the power of social media, the press, MPs, the local authority, business leaders and key industry stakeholders.

Six lessons emerge from Rachel's campaign that can be applied by anyone looking to transform conflict into positive action:

- **Manage your emotional state.** Staying calm and curious enables you to work through negative interactions confidently so that you remain in a flow state (see Chapter 9 for more on flow).

- **Focus on a positive outcome.** Know what you want and then plan and implement a strategy to get there with tenacity (see Chapter 7 for more on goal-setting).

- **Unlock resources.** Make the most of your own creativity, sense of fun and contacts. Look to other people to serve as role models.

- **Develop stronger beliefs.** Remind yourself often that 'I can do this' or 'I'm doing this for the greater good'.

✔ **Honour values.** Pay attention and respect both your own values and other people's.

✔ **Work with passion and purpose.** These forces can guide you to take massive action.

# Developing appreciative habits

What gets lost during conflict is the fundamental appreciation of other people, that diversity of views and cultures that enriches the experience of being human. In particular, listening at a deep level closes down in the face of anger and frustration.

As a coach, you're in a privileged position to feel empathy for your client while taking a more impartial view of the whole situation. Exercises or activities that engender an appreciation of the person, group or organisation with whom your client is in conflict can defuse the situation and make the client more flexible.

Invite your clients to reflect about the people with whom they differ. Ask questions such as:

✔ What are five good things that they've done?

✔ What are their best qualities? What are their hidden strengths?

✔ What are you glad that you've discovered from this situation that you wouldn't have without this opportunity?

Leave your clients working through conflict situations with longer term inquiries to mull over outside the coaching sessions. Ask questions that shift their thinking, such as:

✔ How can you be the catalyst for empathy and understanding here?

✔ What are you willing to let go of? Where could you become more flexible?

✔ How might you and others benefit when you look for similarities with the other party?

✔ Who can you become through this conflict?

Ultimately, when you provide space for your clients to raise the quality of their thinking and listening to reflect on other perspectives, you create the potential to transform conflict into co-operation. Beyond the particular troublesome situation, such lessons change how your clients behave in future interactions.

# Chapter 15

# Smoothing Career Peaks and Troughs

## In This Chapter

▶ Taking ownership of your career

▶ Planning for the unexpected

▶ Developing an attractive professional reputation

▶ Connecting with others online and in the real world

*W*ork has always been a defining factor in people's identities: the first question on meeting someone after you say hello is inevitably 'What do you do?' While the precise nature of work is different for each generation, change and uncertainty have always concerned anyone with a working life. Just now the levels of unpredictability in work are the highest in decades. Cutbacks and redundancies in both the public and private sectors have led to mergers and outsourcing in an effort to reduce costs. Such moves have far-reaching impacts on jobs, services and those just entering the workforce.

As a coach, you support clients whose working lives are likely to extend far longer than many expected when setting out on their careers. Additionally, technology and globalisation are making the world a smaller place, and in this digital age, everyone is continually available, on the move and online. You're as likely to be coaching a client about his career in Bangalore or Buenos Aires as Birmingham or Brighton. Change brings amazing opportunities in its wake.

These economic and social contexts affect the specific challenges your clients bring to coaching, especially where career issues are concerned. Jobs for life don't exist for most people, so your clients are likely to move through a range of jobs with the inevitable challenge of frequent transitions. They may move in and out of self-employment and set up and close down businesses, as well as move within and between different organisations.

The psychological contract between employers and employees is taking a new shape along the way. The one certainty is that individuals must take full responsibility and ownership for their working lives and careers because nobody else is making that commitment. Having a coach alongside makes this entire process so much easier.

In this chapter, you read how you can support clients to clarify their strengths, manage their own careers and attract opportunities that are the best fit for them.

# Playing to Strengths

Not everybody wants to do the same job. A world of carpenters and no electricians, or superstar actors and no one to manage the cinemas, would be crazy, indeed. Luckily, one person's dream job is another's nightmare. Yet how often do you meet people who are drifting through their working lives, putting up with what they're doing because they feel they have no choice and that their current jobs are what they should be doing. For many, their jobs are what the world and other people expect of them. They're fulfilling someone else's dream and not their own.

When you hear the language of *shoulds*, *musts* and *have-tos*, you're tuning into a language pattern that NLP refers to as the *modal operators of necessity*. The counter-questions to this kind of thinking are: 'Who says you should/must/ have to?' or 'What would happen if you didn't?' See Chapter 8 for more on dealing with life's *shoulds* and *musts*.

For many workers, their dream jobs always remain out there somewhere, if they could only find them. The real dream job comes to life when people shape and pursue their own careers by playing to their strengths and listening to their intuition. NLP coaching helps people to access these dreams, articulate them clearly and then take action that moves them towards achieving their goals.

Dream jobs are not always about being the next chief executive, high profile figure or star performer. Rather, they're about creating satisfying and purposeful work. When people are aligned with their personal values and skills, they behave with confidence and integrity and enjoy a sense of fulfilment.

## Creating a career recipe

Like food, tastes in work are extremely individual, which is why good cooks like to adapt recipes for different palates. Great recipes begin with taking the time to explore a mix of ingredients and flavours so that surprising things happen. A similar approach applies to crafting a great career.

# Life in *The Office*

A British TV programme about the daily life of office workers in the twenty-first century, *The Office* (2001–2003), became an award-winning and international favourite for its excruciatingly accurate portrayal of its characters' grey and drab living-dead lifestyle. Although the programme is a fiction scripted and directed by Ricky Gervais and Stephen Merchant, it utilises documentary-style filmmaking in which the characters play to the camera as reality TV.

*The Office* stars Gervais as the petty, pompous and badly behaved David Brent, general manager of the Wernham-Hogg paper company based on a Slough trading estate. Brent sees himself as a philosopher and intellectual with an acute sense of humour. Alongside Brent, Tim Canterbury (played by Martin Freeman) is the likeable sales rep who does a job that he considers completely pointless and pursues romance with the office receptionist Dawn Tinsley. Meanwhile Dawn is also acutely aware of her unfulfilling work; she gave up on her real love of illustrating children's books and is engaged in a better-than-nothing relationship with the warehouseman Lee. Another familiar caricature is Gareth Keenan, who's obsessed by petty job titles and annoying others with his silly and pretentious comments. He's the ultimate 'more than my job's worth' character with few endearing qualities.

Throughout the episodes a parade of characters from office life provide the interest and humour. They range from a handful of competent and energetic professionals to the bubbly, bullying and downright boring employees: the whole fabric of contemporary office life. If you're looking for lessons in what to avoid doing as a manager, worker or within your career, this show is filled with some great examples – painfully recognisable as what really happens in an office near you!

The TV programme has become one of Britain's most successful media exports, spawning national versions in the US, in France as *Le Bureau*, in Germany as *Stromberg*, Brazil as *Os Aspones* and Canada (in French) as *La Job*. Such is the international appeal that the series has been sold to broadcasters in more than 80 countries, clearly hitting a nerve with viewers who recognise the inane experiences of office life.

The following creative exercise helps clients explore the types of work that engage them. You can use it to complement more conventional strengths-finding psychometric tests and talent inventories. The client can do this alone or with you as coach capturing the answers for him in a notebook.

Allow plenty of time for this exercise. Situate your client in a quiet and relaxing place that allows for calm thinking outside the normal work environment.

1. **Conduct an initial exploration.**

   Write the answers to the following questions in a notebook.

   - What activities engaged you while growing up that you may have pushed aside, yet you still love?

   - What would you like to have more of in your job?

   - What must you absolutely have in order to be happy at work?

- What have you always found easy that others find difficult?
- What boosts your energy and gives you the most satisfaction?
- What can you give to others and give to yourself at the same time?
- What would you like to give up that's not really the true you?
- In your dream, what would you really love to be doing?

From the answers, have the client highlight five or six key words that stand out for him as the elements he wants to include in his personal career recipe. Make a note of these key words.

Your client may highlight words that represent values such as collaboration, challenge, technology, innovation, outdoor space, leadership or excellence. Or he may be quite specific in terms of the people, things or places that he wants included in the career recipe. The important thing is to capture the client's own language, not the coach's words.

2. **Delve into a past experience.**

Have your client think of a time when he was happiest in his work. Find a moment that he could describe as being in a state of *flow* – stretched without being anxious, using his skills without being bored. See Chapter 9 for more on flow.

After the client identifies a specific time, ask the following questions and make notes for him:

- What kind of place was it, and what kind of people were you with (or maybe you were alone)?
- What activities were you engaged in?
- Which of your particular skills did you use?
- What was most important to you?
- How were you being? What was your sense of self?
- What was your contribution to others?

From the answers, have the client highlight five or six key words that call to him. Some overlap with the first list is likely, but you're aiming to capture a variety of ingredients to include in the mix.

3. **Create the career recipe.**

This exercise may be done in one long coaching session or split into two shorter ones with the client working on it as an assignment between sessions. With your client, look at the two lists of words you created. Ask the client what sounds, images and feelings the words conjure up. Allow your client time to absorb and enjoy these sensations.

Give your client a blank piece of paper and have your client write 'In my work, I truly want . . .' at the top.

Encourage the client to freely write a job description of what that work will be like. Have him consider the kind of places he wants to be, the people involved, the typical activities, the skills he makes use of and what he'll learn.

Ask your client to consider how this job fits with his values and what a difference the client can make for others or for himself through the work.

Work with your client to make the description specific, so that anyone reading it can follow the recipe. What are the absolutely essential core ingredients? How do they mix together? What's the end result? Describe how the situation smells and tastes.

After your client creates his personal recipe, the unconscious mind naturally gets to work on attracting the desired outcome. Your role as coach is to encourage practical action to take the dream into reality: checking for well-formed outcomes, overcoming the interference that clients put in their own way and taking the first step forward.

## Preparing to lose a job

Even the best-laid plans for careers don't always work out as you expect. Anyone who's been made redundant can vouch for the initial feelings of shock and loss, even if change was inevitable.

People who live in the moment, what NLP calls *in-time individuals*, are less likely to have back-up plans in place compared to those who take a longer-term view; these *through-time individuals* may well have contingency plans in place. (Flip to Chapter 16 for more on NLP and time.)

Just as most sensible people have some kind of insurance policies for cars or possessions, having a career Plan B in place in case of career glitches offers additional security and ultimately freedom of choice to your clients.

A good career Plan B includes:

- ✔ An up-to-date CV.
- ✔ A list of agencies and prospective companies to target.
- ✔ Testimonials and evidence of career successes.
- ✔ A network of personal contacts to inform of availability.
- ✔ A financial buffer of savings to cover essential living costs.

For some people, the Plan B also includes a plan for the new business they could set up or role they'd love to do if the opportunity presented itself.

ANECDOTE

## Fashioning a new career

Annette didn't have a Plan B in case of job-loss. She already had what she considered to be her dream job as an accessories buyer for a chain of department stores. She loved the job, especially travelling internationally, selecting merchandise and managing suppliers. She expected her work to go on for ever because she felt she was popular and very good at what she did.

After one trip to India, she was taken ill and need to take six weeks off work to recover. On her return, she discovered her role was being cut. Some of her work was divided up amongst a couple of new graduates who'd meet with suppliers online rather than face-to-face and negotiations on prices and delivery were centralised. Her vast experience suddenly seemed to count for nothing.

'This was crunch time for me,' says Annette. 'The real joy in my job had been meeting the local producers in their countries and feeling that I was creating a livelihood for them, as well as giving the customers beautiful and unusual goods.'

Initially, Annette returned to her company and took on the administrative job she was offered as an alternative. During this time, she worked with a coach to support her in setting up a new business. She built up her IT skills (in particular online trading), and a year later she left the company to launch an online business capitalising on her long-term relationships with her supplier base. She's also supplementing her income by giving language tuition to business people. 'It's scary at times being self-employed, yet I'm enjoying the freedom of doing what I'm best at,' she says. While Annette is still working in the fashion business, she's using a range of established skills (languages and supply-chain management) and learning new ones (online retailing, business management and website development) that can open up new opportunities in the future.

# *Owning an Engaging Reputation*

People who seem to move effortlessly from one job to the next attract opportunities based on their reputations for doing good work. When you're looking for a plumber to install your bathroom, you probably first ask your friends 'Who do you know who's done a good job?'

The same happens in the workplace. Whether you're looking for a new Chief Executive, project manager or PA, you're more likely to trust word-of-mouth recommendations than any unproven candidate at interview. Many jobs are never even advertised, but rather *created* for the right person. Even if the position is advertised, the people recruiting are much more likely to be influenced by reputation over an impressive CV.

Every individual, like it or not, has a reputation, or *personal brand*. Any coach working with clients on their careers needs to dispassionately help clients to manage their brand reputations. You may be very fond of your clients, yet you need to see them objectively from an independent position. The brand-awareness process begins with establishing how others perceive your clients, supporting them to develop the stories that they want others to hear about them and helping your clients communicate those stories confidently through networking.

## Gaining insight from others' feedback

Coaching enables your clients to discover things about themselves. This process begins with getting curious and opening up to how others see you.

In business coaching, some clients arrive with folders full of performance evaluations from various managers. They may have been subject to a 360-degree feedback questionnaire where colleagues at all levels in an organisational hierarchy give feedback.

Whether you're working with private or organisational clients, it's important that your clients know how others really perceive them. People naturally filter out information from others, either overlooking their strengths or their weaknesses.

Angie was a highly skilled business analyst in an international bank, yet she lacked self-esteem and always avoided getting feedback from colleagues. She came from a family where her father had told her that she'd 'never be as bright as her elder sister' who'd become a doctor. When her coach invited her to get some feedback from a range of colleagues, Angie was genuinely shocked and humbled by the positive affirmations she read. Receiving feedback enabled her to notice that she was extremely astute with company data and business strategy and thus steer her career to the part of the organisation specialising in mergers and acquisitions.

Use the following questions to help your clients gain feedback from others. Invite your clients to choose five or six people in their networks and ask these questions face to face, on the phone or by email. They may choose colleagues, the boss, team members, friends, family, or members of a sports team or community group.

Remind your client to just accept the feedback with thanks and not try to justify anything he receives or ask for justification from others. (See Chapter 14 on giving and receiving feedback.) Prepare him for the fact that he may not like what he hears and that's fine: the exercise is about being open to subjective opinions rather than feeling good.

Five feedback questions:

1. What are my strengths?
2. What are my weaknesses?
3. What can you always rely on me for?

4. What can you never rely on me for?

5. What does everybody know about me?

After your client gathers the feedback, look at it together to decide where your client can put his strengths to better use in career development. Ask whether your client really wants or needs to work on the weaknesses or whether he can just allow himself to let go of trying to be something he's not.

## Developing personal stories

The challenge and joy of a career reputation is that you can carry on getting more opportunities from your previous work. This phenomenon can be great for job security, but the experience can also be rather like an actor who gets typecast as the brave hero or slimy villain in films but yearns to do something different.

If your clients want to break out of a mould into new career opportunities, he must become selective about the stories he tells about work. He needs to stop talking about anything he doesn't want to do in the future and focus on what he does want to do. See the earlier section 'Creating a career recipe' for more on clarifying the work your client wants to do in the future.

Also, everyone benefits from talking more about successes and positive experiences than failures. Some hiccups make a person seem real, but too many don't do any favours. A person in the midst of constant struggle and strife can come across as incapable or a complainer.

Work with yours client to develop mini case studies of his work successes, being careful to choose the kind of work he'd like more of. Use the following structure to shape up those stories:

- Describe the kinds of people or organisations you work with by completing the statement:

  - I work with . . .

- Describe the kinds of work that you do best by completing the statement:

  - What I do is . . .

- Describe the benefits that others get from working with you by completing the statement:

  - So that . . .

- Describe how you bring your unique skills to the situation by completing the statement:

  - What makes me different is . . .

# Thorough prep work

John was the Deputy Head of a school in Aberdeenshire when he contacted me for telephone coaching. He was extremely apprehensive about the interview panel that he'd face when going for his first headship and asked for a series of three short telephone coaching sessions to prepare for that interview.

Through the sessions, we looked at the outcome John expected from the interview and how he'd look, sound and feel if he were to present at his most confident.

✔ We explored John's values and motivation for the job, specifically, what he'd be able to achieve in the headship if he got it, so that John could talk with passion about his current work and future goals. Separately, John practised telling his stories about his career achievements to his wife at home.

✔ Using NLP anchoring techniques, we anchored various positive states for him to manage his nerves and perform at his best. One positive state helped him stay calm, another encouraged him to be strong and forthright in the way he spoke. (I discuss anchoring techniques in Chapter 18.)

✔ We moved through the three NLP perceptual positions, stepping into the shoes of the members of the interview panel and imagining what was going on for them as well as taking advice from the third-person observer position. (Flip to Chapter 12 for more on perceptual positions.)

By the time John went for his interview, he was fully prepared yet also philosophical about the end result. He believed that if this job wasn't right for him, he could attract plenty more opportunities. He did get the job and has been happily employed at the school for two years.

Combine all four of the preceding phrases into a single statement and you have the start of a great story that clients can share within their networks.

Imagine that you're coaching Annette (see the earlier sidebar 'Fashioning a new career') to find another job that she loves in a new organisation after she was made redundant. Her stories can read:

> *I work with . . . retail organisations that want to sell an exciting range of good quality, well-priced accessories to their clients.*

> *What I do is . . . travel through India, South America and Asia setting up relationships with reliable local producers and getting them to design and manufacture goods that appeal to European customers.*

> *So that . . . the retailer is profitable, the suppliers are well treated and customers are delighted.*

> *What makes me different is . . . I have ten years' experience in the market and speak French, Spanish and Portuguese fluently. I'm particularly good at working with different cultures.*

In addition, you can coach Annette to develop more specific stories about her work using the same basic framework. For example, she can create other stories about specific countries she's worked in or the types of accessories she knows about – bags, scarves and jewellery. As she develops her own online business and goes out looking for new customers, her story can evolve to promote the way she works online and the kinds of customers she serves. Likewise, if she wants to build the part of her career portfolio that offers language lessons, she needs stories to tell that explain the kind of people she works with and what difference she makes for them by teaching language skills.

## Communicating confidently

Confident communicators don't just rehearse their words; they're aware of how their stories come across in terms of the way they tell their stories convincingly. Tone of voice and body language count too.

Job interviews can leave quite confident people quaking in their shoes because they're so fixated on getting the job they want. The art to communicating effectively at interview is to be well prepared and also to be authentic. This combination begins with breathing well and using the whole body, noticing your physiology and the effect of the body on your emotional state.

# Recognising the Power of Networks to Support Growth

The very thought of networking sends some clients into a panic: people love to network or hate it. Networks play an important part in managing careers, especially at key transition points. When people with work opportunities to offer are looking for someone good, they naturally defer to their network of trusted advisors. Candidates with strong networks find opportunities come to them when they least expect it, and they're also in a good place to ask for help when they need it.

Luckily for more introverted clients, online networking is extremely powerful. Those who struggle with meeting people in a crowd can strike up virtual conversations and reach a much larger audience than is possible face to face. In fact, the whole idea of networking has changed enormously in the last ten to twenty years; it used to be about attending formal cocktail parties and dinners where you wanted to be seen to look good and made small talk with useful contacts. Today, you still need to be professional and prepared, but connecting with like-minded people across a greater area is much easier. Phew, thank goodness networking has moved on!

## Connecting online

The world of online communities and social media – from blogging to joining groups such as LinkedIn, Twitter and Facebook – is familiar for some and scary for others, depending on your client's age group and comfort levels with technology. In addition to public networking sites, many large organisations have their own internal online social networking groups, which are important for professional contacts.

Online communities will only expand as technology spreads, which makes them powerful resources for people to find career opportunities – and also potential places to damage their precious reputation.

For clients new to the online social networking world, I advise choosing one site to get comfortable with rather than trying many at once. LinkedIn has become a popular professional network to build contacts that can help with career development. Facebook is usually used for friends and less formal business relationships, but can be a useful first step for making other, more professional contacts.

After you're familiar with a network, you can begin to play and go deeper, joining specialist groups, setting up your own groups and posting questions to build a community of like-minded individuals.

People posting information about themselves online need to protect their reputations and personal privacy. Just as any email message potentially becomes public after you hit the Send button, you must assume that after you post anything – including pictures or short comments – it becomes part of the public domain for all to see. So no matter how much fun you had on vacation or out with friends last weekend, never post anything you don't want a prospective customer or employer to see or read about you.

## Getting known

Whether your clients are looking at online or face-to-face networking, explore the following questions together to help them get the best out of every networking opportunity and further their careers.

🖊 **What is your outcome for this network?** Clients need to clearly articulate their personal goals. Are you looking to build or share knowledge, or to build a support group of like-minded individuals? Are you looking to find new career or business opportunities, or to offer them to others? Or do you simply want to have some fun getting out and meeting new folks to see what happens?

Take the pressure off yourself and join a network with the mindset of 'What can I give?' rather than 'What can I get?' People naturally warm to generosity rather than neediness.

✔ **What do you want to communicate?** Going to a real-world networking meeting or event can leave people tongue-tied. So help your clients feel prepared with stories. See the earlier section 'Developing personal stories' for a useful story structure that sends out a clear and simple message when invited.

Communication is two-way. Often people venture into networking situations thinking they have to say a lot. However, being *interested* in others rather than *interesting* is the name of the game.

✔ **Who do you want to meet up with?** Choose people in the group who look interesting and different to yourself – people who may give you a different insight or connect you to a different world. You can't connect with everyone, so push outside your comfort zone to meet people you don't already know.

✔ **What image do you want to convey?** Whether you're out in person or online, you have your reputation to protect and your brand to project. Your image leaves a mark from the way you dress, speak or come across in online messages. Consider what you'd like others to say about you. How can you stand out from the crowd to be memorable?

As clients get into the habit of networking without trying to impress, they build their brand reputation and more easily attract career opportunities that can serve them through the peaks and troughs that naturally occur.

Christopher describes himself as quite shy and private, yet he becomes very animated when talking about his passion for light aircraft. Some years ago, he volunteered his services at his flying club to organise regular talks from interesting figures in the aviation world and trips to other clubs that he was keen to see. When he was made redundant unexpectedly, he was offered a temporary job at the flying club that led into the role of the club general manager for nearly ten years. Of the direction his career took, Christopher says:

> *I wouldn't say I'm a networker at all. I'm just interested in people. Being known in the group meant that the club gave me an opportunity I would never have considered otherwise. People knew that I really cared about flying and only wanted the best for the club and its members, so my career took an unexpected path of its own.*

Now Christopher attends various local business networks on behalf of the club. He focuses on being interested in other people at these events and finds that this shift in focus brings him out of his natural shyness.

# Part V
# Advancing Your NLP Coaching Repertoire

The 5th Wave                                    By Rich Tennant

"I reframed his problems to eliminate negative
thinking, remapped his sensory perceptions,
and gave him a kick in the butt."

# In this part . . .

In this part, you'll discover how to bring proven NLP tools into the coaching space including working with different concepts of time. Planners will discover spontaneity, while the less organised will get on track. You'll see how classic NLP exercises in submodalities and anchoring empower your clients to confident action. You'll delve further into shifting beyond limiting beliefs that hinder progress. Here you find out how to solve internal battles that pull your clients in more than one direction at the same time with some neat parts integration and re-framing exercises.

# Chapter 16

# Turning Time to Your Advantage

## In This Chapter

▶ Understanding your relationship with time

▶ Playing with time lines

▶ Cleaning up negative experiences

▶ Creating an exciting future

*A*re you the kind of person for whom whole days or weeks drift by, or do you like to account for every minute in your schedule and book yourself solid without wasting a minute? Does time sit heavily on your shoulders or slip through your fingers like sand?

You constantly make choices about how you spend your time and how you relate to it: the hours you spend in one place compared to another, the moments you spend with one person compared to someone else. Becoming aware of how your approach to time differs from other people is interesting. For example, if you've faced a life-threatening experience, you may find each moment more precious than those around you.

When you first begin coaching others, you may be surprised at how time takes on a different dimension. You're working with the arc of time that spans from the start of a coaching conversation, through the coaching itself and into the conclusion. Substantial change happens in minutes. Just a 30-minute telephone call can shift a client from chasing her tail in circles to contentedly knowing that she's arrived in a better place. Time invested by both parties in being fully present and attentive in the coaching space yields results.

People often turn to coaching when the pace of their lives takes a toll, arriving at their initial sessions with quests to sort out their time management. Yet increasing efficiency – getting more done in less time – isn't the answer to contentment in life. Rather than doing things faster, you need to do the right things; the ones that energise you, that fit with your values, your needs and true sense of self. You also need to have the courage to let go of the rest.

## Contemplating time

The language you adopt when considering time directs attention in different ways. Consider the difference between two basic coaching questions that may initially seem similar:

✔ **What did you get done?** This question is about time management. It comes from the *chronos* perspective, in which the Ancient Greeks defined time as linear and sequential. Here lies the world of activity and doing, you get caught up in efficiency and accomplishment.

✔ **How have you been?** Whole cultures – such as African and Middle Eastern – take the *kairos* perspective. *Kairos* is another Ancient Greek word and describes an undetermined period of time in which something special happens. Time is an existential concept that people experience. You notice the quality and value of your time, how you are *being* in the moment.

Typically the coaching client from the western world arrives with the *chronos* perspective, focused on getting things done, while coaching can open up the *kairos* perspective to achieve a strong sense of well-being. *Chronos* is akin to the world of through time while those with a *kairos* perspective are more naturally in time.

In this chapter, you discover how to work with the two NLP aspects of time known as *in time* and *through time* and how to shape lives with the powerful tools of time lines.

# Creating a Personal Time Line

You can view the way people hold their memories as a pattern based on both time and direction. Clues about how your clients conceptualise time crop up in the language they use. Statements such as 'That's all behind me now' or 'I'm looking forward to that next week' imply that they hold memories of the past behind them and thoughts of the future ahead of them. They may also look to or indicate a particular direction when talking of an event.

When you understand how people organise their concepts of time, you can more easily coach them according to their natural patterns. You can also teach them ways to be more flexible in their approaches, to separate from painful memories and to make their dreams of the future more compelling.

## Visualising time

To help your client get a sense of the way she experiences time, help her identify her concept of time.

1. **Have your client think of an event from the past.** For example, something she did last month or last year or an event she attended.

2. **Ask the client to point anywhere in the room to indicate the identified event.**

3. **Have the client think of an event that's going to happen in the future.** For example, a meeting coming up or something she plans to do next month.

4. **Ask the client to point to this second event anywhere in the room.**

5. **Ask the client to point to where the client sees 'now'.**

6. **Work together to consider the three points – past, present and future – and develop the client's concepts of a personal time line.**

   Share with her the two typical positions of in-time and through-time time lines. Ask whether your client has a sense of standing looking at the line spread out from left to right in front of her or whether it runs through her. Most people have some kind of linear concept, which may be not be straight, and very occasionally their time is shifting around them.

   - **A through-time line** stretches out in front of clients. They must turn their heads to the left or right in order to look towards the past or future. See the later section 'Working with through-time clients' for more.

   - **An in-time line** runs through the body. Clients have to physically turn their bodies to look back at the past or toward the future. See the later section 'Working with in-time clients'.

---

## Just in time

When Mark went to university, he failed his first year by being highly disorganised and not getting his assignments in on time. He'd come from a home where his mother was very organised, reminded him constantly of deadlines, and kept track of his work. At university, with a lack of structure, Mark simply lived for the moment, getting up when he felt like it and enjoying a social life with late night concerts and evenings in the bars.

Mark's mother had a coaching friend who told Mark about time lines and invited him to switch his time line to see his future span out in front of him. Mark saw that unless he paid some attention to the future, his graduation ceremony didn't figure on the time line and he wouldn't get a decent job. The friend also helped him to work with a large paper schedule for each term on which he could mark essential lectures and seminars and break his essay work down week by week so that he could see what he needed to do and still allow time to socialise.

7. **Invite your client to draw a picture or demonstrate to you with her hands what her personal time line looks like.**

   Your client may not envision the time line as an actual line, but rather as a series of symbols in a pattern, rings or swirls – like a galaxy of stars. If this is the case, invite her to identify with the in-time and through-time concepts for the purpose of the exercise as she can imagine and work with these easily.

## Working with in-time clients

Figure 16-1 shows a straight in-time time line. This type of time line may also show up as a V-shaped drawing with the past on one side and the future on the other. The key thing to check is whether the line actually passes through some part of the body.

**Figure 16-1:**
An in-time
time line.

Past

Future

Present

In-time clients typically:

- ✔ Are laid-back about time.
- ✔ Have an aversion to schedules and plans.
- ✔ Follow their hearts in the moment.
- ✔ Take one day at a time.
- ✔ Easily let go of the past and future.
- ✔ Keep options open to make up their minds later – often at the very last minute.
- ✔ Drive through-time people nuts!

## Power through the hour

In his classic work *The 7 Habits of Highly Effective People* (Simon and Schuster), Stephen R. Covey reminds readers to spend time on *Quadrant II activities* – things that are important and not urgent. These activities are the strategic things in life, like planning your finances, undertaking large projects, investing in learning and relationship-building. While important, these activities are all the kinds of things that get put on hold until you have more time.

NLP asserts that anything is possible in small-enough chunks. For in-time people, chunks provide focus rather than going with the flow in the moment. For through-time people, the process provides some impetus to get on and do something in the moment rather than waiting until time miraculously becomes available.

One of the most powerful ways to spend time on Quadrant II activities is to allocate power hours in the day, during which you focus purely on these important areas. Try the following:

✔ Decide when your most productive time is and book that time for yourself to focus on only your top priority. Book just one hour to start with.

✔ Find a place where no one can disturb you and you won't drift off to surf the Internet or get involved in something else. Settle down with your favourite cup of tea or glass of water.

✔ Focus without any distraction on working on your top-priority activity for 50 minutes, then stop and give yourself a pat on the back. You may just bite off one chunk of a project, yet even that is moving you towards completion of the whole project. Reward yourself with a ten-minute break.

After you get into the swing of working this way, you can schedule more power hours in the day or week. Bit by bit, you can sort your finances, write your book, learn a language or build your network of contacts.

In order for in-time clients to get a sense of operating in through-time, invite them to imagine stepping off their time lines and placing the past to one side and the future to the other. Send them off with tasks to perform in a through-time style. For example, draw up a schedule of activities together for planning a party, with a list of tasks placed in order of the completion date for each step. Warn them that they may become slightly disoriented while trying out a through-time work style. Encourage them to notice what improvements the new time line brings.

## *Working with through-time clients*

Figure 16-2 shows a straight through-time time line with the person standing off from the time line. As with the in-time line, the through-time time line may show up as a V-shaped drawing – only in this case, it stretches out from left to right in front of the person and doesn't pass through the body. Here, the client is watching time pass in a detached way. The later sidebar 'Scheduled spontaneity' explores the experience of a strongly through-time individual.

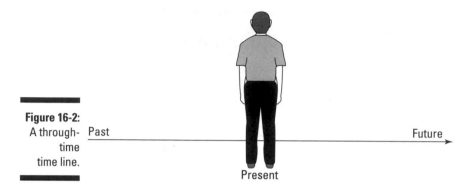

**Figure 16-2:**
A through-
time
time line.

Past

Future

Present

Through-time clients typically:

- ✔ Value punctuality.
- ✔ Like to see a time plan, schedule and diary.
- ✔ Think logically.
- ✔ Have life planned out and then follow their plans.
- ✔ Remember the past and are always looking to future improvements.
- ✔ Have high need for closure.
- ✔ Drive in-time people nuts!

In order for through-time clients to get a sense of operating in-time, invite them to imagine stepping on to their time lines so that the lines run through their bodies. Send the clients off with tasks to perform in an in-time style, with the emphasis on spontaneity rather than planning to the *nth* degree. A really challenging example is to tell a client to allow one day when they get up when they feel like it and have nothing planned to do that day. They simply do exactly what they feel like doing next according to their mood. Warn them that they may become slightly disoriented while trying out a through-time work style. Encourage them to notice what improvements the new time line brings.

# Becoming a Time Traveller

After clients have a sense of their time lines (see the earlier section 'Creating a Personal Time line'), they can put their time lines to work in various coaching exercises involving time.

## Scheduled spontaneity

Cheri lives life by the clock with a classic through-time pattern. Ideally, she'd have her life mapped out for the next ten years – at least. Planned, organised and with all the details under control to the last minute, she thrives on organising complex trade shows and corporate events. She hates to waste a minute doing nothing. She hired an NLP coach when she began suffering mild panic attacks after being made redundant and worrying about finding her next job.

One positive aspect of losing her job was that Cheri now had time to take her dog for a walk in the local woods instead of paying the dog walker she'd hired when working in the City. However, she felt guilty that she ought to be job-hunting more furiously all day instead of enjoying herself.

Cheri's coach began with a time line session to work through unhelpful negative emotions that may have caused her panic attacks; they also worked on letting go of fear, guilt, anger and anxiety from the past.

Cheri also worked to switch her time line from through-time to in-time. Cheri's coach suggested she experiment with being in-time for at least half of every day, just allowing the days to unfold and responding to spontaneous events and requests that she'd normally be too busy to accept. For the rest of the day, she could revert to her through-time pattern of being highly focused and organised about her job search.

With more scheduled spontaneity, Cheri stopped to help an elderly neighbour clear the autumn leaves from his driveway. They got chatting, and two days later the neighbour's son hired Cheri to work for his company as his new conference organiser.

- One approach is to lay out a client's time line spatially on the floor with pieces of paper to denote past, present and future. (I describe a similar technique in 'Creating the Desired Future' later in the chapter.)
- Another approach is to head into the skies (metaphorically speaking), in charge of an imaginary flying machine such as a hot air balloon or a custom-built Tardis, as in the popular *Doctor Who* TV series.

The following sections take the flying machine approach, allowing clients to land in their experiences or to get lift off and detach themselves from the surrounding emotions.

 NLP defines being in the moment as *association* and detaching from a moment as *dissociation*. Both terms appear frequently in the following sections, and explaining the terms to clients so that they can be aware of their own experiences is helpful.

# Taking off at will

In the following exercise, you teach clients to be time travellers.

- ✔ **In-time people** experience dissociating from the emotion of the moment in order to gain a broader perspective. In-time people can get the useful aspects out of strongly emotional experiences, such as anger with a loved one.

- ✔ **Through-time people** get closer to the moment, stopping to notice their feelings about a particular situation rather than retaining their normal detached style.

To help a client travel through time:

1. **Have the client sit down comfortably with her eyes closed, breathing in and out slowly five times until she feels relaxed.**

2. **Talk the client slowly through the following instructions, checking that your speed matches your client's.**

   Use the following script to guide the client through time:

   *Begin to feel yourself floating. Imagine yourself drifting up, up above yourself. Notice how you can travel way above this building to see the roofs . . . and then float up through the clouds . . . and now way above the clouds.*

   *You are in space. Your time line is way below you, like a ribbon. Look closely and you can also see yourself down there in the time line.*

   *Now, float back over your time line until you are directly above an event that happened last week or last month or last year. Hover there as long as you like.*

   *Float forward over 'now' and into the future until you are directly over an event that you know is going to happen.*

   *You can hover here as long as you like and move between your past and your future, knowing that you can travel down to the time line whenever you wish and then come back up again.*

   *When you're ready, float over your time line until you're directly over 'now'.*

   *Come gently back into the present and into your own body in the room.*

3. **Tell the client that she's now a competent time traveller and she can access this skill any time she finds a situation challenging.** Invite her to think of a time in the future when this technique will be useful and tell you what she'll do differently.

## Letting go of the negative

Time-line therapy techniques suggest that negative emotions such as guilt, sadness, anger and fear have a time element attached to them. If somebody in the past told you: 'Don't do that, stupid girl,' you may be holding on to that memory unconsciously, which can hold you back from achieving your potential.

If you remember a lot of anger in your childhood, those memories may still be affecting you. The memories can prevent you from entering into conflict or may encourage you to deal with issues angrily because that's the model you were brought up to understand.

NLP-trained coaches have a repertoire of time-line techniques and the experience to deal with strong and traumatic emotions. Only use techniques that you feel are within your level of capability as a coach. If in doubt, talk through your concerns and potential techniques with a coaching supervisor or NLP Master Practitioner instead of experimenting with a client.

If you ever run into difficulty during a time-line activity, get your client to distance herself from painful emotion by rising higher and higher above her time line.

In a regular coaching conversation, a simple and safe intervention to work with a time line is to teach your clients how to time travel (see the preceding section 'Taking off at will') and then invite them to travel along their time lines to a point where they feel stuck and then identify the resources they needed at that time. Flip to Chapter 18 for more on resourceful states.

For example, the client who says: 'My mother told me I was lazy when I was fifteen, so I've always worked to prove her wrong', is holding on to a limiting decision from those years that may no longer serve her as a hardworking adult. Ask your client to drop down into that event and check on the resources she needed back then. Invite her to identify the resources that would have made the difference then (such as more fun or compassion) and then imagine beaming them down into the past situation. She can go back to her 15-year-old self and accept the resources from her older and wiser self, taking on board the experience of her adult years.

You may want to do a lot of cleaning up with clients in regard to limiting decisions that they've made about themselves over the years. Clients may have had several unpleasant experiences where they felt bad about themselves and still hold on to those memories, which in turn hold them back.

# Creating the Desired Future

Time lines offer a powerful way to create an exciting future as well as overcome limitations from the past. This section offers a longer exploration to work with your clients to create the kind of lives they want in the future.

In particular, you can enable them to define how they'd like to be:

- Physically.
- Socially and emotionally.
- Intellectually.
- Spiritually or purposefully.

## Touring various aspects, at various points in time

You can physically lay out a time line with your client, identifying three distinct spaces where they experience:

- The past: five years ago.
- The current time: now.
- The future: five years from today.

Do this activity in a clear room where you can place pieces of paper on the floor or use different chairs for the client to sit in. If space is restricted, invite clients to imagine they have a magic carpet that they roll out to take them to different points in time.

For each of the following activities, have a notebook and pen handy to capture your clients answers for them. You can work through the activities in the following sections in turn or jump from section to section as appropriate.

### Fine-tuning the body

Explore your clients' physical health at the three different time points by moving through the three different spaces on the time line, observing how their approach to health was in the past, how it is now and how they'd like it to be in the future.

Ask the following questions about the past, present and the future:

- ✔ How do you experience your health?
- ✔ What do you do to look after yourself physically?
- ✔ What's essential for your physical well-being?

Capture your clients' answers, paying most attention to the adjustments they want to make now to safeguard their futures by asking: What are some adjustments, if any, you'd like to make to safeguard your health for the next five years?

### Assessing the social and emotional connections

Explore your clients' social and emotional well-being at the three different points in the three different spaces on the time line, observing how their approach to this aspect of their lives was in the past, is now and how they'd like it to be in the future.

Ask the following questions about the past, present and the future:

- ✔ How are your relationships at this point in time?
- ✔ How are you emotionally?
- ✔ What's essential for your social and emotional well-being?
- ✔ What do you do to look after yourself socially and emotionally?
- ✔ What are some adjustments you'd like to make over the next five years?

Capture your clients' answers, paying most attention to the adjustments they want to make now to safeguard their futures.

### Developing intellectual capability

Explore your clients' intellectual well-being at the three different points by allowing them to stand in three different spaces on the time line, observing how their approach to this aspect of their lives was in the past, is now and how they'd like it to be in the future.

Ask the following questions about the past, present and the future:

- What do you do to look after yourself intellectually? What about learning?
- What's essential for your intellectual well-being?
- How do consider yourself to be intellectually today?
- What are some adjustments you'd like to make over the next five years?

Capture your clients' answers, paying most attention to the adjustments they want to make now to safeguard their futures.

### Raising the sense of spiritual connection

Explore your clients' sense of purpose and spiritual well-being at the three different points by allowing them to stand in three different spaces on the time line, observing how their approach to this aspect of their lives was in the past, how it is now and how they'd like it to be in the future.

Some clients may be sensitive to exploring the spiritual domain, so check whether they're okay with sharing this. They may find it more acceptable to talk about the idea of spiritedness and what makes them feel most alive or excited.

Ask the following questions about the past, present and the future:

- How do consider yourself to be spiritually today? How do you connect with the bigger picture of your life?
- What do you do to nurture this sense of yourself?
- What's essential for you to connect with your spiritual or more purposeful self?
- What are some adjustments you'd like to make over the next five years?

Capture your clients' answers, paying most attention to the adjustments they want to make now to safeguard their futures.

Exploring the spiritual dimension can be very challenging for clients because they're shifting into more existential questions around the purpose of their lives. Chapter 9 talks more about living with purpose and relating that to everyday experience.

## *Increasing the sparkle dust*

After you capture information from the preceding section on the physical, mental, emotional, intellectual and spiritual dimensions of your clients' desired futures, you can work with them to make their visions of the future even more compelling.

Invite your clients to step on the time line into the future. Read back to them how they've described how they want to be five years from now. Let them notice the images, sounds and feelings coming to them and wrap those into one image, word or feeling that they can hold and remember, and then invite them to sprinkle this experience with a magic sparkle dust.

Your client naturally remembers this experience unconsciously without you needing to prescribe any additional action. If they want to find a symbol or draw a picture to remind themselves consciously of their future self, that's also fine.

---

# The future of time?

Most people have a mechanistic view of time, in which life ticks away just as the hands on a clock move. For instance, if you get on a train in London's St Pancras's station, you expect to arrive at Paris's Gare du Nord less than three hours later.

Yet from a physicist's viewpoint, time depends on the observer's frame of reference. Take, for example, an astronaut travelling the universe in his spacecraft, accelerating close to the speed of light. He doesn't age at the same rate as his colleague back on planet Earth.

Quantum theory examines the behaviour of very small objects and very high energies, demonstrating the unpredictability of concepts such as time and space. Even today's most eminent scientists like Stephen Hawking and Roger Penrose debate cosmological models to decide whether time has a beginning or an end. Did time begin with a Big Bang? Will the universe expand for ever or all collapse to nothing?

While *The Origins of the Universe For Dummies* by Stephen Pincock and Mark Frary (Wiley) tackles these (and many other) big questions, great minds always have – and always will – seek the truth about the deeper structure of time.

# Chapter 17

# Shifting Experiences with Submodalities

## In This Chapter

▶ Coaching beyond the content of stories

▶ Tapping deeper into the senses

▶ Tackling problems by accessing inner resources

▶ Transforming limiting beliefs to empowering ones

*H*ave you ever had someone who let you down badly? A supplier, friend, colleague or lover who left you in the lurch? Notice how much emotional energy shifts through your body as you recall the original let-down. Thoughts and emotions tumble around and interfere with your well-being.

Just as I sat down to start this chapter, I noticed how cross I felt about an unreliable web-developer who'd reneged on his commitment for a project in the last week. Furious at his slap-dash behaviour, the fire in my belly raged. I wanted to name and shame him on Facebook for the entire world to see. Luckily, my Pause button kicked in with timely logic. I asked myself how my efforts could achieve any positive results. When I was unable to come up with any possible positives, I realised that I needed to sort through the situation in an effort to gain new understanding for myself.

NLP enables you to shift an experience from shock or anger to acceptance and moving on, putting you back in the driving seat. In my case, by making my image of the situation with the web-developer smaller and smaller in my head, I can eventually shrink it down to a little black and white document and then file it away, just as I do old receipts.

Reframing painful experiences helps clients break their unhelpful patterns. The tools and techniques in this chapter are fast and fun, like holding your own remote control for life. Most importantly, they give you freedom to work on sensitive issues without sharing a lot of intimate details or getting bogged down in a lot of drama.

## Structure, not content

NLP goes beneath the surface details of life to uncover the structural foundation of experiences.

Indeed, NLP co-creator John Grinder says that he doesn't need to hear the detail of his clients' stories in order to help them. If the Chief Executive of a global corporation finds his colleagues cheating and wants to discuss the situation with Grinder during a coaching session, Grinder typically stops the client and instead works to resolve the issues content-free (see Chapter 6 for content-free questioning).

The danger of allowing clients to pour out detailed histories during coaching sessions is two-fold: the clients get caught up in their own circular web of stories, and coaches often become entrapped, connecting with similar experiences of their own. 'How awful. That reminds me of the time that happened to me too,' you think as you become part of your client's issue. See the later section 'Shifting Positions' for more helpful tools to avoid getting pulled into clients' experiences.

# *Understanding the Submodalities*

In your mind's eye, think back to an event that happened yesterday. You don't need to think back to a major event, just consider some food you enjoyed, a movie you saw or a conversation you had with a friend. Notice the images, sounds and feelings that come to mind. Which sense is strongest for you? Imagine that you have your own control buttons to change the quality of the images, sounds and feelings. Take the image and make it a different colour, turn up the volume or lower it, change your feelings to a different emotion, change any textures or tastes. Notice what effect each of these changes has on you. You can think of a pink elephant, a sunny day or the sound of the wind without experiencing it in the moment. Playing with your senses demonstrates the fantastic power of your playful mind.

NLP suggests that everything you experience is as a result of information that you take in through your senses: Visual (V), what you see; Auditory (A), what you hear; Kinaesthetic (K), what you touch and feel emotionally and physically; Olfactory (O), smell; and Gustatory (G), taste. These senses are the *modalities* and are referred to as the *representational system* of VAKOG (read more in Chapter 2 on representational systems).

Each modality has a level of fine-tuning called the *submodalities*. For example, a picture can be bright or dull, black and white or colour. A sound can be loud or soft and have a particular rhythm. In coaching with submodalities, you pay attention to your clients' predominant visual, auditory and kinaesthetic experiences to work with the structure without needing to know the content.

The following three sections look in detail at how someone stores a particular experience in the main VAK submodalities. Each submodality has a question you can ask in coaching in order to delve into the structure of your client's experience.

If your clients aren't familiar with exploring submodalities, the process may seem strange. You can advise them that you'd like get to the deeper structure of their thinking by using a different type of question than they may be familiar with, and check that's okay. Say that you're trying to get a sense of the kinds of images, sounds and feelings associated with their experience because your clients get good results when they learn how to see, hear or feel things in a different way. Giving an example can help.

The later section 'Mapping across from other resources' shows you how to bring together – or *map across* – these three submodalities using a contrastive analysis.

Sandra came for career coaching, fuming about her old boss at a motor trade dealership, in which the macho culture verged on sexual harassment. She'd left one company primarily to get away from him, then six months later he appeared in the new company and once again she was reporting to him. His presence loomed large in her head. I invited her to hold the sense of this man in her mind's eye, imagine putting a picture frame around a photograph of him, make him smaller and smaller so that he was only a small dot and then see whether her feelings of anger had shifted. Unprompted by me, she said that she now saw him as an annoying spider and was flushing him down the sink in her mind's eye. Such wizardry in the mind! After that, he never appeared troublesome again. You can find more examples of this kind of wizardry in *Neuro-linguistic Programming For Dummies* and the *Neuro-linguistic Programming Workbook For Dummies* (Wiley), by Romilla Ready and Kate Burton (me!).

When clients explore their submodalities in coaching, you empower them with tools to manage other future experiences.

## Seeing the distinctions

In this section, you begin to identify the visual submodalities of an experience. Table 17-1 summarises the various questions.

If you want to try a simple visual intervention in conversation without doing an in-depth exploration of the visual submodalities, invite a client to change the colour and brightness of his experience. Ask 'What happens to how you think about this situation when you add bright lights or make it dim and dark?'

| Table 17-1 | Questions to Identify Visual Submodalities |
|---|---|
| *Submodality* | *Question to Ask* |
| Location | Point to where the image is located. Is it close to your body, somewhere else in the room or outside? |
| Brightness | Is it bright or dim? |
| Two- or three-dimensional | Is the picture in two or three dimensions? |
| Size | Is the picture small or big? |
| Distance | Is the picture close or far away? |
| Framed or panoramic | Is there a border around the picture or is it as if you're standing on a hilltop looking around you? |
| Colour/black and white | Is the picture in colour or black and white? |
| Movement | Is it a movie or a still picture? |
| Orientation | Are you holding the image horizontally or vertically? |
| Associated/dissociated | Are you looking out of your own eyes or are you observing the picture as if on the television? |

## Hearing auditory signals

In this section, you explore the auditory submodalities of an experience. Table 17-2 offers some questions to identify auditory submodalities. A simple auditory intervention during a coaching conversation is to ask the client what kind of soundtrack accompanies the experience. You could explore what happens if he changes the soundtrack.

| Table 17-2 | Questions to Identify Auditory Submodalities |
|---|---|
| *Submodality* | *Question to Ask* |
| Location | Is the sound inside or outside your head? |
| Pitch | Is the sound high- or low-pitched? |
| Volume | Is it loud or soft? |
| Duration | Is it short, quick, broken notes or continuous? |
| Tempo | Is it fast or slow? |
| Mono/stereo | Is the sound coming from one direction or from all around? |
| Rhythm | Does the sound have a beat? |

## A grey world

The world contains fewer pleasures when people suffer from depression. Scientists at the University of Freiburg in Germany discovered that people dealing with depression are less capable of detecting the contrast between black and white. As a result, they see everything, quite literally, in greyscale.

The research, reported in *New Scientist*, measured electrical impulses to gauge the activity in the retinas of 40 depressed individuals and in volunteers who were not depressed. The depressed patients were found to be less able to perceive contrast than the other volunteers, even if they were taking anti-depressant medication.

Researchers also found that the more depressed the individual, the less able he was to detect contrast. They even suggested electro-retinograms as a potential test to diagnose depression.

As a coach, if you find your client is unable to access submodalities in colour, it may be an indicator that he's depressed and could benefit from a medical check-up.

Marathon runner Michael practises playing his favourite music over and over in his head as he runs. When he hits the wall in a race, he turns up the volume on the classic Queen song 'A Kind of Magic' to crowd out the inner voice telling him how tired he is. He imagines himself on the finishing line punching out the lyrics 'One dream, one soul, one prize, one goal'. His strategy has served him well for 20 years of competitions, enabling him to raise many thousands of pounds for charity.

## *Feeling the kinaesthetic differences*

Elaine called in for a weekly coaching session saying she was shattered by the uncertainty of not knowing where her husband's next international posting would be. She was experiencing her feelings as a cool expanse of cloud enveloping her. After doing a brief check on her kinaesthetic submodalities, she decided that by making the mist warmer and imagining a cylinder containing the cloud, she could enjoy just being with the uncertainty. Making these submodality shifts gave her time to explore the various options of locations rationally with her husband.

In this section, you explore the kinaesthetic submodalities of an experience. Remember that kinaesthetic refers to both touch and feelings. The questions in Table 17-3 guide you through identifying various kinaesthetic submodalities. A simple submodality intervention in a coaching conversation is to have the client allow a pleasant feeling to wash through his body from the top of his head through to the tips of his toes. This exercise is helpful if a client is feeling a little anxious and would benefit from letting go of worries to feel calmer.

| Table 17-3 | Questions to Identify Kinaesthetic Submodalities |
|---|---|
| **Submodality** | **Question to Ask** |
| Quality | Is the sensation tingling or dull, relaxed or tense? Is there any texture associated with the feeling? |
| Intensity | How strong is the feeling? |
| Duration | Is the feeling continuous? |
| Location | Where is the sensation in your body? |
| Still or moving | Is the feeling in one place or does it move around your body? |
| Size | What is the size of the feeling? |
| Temperature | Is the feeling hot or cold? |

# Mapping across from other resources

Mapping across is a coaching technique that works by finding the specific submodality qualities of a client's problem area and contrasting these qualities with another area where the client is successful. After you and your client observe the differences, you can make adjustments to see how the experience changes when the client thinks about the situation differently. See the later sidebar 'Roll on, grand designs' for more on my own experience with mapping across submodalities.

Following are just a few areas where you can map across resources from one place to another:

- ✔ **Action versus procrastination.** When clients are stuck, identify examples of when and where they take action.

- ✔ **Good mood versus bad mood.** When negative emotions are interfering with well-being or the ability to move forward, identify areas where clients are content and happy.

- ✔ **Fun versus serious.** Make difficult or boring tasks, like that tax return, more fun by accessing times when clients had fun.

- ✔ **Understand versus confused.** Create ways that make learning easier by tapping into experiences where clients understood something new.

The following steps help you guide a client through a *contrastive analysis* that checks on all three of the visual, auditory and kinaesthetic submodalities in order to map across from a positive experience to one where a client desires change.

Before trying the following exercise, ensure that you're familiar with the specific submodality questions in the previous three sections. When doing this exercise with a coaching client, having the questions in front of you to aid your memory is perfectly acceptable.

1. **Have the client identify the issue and a resourceful state that can be useful in that context.**

   For example, if the client can't get motivated about a project, find a time when he was motivated to do something else as the resourceful state. (See Chapter 18 for more on resourceful states.)

2. **Using Table 17-4 as a guide, contrast the submodalities of each context.** Take each question in turn for each of the three submodalities to capture a full profile so that you have two lists, one for resource space and one for problem space. However, if the client really struggles in one area, don't push that question. Perhaps he has a stronger sense in one area than another, and you don't need to have every submodality on the list completed.

   You can contrast the two situations without knowing any content. Simply refer to the contexts as *A* and *B*, or resource space and problem space.

3. **Map across the submodalities.**

   Keeping the client thinking about the issue, change the submodalities across from the resourceful state to the problem state.

   Work through the list one at a time, inviting him to think about the problem, and talk him through each of the submodalities of the resourceful space that he came up with. For example, 'Thinking about the image, bring it closer to you, make it bright, see it in 3-D and colour. Notice the sounds are gentle and soft now, and you have a feeling inside your body of a warm, smooth, flowing liquid.' This process can happen very quickly, taking just a minute or so.

4. **Test**.

   Check how the client thinks about the issue after mapping across the submodalities. Ask 'What is your sense of the problem now?'

   Normally, you'd expect the client to say that it's much better, and he feels quite resourceful. If that's the case, the work is done. If the result is not so good, you can do some fine-tuning by going over the submodality list more slowly and checking if each one in turn makes it better or worse. Change back any submodalities to the original one unless those from the resource space improve the situation.

   If you've ever had an eye test, think of switching submodalities as being the optician testing which lens is better or worse. You're just making fine adjustments to the experiences.

Take copies of Table 17-4 and write down the submodalities as you work through these steps with your client. Give your client the completed table at the end of the session so that he can remind himself of how to access resources himself in future if another problem arises.

| Table 17-4 Contrastive Analysis of Resourceful and Problem Space | | |
|---|---|---|
| *Submodalities* | *Resourceful Space* | *Problem Space* |
| **Visual: what aspects of the images are important?** | | |
| Location | | |
| Brightness | | |
| Two- or three-dimensional | | |
| Size | | |
| Distance | | |
| Framed or panoramic | | |
| Colour/black and white | | |
| Orientation | | |
| Movement | | |
| Associated/dissociated | | |
| **Auditory: what aspects of the sounds are important?** | | |
| Location | | |
| Pitch | | |
| Volume | | |
| Duration | | |
| Tempo | | |
| Mono/stereo | | |
| Rhythm | | |
| **Kinaesthetic: what aspects of the feelings are important?** | | |
| Quality | | |
| Intensity | | |
| Duration | | |
| Location | | |
| Still or moving | | |
| Size | | |
| Temperature | | |

# Roll on, *Grand Designs*!

When I worked as a marketing executive responsible for my company's stands at trade shows, an exhibition designer typically gave me flat plans for the very expensive stand constructions. The drawings left me bemused and befuddled. Specifically, I struggled to connect how the black and white flat drawing would work in three dimensions in the real world, for example, at the National Exhibition Centre in Birmingham with thousands of visitors passing through every day.

Initially, not wanting to look ignorant, I put my trust in the experienced designers and figured things would work out on the day of the show. Later, as I got to grips with the designs, I asked for a scale model of the major projects to aid my understanding. Similarly, when I took an evening class in garden design, I struggled to create 2D black and white construction plans and planting layouts, although I loved creating watercolour sketches of garden planting on thick art paper.

Ten years ago at a submodalities workshop, NLP developer and trainer Suzi Smith invited participants to work with partners to examine subjects they found confusing. I was about to embark on some redesign work of my kitchen, so I chose my frustration with translating 2D into a 3D visualisation.

My magic a-ha moment came in the mapping across stage of the exercise (see the earlier section 'Mapping across from other resources' for more on this technique). First my partner and I looked at the submodalities of the problem space, where I struggled to understand two-dimensional drawings. Then by contrast, we captured the submodalities of a resourceful space, where I really found learning easy and fun in a different context, this time in training design. Then my partner mapped across the submodalities I talked about in designing workshops where I could plan something and then imagine it coming to life.

I realised that if I tilted the orientation at which I viewed a drawing from flat to upright (as in pinning it on a wall or flipchart) and then annotated the drawings myself with coloured pens, I suddenly saw the final design in my mind's eye. I could make the experience even better by imagining the paper was textured, not smooth. Now I was really engaged with the design; it was tasty and exciting. I felt empowered to own the design rather than allow others to dictate their ideas to me. From that day, design work sprang into life.

As you become familiar with the submodality distinctions, you develop favourites to work with. Try feeding questions around submodalities into a coaching conversation without doing a full submodality checklist. Asking if someone sees an issue in colour or black and white or where the issue is located in the body acts as a catalyst to get your clients curious about their experiences.

# Shifting Positions

Have you ever cried at a sad tale because you identified with a character? It's one thing to shed tears alone on your sofa in front of a sentimental movie, another to cry uncontrollably in a public gathering.

- ✔ **Association** is the ability to really live an experience in the moment and also to keep on re-living it as if it's happening again right now. For example, the ability to enjoy being on a mountain top admiring the stunning views all around you and accessing that memory at will.

- ✔ **Dissociation** is the ability to watch yourself quite separately from the experience as an impartial observer. For example, developing the ability to dissociate from emotional episodes saves you the embarrassment of red eyes when you want to look calm and professional.

As a coach, you need to be able to do both: step into situations and then step out and encourage your clients to do the same. Being empathetic to your clients' experiences is appropriate for you in order to understand what they may be experiencing, yet coaching also requires that you keep your professional distance to hold the space and remain objective.

## Associating with the moment

Being present in the moment and paying full attention to the coaching session is absolutely essential; wondering what's cooking for supper is no use. In order to get your client associated into the coaching, choose a time and place for coaching when and where they can concentrate on being in the coaching space particularly for business people. If you coach them in their offices, they're likely to be distracted. When coaching, as you step into your clients' worlds, you really get in touch with what's happening for them. NLP encourages walking in someone else's shoes through close modelling of verbal and non-verbal body language.

To associate into a context, step into it. Be there and notice all the colours, textures and sounds. Enhance these while slowing down to half the speed so that you're really savouring the moment as if in slow motion. (See Chapter 7 for tips on engaging the senses.)

## Dissociating from the moment

During a coaching session, you mentally step in and step out of the client's world to aid him to find the answers he seeks. After a session, you must distance yourself and not run the movie of your client's life or you'll never have a life of your own! (Getting too involved in your client's story is a good topic to raise in coaching supervision; see Chapter 1 for more on supervision.)

Create a film in your mind of the context you need to dissociate from. Imagine yourself in colour and the context or backdrop fading away in black and white. Run the backdrop at double speed, going forwards from the start of the film to the end. Run the colour images of yourself at half speed, going backwards. (Read more about dissociating what you see from how you feel in *Neuro-linguistic Programming For Dummies* (Wiley) by Romilla Ready and me, Kate Burton.)

# Changing Beliefs through the Senses

NLP considers beliefs as pivotal to change because beliefs drive behaviour powerfully. (Chapter 5 demonstrates the link between beliefs and behaviour with Robert Dilts's Logical Levels model.) The deep structure of beliefs shows up in the surface structure of everyday speech and action. One of my most successful business coaching clients believes that 'money is everywhere I look'. This belief has led him to set up and sell profitable businesses from Scandinavia to the Baltic, China to Europe; he's always finding opportunities.

## Distinguishing between limiting and empowering beliefs

*Beliefs* are assumptions that may or may not be true; however, you act as if they are true. *Limiting beliefs* hold clients back, while *empowering* ones shift them towards their goals.

As a coach, challenge assumptions or limitations that you hear in your clients' conversation and sponsor the ones that enrich their lives. Yet be aware that the most influential beliefs are held at an unconscious level.

NLP offers various processes to unpack the structure of limiting beliefs and generate more useful ones that empower clients. In the following section, you discover the role submodalities can play in shaping beliefs.

A client holds on to a limiting belief for a reason. Discovering the benefit he gets from a limiting belief and honouring his intention underlying the belief (for example, to need to feel included, safe or in control) is an important prelude to the work in this section.

Following are some common limiting beliefs:

- ✔ Nobody likes me round here.
- ✔ I'm no good at delegation.
- ✔ I'm too scared to leave my job.
- ✔ That's the kind of thing that rich people can afford.
- ✔ I'll never be able to drive.

When you hear these kinds of statements, enquire as to the benefit the client gains from the belief first and then invite him to consider what would be a more empowering belief to develop going forward.

## Getting beneath the surface and empowering the client's potential

Given that beliefs aren't always logical or true, they prove resistant to conventional questioning and logical evidence-based approaches to disproving them.

To create change requires changing the structure of the belief – via submodalities – so that the belief no longer holds up. After submodalities shift, the client can no longer hold the old belief in the same way; the process of working with submodalities destabilises the structure.

The following coaching exercise creates empowering beliefs through shifting submodalities. The steps rely on visual submodalities because research shows that people process pictures faster than sounds or feelings. If you have a client who responds better with auditory or kinaesthetic approaches, you can adapt the exercise to suit him better, making notes of sounds or feelings instead. You can photocopy blank charts of Table 17-5 to take to coaching sessions.

1. **Identify a limiting belief.**

   Work with your client to verbalise a belief that holds him back. Write this down under Limiting Belief in Table 17-5. Make a note of the picture that comes to mind when the client considers the belief. The client can keep the image to himself or share it with the coach.

   For example, the belief 'I'm never going to be a good presenter' or 'I'm financially irresponsible' may be represented by an image of giving a poor talk or credit card bills piling up.

2. **Identify an old belief that the client no longer finds true.**

   Have some fun with this. Old beliefs you no longer hold true may be 'The tooth fairy will leave a silver coin tonight' or 'My life will always be perfect'. Allow an appropriate image to come to mind. Again, write this under Old Belief in Table 17-5.

3. **Ponder a belief that your client considers an absolute certainty.**

   Need help finding a certain belief? Try this: you know the sun will rise even if today's grey and cloudy. Picture the sun rising behind – and perhaps peeking out from – the gloomy clouds.

4. **Have your client think of a belief the client wants in place of the limiting belief he or she pictured in Step 1 – a desired belief that's more empowering.**

   This belief may be the opposite of the limiting belief in Step 1, stated in the positive. For example, 'I can be a confident and entertaining public speaker' or 'I'm taking good care of my finances'.

   Ask your client to notice the picture that accompanies the new desired belief and write this down in Table 17-5 under Desired Belief.

5. **Identify the submodalities of the limiting belief from Step 1, the old belief in Step 2 and the certain belief in Step 3.**

   Capture the client's submodality details in writing in Table 17-5. Refer back to the visual submodality questions in Table17-1 to remind yourself of the questions you need to ask about submodalities. The Desired Belief column is still blank.

6. **Change the submodalities of the limiting belief from Step 1 into those of the old belief in Step 2.** Do this in the same way as in the mapping across exercise in the earlier section 'Mapping across from other resources'. Invite your client to think about the limiting belief as you talk him through the visual submodalities to those of the old belief.

7. **Change the submodalities of the desired belief the client would rather have (from Step 4) into those of the belief of which the client is absolutely certain (Step 3).** Do this by inviting him to think of the desired belief and talking him through the visual submodalities of the certain belief so that he can now create his own sense of this new belief.

   The sequence of the exercise is important. The client arrives with a limiting belief that prevents him achieving what he desires. He needs to let go of the limiting belief first before he can feel empowered about the desired belief.

8. **Notice the difference.** Ask the client what he now believes to be true, what's different for him? You can expect to find that your client now has a new empowering belief in which he's confident. Work with the client to make any adjustments to the submodalities that will strengthen the desired belief. Capture the final submodalities in the Desired Belief column of Table 17-5 and invite him to hold a new image in his mind's eye to remind him of this belief.

The exercise can reveal other limiting beliefs. If so, work through these by repeating the same process.

| Table 17-5 | Switching Limiting Beliefs to Empowered Beliefs with Visual Submodalities | | | | |
|---|---|---|---|---|---|
| *Submodalities* | *Limiting Belief* | *Desired Belief* | *Old Belief* | *Certain Belief* | *New Empowering Belief* |
| **Visual: what images are important?** | | | | | |
| Location | | | | | |
| Brightness | | | | | |
| Two- or three-dimensional | | | | | |
| Size | | | | | |
| Distance | | | | | |
| Framed or panoramic | | | | | |
| Colour/black and white | | | | | |
| Orientation | | | | | |
| Movement | | | | | |
| Associated/ dissociated | | | | | |

# Is it true?

In her book *Loving What Is* (Rider, 2002), Byron Katie shares four simple questions known as *The Work* that shape the way she's moved through her own personal pain and suffering. By shifting how she *thought* about her own situation, she dramatically changed her own clarity and perspective on life. Katie now teaches this deceptively simple process to others.

She has four main questions she asks clients to consider about any difficult situation that question the way they think about their current dilemma, whether their thoughts are the truth, what effect those thoughts have and how the client might be different if they didn't have those thoughts. The questions are:

- Is it true?
- Can you absolutely know it's true?
- How do you react when you think that thought?
- Who would you be without the thought?

Here's how Katie's approach works in coaching: a client makes a statement that doesn't seem to serve him well. An example is a complaint about someone else being unkind, such as 'Stephan is unfair to me.'

Gently exploring this statement with the first two questions gives the client the chance to unearth the truth and reflect on the statement. Is it really true or just a story the client is telling himself?

With the third question, invite the client to explore the specifics of his behaviour. What does the client do specifically when he thinks that Stephan is behaving unfairly? Make a list and examine it.

With question four, invite your client to imagine who he'd be if he couldn't have that thought. Notice what the client sees, hears and feels. Give your client the possibility that he can't blame Stephan for the problem. Suggest that your client can release himself from that hook, as well.

Katie's final activity is to *turn around* the original statement, to re-write it. Using a series of turnaround techniques (similar to NLP reframing), you rephrase the original thoughts in several different ways. Here are a few examples:

- Stephan is not unfair to me.
- I am unfair to Stephan.
- I am willing to be fair to Stephan.
- I need to be fair to myself in order to be fair to Stephan.

In its own style, this process transforms limiting beliefs through simple conversational exploration. As Katie notes:

> *The power of the turnaround lies in the discovery that everything you think you see on the outside is really a projection of your own mind. Everything is a mirror-image of your own thinking. In discovering the innocence of the person you judged, you eventually come to recognise your own innocence.*

# Chapter 18

# Managing Emotional States

. . . . . . . . . . . . . . . . . . . . . . . . . . . . . . . . . . . . . . . . . . . . . . . . .

*In This Chapter*

▶ Keeping clients resourceful under pressure

▶ Working from the inside out

▶ Cleaning up interference

▶ Championing natural potential

▶ Conquering fears and phobias

. . . . . . . . . . . . . . . . . . . . . . . . . . . . . . . . . . . . . . . . . . . . . . . . .

*A*t last, people within organisations are beginning to be able to talk about emotions at work rather than trying (and often failing) to leave them in the car park. Leaders know that people need to be emotionally intelligent as well as intellectually or technically strong. Emotional intelligence involves the skill of tuning into your own emotions and those of people around you.

In this chapter, I explore emotional states and how you can encourage your clients to anchor positive states and deal with pesky gremlins who can interfere with people's resourcefulness. I also delve into dealing with fear and improving confidence.

# Saying Hello to Emotional States

The four core emotions of anger, joy, sadness and fear can each trigger an *emotional state*. An emotional state encompasses thoughts, feelings and sensations in the body. *State* describes a way of being, whether that's unhappy or peaceful, terrified or elated. In coaching, you encourage your clients to pay attention to emotional states, taking it as valuable information about what's going on for them at a deep level. For example, if someone's waking up at night in a hot sweat and going over conversations, she's clearly anxious about something that would be useful to explore. Emotions drive action and affect health; they direct attention and behaviour. If you're feeling sad or fearful, the emotion may well drive you to do something that you wouldn't otherwise consider doing.

# Coach, consider thyself

As a coach, you need emotional awareness of both your clients' emotions and your own because your state affects your clients' states and vice versa. States change frequently during a day – even during a coaching session. When you're talking about the issues that your clients bring to coaching, you need to be aware of how you react emotionally and whether your reactions serve or hinder clients' progress.

As you read this chapter, consider how you've been feeling today. Mad, bad, glad or sad? All of them? Did you even notice how you were *being* or were you more caught up in what you were *doing*? What emotions did you express or suppress?

Beware of labelling emotions as good or bad; they are what you feel in the moment and you need to examine where they lead you. For example, a touch of angry resentment may be what someone needs in order to kick-start a change she's been avoiding. By contrast, pure joy may lead someone else to take a decision with rose-tinted specs on that she later regrets.

Persistent negative emotions take their toll on clients, draining energy and creating unhealthy levels of stress. If somebody is persistently angry or sad, advise her to discuss this with her doctor who may refer her for therapeutic work or give medication.

Emotional ups and downs are natural; they show that you're just human. Some people love to ride through life on an emotional roller-coaster where their moods are unpredictable to others, only feeling alive at the extremes, while others prefer a steadier approach. While moods and states are similar, a state is more enduring than a mood. States are highly infectious, affecting your relationships, performance and health.

Have you ever considered how many people your state affects in any one day? Your one action can have an immense ripple effect on others. James recalls the anguish of his son when he collected him from school on a Friday evening. He could feel the bad vibes when 8-year-old Tom came rushing towards him in a horrible tantrum. 'Sir's been mean again today,' his son complained. 'Sir was in a temper, so nobody could do sports this afternoon. We all had to stay in the hall and tidy up the equipment instead.' After a couple of children misbehaved, the punishment stretched to all the pupils in the school. The headmaster's miserable *state* affected 120 small children and half-a-dozen members of staff, and then spread out to their families.

# Changing Emotional States

The good news about states is that you can change state when you feel that doing so is appropriate. In particular, the following sections cover the classic NLP approach known as *anchoring*, which enables you to access the precise states that serve you best, regardless of what's happening in the world around you.

For coaching to be most effective, both client and coach must be in *resourceful states*. You can describe a resourceful state as being alert, present, calm, clear, curious or creative – whatever words epitomise the best state for you.

## Checking the baseline state

To change state, you need to first tune into your *baseline state*, which is your normal, most familiar way of going through the day.

The following self-awareness exercise helps clients capture information about their baseline state and note how it shifts throughout the day.

1. **Have your client check in with herself for seven days, noting feelings at morning, noon and night.**

   Your clients may choose to write down the baseline state in words on a chart, put a colour code in her diary, drop pebbles in different jars, affix coloured sticky notes to a calendar or draw symbols such as smiley and sad faces. Be as creative as you like in co-creating this bank of information.

2. **After gathering enough information, analyse the data.**

   Have your client review the data herself prior to session so that she can answer the following:

   - What specific activities affect her baseline states for better and worse?
   - How have her states triggered behaviour?
   - What effects do various people or situations have on her states?
   - When is she at her best and her worst on a regular basis?

3. **At a subsequent session, ask questions about the client's observations and what the client might *want* to have happen differently in future.**

   If she identified that she regularly feels glum, for example, then the coaching could focus on ways to rise above that rather lonely place.

Or if she finds that certain activities make her feel really good, she may want to consider how to allocate more time to those things.

4. **Design actions together that give the client the opportunity to try on new ways of behaving and being.**

   Perhaps she sets her intention to celebrate successes as she goes along and have more fun. (Chapter 5 offers useful advice on taking action.)

When clients are aware of their natural baseline states, they have a reference point from which they can consciously change how they operate. In the next section, I explore changing states through the process of anchoring.

## Anchoring positive states

An *anchor* is an external stimulus that triggers a particular inner state or response. You respond to anchors all the time; you know to check your phone when you hear a text message alert or to head to the kitchen when you smell dinner cooking. You may have inadvertently set negative anchors like shouting or scowling when something displeases you. You've stored these stimuli and responses in your memory bank over a period of time as you develop habits.

Memories offer powerful resources to trigger a positive shift in emotional state, and NLP taps into these with anchoring. Various NLP techniques enable you to set an anchor to create a particular state. Most usually, NLP coaches encourage clients to set an anchor such as a distinctive hand movement to trigger a particular state. Some clients prefer to use sounds and images as anchors. See the following sidebar 'Circle of Excellence success' for just one example.

The following Circle of Excellence exercise works by anchoring a positive experience enjoyed in one context to a hand movement. After an experience is anchored, clients can then fire off this anchor to change state when they're in challenging situations.

Describe the following steps and anchoring process to clients before going through the actual steps. You may want to show clients a few hand movements commonly used in anchoring.

Suggested things to say to the client throughout the following steps appear in italics.

1. **Invite the client to describe a situation that she finds challenging and where she'd like to change her emotional state.**

ANECDOTE

## Circle of Excellence success

Hayley knew that she wanted to lead project management workshops for a high-tech business with infectious energy. However, she found creating this high-performance state tough, particularly on days when she left for work early, so she asked her coach to help create this desired state. Hayley also wanted to be able to create some calm and reflective states for times later in the training, during which she could encourage people to quietly reflect on their project work.

Her coach took her through the Circle of Excellence exercise to anchor a series of positive states. First Hayley recalled a day when she was tired, yet found the energy to play a strong game of tennis. As she relived the experience, she found her hands naturally moving as if gripping her tennis racket. This generated her alert-and-energetic anchor to call up whenever she gives her introduction to the workshop.

She accesses this state by repeating the same hand-grip on an imaginary tennis racket.

For her calm and reflective state, Hayley recalled a particular piece of music that she hums in her head when all is calm for her. She anchored this experience by touching an imaginary CD in the palm of her left hand while the forefinger of her right hand made circular movements on the disc. She sets off the hand anchors discreetly without anyone noticing.

Her coach repeated the exercise with Hayley, accessing various memories for each resourceful state until both were confident that Hayley could change state at will. Hayley subsequently found that she could trigger a change in her state to consciously raise her energy levels for times in her workshops when she found her energy dipping a little and could shift quickly into the calm and reflective state when she wanted delegates to be calm and reflective too.

*Think of the situation in which you'd like to be different and imagine a circle on the ground in front of you about one metre in diameter.*

This imaginary circle is the client's Circle of Excellence.

2. **Stand outside the circle with the client and have her identify the positive state she wants to create.**

   *Identify your best state. Tell me what that state is in your own words.*

   Allow time for the client to describe the positive state. All you're looking for here is a couple of sentences of description or some key words.

3. **Have the client experience the positive state again.**

   *Remember a time when you were* [repeat back the client's descriptive words] . . . *Go back to it strongly . . . See what you saw then. Hear what you heard.*

   Ask the client to step inside the circle and experience the positive state even more vividly.

*Re-live that experience. Make it vivid; be there in it with all your senses. Feel what your hands are doing. Now, hold or* anchor *that state with a hand movement at the point when the memory is most vivid.*

After the client anchors the experience, ask her to step outside the circle.

4. **Repeat the exercise with a second experience of a positive state, anchoring the most vivid experience of the feeling with the same hand motion.**

5. **Invite the client to describe the time in the future when she wants to access this state.**

6. **After identifying the future event, ask the client to step inside the circle again as if stepping into the actual event and do the anchored hand motion.**

*With your hand in your anchored position, move into the circle. See, hear and feel how the experience can be for you now.*

Give the client time to enjoy and integrate the feeling of the positive state.

7. **After the client experiences the positive step, ask her to step back out of the circle.**

*Relax . . . you've got it!*

Encourage clients to practise using this hand movement a few times between coaching sessions to remind themselves of the technique.

## *Allowing negative states to slide away*

Historically, the annual performance evaluations that managers gave to their subordinates dwelled on negatives, utilising a 'things you could do better' approach. Fortunately, this attitude is starting to change as more managers become trained in coaching and understand that personal transformation happens when you champion other people's strengths and successes in order to harness their potential.

As people are encouraged to pay more attention to what they're good at, the negatives slip away. Clients shift into *flow states*, finding a sense of ease and self-confidence. (Read more on flow states in Chapter 9.)

When you're working with teams, the best scenario is to acknowledge and celebrate the strengths of individuals and the diverse qualities each team member brings. The power of the team is more than the sum of the individuals in it. As you notice what's working, the negatives slide away and the positive emotional connections grow.

The following exercise is based on one used by US coach Jan Elfline in her master classes. I present the exercise as a team activity, but you can adapt it for an individual coaching session by inviting your clients to talk through or write about their successes.

1. **Ask each member of the team to privately identify three personal successes and three business successes and make a brief note of them. Have them prepare to be interviewed about the successes.**

2. **Have each team member interview colleagues, asking them to share one success.**

   Have each team member interview up to six colleagues. If the team is six individuals or smaller, allow everyone to share one example each in a series of rounds.

3. **Complete six rounds of interviews, allowing each team member to share one story per round.**

   Each person should tell a story only once.

4. **Reconvene in a circle and highlight the successes of each team member.**

   Go round the group, team member by team member, and have others share a success story that relates to that person.

# Tackling Interference from Gremlins

*Gremlins* are the aspects of people's identities that may get in the way of their natural resourcefulness by playing havoc with their emotional states. Gremlins hold you back from action or criticise what you do. They're like little pesky goblins who dance around and make mischief, nagging at your clients and amplifying their insecurities.

Gremlins play on your emotions in a negative way and take on various forms. The following sections look at three examples of gremlins that often pop up.

- ✔ **The peacekeeper gremlin** avoids confrontation at any cost.
- ✔ **The perfectionist gremlin** is impossible to please because perfection is unattainable.
- ✔ **The procrastinator gremlin** wants to put off today's task until tomorrow.

Many other gremlins are out there, so keep watch for them in coaching conversations and point them out to your clients if you sense a gremlin is lurking. While some coaching models get rid of the gremlins, the NLP approach is to honour them as an important part of your identity. When you treat gremlins as offering valuable information, you can gain wisdom from their gifts. I prefer to treat them as inner team members who bring a different quality to my clients' goals. Clients can take gremlins out of their boxes when needed and keep them in place if not invited. In Chapter 19, I look at integrating different parts of a person's identity, noticing that each part has a positive intent for the whole. The challenge is to find the positive aspect of a gremlin keep it out of mischief unless useful.

## Shaking up the peacekeeper gremlin

The peacekeeper gremlin fears taking any action that may rock the boat and wants to wave the white flag at the first sign of a battle. Its job is to keep a person safely out of danger. However, 'put up and shut up' is the implicit message from the peacekeeper gremlin when taken to extremes:

- ✔ Why file for divorce when you can put up with a toxic marriage?

- ✔ Why tell a friend she's outstayed her welcome when she'll leave eventually?

- ✔ Why discipline an employee when you're changing jobs anyway?

- ✔ Why tell your boss she's being unreasonable if you can just quietly ignore her?

Peace in itself is a worthy goal, yet fear of any conflict or willingness to air a different view means you settle for a better-than-nothing kind of life.

At 19, Alex married a much older man with whom she had four children. Her husband held a responsible middle-management job in banking and refused point blank to support Alex's desire to go to college, study, get a job and have money she could call her own. He wanted a gorgeous wife at home, responsible for doing the cooking, cleaning and making the home attractive for entertaining his clients. By her early thirties, Alex decided that divorce was the only way to create a better life for herself because her husband would never discuss any problems with their marriage. (Indeed, he's never spoken to her or the children since the break-up.) Alex recognised that her strong peacekeeping desire came in the form of her mother's voice telling her to keep quiet and don't make a fuss. Her mother, who remained in a controlling marriage of her own, believed Alex was lucky to have a comfortable home and children. Alex recognised that her peacekeeper gremlin had served her well, yet it was time to be more challenging and face confrontation. When she found herself feeling that she couldn't air her views, she learnt to park the gremlin. Alex is now a teacher in a special needs unit living in a smaller, more chaotic home, yet she's very happy to be independent.

One way to tame the peacekeeper gremlin is to learn to have courageous conversations. Clients can prepare for these emotionally with the anchoring techniques described earlier in the section 'Anchoring positive states' and by planning out the words to give feedback without confrontation (Chapter 14 offers a valuable structure). When clients are in touch with their values, choosing which battles they want to fight to honour those values is easier.

## Messing with the perfectionist gremlin

Many clients recognise their perfectionist gremlins and realise that they take huge amounts of energy. Not only is perfection impossible, it causes you to agonise about and go over tasks and projects so that they never get completed. Nothing is really good enough as you seek examples of perfect lives portrayed in glossy style magazines or glowing celebrity profiles.

One way to counter perfectionism in your clients is to share Pareto's principle or the 80/20 rule. This states that 80 per cent of your results come from 20 per cent of your effort. The cost of perfection is that it takes 80 per cent more time to squeeze out the extra 20 per cent of result. This principle leads you to pay greater attention to the opportunity costs of going the extra mile all the time.

Of course, perfectionism may also have its roots in the past where a person perceived her efforts weren't good enough to please a parent, teacher, partner or boss. In this case, you can uncover the limiting beliefs and support your clients to create new, more empowering ones for themselves. (Chapter 17 gives you ideas.)

## Firing up the procrastinator gremlin

The procrastinator gremlin thrives on creating distractions, causing noise and activity that diverts you from your main focus. Procrastinator gremlins can be quite entertaining and even provide much needed relaxation or thinking time. 'Let's go shopping instead of doing that job now' or 'Let's just have another cup of tea and chat' are some appealing versions of this gremlin.

The counter-tactic for the procrastinator gremlin is to introduce more structure and bursts of focused time on identifiable activities.

Ask your clients to identify how specifically the procrastinator distracts them. What temptations does this little gremlin offer? A chance to go shopping? Spend time gossiping over coffee? A temporarily satisfying trip to raid the fridge, read a magazine or surf the net? Then invite your clients to:

- ✔ Measure the time spent on distractions.
- ✔ Decide what benefits you want to keep and what you want to let go of.
- ✔ Assign a cost to your distractions in terms of money or lost opportunities elsewhere.
- ✔ Identify ways to diminish the distractions.

When clients are procrastinating, I invite them to allocate just one power hour each day to the critical task in hand. It's not even a whole hour of work; just a commitment to spend 50 minutes of dedicated time and then take a ten-minute break. Clients who follow through with this technique have permission after one hour to stop or keep going. Most often, after starting, people spend longer on the task and get into the groove, leaving their procrastinating behind.

## Drawing your gremlins

The following exercise can help clients identify a group of gremlins that are causing trouble and decide how to get these pesky critters working for a living.

1. **Give your client a large sheet of blank paper and several coloured pens.**

2. **Invite her to identify her cast of gremlins with pictures and words.**

    Encourage your client to give the gremlins names and personalities. Start with the top three, and she may come up with two or three more.

3. **Discuss with the client each gremlin's attributes, observing all the positive benefits that they bring.**

4. **Ask the client to decide what positive role to allocate to each gremlin and find a way that each can be of service to the coaching agenda.** One client, Tessa, who called one gremlin Scaredy Cat, says this character is in charge of highlighting risks when big decisions loom.

5. **Identify how each gremlin may creep in unwanted and list strategies to keep each one at bay.** The Scaredy Cat gremlin can prevent Tessa enjoying parties, so she imagines tucking the gremlin in a pet-carrier on social occasions when he can be a nuisance.

By personifying gremlins, you have a shorthand way to identify and discuss them. Being able to say something like 'Ah, sounds like Penelope Perfectionist has just popped up' or 'That's Peter the Fixer speaking again' helps you recognise when the gremlin is butting into a situation without an invitation to do so and reduces non-productive self-criticism.

# Overcoming Fear

Fear centres on the expectation of something unpleasant or undesirable happening in the future. Fear can freeze your clients to the spot or trigger frantic action to get away from the fear. Fear is a proven motivator, yet it's one that leaves people feeling drained of energy and operating below their potential.

Sometimes the fear isn't tangible or even rational to articulate – a sense that things aren't right. Although fear can keep you from achieving some goals, it can also serve as a useful warning mechanism.

When Jason was on holiday with a group of friends, several of them decided on an adventure activity – swinging through woodland on ropes – but as it came to Jason's turn to jump off a high ledge, he felt inside that he shouldn't do it and refused to go ahead, not really knowing why. The following day he had problems seeing out of one eye and ended up in hospital with a detached retina. The specialist told him that if he'd jumped, he may well have lost his sight permanently. He subsequently pays a lot of attention to his instinctive feelings.

To let go of fear and build confidence, clients must recognise the sensation of fear and face up to what may be unnerving them. Some common fears that people bring to coaching include:

- **Finance and possessions.** Do I have enough money? Can I buy the right car, house, clothing, treats? What if I lose my treasured belongings?

- **Loneliness and rejection.** Will anyone like/love me? Does anyone care about me? Will I lose my job?

- **Knowledge.** Do I know enough? Am I clever enough? Will others find me out?

- **Judgement.** Will I hear something critical about me that I don't like?

- **Privacy.** What happens if I tell people about a personal aspect of me? Can I hide in the wings quietly?

- **Bad experiences.** Will I repeat past mistakes yet again?

- **Courage.** How can I say what I really think and state what I want?

Ask any of the following questions in coaching sessions to explore fear:

- How are you experiencing the fear?
- Is your fear – or someone else's – driving you?
- What does your fear give you?
- What would you rather have in place of the fear?
- How will life be better for you as soon as you let go of this fear?
- What ideas do you already have for getting rid of this fear?
- What's one small and easy step you can take right now to release yourself from the fear?
- How would you leapfrog your fear?

## Championing natural confidence

When clients come to coaching saying that they have no confidence, they are generalising from one or more specific incidents to a broader sense of stuckness in which they no longer acknowledge themselves. They've lost connection with their natural, healthy state of emotional well-being.

Confidence requires the feeling that everything will be okay, regardless of events, people and circumstances. It requires you to trust yourself from your very core and not allow negative emotions to get in the way of getting on with what you want or need to do.

Sadly, no magic confidence pills and potions exist; ultimately, developing confidence is in your clients' hands.

In *Building Self-Confidence For Dummies* (Wiley), my co-author Brinley Platts and I give this definition of confidence:

> *At its heart, confidence is the ability to take appropriate and effective action in any situation, however challenging it appears to you or others.*

In order to take action, clients need to recognise themselves at their most confident. Unfortunately, under stress they delete this information. 'I'm never confident' or 'I've lost it' they say. Yet given time and space to relax and think about their previous experiences, they can find times when they were extremely confident. For example, one coaching client suffered a loss of self-confidence due to a micro-managing boss and job that required busy reactionary work, yet she had enormous confidence in setting up a charity.

As coach, encourage your clients to notice for themselves times when they felt confident. Have them describe these experiences as precisely as possible. Table 18-1 provides a form to capture these times and shows an example. Such experiences act as references that can then be anchored using the Circle of Excellence technique in the section 'Anchoring positive states' earlier in this chapter.

If people really struggle with identifying their own states of confidence, invite them to find role models who demonstrate the qualities that they'd like to adopt. Then get them to imagine behaving as if they were the role model, noticing what they'd be thinking or experiencing.

| Table 18-1 | Confident Experiences | | |
| --- | --- | --- | --- |
| *Where was I and what was I doing when I felt most confident?* | *What assumptions did I make about myself and others?* | *What enabled me to feel confident?* | *Give a label to this state of confidence. How exactly did I feel?* |
| When I posed for my graduation photograph with my parents. | That I could achieve something difficult through my own efforts. | Knowing that my hard work had paid off. | Excited and contented. |

After clients create their set of positive reference experiences, work with them to anchor the experiences for the future or to remind them of these experiences when they are struggling.

## Releasing phobias fast

Clients bring all kinds of insecurities to coaching that can be talked through and dealt with logically. Occasionally someone arrives with a phobic response that gets in the way of her everyday life. Her emotional state is destabilised by thinking of the thing she fears. I've had clients who fear travelling on escalators or in lifts, driving across motorway bridges and flying. Their extreme emotions create strong physical reactions including stomach cramps and panic attacks. Such fears aren't logical, and they can have a debilitating effect on everyday life. Yet when they're overcome, the clients experience a sense of freedom that's a joy to see.

### Separating emotion and memory cinematically

NLP offers a very helpful technique called the *Fast Phobia Cure* that desensitises clients from trauma or phobia. The technique works by separating – or *dissociating* – images from emotion in the client's memory. This dissociation occurs by having clients watch themselves sitting in a cinema (dissociation), while watching themselves on a cinema screen (double dissociation). The technique is also useful if someone has had a bad experience, such as doing a presentation that didn't go well.

Only use this technique in a place where clients feel very comfortable and safe and if you feel competent to keep your client relaxed and calm if she feels panicky. Read through this section carefully and practise on a coaching buddy to be clear on the process. Ensure that before you begin, you create a safe spot where your client can stop the exercise if it feels too challenging. Remind the client that she was safe before the unpleasant experience and that she's safe now.

After you identify a client's phobic response to a stimulus or a traumatic or unpleasant memory, go through the following with her to help her overcome her phobic responses. This technique works well sitting on a comfortable sofa in a quiet, private room.

1. **Imagine yourself sitting in the cinema, watching yourself projected as a small black and white image on the screen.** Invite your client to think about having a drink and some popcorn to get her into the experience; you could hand her a TV remote control and do the exercise imagining looking at a TV screen.

2. **Imagine floating out of the you that's sitting in the cinema seat and into the projection booth.**

3. **See yourself in the projection booth, watching yourself in the seat as well as watching the film of you on the screen.**

4. **As the projectionist, run the film in black and white, as a very tiny image.**

   Start the film at a point before you experienced the unpleasant memory you want to overcome and run it through until after the experience when you were safe.

5. **Freeze the film or turn the screen completely white.**

6. **Float out of the projection booth, out of the seat, up onto the screen and into the end of the film.**

7. **Run the film backwards very quickly, in a matter of a second or two, in full colour.**

Experience the film from end (where you are safe) to beginning (where you also are safe).

8. **Run the film backwards and forwards several times, always stopping at a safe spot.**

   Repeat this step until you're comfortable with the experience.

9. **Test for completion.** Ask the client to leave the cinema and come back to the present time. Have her imagine a time coming up when she may experience the phobic response, such as a flight if she fears flying. Ask how she feels about it now. If she doesn't display the phobic response, then the phobia cure has been effective. You can repeat the exercise until your client is fully desensitised to the unpleasant experience.

If you don't feel confident in doing this exercise with a client, consider inviting an NLP-trained coach to work with and support your client to find the secondary gain of the phobia.

---

# Exploring the mind-body link

For centuries, the medical profession has treated the mind and body separately, and this division affected how people think about emotions on a daily basis with the brain and the body split. However, NLP has always argued that the mind and body are inextricably linked, and contemporary research developments in neuroscience prove this to be true. Now we have scientific evidence of the integration of emotional and physical health.

Science has traditionally asserted that the limbic system in the brain controlled emotion, conveying feelings from one neuron to the next via the synaptic gaps between neurons. However, painstaking research by Dr Candace Pert and other leading neuroscientists shows that *peptides,* the chemical keys that take information to the cells, and their receptors are not necessarily communicating across the synaptic gap. In addition, peptides and receptors are not communicating exclusively in the central nervous system (brain and spinal cord). In fact, these peptides and receptors appear throughout the body's cells, allowing communication across systems. Often the brain is last to know what's happening in your body!

Dr Pert's popular book *Molecules of Emotion: Why You Feel the Way You Feel (Scribner, 1997),* details her research and theories. Today she lectures worldwide on how humans hold emotion in each cell in their bodies.

At a practical level, her advice makes perfect sense. To be healthy, people must be aware of their mental, emotional and physical experiences. In particular, she advocates noticing the effects of emotional states on your body, paying attention to messages from your unconscious mind via dreams and getting in touch with your body via body work, movement or touch. To reduce emotional stress, she recommends exercising and eating wisely, which includes avoiding substances such as sugar and caffeine – all good advice for coaches to share with clients to manage their emotional states.

### Identifying – and substituting – secondary gains

As a starting point to defuse the emotional over-reaction, you can support your client conversationally without tackling the phobia directly. Simply find out the phobia's *secondary gain*. What are the positive benefits your client gets from the phobia? If these benefits can all be met in other ways, the phobia may disappear of its own accord.

Lucas had a fear of flying that threw him into a panic when he was about to board an aircraft. He worked in an office where he didn't have a lot in common with his co-workers; they were much older ladies and more interested in their children and grandchildren than work. However, they were always interested to hear about his holiday or business trips and how he'd coped with the travelling. He realised that this was the one time when he had proper conversations with his colleagues. His fear also gave him plenty of sympathy from his travelling companions who went out of their way to make his journey less stressful and gave him the seat of his choice.

# Chapter 19

# Connecting All Parts of a Person

● ● ● ● ● ● ● ● ● ● ● ● ● ● ● ● ● ● ● ● ● ● ● ● ● ● ● ● ● ● ● ● ● ● ● ● ● ● ● ● ● ● ● ● ● ● ● ● ● ● ● ● ●

## In This Chapter

▶ Supporting clients through change

▶ Integrating personal parts to create a whole person

▶ Overcoming internal conflicts

▶ Placing a different frame around a situation

● ● ● ● ● ● ● ● ● ● ● ● ● ● ● ● ● ● ● ● ● ● ● ● ● ● ● ● ● ● ● ● ● ● ● ● ● ● ● ● ● ● ● ● ● ● ● ● ● ● ● ● ●

*W*henever you hear your client say 'Well, part of me . . . and another part of me . . .', you have wonderful material to work with. 'Part of me wants to be a pop star and part wants to be a plumber,' one client says about her dream career. 'Part of me is feeling angry and part of me is relieved,' another client says when he loses his job. Venturing into the tensions, desires and challenges of these different parts can yield rich information and newfound self-awareness for your clients.

In this chapter, I look at ways you can identify and integrate your clients' seemingly conflicting parts, and in the process, help clients move safely through transitions, overcome the conflicts and tap into new resources.

## Splitting into Parts

In life, you split yourself into many parts. Some of the splitting happens within conscious awareness. Perhaps you already know a part of you likes a challenge, yet you may be less aware that another part gets troubled by conflict until this part of you becomes problematic because you don't like giving bad news to colleagues or feeling you haven't done the best possible job.

Splitting off part of yourself to the point where you ignore that part isn't successful. Danger lies in not honouring the value that one part contributes to the whole. As a coach, you're encouraging your clients to accept their whole selves without judgement and to acknowledge the disconnect between different parts as they work to find a coherent sense of identity. Your clients progress as they work to accept all aspects of themselves without judgement.

NLP suggests that these parts are *non-integrated fragments* of the client's whole mind. Each has its own purpose and function and presents different intentions that show up in behaviour. Often these fragments appear as if they're involuntary. You may hear your client say, 'I don't know what came over me!' or 'That's not me talking.' A part may take on the identity of a disapproving parent as in 'That part was my father talking.'

Each part is likely to have its own beliefs and value system. Parts bring trouble when the behaviour of one part doesn't match up with – or is *out of alignment with* – desirable adult behaviour.

Parts often split off as a result of significant emotional experiences when you are young. Marco talked about the part of himself that feels guilty for not doing enough for his mother. He traces this feeling back to the time that he saw his mother crying in distress when he was a small lad and felt helpless to soothe her. His part that 'can't do enough for others' caused him problems until he identified it and resolved it with the NLP parts integration exercise, which appears in the later section 'Integrating conflicting parts'.

# *Keeping Everyone Supported during Change*

Just imagine how life would be without change. Everything is predictable and under control – but nothing is fresh or new either. Perhaps most significantly, no growth happens. However much a Peter Pan type of existence in the idyllic world of Neverland might appeal, you have to grow up and face change at regular points in life and work.

Some changes are welcome; others are shocking and most unwelcome. Times of transition cause heart-searching and confusion even when the change is desired and welcome. 'Part of me knows the old way has gone, and part of me fears the new' is the implicit message when split emotions, split loyalties and split identities show up.

Coaching offers a fabulous resource to your clients going through times of transition when they need to let go of one part of their lives in order to embrace another. Coaches understand the value of a safe *bridging space*, a supportive place with a competent professional who wants the best for you where you can make adjustments, explore dilemmas and experiment with new approaches. It's a place where clients feel acknowledged and respected for their whole selves without having to have all the answers.

# Building on past experiences

Often people aren't aware they've even been through a transition until they find they've reached the other side and are able to look back and see how they grew and changed.

The following exercise enables your clients to pay attention to their natural ability to make the most of knowledge they gained from earlier transitions and apply them to current and future situations.

1. **Invite your client to note down seven events in his life that he considers transitions.**

   Some examples of transitions include:

   - **At home:** going to school, shifting from the teenage years into adulthood, learning to drive, leaving home, getting married, having children, changing partners or spouses, losing a loved one.

   - **At work:** starting your first job, losing a job, hiring or firing an employee, going through a merger, experiencing reorganisation, being promoted or demoted, changing careers.

2. **For each experience, ask the client a series of questions.**

   - Did you plan for this experience?

   - Did you recognise it as a transition at the time?

   - How did you experience it?

   - How did you adjust to the new situation?

3. **Invite the client to create a summary of what he discovered about himself from the earlier transitions.**

   Pay particular attention to (and if necessary guide the client to identify) what or who supported him and what or who held him back.

4. **Get the client to identify possible changes he'll face in the future and ask what action the client can take now to build resilience.**

   Encourage the client to identify what he needs to remind himself of in the moment. This can include asking for additional help from someone, increasing exercise or sleep, building up a financial buffer or learning new skills.

5. **Plan with your client what he needs to keep on track when challenges arise.**

For example, does the client need a visual or written reminder? Some people like to have an image or small object, others a list of tips or a spreadsheet or other document that they complete to stay on track.

## Checking for ecology

During transitions, the coach is looking at the whole person, holding the space for the individual and gently reminding the client of the complete picture of his identity. Clients, by contrast, are often focused on one part of their identities.

The classic question 'What do you want?' needs to take especial account of what the whole person wants at times of change, not just the part that's dominating at one time. What else is going on in the bigger context?

The unspoken Hippocratic oath of coaching is to leave the person in a healthy place – and definitely not in a worse place than when you started.

Consider a situation where a corporate client in the midst of a merger is angry at one of his subordinates and says: 'I want this person out of here today,' in a fit of frustration. Before the client speeds into the how of going through an exit process, you as coach can hold the space for the client to assess what is lost or gained by going for this outcome. This is the ecology check of a well-formed outcome. You can invite all parts of the client to the discussion. Is the client speaking from a rational place or from a hurry-up impatient part that the client may regret later?

Likewise, when a client going through redundancy announces an intention to leave his life partner in a blaze of anger, the coach can give the client the breathing space to check if this is the real desired outcome.

To check for ecology, ask your client the following questions:

- ✔ What will that outcome do for you?
- ✔ What's the impact on others around you if you go for that outcome?
- ✔ What's the real value to you?
- ✔ What do you stand to lose or gain?
- ✔ Is this the best or only way to achieve the outcome you want?

The answers highlights warning signals if a client is about to make a decision he'll regret. Then you can work with him on finding better approaches that fit with his values and meet the well-formed outcome conditions from Chapter 7.

# Establishing the bale-out position

Coaching provides a safe space for your clients to escape and take a breather from the rough and tumble of everyday life. Your sessions may be the only quiet space your clients have. Knowing that they can find that sense of calm and reflection in their coaching time with you can encourage them to replicate further bale-out space to think or recharge themselves elsewhere in their schedules.

When people are going through a particularly unwelcome situation, such as a family conflict or redundancy, the key questions are 'What will make you more resourceful?' And perhaps even: 'What will make this transition more fun?' or 'How can you take real value and new growth from this time?'

Julia found herself in a state of transition after she gave up her job in the UK as a hospital pharmacist because her husband took an international assignment. Much of her time was spent in a company-owned apartment in the US, and the rest was spent on planes to and from the family home in the UK. She took the opportunity to arm herself with dozens of books that she'd wanted to read for years. She also hired a private trainer to get her running longer distances, something else that she'd never had the chance to do when working full-time.

The following sections explore some ways that people can create bale-out spaces.

### Find an engrossing project or hobby

Your clients have amazing, untapped talents. Encourage them to pick activities that are more extreme than normal, ones that shift them out of their normal sphere and take them to different places physically or mentally.

Finding an activity that shifts focus into a completely different sphere unlocks creativity. Consider off-the-beaten-path hobbies such as building model airplanes, constructing garden gazebos, designing free software, creating patchwork quilts, cooking exotic meals, creating mosaics, pole dancing, producing rap music, visiting old train routes or exploring hidden churches – whatever seems fun and different. Consider something you dreamed of as a child and never had the opportunity to pursue, or something you used to do when young and don't any more.

### Take time to recharge alone

Disjointed lives gobble up huge amounts of energy. People benefit from factoring in real down-time into their schedules with no commitments to do anything. Just like an athlete who needs to rest in order to operate at peak performance, so too more regular mortals need to balance rest with exertion.

During transitions, people's natural rhythms get disturbed, especially sleep patterns. One of the first questions I ask clients under stress is how much sleep and rest they're getting. And I don't mean slouched on the sofa in front of the TV. Calm, relaxing space and undisturbed sleep make a huge difference to people's resilience.

Invite your clients to award themselves with as much sleep as they can possibly handle and create a down-time routine at night that shuts off phones, TVs and technology before moving into their clear, quiet spaces where they can sleep well and dream to their heart's content. Just making a commitment to 30 to 60 minutes more sleep a night can start to yield results in a week or so.

Dreams offer great insights for coaching. Just asking the simple question 'What do you dream of?' may open up an unexpected line of enquiry.

### Identify other people with similar experiences

Real value comes from a client connecting with someone else who knows exactly what the client is experiencing. This connection is not about expert advice, but simply having access to an ordinary person who knows what it's like to go back to work after a break, lose a home, suffer a health setback, leave a child at a nursery for the first time or work in a disaster zone.

### Set aside thinking time

People need time alone for thoughts to bubble around and settle, time when the world isn't coming at them.

One executive I know walks off into the tall glass stairwell of his office building to give himself private thinking time away from his desk. Another uses her time when travelling by train to switch off from doing work to thinking alone with gentle background music on her headphones. Yet another chooses his quiet moments by walking his faithful old Labrador dog slowly across the fields and connecting with the outdoors.

Through coaching, people realise that the answers they seek are accessible to them when they give themselves space to think. Encourage your clients to create more of this time for themselves beyond the coaching environment. Clients need time to ponder some of the questions that arise in sessions and explore the larger life inquiries you leave them with. (See Chapter 6 for more on inquiries.)

### Lay the foundation with physical self-care

Eating and exercise rituals go haywire during times of transition, and people forget how important these are to maintaining equilibrium. You hear that some people completely overeat when anxious, packing in the food as if famine beckons. Yet for others, the opposite is the case as they lose their appetite or forget to eat.

On the exercise front, your clients may find it tough to commit to a regular routine when life is unsettled – maybe when they're commuting between countries or jobs, in the midst of a house move or recovering from an accident.

In both diet and exercise, you can support your client to find healthy ways to fuel mind and body. Get them to consider other rewards such as a massage or nail and hair treatments, which can make all the difference between feeling neglected and cared for. (This recommendation goes for the men as well as the ladies!)

Monica's high-powered job as an adviser in international development takes her all over the world to meetings and conferences. Like many with her lifestyle, she find herself torn between wanting to be at home with family and the dog in her native US and doing the job she loves that takes her into some impoverished developing countries. As a result, she pays particular attention to keeping herself fit and well. 'It may sound selfish, but long ago I recognised that unless I'm well, I can't do the job to look after the people I want to support.' Wherever she goes, Monica's suitcase is packed with supplies of healthy snacks from her favourite wholefood supplier, such as almonds and seeds for a speedy meal on the move. She includes an array of colourful warm scarves that make her feel good and seeks out a local masseur for a neck and shoulder treatment between meetings. Each day, she begins with a 15-minute yoga session followed by a short tummy tightening routine she's developed to do on the floor of her hotel bedroom. 'Work can be punishing, so I need my creature comforts and routines,' she says.

# *Developing a Unified Identity*

While this chapter's preceding sections focus on recognising the various parts of people's personalities, this section examines ways to shift to a sense of wholeness at an identity level – ways to integrate all those disparate bits and quirks to establish a unified person.

As you go through the following sections, consider situations where you sense tension, perhaps even in your own life. You may sense conflicting roles, values that are hard to honour and unhelpful ways of behaving. For example, you may have a client who talks about a problem behaviour that conflicts with a better one, such as smoking conflicting with healthy eating. Or you may experience *role conflict*, such as when a client is someone's manager as well as his personal friend.

# Integrating conflicting parts

NLP assumes that all behaviour has a positive intent, so when working on behavioural change, you must recognise the positive side of the things you want to change. Parts integration activities work by honouring and keeping the positives and finding the common ground between separate parts.

The following parts integration exercise adds insight for the client who has two or more parts that are in conflict with each other. It involves chunking up each part to a higher level of positive intent (see Chapter 14 for more on chunking). In this way, you can find the connection between two apparently conflicting parts. (The later sidebar 'Saving the good through change' details a client's experience with this exercise.)

1. **Clearly identify two parts that are in conflict with each other.**

   Encourage the client to use all his senses to give some personality to each part. For example, like a little plastic character that comes in a cereal box or Christmas cracker, an image or a symbol.

   Invite the client to consider each part in turn, find the character or symbol that represents that part and imagine placing the symbol on each hand. For example, I might imagine having a pen that represents my writer part on one hand and a glittery dancing shoe symbolic of my party-going side on the other.

2. **Find the positive intention of each part as separate from the behaviour.**

   Start with a part that seems problematic and ask the client: 'What is the positive intention of this part of you? What does it want for you?'

   Make a note of the client's responses. With each answer he gives, chunk up to the higher positive intention by asking: 'And when you have that, what will it do for you?'

   Keep going higher and higher until you reach a fundamental concept or come up with one or several core values, such as love, security, freedom, connection, and so on. (See Chapter 8 on values.)

3. **Invite each part to inform the other of its positive intention.**

   Encourage the client to have the characters or symbols look at each other and talk to each other. Let the characters share with one another what they need.

4. **Have each part notice that they're part of a larger whole and share the same higher-level intention, such as having fun or feeling secure.**

ANECDOTE

# Saving the good through change

Dave likes to compete in cycle races and triathlons, yet this sporting part of him felt in conflict with his role as a dad with two small children. Dave's coach took him though the parts integration exercise I cover in the earlier section 'Integrating conflicting parts' and helped him identify the positive intention of the two parts of himself that were in conflict.

| *Part: Good Dad* | *Part: Competitive Sportsman* |
| --- | --- |
| Makes me take care of my family | Gets me outdoors |
| Gives me a sense of doing the right thing | Clears my head and keeps me fit |
| Makes me feel proud | Gives me space to let go of duty to anyone else |
| Makes me feel connected to them | Makes me feel free and connected to the world |
| I feel really grateful to have a loving family | Gives me a sense of love and gratitude |
| Makes me feel alive | Makes me feel as if I have a purpose |
| Shows me I have a sense of purpose | |

By going through the exercise, Dave realised that both parts of him had complementary intentions – a strong sense of purpose, connection, love and gratitude. Dave acknowledged that these are core elements to his identity and that they don't have to be mutually exclusive. He saw that he was able to enjoy both roles, yet he also needed more creative ways to connect his family life and sporting interests.

When his coach asked whether there were any other parts or qualities he needed, Dave realised that both parts needed extra fun and patience. With this in mind, he worked to find some practical ways around the time issue involved in pursuing both roles, keeping the need for a sense of humour and patience.

Inspire integration by telling the client, 'Each part needs the other parts to be complete. You aren't compromising. Each part of you is getting your fundamental needs met.'

Allow your client plenty of time and space for the internal processing that's happening.

After a few minutes, ask whether any part or quality needs to be added to make the whole complete. If so, bring that quality into the mix, introducing it to the other established parts.

5. **Integrate the parts.**

Gently suggest the client allows his hands to come together. The movement can be quite slow and deliberate. After the client sees his hands connecting, have him bring the parts inside symbolically by bringing his hands to his chest.

6. **Assist the client in planning for the future.**

Ask the client to think of a time in the future when a potential conflict may arise. Ask your client, 'What will it be like to have the two parts working together?' You can expect some positive affirmation that the two parts have a strong understanding of each other's needs.

If there are any qualities the client still needs after considering the future, invite him to identify the qualities and bring them inside too.

## Bringing the whole self into play

People who really take leading roles in their lives demonstrate *congruence*, the NLP idea of wholeness. A congruent person doesn't split into different characters. The person you see on Saturday is completely at ease with the person who's at work on Monday, regardless of the different roles he plays. When a person is *incongruent*, he's at odds with himself. An internal struggle is raging. On one day you see him act compassionately, on the next he gets angry about the same issue.

Congruence involves clarity, consistency and confidence. You recognise congruence in your clients when they:

✔ Say what they mean and mean what they say.

✔ Know their strengths and weak spots.

✔ Know where they're going and how to take others with them.

✔ Stay focused without succumbing to distractions.

✔ Have self-awareness and sensitivity to others.

✔ Are open to holding difficult conversations.

✔ Behave in consistent and confident ways.

✔ Know what their end goals are – their real purposes in life.

The following self-assessment exercise reveals insights into whether the whole self is coming into play. Use it to open up a conversation about how part of a client may not be aligned with the whole so that you can review new possibilities.

On a scale of 0 to 10 (where 0 is low and 10 is high), rate yourself on the following statements:

✔ I know why I'm doing what I'm doing.

✔ I feel that I'm confident and consistent in my activities.

✔ I know what my strengths are and where I need the support of others.

✔ I know how to ask others for what I want.

✔ I stay focused on where I'm going even if I hit difficult times.

Examine the areas with low ratings and invite your client to be curious about what's preventing him from getting higher scores here. These statements make good topics to bring to coaching to determine changes the client wants to make.

## Keeping a journal

Coaching sets clients on a path of self-discovery that unfolds with the coach as a trusted ally along the way. In the words of Joseph Campbell, they're on a Hero's Journey. By signing up for coaching, clients take that brave first step across the threshold from one world into another. Yet many journeys whizz by so fast that key landmarks get missed along the way.

---

### Embracing the dark side

Debbie Ford, author of *The Dark Side of the Light Chasers* (Mobius), argues that we'd like to disown parts of ourselves, and as we go through life we've tried to bury these aspects of ourselves beneath the surface. Yet like giant beach balls, they pop up to the surface the minute you try to keep them down.

'When we come face to face with our dark side our first instinct is to turn away and our second is to bargain with it to leave us alone,' she says.

Yet the hidden sides can offer the most valuable treasures.

She argues that we need to truly embrace all aspects of ourselves, loving our faults and all they have to teach us. 'We can't have the full experience of the light without knowing the dark. The dark side is the gatekeeper to true freedom.'

By reconciling the darker impulses, you can find the gifts they offer and reclaim wholeness once more.

Journaling simply involves capturing thoughts regularly in a notebook. It provides one way to pay greater attention to the coaching journey clients are undertaking. Often people fail to look back and see how far they've come.

In the pages of a journal, you can capture practical information – the goals, inquiries, actions, successes and challenges. However, an even more powerful role for this activity is when a journal provides blank space for clients to allow their free-ranging thoughts to come tumbling onto a page between coaching sessions. At these moments, journaling becomes an open conversation with yourself.

Writing doesn't immediately appeal to everybody as a way of noticing experiences. Many people feel blocked when confronted with the blank page of a new journal because they believe they aren't good enough to be writers. In a similar way, people who don't think they are artists avoid drawing or even doodling for fear of going public with their work. Remind reluctant clients that writers and artists hone their crafts from basic first attempts. Creative work isn't about perfection or judgement on anyone's part. Using tools such as journaling enables unconscious thoughts to become conscious.

Dive into any stationery or book shop these days and you'll find a wonderful range of notebooks and pens. Invite your clients to choose the most appealing ones they can find and encourage them to write free hand anything that occurs to them between sessions about the topics and inquiries that come up. They may well enjoy illustrating their ideas too. The physical action of connecting pen to paper – rather than fingers to keyboard, phone or screen – offers a pleasurable way to tap into their creativity and capture the lessons along the way.

Journaling works best as a regular habit. Set aside a time in the day to write, on waking or before going to bed.

# Reframing the Situation

You may have heard the famous tale told in NLP circles about the therapist Milton Erickson meeting a patient in a mental institution who was under the delusion that he (the patient) was Jesus Christ. Erickson is reputed to have said to the patient that it was good to find a carpenter and set him to work on fixing the building.

In this interaction, Erickson shifted to the *as-if frame*, behaving as if the client's perception were true. Doing so actually supported the patient's return to health. In the context of the institution, the client is mad; in the context of the client's own beliefs, he is a carpenter called Jesus.

NLP suggests that the meaning of any interaction is dependent on the context, so by changing the context you can change the meaning. Think about it: in one political system, a person may be considered a hero for killing someone else, while in another system he's punished as a villain. In one organisation certain behaviours are expected, in another they are frowned upon. One person complains about having a painful leg, while another is delighted to have legs to swing out of bed in the morning.

This idea of *reframing* involves putting a different frame or context around what you're working with in order to change the way you think and experience a situation. The following sections cover the key aspects of reframing that you can utilise with your clients.

## Adopting various frames

Many frames exist that offer a sense of structure to your client's experience. Some typical frames that you can adopt in your coaching conversations include the:

- **As-if frame,** which allows people to explore future options as if they were already happening. What you can say here is: 'Let's act *as if* you had already achieved your goal and look back on what you did to get there.'

- **Contrast frame,** which compares two different experiences and enables clients to discover new things by checking for difference. To use this frame, you might ask: 'What was it that made a difference there that could really help you now?'

- **Back-track frame,** which focuses on what you've just heard from your client to clarify a situation. You might say: 'If I can play that back to you, this is what's happening in a nutshell . . .'

- **Outcome frame,** which shifts the attention to what is desirable rather than staying caught up in the problem. Base the questions you ask on the well-formed outcome process in Chapter 7, particularly 'What do you want?' and 'What will that do for you?'

Verbal frames offer tools for coaches to shape up their words in a conversation. Sometimes sharing the power of different frames with the client is valuable, as in Chapter 14 which compares the use of problem or blame-frame questions to the outcome frame. Work by Robert Dilts in his book *Sleight of Mouth* demonstrates the power of subtle changes in the use of language to determine the quality of people's experience. Even simple connective word like 'and' or 'but' focus a listener's attention in different ways. NLP calls this verbal reframing.

# Reframing in six steps

This section looks at the classic NLP Six-Step Reframe exercise for changing a behaviour that isn't congruent with the rest of the person. In this six-step frame, you work with your client to find creative ways to change this behaviour by accessing a part of the client that knows inside, unconsciously, what needs to happen.

1. **Identify a problem behaviour.**

   Get clear about what it is that the client wants to change.

   Some examples of behaviours that aren't congruent with the whole person include inappropriate behaviours with other people, with money, with alcohol, food or substance use. You can use this exercise to address unwanted physical symptoms such as headaches and involve the unconscious mind in healing.

2. **Help the client connect with the part of himself responsible for the problem behaviour and find the positive intent.** Typically one part is responsible, but if there are several, treat them as one responsible group.

   Invite your client to 'Go inside and say hello to the part of you that's responsible for this behaviour. Do this without any blame or criticism to that part – make it feel welcome to come forward!'

   Allow your client time to find and connect with the responsible part. During this part of the process, your client may hear a sound, see an image or experience a feeling connected with the behaviour. (For example, the client may hear a jarring noise, see an image of a mountain or feel a churning movement in his stomach.)

   If your client struggles to connect with the responsible part, explore the submodalities of his experience. You can read more about submodalities in Chapter 17.

   After connecting with the responsible part, ask the client to thank the part responsible for responding.

   Have the client ask the part 'What is your positive intention for me?' Expect to hear answers such as 'protects me', 'keeps me on my toes' and so on.

   After the client's response, probe further by asking 'What does this do for you?' Keep going until you arrive at a fundamental concept or core value such as love, security, connection or peace. (Refer to the exercise in the earlier section 'Integrating conflicting parts'.)

3. **Enlist the creative part of your client's brain.**

   Ask your client to find three positive ways in which he can meet this positive intention.

   At this point, the client may not be able to articulate out loud what the three ways are. If this is the case, tell him that it's okay to have this awareness at an unconscious level even if he can't articulate it in words.

4. **Come to an agreement about new behaviours.**

   Invite your client to have an internal conversation and secure agreement from the positive intention part that he'll carry out these new creative actions.

5. **Plan for the future.**

   Ask the client to envision a time in the future when things are different. Invite the client to put up an imaginary movie screen in which the client appears doing the new behaviour. How does the new behaviour feel? Does the client need to make any further change in order to do the new behaviour?

   If the client didn't articulate three specific behaviours in Step 3, the client won't see himself doing anything on the screen. Instead, let him go with the sense that his unconscious mind can be trusted to guide him to the new behaviours.

6. **Perform an ecology check.**

   As a final check, invite your client to 'Go back inside and check if any other parts of you aren't happy with these new behaviours'.

   If the client encounters any objections, identify the part or parts responsible and return to Step 2, working through the rest of this exercise.

# Part VI
# The Part of Tens

## The 5th Wave

By Rich Tennant

"I've always been impressed with Larry's ability to control his audience."

# In this part . . .

The famous *For Dummies* Part of Tens puts valuable insights into coaching at your fingertips. This part gives you ten questions to set your coaching repertoire in the right direction and cool advice so you don't race ahead of yourself when it's best to stay open and curious. Great coaches recognise they can always learn more, and this part offers key suggestions to keep learning.

# Chapter 20

# Ten Powerful Coaching Questions

**In This Chapter**

▶ Discovering effective questions to ask

▶ Delving beneath surface answers

▶ Noticing the effects of your questions

Great coaches ask powerful questions that linger in clients' minds. The art of questioning lies in creating awareness for the client. A good question may invoke a deeper understanding of who clients are, help them connect with something that makes them come alive or inspire a sense of how they'd like their lives to unfold.

In this chapter, you can explore ten powerful questions. Ask them of your clients and try them on yourself too.

As you find ways to feed these questions into your coaching conversations elegantly, stop to consider the purpose of asking a certain question at a certain time to ensure that it lands effectively. The key point to remember is to keep listening to your client with all your senses attuned. Work to feel what's going on for her rather than weighing up the next question you'll ask. You find more about asking effective questions and listening to clients' answers in Chapter 6.

The questions form a natural sequence, but you can jump around them if you prefer. Just choose what feels right in the moment.

## What Do You Want?

This classic NLP question shifts clients into investigative mode, encouraging them to become curious about what they indeed want. Asking it is particularly effective when clients seem stuck in the opposite scenario: what they don't want.

Very often people respond initially to this question with more negatives:

- ✔ 'Well, I don't want X.'
- ✔ 'I know that I don't want Y.'
- ✔ 'I certainly don't want Z.'

Until they come to coaching, many people haven't experienced the luxury of questioning what they really want. They've been what NLP terms *at effect* rather than *at cause*. They're always reacting to circumstances or demands placed on them rather than taking responsibility for creating their own experiences. Shifting clients to a place where they give themselves permission to consider what they want can be a challenge. You may be pushing them in this direction for the first time in their lives.

If clients struggle to articulate what they want, try some alternative ways of asking this question such as:

- ✔ What would you like more of?
- ✔ What would you like less of?

Also consider framing the question within a specific context such as: 'What do you want . . .'

- ✔ In your job?
- ✔ In your marriage?
- ✔ In friendships?
- ✔ In your health?
- ✔ In your next holiday?'

# What's Important to You about This?

So often people want to do it all or have it all, even though they know that's not possible. Clients may look to their coaches to wave magic wands to save them from making difficult choices.

Classic conflicts of values arise when demands put pressure on you to choose between values such as work and play, health and wealth, family life and work demands. Ultimately, people have to decide which is most important to them, and clients naturally bring dilemmas that represent conflicts of values to talk through with their coaches.

Not many people go through each day talking about their values, and yet values drive your thoughts, decisions and actions. This question brings unspoken values, criteria and beliefs right up front and forces them to be debated. Turn to Chapter 8 for more about the power of values.

When you ask 'What's important to you about this?', your clients must consider the values that they live by. At a practical level, this question helps prioritise their requirements and aids decision-making.

An alternative way to ask this question is: 'What matters to you?' or 'What values are you honouring?'

This question is equally valid and useful to ask whenever you're in a quandary: when you're deciding how to grow your business, whether to hire a new employee or make a major purchase such as a new car or computer.

# How Will You Know When You've Got What You Want?

When I ask you what you want, you can respond in many ways:

- ✔ I want the partner of my dreams.
- ✔ I want the holiday of a lifetime.
- ✔ I want a supportive team.
- ✔ I want satisfied clients.
- ✔ I want the perfect job.
- ✔ I want to be happy and successful.
- ✔ I want a system that works.

All these answers sound fine, but they can mean totally different things to different people. As a coach, your role is to challenge others to shift from vague concepts to specific details. After I hear what clients are aiming for in big-picture terms, I start work to gain precision. With specific details in place, clients are much more likely to get what they want and recognise when they've arrived rather than live in a world of vague future possibilities.

The question 'How will you know when you've got what you want?' transforms lofty strategic directions into tangible goals with measurable outcomes by moving clients toward specific evidence. The process of gathering evidence engages clients' senses so they really see, hear, feel, touch, taste and smell what they'll experience in the future after they achieve what they want. This question also forms part of the well-formed outcome process that I outline in Chapter 7.

Anna, a lawyer with two young children, told me in a coaching session that she desperately wanted more time to herself. I could have made assumptions about what more time meant, but instead I asked her to describe her goal with the question: 'How will you know when you've got more time to yourself?' Anna got specific on what shape she'd like that time for herself to take, and then began to carve time in her schedule where she put herself first. Her evidence that she'd achieved her goal involved picturing herself spooning the froth off a small cappuccino in her favourite Italian coffee shop, novel in hand for 15 minutes each day, while allowing the sounds of fellow commuters to drift past her. She then talked about booking two hours at the weekend to go to a gym class, picturing herself on the bike, feeling the stretching in her legs, hearing the music playing and the instructor's encouragement as well as enjoying time to shower and dress without the little ones tugging at her for attention. She also mentally rehearsed the conversation when she'd ask her partner if he'd look after the children for a fixed slot each Saturday morning.

Anna engaged her senses of sight, smell, taste, sound and feeling. See Chapter 7 for ways to engage the senses.

# What Is Getting in the Way for You?

Top coach Timothy Gallwey, author of the classic *Inner Game* book series has a simple formula for coaching clients to be at their best:

$$P = p - i$$

The formula proposes that performance ($P$) equals potential ($p$) minus the interference ($i$). In order to reach potential, you need to tackle whatever gets in the way. This interference may include:

- **External factors,** such as choosing the wrong place, hanging out with the wrong people, having bad timing, lacking resources such as staff, equipment or funding.

- **Internal factors,** such as personal skills and attributes, thoughts and beliefs.

This coaching question pinpoints the interference factors that need to change in order to turn a situation around. For example, if you're coaching an executive in an organisation, asking this question determines whether she needs to focus on what isn't working in the practical infrastructure in terms of a team and technology, or if she needs to pay attention to her leadership style and behaviour. Often the answer to this question involves a combination of making changes in both the environment and one's personal approach.

# What Resources Have You Got that Can Support You?

NLP coaches assume that their clients are resourceful and adopt the presupposition: 'You have all the resources you need to achieve your desired outcome.' This belief empowers clients at times when they're struggling and thinking that the answer is out there, or that somebody else can tell them what to do. In fact, they already know what to do, deep down within themselves; they've just forgotten it in the moment.

Like interference, *resources* come from different places:

- **Internal resources** include personal beliefs, memories, values and energy.
- **External resources** include people, sponsors and mentors, possessions and money.

In NLP coaching, you draw on someone's previous experiences, often called *personal history*, to find internal and external resources that support the client in moving forward. The SCORE model, which I cover in Chapter 5, is an effective tool to identify resources.

When coaching clients through situations that test their confidence, I invite them to access times in completely different contexts when they were confident. I once coached a young woman whose pre-wedding nerves threatened to spoil the build up to her wedding. She was concerned about the behaviour of the young bridesmaids who were likely to become distracted in the excitement of the occasion. She also wanted to make a speech at the top table in a relaxed and humorous way. During our sessions, I invited her to find times in her memory when she'd been confident, relaxed and humorous and then *anchored* those same states with her so she could immediately switch on those qualities under pressure on her wedding day. You can read more about anchoring states and increasing resourcefulness in Chapter 18.

# When You Accomplish Your Goal and Look Back on Your Success, What Will You Experience?

The wording of this question assumes positive results: success, accomplishment and knowledge. You're acting as a sponsor or champion, encouraging your clients to achieve what they've set out to achieve by having them envision the end-point on their time lines or their *desired state*. You're also implicitly demonstrating that the results they envision are not only possible, but also that you believe they can reach them, even if they are feeling some doubt. You're inviting them to taste success – the completed project, the culmination of the hard work and everything they strive for.

Help them to explore the future experience in sensory detail by asking follow-up questions including:

 ✔ What will it look like?

 ✔ What will it sound like?

 ✔ What will it feel like?

The main question also acts as a test of whether clients have chosen goals that they truly want to pursue. By shifting their thinking into the future, which NLP calls the *as-if frame*, you're testing their choices. Sometimes a client decides that the goal doesn't justify all the challenges along the way and changes the goal.

# What's the Question You Don't Want to Ask Yourself Right Now?

This question's valuable when you feel that a session has reached an impasse and aren't quite sure how to move forward. Asked with curiosity and sensitivity, it gets beneath the surface of the conversation and gives clients permission to articulate something that hasn't been said before and which may be troubling them.

Paul's client Ramon described the offer of a dream job as the Chief Operating Officer of an international banking organisation: the role he'd been working towards for some years. Paul, however, felt something was amiss and asked Ramon, 'What is it that you don't want to ask yourself right now?' Ramon's voice became surprisingly hesitant, even out of character, as he splurged out his fears about his family's acceptance of the changes the new role would bring to their lives. In particular, Ramon was concerned about who would manage the care of his elderly parents, the increased pressure on his wife who hadn't been well and dilemmas about the house move. After this raft of fears surfaced, Paul worked with his client steadily on practical plans to bring in extra assistance on the home front. 'Pandora's box had sprung open,' says Paul. 'My role was to be there and provide a stable sense of perspective as Ramon examined the contents.'

# What's the Way to Make This Really Easy?

With this question, you make the positive assumption that solving a situation or achieving the end result can be easy. This question is particularly useful when someone is faced with something that feels like a difficult uphill battle that threatens to overwhelm. I also keep it posted as a note on my desk to remind me to make things easy – a variation on the KISS formula (Keep It Sweet and Simple).

Sometimes people create complexity and forget to look for an easier way. Asking this question invites the client to come up with strategies that increase focus and fun. This is the kind of question to leave clients with to ponder, so that they come up with their own solutions in their own time, often outside the coaching session.

# What's the First Step?

Coaching sessions conclude with an action of some kind, even if that action is an inquiry, something for clients to think about, rather than a to-do list.

An example of an inquiry is: 'How would it be to relax and take your time more often?' By comparison, an example of a to-do list is: 'Identify three favourite ways to increase your relaxation.'

Taking the first step is often the most difficult one because after you take it, you're committed to move and take another step. You can't go back. The first step honours the challenge of change and the ownership of responsibility. The first step to a clear desk is throwing away a piece of paper. The first step to a weight-loss programme is (literally) stepping on the scales.

With the first step comes a sense of relief and the recognition that momentum can build. In the parlance of Joseph Campbell's classic work *The Hero with a Thousand Faces* (Fontana Press), taking the first step involves the hero stepping over the threshold and venturing into the unknown. In NLP terms, the first step moves clients from the present state to the desired state, shifting from being *at effect* to becoming *at cause* in their lives. There's no correct or best first step, simply something that clearly shifts the client into action towards the goal rather than perpetuating procrastination.

# *And What Else?*

This simple little question is amazingly powerful, especially at the end of a session that covers a range of topics, because it allows space to think beyond the immediate issue. This question drills down, giving clients' permission to raise another issue that wasn't on the agenda, yet is the real thing that's troubling them.

The issue that clients say they want to work on is often not the real issue; this question gives them time to reveal what's really going on.

In a previous life before becoming a coach, I spent many years interviewing executives about their work in the corporate world and made an interesting discovery. We'd have a formal meeting for an hour when a person gave me all the facts and figures, the official story I needed to write up for an article. Yet the most intriguing tales, the best one-liners, emerged on the informal walk to the coffee machine or the lift out of the building after I tucked my notebook out of sight. In these moments, I captured the best headlines and off-the-record stories. Similarly in coaching, the most important discoveries often come at the end of a session, when clients feel they've off-loaded what they thought they ought to work on. Now relaxed, their unconscious minds come up with the most useful information.

Michael coached a senior business leader for nearly a year on how he'd transform his organisation and gain himself a new job in the organisation. One session was drawing to a close earlier than usual, and Michael asked 'And what else would you like to talk about?' The client shared the news that his wife was having suicidal thoughts; a topic that had never been aired before in sessions. This moment of revelation took the coaching relationship to a deeper level of trust where Michael supported his client to find therapeutic help for his wife and the courage to ask for time away from the business for himself.

# Chapter 21

# Ten Traps to Avoid in Coaching

## In This Chapter

▶ Raising your game as a coach

▶ Maintaining healthy, helpful relationships with clients

▶ Paying attention to your process

Coaching is a highly sought after skill and like all skills, it needs to stay sharp to stop you getting into bad habits. If you're honest, you accept that your skills aren't perfect. Thank goodness! You're only human and sometimes you get it wrong.

Part of developing as a coach is to engage in regular self-reflection on the quality of your coaching and notice where you come unstuck. Ask yourself, 'What's the interference that trips me up at times?' and 'If I were being observed right now, am I walking the talk?'

In this chapter, you can read about some common pitfalls and identify some helpful first steps to begin correcting your course.

Engaging in a regular coaching supervision group is a brilliant way of gaining new insights from other coaches and noticing what you may be missing with your own practice. You can read more about supervision in Chapter 1.

## Racing into Detail without Seeing the Bigger Picture

By its very nature, coaching gives people time and space. So allow your clients that space to think. Avoid the temptation to hurry along one line of inquiry before the client's had the opportunity to set out what's on his mind. Racing through coaching is rather like asking someone to choose one location to visit for a holiday before he's had time to look at the options on a map and evaluate several choices.

NLP reminds coaches to pace and lead people. *Pace* your clients' current reality by listening to them, then listening more and finally *leading* them along one particular path with your questions. This approach requires the coach to achieve the fine balance between uncovering what's happening overall for the client and targeting the core issue. (You can read more on pacing and leading to build rapport in Chapter 2, while Chapter 6 looks at the core coaching competency of listening in more detail.)

A thought to hold while listening to clients is that the presenting issue isn't the real issue. By dallying a while in the space with patience, you get to the place where the client says, 'I think this is really about *Y*,' and you then have something deeper to work with than the superficial topic the client first put forward. Don't push your clients to go too fast too quickly: they need to trust you and the coaching process. The chapters in Part III are full of suggestions about how to shift to a deeper level of work with your client.

Stay curious as to how the topic that the client first brings to coaching is part of a larger issue or pattern for him involving his beliefs about what's possible for him, his values, sense of identity and purpose.

# Getting Caught with Long-Winded Tales

One of the challenges all experienced coaches admit to is the temptation to get caught up in listening to their clients' stories. Everyone loves a good story, and if you're a good listener in rapport with your client, you can fill the majority of coaching sessions listening to tales.

Coaching isn't the same as a coffee chat with a friend. Listening to distracting stories isn't what you're being paid for as a coach. Your clients already know their stories. They've been living with them and telling them to themselves over and over. They're now looking for finer stories and finer lives. If you don't redirect them from 'this happened and then that and then . . .' types of conversations, they eventually become dissatisfied with the entire coaching process.

One way to break through never-ending tales is by having phrases ready in your mind to shift from the storytelling. For example:

> *It's a wonderful story, and I could spend all your session being entertained. That's not going to be most valuable to you. Can I ask that you just tell me only as much detail as you need to in order to get clarification for yourself on the real issue?*

Or you can raise a hand to signify a cut or pause and say:

> *Can we hold it there for a moment? What's the essential question on your mind as you're telling the story?*

Or you can use the more direct:

> *What do you want to do about this?*

Stopping a story and refocusing a conversation is a form of intrusion – a skill that takes time to develop and sensitivity to maintain rapport. Always intrude with a smile and some humour. Remember the power of non-verbal communication – your shift in gestures and tone of voice signifies the change of pace needed to forward the conversation. See Chapter 10 for more tips on intruding tactfully and successfully during a coaching session.

# *Rescuing the Other Person*

Coaches tend to be very decent people who want the best for others! They may slip inadvertently into the rescuer role in which they take on more than their fair share of the work involved in coaching. Some warning signs of rescuer-mode include:

- ✔ **At a practical level:** You take lots of notes that you then send to the client after the session. You take on actions to contact people on the client's behalf.

- ✔ **At an emotional level:** You find yourself worrying about the client's well-being between sessions. You over-empathise with the client's situation.

Coaching works best when you have a series of mental models to ensure that you remain true to the coach role. Chapter 13 examines Stephen Karpman's Drama Triangle – how you can get caught in a trio of roles known as Rescuer, Victim and Persecutor and how to get out of these unhelpful roles.

The coach who rescues the vulnerable client reduces the client's power so that the client emerges as a victim of circumstances. The script is 'Poor client, let me help you.' Also, coaches who take on responsibility for their clients end up switching to Victim or Persecutor mode later on when they've had enough.

# Dramatising What You Hear

An insurance company had an advertising slogan: 'We won't make a drama out of a crisis.' This is a good slogan for your coaching sessions too!

When you dramatise, you shift into the realm of entertainment through action and excitement that's engaging. If you become really animated and entertained by the drama, then unconsciously, your client takes on the message that the coach wants to be entertained by one crisis after another. He'll get into the habit of bringing drama to coaching to entertain you further, so the coach becomes part of the problem.

Drama is an act that masks the deeper and more important issues. It's fun, but ultimately, it's a distraction. As with storytelling, you can find yourself caught up in the drama of your clients' lives where the emphasis is on all the buzz of interesting characters and their activities.

Your clients need to step from acting into the directing roles, finding the perspective to recognise 'What are the underlying patterns here?' and 'What is the movie I really want to create for my life?' NLP offers various tools for clients to step back and look impartially at their lives, including time lines (see Chapter 16) and perceptual positions (refer to Chapter 12).

# Being the Know-all

One of the most liberating early lessons for novice coaches is that you don't need the answers, only good questions. You don't need to come up with the solutions to be a good coach. In fact, if you do, they're unlikely to add much value. Unlike so many areas of life and work, coaching is one field where arriving as the expert trouble-shooter produces the worst results.

As a coach, you need to haul yourself up when you find you're asking leading questions such as: 'Don't you think you should try this?' Instead, shift your vocabulary to messages such as 'What ideas have you thought of?' Doing so sets the tone for your clients' creative exploration and ownership of the agenda. See Chapter 6 for more on phrasing effective questions. Chapter 20 features some of the most powerful coaching questions.

Coach and client are collaborators in the client's success. By coming from that place where you as coach know nothing, you create the conditions for the client's self-confidence and self-directed change.

# Slipping into Parent or Child Role

In life you assume many roles other than coach. You were once a child and may well be a parent now. Even without children of your own, you know how to play the parenting role from witnessing your own or other people's parents. As you engage with your clients' experiences in coaching, you also draw on your emotional history of family relationships.

If you're naturally an indulgent parent or experienced in that kind of parenting, a tendency to let your clients off the hook and prevent them taking ownership for their actions may come out in your relationships with clients. Likewise, if you had strict parenting, your coaching may take on a bossy style.

Another role to avoid slipping into as coach is to be the adaptive child trying to please your clients: this gets in the way of challenging them. If you're coaching someone who you feel is more experienced than you or are in an unfamiliar business context, remind yourself that you're not hired as the expert in his world, but as a coach bringing a fresh perspective.

When you encounter a difficult situation with a coaching client, check whether you're slipping into being an indulgent parent or an adaptive child. If you happen to be coaching a client who's part of a family business, be aware that you very likely to pick up the unconscious family patterns during sessions as well.

# Losing Track of Time

Managing the time within each session is an important way for you to create structure for your clients. Establishing a definite start and finish time sets the parameters in which coaching is most effective.

As part of your initial contracting (see Chapter 3), you have the opportunity to emphasise that both you and your client are responsible for arriving on time. Agree the implications if the client is late upfront.

During the session, you as coach are responsible for managing the time to give the client the greatest value. Doing so means you establish a focus for the session after some initial exploration as well as allow time for an elegant closure, rather than an abrupt 'Okay, time's up now!'

Have a structure for the session planned, such as a mind map that guides you from time for the introductory niceties and opening questions through time to coach the topic and time for action-planning and then closure, including diary and payment administration. With telephone coaching, you can check the time as you go along. With face to face coaching, sit facing a clock on the wall or have a watch on the table in front of you to keep an eye on the time without the need to look at a watch on your wrist.

# Falling into Love and Friendship

Having close and fruitful relationships with other people in which they share their intimate thoughts can be endearing. Yet remember that coaching is a professional relationship, just as doctors, accountants and lawyers have with their clients. Your responsibility is to work ethically within professional boundaries.

Here's a health warning. Beware of falling in love and expecting to run off with a client to a long and happy life together! While it's impossible to say that coach-client personal relationships never succeed, switching from coach to lover rarely leads to satisfactory long-term results.

Of course, you can become friends with your client after the coaching contract is complete. For coaching to be successful, gently tell clients that you're not going to become great buddies with them while coaching them.

 Coaching is a lop-sided relationship in which clients open the box on their vulnerabilities. Meanwhile, the coach's own life and issues are kept private. Re-balancing that history and redesigning the relationship involves close self-scrutiny, which is very difficult to achieve in the face of an established pattern and history between two individuals.

# Engaging in Over-Enthusiastic Action-Planning

Even though action-planning is an integral part of the coaching competencies (refer to Chapter 3), I'm not a great fan of long action lists for clients. Many people come to coaching when they're already busy; adding to their tasks doesn't support them. Ending with a couple of key items to follow up on and a self-reflective inquiry is more likely to be successful than a long to-do list that never happens. All too often, clients become disillusioned with their failure to complete the actions and then abandon coaching.

Help your clients notice the resistance to do what they need to do, while recognising that these are the tough places where personal transformations happen.

You do your clients the greatest service by shining a light on just one action that can have the most impact.

# Being Scared to Say Goodbye

All good things come to an end, including a coaching relationship. Coaching exists for an arc of time; it's not an open-ended arrangement, even though it's a process that takes place over weeks and months. Most coaching relationships involve a commitment to three months of working together, and you may extend that to an assignment of six or even nine months. For some clients who are highly committed to the power of coaching in their lives, the coaching relationship may last into a period of years while meeting at less frequent intervals.

Initially, you can anticipate excitement in coaching assignments as your clients achieve new insights and breakthroughs and see dramatic change. They're developing new skills, experimenting with new behaviours and moving creatively into discovering themselves. If they stick with the coaching, as time progresses, they shift from doing mode into being mode, finding new ways of connecting with the bigger picture of their lives.

At some point, your clients are satisfied that they've had enough from their coaching relationships and are ready to move on. Acknowledge that parting can be sad because you shared many experiences together over your sessions. Send clients on their way with gratitude for the shared experience.

As coach, you may be tempted to carry on beyond the best-before date, so set up a closure session from the outset; don't just walk away from a coaching relationship. Closure sessions are a chance to wrap up the coaching and allow clients to acknowledge the journey they've taken with you. During this final meeting, plan to discuss the following:

- What has the client discovered about himself?
- What worked best for the client during the coaching? What tools will help him respond to future challenges?
- What can the client take forward into other aspects of his life for the longer term?

When you close the door behind one client, you open space for another one to appear.

# Chapter 22

# Ten Ways to Enhance Your Coaching Skills

## In This Chapter

▶ Making on-going discoveries

▶ Staying curious and open to everything you don't know

▶ Gaining insights from other coaches and professionals

▶ Giving back to the coaching community

*I was like a boy playing on the seashore, and diverting myself now and then finding a smoother pebble or a prettier shell than ordinary, whilst the great ocean of truth lay all undiscovered before me.*

– Isaac Newton

*C*oaching involves a commitment to continuous personal growth by the coach, and this development can take place in a variety of settings. An accredited coach-training programme is a good starting point to build your skills, even though not all established coaches have any formal coach training. To be an NLP coach, you need to precede the coach training with NLP training until you reach Master Practitioner level.

You can find details of accredited training programmes by looking at the websites of the key professional coaching bodies:

✔ The International Coach Federation (ICF): www.coachfederation.org

✔ Association for Coaching (AC): www.associationforcoaching.com

✔ European Mentoring and Coaching Council (EMCC): www.emc council.org

As you pursue your interest in coaching, every client and coaching session teaches you something new. When you relax, approach what you don't know with humility, and stay curious and uncertain about having the answers, you discover the most – and have the most fun.

Making the habit of opening yourself to new opportunities rekindles your love of acquiring knowledge – a love that you may have pushed aside during a career devoted to getting on with a job or while raising a family. Here are my top suggestions to keep building your skills.

# Enrol in Diverse Courses and Workshops

Taking part in both coach and NLP training is fun and enlightening for new-comer coaches, to the point that further training becomes slightly addictive. You want to recapture the buzz of uncovering new knowledge with like-minded people and practise your skills.

As you choose more workshops and courses, be adventurous and see how something totally different can extend your ability to stay present in the moment. Consider a course in acting, art, aviation or aikido, for example. Seek out courses that engage the body, not just your mental faculties, so that you engage the different senses. Try a pottery course, drumming or a dance workshop as well as the more logical academic programmes.

Even if you don't have time to participate in a full-length course right now, you can still attend interesting and random events from the arts, music, language, literature, law, leadership, history, engineering, education, science, sport, dance, martial arts, philosophy, psychology – the list is endless. With each new experience, ask yourself how your coaching can benefit from this unfamiliar world compared to the one in which you typically choose to inhabit.

# Share Your Knowledge with Others

When you're invited to teach somebody else what you know – guess what! – you have to unpack your knowledge in fine detail, a process that ultimately improves your own understanding.

Find opportunities to talk about coaching in general and how you coach. Run through your favourite tips and tools. Put yourself in the hot seat and do live demonstrations of your coaching, coaching someone through a life or work goal using the well-formed outcome process in Chapter 7 or assisting in planning for a difficult conversation or meeting, which is covered in Chapter 14.

Another way to share your coaching knowledge is to teach someone what you know about the core coaching competencies, such as asking powerful questions or active listening.

Think back to something you recently learnt. Or consider when you learnt to ride a bicycle or drive a car. Notice how your learning naturally goes through four stages:

1. Unconsciously incompetent: before you began to study.

2. Consciously incompetent: the wobbly time when you're suddenly aware of what you don't know.

3. Consciously competent: when you proceed with caution and are aware of how to follow a process.

4. Unconsciously competent: when you relax, let go and can do it!

As you teach others, you realise how far you've come.

# Practise on Willing Guinea Pigs

Top international golfer Gary Player said, 'You must work very hard to become a natural player.' Just like any professional, the more hours of practice you put in, the better you become. The way to improve at coaching is practice. The more practice you put in, the better you become.

Find people to practise your coaching skills with. Many people would love to have some coaching, but can't normally afford it. Even if you're not charging, contract with your guinea pigs that they buy the coffee or make some contribution so that you feel you have a commercial contract. Chapter 3 has many more ideas about contracting.

Your family and friends don't make the best guinea pigs because you have established relationships with them. They don't see you as a coach, and the knowledge you already have about them can get in the way of your coaching. Look for people that you don't know so well. Volunteer your services at work, through community groups, clubs or friends of friends.

When people pay for coaching, even a token amount, they're more likely to be committed than when it's completely free. Consider offering coaching at a very modest fee or in return for a light meal. This is very reasonable when you're a novice or want to extend your experience in a new field. Don't be afraid to say you're new to this work and want to hone your skills, just like any apprentice.

# Model Other Coaches in Action

NLP began by modelling excellence. To enhance your skills, follow the example of NLP's founders: find the top performers in the field and become curious about what they do and how they think. Chapter 11 explains more about modelling.

Use a framework such as the NLP Logical Levels to observe how coaches operate at each level, from the environment in which they work, right up to their sense of purpose. Turn to Chapter 5 for a quick review of questions to ask at the different logical levels.

When Richard Bandler and John Grinder modelled the great therapists, they found that one model of excellence wasn't enough. Each of their exemplars achieved results in his or her own unique way. So choose two or three different people to model who come from a variety of backgrounds. Create your own model of what works for you.

You can also refine your skills by attending master classes and teleclasses from top coaches. Look for offerings through coaching associations or watch videos of their work.

# Experiment with New Ideas

Be brave and experiment with different approaches to your coaching so that you and your clients avoid getting stuck in predictable routines. For example, put on your NLP hat and consider how you can engage sight, sound, taste, touch, movement and smell.

Try any – or all – of the following suggestions to vary your coaching:

✔ **Change the venue.** Walk and coach by the river, in a park, in a coffee shop, or on comfy chairs in a concert hall reception. Trying different spaces can prove valuable, particularly if you're coaching in the corporate world and your clients are office-based. Putting them in a different environment also puts them in a different frame of mind.

✔ **Work with photos and favourite objects.** Invite your client to bring a favourite photograph or important object and share a story about it. Choose some questions to deepen the significance of the chosen image or object. How does it relate to the client's current situation? What does this say about who the client is and what's important to her now? What is your client carrying from the past? And be sure to check out Chapter 13 for ideas on letting go of the past.

✔ **Introduce toys and art materials.** Instead of talking about a situation, invite your client to draw it or map it out with bendy toy characters or plastic animals as the key stakeholders. Explore why the client chose specific characters or animals to represent various people. (I often use bendy frogs, owls, monkeys, cats, dogs and tigers!)

✔ **Extend the coaching session to include a meal.** Sharing food introduces a note of informality and the opportunity to relax and open up.

✔ **Play music.** You can change people's state by playing music. Baroque-style tunes create a state of relaxed awareness, known as the *alpha state*: the most famous of this type of simple, clear music is Pachelbel's Canon. If you don't have control over the room where you're coaching, find the client's favourite music that takes her to a good state and suggest the client listen to that before your coaching session.

✔ **Introduce stories and poems.** Read a short poem or story that may resonate with your client. You can find wonderful books of poems that arouse curiosity or amusement. For example, I often share work by the poet David Whyte and stories from Nick Owen's books, including *The Magic of Metaphor*. You can also invite the client to create her own poetry or short story as homework between sessions.

✔ **Vary your pace.** If you're naturally slow and reflective in coaching conversations, introduce some quick exercises. Ask a client to 'Tell me what this is all about in 60 seconds' and see what happens. Set a time frame of seven or seventeen minutes for a topic and then move on. If your tendency is to dive in with a very directive style, introduce some variety by staying silent and listening for longer.

# *Record Yourself and Play It Back*

When you record a coaching session and play it back, you become the observer of your own performance as a coach.

With a client's permission, record a session. Draw up a list of the core competencies of coaching based on material in Chapter 3 and then go through your recording, checking how you fare on each one. Ask yourself:

✔ What were the questions that worked for this client?

✔ What is the evidence that you covered each competency?

✔ Where do you play safe? How can you stretch yourself as a coach to the edge of your comfort zone to improve your skill?

With an audio recording of a session, concentrate on the quality of your dialogue. Listen for speed, silences and tone of voice, as well as the actual words. With a video recording, try to spot the nuances of body language. What habits show up that are particularly useful or a hindrance? See Chapter 2 for much more on non-verbal communication.

You can also use the recoding for your client's benefit by inviting the client to re-visit the session and notice what she sees, hears and feels about it from an independent observer standpoint. What questions shifted the client's thinking? Where might the client be getting in her own way? How could the client have made better use of the time?

Erase the recording after you (and perhaps the client) review it in order to maintain confidentiality.

# Set a Quality Target

In order to improve your skill, you gain most if you have a clear sense of what the improvement will be like in the future. The aim 'to be a better coach' is vague. More specific goals may include delivering a course assignment, passing an accreditation, logging a number of coaching hours or doing a personal competency check after each session.

Setting well-formed outcomes reminds you to set specific evidence criteria. Get clear on what that quality improvement is like and how you know when you arrive. Chapter 7 covers fulfilling the well-formed outcome conditions, which you can apply to your own coaching.

After you reach one level, stretch yourself even further to master the next. There's always more to learn.

# Work with a Supervisor or Mentor

Supervision began in the therapeutic world to give therapists a space to offload their cases by talking through them with supervisors. Supervision is now increasingly popular within the coaching profession as a way to deepen a coach's practice and awareness. You may work with a supervisor on a one-to-one basis or within a group in order to step back, reflect on how you work and get support on the more challenging situations you face.

Supervision offers a way to allow a coach to break through the illusions, delusions and collusions that can happen in coaching. A supervisor may also take on a mentoring role with you to guide your professional development and practice-building. Supervision is not the same as coaching, yet a coaching supervisor is an experienced coach who provides the space for you to reflect and gain insights.

To find a qualified coaching supervisor, ask around other coaches you know for personal recommendations or contact the coaching bodies mentioned earlier in this chapter.

Peter Hawkins and Robin Shohet created the seven-eyed coaching model, one of the classic models of supervision, so named because it addresses coaching from seven perspectives. This model examines the relationship in coaching between the various elements, from what happens in the actual sessions through the coach's unspoken experience, interpretation, the actual interventions used, the system in which she's working, the supervisor's role and feelings she picks up on, and the wider context.

# Join a Coaching Network

As interest in coaching builds, so do coaching groups, circles and networks. These bodies provide friendly forums of knowledge-sharing and co-coaching practice as well as potential joint business-ventures.

Some groups form as alumni of coach-training programmes, while others are organised by members of the main coaching bodies such as the International Coach Federation and the Association for Coaching (see Chapter 3 for their details).

If no coaching groups exist in your area, how about setting one up? You can also consider establishing a virtual group that meets online, as well as one that functions through regular real-world meetings.

# Volunteer with a Professional Body

All professions depend for their existence on the enthusiasm of their members. The various coaching bodies will welcome you with open arms when you're ready to volunteer your skills. Consider what particular talents and experience you bring and how much time you can commit to regularly.

Can you volunteer to help with events, man conference stands or give talks? Do you have the time to run for office, train as an assessor or set up a local group? Choose something that you want to do rather than from duty or you resent the time. You can find out more on the websites of the professional bodies mentioned earlier in this chapter.

As you become more involved in a professional coaching organisation, you'll be surrounded by opportunities to further your own skills as you share your own with others.

# Index

## • *Numerics* •

4-step Communication model, 211–212
*The 7 Habits of Highly Effective People*
  (Covey), 214, 275
8-second rule for questions, 112
80/20 rule, 155, 309

## • *A* •

AC (Association for Coaching), 11, 51, 351
accountability, 61, 203
accredited training programs, 351
actions
  forwarding awareness into, 101–102
  planning, 348–349
  powerful questions about, 113
  questions to develop, 101
  transforming conflict into, 255–256
*The Adventures of Tom Sawyer*
  (Twain), 215
agenda for coaching
  keeping clients on track, 85–86
  personal aims in, 85
  professional aims in, 84–85
  refining, 84–85
  setting at intake, 83
  staying in the moment, 86
*Alice in Wonderland* (Carroll), 93
alliances. *See* client-coach alliance
alone time, as bale-out space, 321–322
anchoring, 22, 303–306
Anecdote icon, 5
Angelou, Maya (poet), 9
anger, in DASE model, 162
appreciative enquiry practices, 155
appreciative habits, 256
Apps, Judy (*Voice of Influence*), 179, 180
as if questions, 113, 126
as-if frame, 109, 328, 329

association
  associating with the moment, 278, 294
  defined, 277, 294
Association for Coaching (AC), 11, 51, 351
audience for communication, 212
auditory sense. *See also* VAK or VAKOG
    senses
  identifying submodalities of, 288
  as lead representational system, 107
  as a modality, 286
  with New Behaviour Generator, 134
  in NLP Communication model, 106
  for representing the future, 111
  submodality intervention using, 288
  words or phrases of, 29
awakening, coaching as, 151–152
awareness
  during disappointments, 228
  of filtering, 108
  forwarding into action, 101–102
  as province of conscious mind, 110
away from metaprogram, 172, 175–176, 219

## • *B* •

background information form, 80–81
back-track frame, 329
Bandler, Richard (NLP co-creator)
  early NLP development by, 19, 29
  eye accessing cues noticed by, 133
  Milton Model creation by, 38
  modelling by, 194–195
  submodalities work of, 238
  voice coaching recommended by, 179
baseline states, 303–304
Bateson, Gregory (psychiatrist), 20
behavioural flexibility
  for coaching agenda, 86
  for conflict resolution, 249
  as key principle of NLP, 21, 28, 86, 168, 249
  mitigating passion with, 168

behavioural level, 98

behaviours. *See also* metaprograms; strategies

being at cause versus at effect of, 32

breaking into manageable sequences, 34–35

establishing new habits, 183–184

every behaviour has a positive intent (presupposition), 68, 222

finding triggers for, 35

of high-performing teams, 224

in Logical Levels model, 98

New Behaviour Generator for, 133–135

in NLP Communication model, 107

people are more than their behaviour (presupposition), 34–35, 222

secondary gain of, 40–41, 68

translating values into, 144

Yes/No lists for, 200–201

being versus doing, 63

beliefs

changing from limiting to empowering, 296–298

defined, 295

developing for teams, 223

empowering, 295–296

limiting, 295–296

in Logical Levels model, 99

of parts of yourself, 318

powerful questions about, 113

for transforming conflict into action, 255

in vision statements, 165–166

beliefs and values level

exploratory questions for, 99

overview, 99

Berne, Eric (Transactional Analysis founder), 20, 234

Big C style of coaching, 15, 151–152

blame-frame, conflict sustained by, 247–248

body language. *See also* non-verbal communication

for first impressions, 72

lead representational system clues, 107

matching and mirroring, 27–28

powerful questions indicated by, 112

when welcoming clients, 74

*Body Language For Dummies* (Kuhnke), 72, 155

Bohr, Niels (physicist), 35

boldfaced text in this book, 2

booking solidly, avoiding, 73

brainstorming, questions for, 113

breathing. *See also* non-verbal communication

conscious, for releasing problems, 232–233

counting monkeys exercise for, 233

finding the good in a situation, 233

for first impressions, 72

matching and mirroring, 28

performance linked to, 232

bridging space, 318

*Building Self-Confidence For Dummies* (Platts and Burton), 312

Burn, Gillian (*Personal Development All-in-One For Dummies*), 152

Burton, Kate

*Building Self-Confidence For Dummies*, 312

*Live Life, Love Work*, 162

*Neuro-linguistic Programming For Dummies*, 38, 60, 172, 189, 287, 295

*Neuro-linguistic Programming Workbook For Dummies*, 60, 172, 287

business coaching, 12–13

## • C •

Campbell, Joseph (mythologist), 327

capabilities and skills level, 99

career coaching, 12. *See also* work

Carroll, Lewis (*Alice in Wonderland*), 93

Cartesian questions, 114–115

causes

being at cause versus at effect, 32, 151

in SCORE model, 92

symptoms versus, 88

change. *See also* parts integration

activities for shifting focus, 321

alone time during, 321–322

bale-out space for, 321
bridging space for, 318
building on past experiences, 319–320
confusion creating a space for, 44
connecting to others with similar experiences, 322
ecology check for, 320–321
incremental and continuous, with coaching, 10, 75–76
necessity of, 318
physical self-care during, 322–323
thinking time during, 322
change work stage of coaching, 19
checking in with another, 203
chest voice, 180
child role, avoiding, 347
*chronos* perspective on time, 271
chunking
  for conflict negotiation, 251–252
  defined, 129, 166, 252
  for integrating conflicting parts, 324
  types of, 129, 166, 252
  usefulness for teams, 167
Circle of Excellence exercise, 304–306
clean language, 40
client-coach alliance
  accepting imperfection, 55
  being enough for the client, 54
  co-creating the relationship, 59–60
  confidentiality in, 49–53
  contracting in, 55–57
  core coaching competencies for, 58–61
  curiosity in, 63, 65–67
  as designed alliance, 47
  development of, 47–48
  ethics and integrity in, 54
  expectations for success shared in, 62–63
  intuition's role in, 65
  motivation in, 62
  power of silence in, 64
  questions for evolving, 48–49
  stages of, 55–56
clients
  detecting flow state in, 152
  executive, 51–52
  internal, 52–53
  as lovers or friends, avoiding, 348
  natural expertise of, 67–68
  private, 50–51
  usage in this book, 1
  yourself as, 1
closure stage of coaching, 19
club, vision statement for, 166
coachee. *See* clients
coaching
  as awakening, 151–152
  Big C style of, 15, 151–152
  booking solidly, avoiding, 73
  colluding versus, 40
  consulting compared to, 16
  content-free, 118–119, 133, 286
  core competencies of, 58–61
  definitions of, 11
  ending the relationship, 349
  enhancing your skills in, 351–358
  mentoring compared to, 16, 57
  NLP compared to, 10
  NLP's ft with, 17–18
  stages of interaction in, 19
  supervision for, 17, 50, 356–357
  therapy compared to, 15–16, 59
  time management in sessions, 347–348
  training programs and courses, 351, 352, 357
  traps to avoid in, 343–349
  types of coaches, 12–13
coaching networks, 357
coaching presence, 59–60
collusion
  asking permission to broach, 182
  as avoidance in coaching, 179
  coaching versus, 40
  intruding to get beyond, 182–183
  voicing what you notice, 179–181
colour-coding schedules and diaries, 202–203
commitment, as key to learning and results, 61
communication. *See also* language; teams
  audience for, 212
  effective, deeper structure in, 60
  four-step model of, 211

communication *(continued)*
  further information, 60
  in job interviews, 264–266
  the meaning of any communication
      is the response that you get
      (presupposition), 112, 222
  message of, 213
  meta-mirror exercise for, 216–218
  metaprograms in, 218–220
  method of, 213
  networking, 266–268
  non-violent, 253
  outcome of, 212
  perceptual positions for, 215–218
  refocusing a conversation, 344–345
  setting priorities for, 212–214
  stages of interaction in, 19
  you cannot not communicate
      (presupposition), 222
Communication model in NLP, 106–107
competencies, client, four steps of, 43
competencies, coach
  co-creating the relationship, 59–60
  communicating effectively, 60
  core coaching competencies, 58–61
  facilitating learning and results, 60–61
  four stages of, 353
  in ICF standards of conduct, 53
  personal checklist for, 61
  setting the foundation, 58–59
concluding questions, 76
confidence, building, 312–313
confidentiality
  with executive clients, 51–52
  facets of, 50
  in ICF standards of conduct, 53
  with internal clients, 52–53
  needed for trust and safety, 49–50
  with private clients, 50–51
conflict. *See also* parts integration
  appreciative habits for resolving, 256
  blame-frame questions sustaining,
      247–248
  chunking for negotiating, 251–252
  defined, 243
  feedback in, 254–255

fight or flight response to, 245
internal versus external, 243
inviting curiosity about reactions, 244
non-violent communication in, 253
outcome-frame questions for
    resolving, 248
panic attacks, handling, 246
perceptual positions for negotiating,
    249–251
physiological changes with, 245
positive and negative sides of, 243
road rage example, 244
role conflict, 323
switching submodalities to defuse, 247
in teams, 250
tension between values, 145
from thoughts alone, 247
transforming into positive action, 255–256
confusion
  mapping across resources, 290
  moving to congruence from, 45
  as pathway to understanding, 115
  space to change created by, 44
congruence. *See also* parts integration
  in client-coach alliance, 59
  defined, 45, 97, 180, 326
  modelling, 45
  recognising in clients, 326
  self-assessment exercise, 327
conscious breathing, 232–233
conscious competence, 43, 353
conscious incompetence, 43, 353
conscious mind, 110
consulting, coaching compared to, 16
contact information form, 79–80
content
  process versus, 40
  structure versus, 18, 171
content-free coaching, 118–119, 133, 286
context
  chunking across, 252
  defining for goals, 125
  metaprograms dependent on, 173, 220
contracting
  defined, 55
  with executive clients, 51–52

finding the best coach, 56–57
in ICF standards of conduct, 53
with private clients, 50
sample forms for intake pack, 79–83
setting the groundwork for, 56
in stages of coaching, 55–56
contrast frame, 329
contrastive analysis, 290–293
Cope, Stephen (psychotherapist), 229
core values. *See also* values
  assessing decisions based on,
      146–147, 148
  discovering yours, 83, 142–143
  as end values, 142
  in everyday life, 148–149
  as guiding principles, 148–149
  responding to violations of, 147–148
  setting priorities for, 143, 145, 146
counting monkeys exercise, 233
counting the days exercise, 202
courses, 351, 352
Covey, Stephen (*The 7 Habits of Highly
      Effective People*), 214, 275
creativity, activities for unlocking, 321
Critic role, 130, 131
Csikszentmihalyi, Mihaly (*Flow*), 153
curiosity
  fostered by coaching, 63
  playful quality of, 65–66
  questions fostering, 66–67
  about reactions under pressure, 244

• *D* •

dark side, acknowledging, 36, 327
*The Dark Side of the Light Chasers*
      (Ford), 327
DASE model, 162–163
debating level of listening, 117–118
decision-making
  ecology check for, 320–321
  questions to ask about outcomes, 320
  values-based, 146–147
deletion, 110
delight, in DASE model, 162

depression, vision affected by, 289
desired state. *See also* goals
  dream future based on values, 149
  lily pads experience for, 109
  outcome as, 93
  powerful questions about, 335–342
  setting expectations for, 78
detail metaprogram, 172, 173–174
diary
  colour-coding system for, 202–203
  during disappointments, 230
  journaling, 327–328
difference metaprogram, 172, 219
digital language, 30
Dilts, Robert (NLP developer)
  Big C style of coaching by, 15, 151–152
  Disney strategy created by, 129
  Logical Levels model developed by, 21, 87
  online Encyclopaedia of NLP, 88
  SCORE model developed by, 87, 88
  *Sleight of Mouth*, 329
  on superficial truth and deep truth, 35
disagreements. *See* conflict
disappointments
  breathing out problems, 232–233
  chain reaction from, 228
  diary during, 230
  Drama Triangle game, 234–237
  as fact of life, 227
  increasing clients' awareness during, 228
  physical symptoms from, 229
  self-care after, 230–231
  staying with feelings during, 228–230
  top ten in Britain, 234
disbanding stage of teams, 225
Disney strategy
  chair arrangement for, 132
  coaching through the roles, 131–133
  creation of, 129
  Critic role in, 130, 131
  Dreamer role in, 130
  questions to ask, 130–131
  Realist role in, 130, 131
Disney, vision statement of, 163
Disney, Walt (filmmaker), 129

dissociation
 as being at effect, not at cause, 151
 defined, 277, 294
 dissociating from the moment, 278,
  294–295
 Fast Phobia Cure using, 314–315
 in grief and loss process, 240
distortion, 108
doing, being versus, 63
downloading level of listening, 116–118
Drama Triangle game
 graphic model of, 235
 meta position in, 235
 persecutor position in, 236–237
 rescuer position in, 236
 unconscious, 234
 victim position in, 235–236
dramatising, avoiding, 346
Dreamer role, 130

## • E •

ecology check
 Cartesian questions for, 115
 for goals, 127–128
 for outcomes of decisions, 320–321
 in Six-Step Reframe exercise, 331
ecstasy, in DASE model, 162, 163
effects
 being at effect versus at cause, 32, 151
 exploratory questions for, 95
 as meta outcomes, 94
 outcomes versus, 88
 in SCORE model, 94–95
effort. *See* trying hard
eight-second rule for questions, 112
80/20 rule, 155, 309
Elfline, Jan (coach), 307
EMCC (European Mentoring and Coaching
  Council), 51, 351
emotional self-care, 231
emotional states. *See also* conflict;
  disappointments; *specific states*
 affects of, 302
 allowing negative states to slide away,
  306–307

anchoring positive states, 304–306
 baseline, 303–304
 dealing with gremlins, 307–311
 described, 301
 labelling, avoiding, 302
 mind-body link of, 315
 as natural, 302
 overcoming fear, 311–316
 splitting yourself into parts
  due to, 318
emotional well-being, time line tour of, 281
empathy listening, 117, 118
empowering beliefs, 295–298
end values, 141–142. *See also* values
ending coaching relationships, 349
ending coaching sessions
 concluding questions for, 76
 inquiry questions for, 77, 115–116
 quick-win sessions, 101–102
 with rapport, 72–73, 76
 reinforcing need for action, 101–102
environment level, 98
Epstein, Todd (NLP developer), 88
Erickson, Milton (hypnotherapist)
 confusion technique of, 44
 Milton Model based on, 38
 as NLP model, 20
 reframing by, 328
 voice use by, 179
Estée Lauder, vision statement of, 163
ethics. *See also* confidentiality
 as core competency, 58–59
 ICF standards of, 53, 54
 for internal coaches, 52–53
 key points for, 54
European Mentoring and Coaching Council
  (EMCC), 51, 351
every behaviour has a positive intent
  (presupposition), 68, 222
evidence procedure
 for goals, 124–125
 for values, 144
executive coaching, 13, 51–52
exemplars
 choosing, 195–196
 external behaviour of, 196, 197

imagining, Wisdom of Mentors exercise for, 198–199

internal processing by, 196, 197

modelling, 42, 196

new strategies from, 196–197

Exit, in TOTE model, 187

expectations

for success, sharing, 62

unclear, conflict from, 250

experimenting, 354–355

exploratory questions

examples of, 67

for fears, 312

for Logical Levels model, 98, 99, 100

for resources, 94, 126, 339

for SCORE model, 91–92, 93, 94, 95

turning information-gathering questions into, 67

external metaprogram, 172, 176–177, 219

external perspective in coaching, 11

eye accessing cues, 133, 190–192

● **F** ●

failure, as feedback (presupposition), 222, 254

falling in love with clients, 348

family, vision statement for, 166

Fast Phobia Cure, 314–315

fear

building confidence, 312–313

common fears, 311

exploratory questions for, 312

of one's potential, 36

panic attacks, handling, 246

releasing phobias, 313–316

feedback

gaining insight from, 263–264

giving and receiving, 254–255

questions for soliciting, 263–264

there is no failure, only feedback (presupposition), 222, 254

fight or flight response, 245

filtering information, 37, 108–110. *See also* metaprograms

first impressions, making, 72

first perceptual position. *See* perceptual positions

first step for goals, 128–129, 341–342

flexibility. *See* behavioural flexibility

*Flow* (Csikszentmihalyi), 153

flow states

allowing space for, 155–156

being in the moment, 156

characteristics of, 152, 153, 154

Csikszentmihalyi's research on, 153

detecting in clients, 152

interferences preventing, 152, 155, 159

maintaining in challenging times, 158–159, 196

questions for shifting into, 156–158

thankfulness practices for, 155

ways of accessing, 155–156

Ford, Debbie (*The Dark Side of the Light Chasers*), 327

forming stage of teams, 221–222

four-step Communication model, 211–212

fourth perceptual position. *See* perceptual positions

Frary, Mark (*The Origins of the Universe For Dummies*), 283

friendship with clients, 348

fun

mapping across resources, 290

powerful questions about, 114

● **G** ●

Gallwey, Tim (coach)

definition of coaching by, 11

equation for performance by, 13, 338

*The Inner Game of Tennis*, 11, 13, 338

on Self 1 and Self 2, 14

generalisation, 108, 109

Gervais, Ricky (TV director), 259

Gilligan, Stephen (Erickson student), 179

global metaprogram, 172, 173–174, 219

goals. *See also* desired state

agenda for coaching, 83–86

conflict from lack of, 250

context defined for, 125

Disney strategy for, 129–133

goals *(continued)*
  dream future based on values, 149
  ecology check for, 127–128
  engaging the RAS for achieving, 111–112
  establishing for teams, 223
  evidence procedure described for, 124–125
  first step for, 128–129, 341–342
  necessary resources identified for, 125–127
  New Behaviour Generator for, 133–135
  positive statement for, 122–123
  questions to ask about, 123, 124, 125, 126, 128, 130–131, 335–342
  self-initiated, self-maintained, and within control, 123–124
  SMART principles for, 122
  value of setting, 121
  well-formed conditions for, 122–129
gremlins
  defined, 307
  identifying by drawing, 310–311
  ill effects of, 307
  peacekeeper, 307, 308–309
  perfectionist, 307, 309
  procrastinator, 307, 309–310
grief and loss process
  described, 22
  development of, 237
  dissociation in, 240
  grief response in, 237
  reestablishing identity, 161–162
  resolved grief, 239–240
  submodality work in, 238, 240, 241
  unresolved grief, 238, 239
  unresolved versus resolved loss, 239
Grinder, John (NLP co-creator)
  on breathing, 232
  content-free coaching by, 286
  early NLP development by, 19, 29
  eye accessing cues noticed by, 133
  Milton Model creation by, 38
  modelling by, 194–195
Grove, David (therapist), 40

gustatory sense. *See also* VAK or VAKOG senses
  as a modality, 286
  in NLP Communication model, 106
  for representing the future, 111
gut voice, 180

● *H* ●

habits. *See also* metaprograms; patterns; strategies
  appreciative, 256
  development over time, 185
  identifying with, 185
  new, establishing, 183–184
  new, ingraining, 202
  for self-care, 231
  structures creating freedom from, 200
  Yes/No lists for, 200–201
handshake, 72
happiness, choosing, 23
having choice is better than not having choice (presupposition), 222
Hawking, Stephen (physicist), 283
head voice, 180
health, time line tour of, 281
heart voice, 180
hobby, for bale-out space, 321

● *I* ●

ICF. *See* International Coach Federation
icons in book margins, explained, 5
identity
  defusing criticism at level of, 34
  exploratory questions for, 100
  inquiry questions for, 116
  Logical Level, 100
  reestablishing after loss, 161–162
  in statement of life purpose, 164–165
if what you're doing isn't working, do something different (presupposition), 222
imagineering, 129

imperfection, accepting, 54, 55
in-combination people, 39
incongruence, 326
incremental and continuous change, 10, 75–76
individuals are resourceful (presupposition), 35–36, 68, 222
influencing, in Communication model, 211, 212
information-gathering questions, 66, 67
informing, in Communication model, 211, 212
Ingham, Harry (Johari window inventor), 104
*The Inner Game of Tennis* (Gallwey), 11, 13, 338
inquiry questions
  ending coaching sessions with, 77, 115–116
  time required for answering, 116
inspiring, in Communication model, 211, 212
intake process
  capturing the current reality, 78
  defined, 78
  intake pack for, 73, 78–83
  models for quick wins, 78
  overview, 77–78
intellectual well-being, time line tour of, 281–282
intents
  every behaviour has a positive intent (presupposition), 68, 222
  honouring, 193–194
  of parts of yourself, 324, 325
  setting for sessions, 75
internal clients, confidentiality with, 52–53
internal conflict. *See* parts integration
internal metaprogram, 172, 176–177, 219
internal perspective in coaching, 11
International Coach Federation (ICF)
  core coaching competencies of, 58–61
  definition of coaching by, 11
  standards of ethical conduct, 53, 54
  training programs from, 351
  website, 51

Internet resources
  accredited training programs, 351
  clean language site, 40
  coaching organisations, 51
  core coaching competencies, 58
  Encyclopaedia of NLP, 88
in-time people
  as associative regarding time, 277
  characteristics of, 274
  described, 39, 261
  dissociating from the moment, 278
  time line of, 273
  working with, 273, 274–275
introduction stage of coaching, 19
intruding effectively, 182–183
intuition's role in coaching, 65
involving, in Communication model, 211, 212
italic text in this book, 2

job. *See* work
Johari window model, 104–105, 252
journaling, 327–328. *See also* diary

• *K* •

Kahane, Adam (*Solving Tough Problems*), 117
*kairos* perspective on time, 271
Karpman, Stephen (Drama Triangle creator), 234
Katie, Byron (*Loving What Is*), 299
kinaesthetic sense. *See also* VAK or VAKOG senses
  identifying submodalities of, 290
  as lead representational system, 107
  as a modality, 286
  with New Behaviour Generator, 135
  in NLP Communication model, 106
  for representing the future, 111
  submodality intervention using, 289
  words or phrases of, 29
'know nothing' space, 42, 346

Korzybski, Alfred (scientist), 33
Kuhnke, Elizabeth (*Body Language For Dummies*), 72, 155

### • L •

language. *See also* communication; Meta Model; VAK or VAKOG senses
  clean, 40
  of global/detail metaprograms, 173–174, 219
  of internal/external metaprograms, 177, 219
  lead representational system clues, 107
  of options/procedures metaprograms, 174, 219
  positive statement of goals, 122–123
  of proactive/reactive metaprograms, 219
  of sameness/difference metaprograms, 219
  sensory-specific words or phrases, 29
  structure versus content, 171
  of toward/away from metaprograms, 175–176, 219
  values words, 143
Lawley, James (*Metaphors in Mind*), 40
lead representational system, 107–108
leading, rapport needed for, 26, 73
learning, facilitating, 60–61
life coaching, 12
life purpose. *See also* purpose
  defining in your own words, 163–165
  questions to ask about, 161
lily pads experience, 109
limiting beliefs
  changing to empowering beliefs, 296–298
  defined, 295
  examples of, 296
listening. *See also* pacing
  active, defined, 116
  developing the skill of, 116–117
  with empathy, 117, 118
  four levels of, 117–118
  non-verbal skills for, 118–119
  patience during, 344

power of silence, 64
refocusing a conversation, 344–345
*Live Life, Love Work* (Burton), 162
Logical Levels model
  behavioural level, 98
  beliefs and values level, 99
  capabilities and skills level, 99
  choosing an appropriate level, 101
  concentrating on a single level, avoiding, 98
  described, 21, 96
  environment level, 98
  exploratory questions for, 98, 99, 100
  identity level, 34, 100
  powerful questions using, 115
  purpose level, 100
  pyramid graph of, 97
loss. *See* grief and loss process
*Loving What Is* (Katie), 299
Luft, Joseph (Johari window inventor), 104

### • M •

the map is not the territory (presupposition), 33, 103, 221
mapping stakeholder relationships, 109–110
mapping submodalities across resources, 31, 290–293
matching and mirroring, 27–28
McDonald's, vision statement of, 163
meaning, finding in work, 159–161
the meaning of any communication is the response that you get (presupposition), 112, 222
means values, 141–142. *See also* values
memories as triggers, 304
mental maps
  engaging the unconscious mind in, 110–112
  growth from coaching, 103
  internal representation of, 107
  the map is not the territory (presupposition), 33, 103, 221
mental self-care, 231

mentors. *See also* exemplars
  coaches compared to, 16, 57
    supervisors for coaching, 17, 50, 356–357
    Wisdom of Mentors exercise, 198–199
Merchant, Stephen (TV director), 259
message of communication, 213
Meta Model
  described, 21
  further information, 37
  modal operators of necessity in, 140
  overview, 37–38
meta outcomes, effects as, 94
meta position
  for Drama Triangle game, 235
  level of listening, 118
meta-mirror exercise, 216–218
*Metaphors in Mind* (Lawley and
    Tompkins), 40
metaprograms
  allowing space for, 183
  breaking unhelpful patterns, 178–179
  as clues to others' motivations, 62
  coaching styles for, 174, 175, 176, 177
  as contextual, 173, 220
  described, 21, 62, 172
  global/detail, 172, 173–174, 219
  insights derived from, 173
  internal/external, 172, 176–177, 219
  listening for, 218–220
  options/procedures, 172, 174–175, 219
  proactive/reactive, 172, 219
  sameness/difference, 172, 219
  time perspective, 172
  toward/away from, 172, 175–176, 219
method of communication, 213
Milton Model, 37, 38
mimicry, matching versus, 28
the mind and body are interlinked
    (presupposition), 222
mind-body link, 315
*Miracle in the Andes* (Parrado), 146
mirroring and matching, 27–28
modal operators of necessity, 140, 258
modalities, 286. *See also* representational
    systems; submodalities

modelling excellence
  benefits of, 22, 41, 195
  for building confidence, 313
  for coaching skills, 354
  exemplars for, 42, 195–197
  for new strategies, 196–197
  presupposition for, 222
  questions leading to, 42
  Wisdom of Mentors exercise for, 198–199
*Molecules of Emotion* (Pert), 315
moment, being in the. *See also* flow states
  associating with the moment, 278, 294
  as association, 277
  choosing happiness and peace, 23
  dissociating from the moment, 278,
    294–295
  as essential to coaching, 294
  flow states accessed by, 156
  during panic attacks, 246
  questions to ask about, 157
  spontaneity allowed by, 86
  for through-time people, 278
  by in-time people, 39, 261
monkey counting exercise, 233
monochronic time system, 39
monofont text in this book, 2
Montgomery, 'Monty' (Field Marshall), 249
moods, mapping across resources, 290
motivation
  as client's province, 62
  lily pads experience for, 109
  Logical Levels model for inspiring, 96
  metaprograms as clues to, 62
  unresolved grief and lack of, 238
  weight loss example, 128

networking
  benefits of, 266
  online, 266–267
  questions for improving, 267–268
*Neuro-linguistic Programming For Dummies*
    (Burton and Ready), 38, 60, 172, 189,
    287, 295

*Neuro-linguistic Programming Workbook For Dummies* (Burton and Ready), 60, 172, 287
New Behaviour Generator
  auditory sense with, 134
  eye accessing cues with, 133
  kinaesthetic sense with, 135
  uses for, 133
  visual sense with, 134–135
NLP Jargon Alert icon, 5
NLP modelling. *See* modelling excellence
NLP (Neuro-linguistic Programming)
  coaching compared to, 10
  coaching's fit with, 17–18
  defined, 17
  development of, 19–20
  dramatic breakthroughs with, 10
  as experiential, not cognitive, 25
  key principles of, 20–21
  online Encyclopaedia of NLP, 88
  stages of interaction in, 19
  tools and models in, 21–22
nominalisation, 62–63
non-verbal communication. *See also* body language; tone of voice
  for first impressions, 72
  for listening, 118–119
  matching and mirroring, 27–28
  for rapport building, 27–28
non-violent communication, 253
norming stage of teams, 224

● *O* ●

*The Office* (TV programme), 259
olfactory sense. *See also* VAK or VAKOG senses
  as a modality, 286
  with New Behaviour Generator, 135
  in NLP Communication model, 106
  for representing the future, 111
'Only do what only you can do' mantra, 199
opening coaching sessions
  effective questions for, 74–75
  intake pack for first session, 73, 78–83
  making a good first impression, 72

preparation for, 73–75
  with rapport, 72–73
  setting intents, 75
  welcoming clients, 73–74
Operate, in TOTE model, 187
options metaprogram, 172, 174–175, 219
*The Origins of the Universe For Dummies* (Pincock and Frary), 283
ought to or should, 140, 258
outcome frame, 248, 329
outcome thinking, 21
outcomes
  of communication, 212
  defined, 93
  ecology check for, 320–321
  effects versus, 88
  evidence procedure for goals, 124–125
  facilitating results, 60–61
  powerful questions about, 93, 114, 335–342
  in SCORE model, 93
  seeking for conflict resolution, 247, 248

● *P* ●

pacing. *See also* listening
  art of, 344
  for mitigating passion, 169
  for rapport building, 26, 73
panic attacks, handling, 246
parent role, avoiding, 347
Pareto principle, 155, 309
Parrado, Fernando (*Miracle in the Andes*), 146
parts integration. *See also* congruence
  described, 22
  ignoring a part, dangers of, 317
  integrating conflicting parts, 324–326
  journaling for, 327–328
  parts as non-integrated fragments, 318
  reframing for, 328–331
  splitting yourself into parts, 317–318
  support during change, 318–323
passion. *See also* flow states
  behavioural flexibility needed with, 168
  DASE model for, 162–163

pacing needed with, 169
for transforming conflict into action, 256
unmitigated, 168
in worklife, 159, 160–161
patterns. *See also* metaprograms
collusion, 40, 179–183
establishing new habits, 183–184
unhelpful, breaking, 178–179
peace, choosing, 23
peacekeeper gremlin, 307, 308–309
Penrose, Roger (physicist), 283
people are more than their behaviour
(presupposition), 34–35, 222
peptides, 315
perceptual positions
for conflict negotiation, 249–251
described, 22, 215
meta-mirror exercise for, 216–218
moving into, 216
perfectionist gremlin, 307, 309
performance
breathing linked to, 232
as potential minus interference, 13, 338
performing stage of teams, 224–225
Perls, Fritz (father of Gestalt), 20
permission, asking for difficult areas, 182
persecutor, Drama Triangle game position,
236–237
personal brand, 262–263
personal coaching, 12
*Personal Development All-in-One For
Dummies* (Burn), 152
personal history, 339
Pert, Candace (*Molecules of Emotion*), 315
phobias
debilitating effect of, 313
Fast Phobia Cure for, 314–315
secondary gains of, 316
physical self-care, 231, 322–323
physicist's view of time, 283
physiological changes with conflict, 245
pictures as reminders, 102
Pincock, Stephen (*The Origins of the
Universe For Dummies*), 283
Platts, Brinley (*Building Self-Confidence For
Dummies*), 312

Player, Gary (golfer), 353
polychronic time system, 39
positive statement of goals, 122–123
potential
fear of one's, 36
performance as interference subtracted
from, 13, 338
powerful questions
building a repertoire of, 113
Cartesian questions, 114–115
eight-second rule for, 112
evaluating the power of questions, 112
examples of, 113–114
indicators of, 112
about life purpose, 161
Logical Levels model for, 115
sequence of ten questions, 335–342
practicing coaching, 353
predicates, 28, 29
pre-frame stage of coaching, 19
presence, coaching, 59–60
present state, 78
present, the. *See* moment, being in the
presuppositions
core principles for teams, 221–222
defined, 21, 32
every behaviour has a positive
intent, 68, 222
having choice is better than not having
choice, 222
if what you're doing isn't working, do
something different, 222
individuals are resourceful, 35–36,
68, 222
informing coaching sessions, 67–68
the map is not the territory, 33, 103, 221
the meaning of any communication is the
response that you get, 112, 222
the mind and body are interlinked, 222
modelling successful performance leads
to excellence, 222
people are more than their behaviour,
34–35, 222
there is no failure, only feedback,
222, 254
you cannot not communicate, 222

priorities, setting
  colour-coding schedules and diaries,
    202–203
  for communication, 212–214
  for time, 39
  for values, 143, 145, 146
private clients, confidentiality with, 50–51
proactive metaprogram, 172, 219
procedures metaprogram, 172, 174–175, 219
process, content versus, 40
procrastination, mapping across
    resources, 290
procrastinator gremlin, 307, 309–310
professional coaching bodies, 51, 357–358
professional wheel form, 81, 82
project, for bale-out space, 321
purpose
  exploratory questions for, 100
  finding after loss, 161–162
  inquiry questions for, 116
  Logical Level, 100
  personal, defining, 163–165
  questions about life purpose, 161
  self-care relating to, 231
  for transforming conflict into action, 256
  vision statement, 165–166

## • *Q* •

Quadrant II activities, 275
quality target for coaching, 356
quantum theory, 283
questions. *See also* exploratory questions;
    powerful questions
  concluding, 76
  eight-second rule for, 112
  as-if, 113, 126
  information-gathering, 66, 67
  inquiry, 77, 115–116
quick-win sessions
  client's need for, 78, 87
  example using SCORE model, 89–91
  forwarding awareness into action, 101–102
  Logical Levels model for, 96–101
  pictures as reminders, 102
  SCORE model for, 88–96

## • *R* •

rapport
  characteristics of, 26
  connecting with the whole person, 30–32
  ending coaching sessions with, 72–73, 76
  as key principle of NLP, 20
  laying foundations for, 26
  non-verbal communication for, 27–28
  opening coaching sessions with, 72–73
  pacing for, 26, 73
RAS (Reticular Activating System), 110, 111
reactive metaprogram, 172, 219
Ready, Romilla
  *Neuro-linguistic Programming For
    Dummies*, 38, 60, 172, 189, 287, 295
  *Neuro-linguistic Programming Workbook
    For Dummies*, 60, 172, 287
Realist role, 130, 131
recording coaching sessions, 180–181,
    355–356
reframing
  back-track frame, 329
  in coaching conversations, 329
  contrast frame, 329
  described, 22, 329
  as-if frame, 109, 328, 329
  outcome frame, 248, 329
  Six-Step Reframe exercise for, 330–331
relationships. *See also* communication;
    teams
  four-step Communication model for,
    211–212
  identifying stakeholders, 208–209
  mapping stakeholder relationships,
    109–110
  perceptual positions in, 215–218
  stakeholders, defined, 207
Remember icon, 5
representational systems. *See also* VAK or
    VAKOG senses
  described, 21, 28
  digital language, 30
  early discoveries about, 29
  lead system, 107–108

as modalities, 286
with New Behaviour Generator, 134–135
in NLP Communication model, 106
notation system for eye accessing cues, 191
notation system for strategies, 189, 190
for representing the future, 111
reputation
getting feedback on yours, 263–264
importance for career, 262–263, 264
rescuer
avoiding the role of, 345
Drama Triangle game position, 236
resolved grief, 239–240
resolved loss, 239
resourceful states, 303
resources
exploratory questions for, 94, 126, 339
identifying for goals, 125–127
individuals are resourceful (presupposition), 35–36, 68, 222
mapping submodalities across, 31, 290–293
in SCORE model, 93–94
results, facilitating, 60–61. *See also* outcomes
Reticular Activating System (RAS), 110, 111
*A Return to Love* (Williamson), 36
Rogers, Carl (therapist), 20, 54
roles
conflict among, 323
conflict from confusion in, 250
in Disney strategy, 130–133
in Drama Triangle game, 235–237
in statement of life purpose, 165–166
traps to avoid, 345, 347

• **S** •

sadness, in DASE model, 162, 163
sameness metaprogram, 172, 219
Satir, Virginia (family therapist), 20
schedule, colour-coding system for, 202–203
school, vision statement for, 166

SCORE model
acronym explained, 88
causes in, 92
described, 21
development of, 88
effects in, 94–95
example form, 95–96
example quick-win session, 89–91
further information, 88
graphic model of, 89
initial use of, 95
outcomes in, 93
questions useful for, 89, 91–92, 93, 94, 95
resources in, 93–94
symptoms in, 91–92
traditional NLP compared to, 88
second perceptual position. *See* perceptual positions
secondary gains
behaviours reinforced by, 40–41, 68
as cause of a problem, 92
ecology check for uncovering, 127
meeting for goals, 127
of phobias, 316
questions for uncovering, 41
Self 1 and Self 2, defined, 14
self-care
after disappointments, 230–231
during times of change, 322–323
self-coaching, 1, 22–23
self-criticism at identity level, defusing, 34
self-initiated goals, 123–124
self-maintained goals, 123–124
sensory awareness principle of NLP, 20
*The 7 Habits of Highly Effective People* (Covey), 214, 275
shadow side, acknowledging, 36, 327
shaking hands, 72
should or ought to, 140, 258
silence, 64. *See also* listening
Six-Step Reframe exercise, 330–331
*Sleight of Mouth* (Dilts), 329
small c style of coaching, 15
SMART principles for goals, 122
Smith, Suzi (NLP developer), 293

Socrates (philosopher), 42
*Solving Tough Problems* (Kahane), 117
spirituality, time line tour of, 282
splitting yourself into parts. *See* parts
    integration
stakeholders. *See also* relationships; teams
  in business, 208–209
  defined, 207
  identifying, 208–209
  mapping relationships of, 109–110
  personal relationships, 209
state of a person. *See also* emotional
    states; *specific states*
  baseline states, 303–304
  challenging, 35
  creation of, 107
  defined, 35
  desired state, 78
  flow states, 152–159
  present state, 78
  resourceful, 303
storming stage of teams, 222–224
strategies
  applying to a new context, 188
  copying, 188
  defined, 185
  exemplars for, 195–197
  eye accessing cues for, 190–192
  honouring the intent of, 193–194
  modelling, 196–197
  notation system for, 189, 190
  questions to ask about, 188
  redesigning, 192–193
  structures creating freedom from, 200
  sub-strategies, 186
  TOTE model for, 187–188
  triggers for, 186
  unhelpful, changing, 188
  unpacking, 22, 188–190
  Wisdom of Mentors exercise for, 198–199
strengths
  confessing in a team, 167–168
  list for intake pack, 82–83
structure
  checking in with another, 203
  colour-coding schedules and diaries,
    202–203

content versus, 18, 171
  freedom created by, 200
  of subjective experience, 196
  Yes/No lists, 200–201
submodalities
  benefits of working with, 22
  defined, 20, 286
  for defusing conflict, 247
  in grief and loss process, 238, 240, 241
  interventions using, 287, 288, 289
  introducing clients to, 287
  mapping across resources, 31, 290–293
  for perceived loss, 237
  power of playing with, 286
  questions for identifying, 288, 290
success
  external measures of, 193–194
  as a nominalisation, 62–63
  powerful question about, 340
  sharing expectations for, 62–63
  stories for career, 264–266
summarising, powerful questions for, 114
supervision, coaching, 17, 50, 356–357
Symbolic Modelling, 40
symptoms
  causes versus, 88
  in SCORE model, 91–92

• *T* •

talents
  list for intake pack, 82–83
  in Logical Levels model, 99
teams
  allowing negative states to slide away,
    306–307
  chunking's usefulness for, 167
  confessing strengths together, 167–168
  conflict sources and resolutions, 250
  core principles for, 221–222
  disbanding stage of, 225
  forming stage of, 221–222
  high-performing, behaviours of, 224
  importance of communication in, 220
  norming stage of, 224
  performing stage of, 224–225
  storming stage of, 222–224

Test, in TOTE model, 187
thankfulness, 155, 156
therapy, coaching compared to, 15–16, 59
there is no failure, only feedback
    (presupposition), 222, 254
thinking time during change, 322
third perceptual position. *See* perceptual
    positions
*The Three Marriages* (Whyte), 145
through-time people
    associating with the moment, 278
    characteristics of, 276
    described, 39, 261
    as dissociative regarding time, 277
    time line of, 273
    working with, 275–276
time. *See also* moment, being in the
    arc in coaching, 271
    association versus dissociation
        regarding, 277
    building on past experiences, 319–320
    *chronos* versus *kairos* perspective on, 271
    common struggles with, 38
    managing in sessions, 347–348
    monochronic system of, 39
    physicist's view of, 283
    polychronic system of, 39
    for Quadrant II activities, 275
    setting priorities for, 39
time lines
    creating the desired future, 280–283
    described, 22
    letting go negative emotions using,
        279–280
    personal, identifying, 272–274
    through-time, 39, 261, 273, 275–276
    in-time, 39, 261, 273, 274–275
    time travel exercise, 278–279
    touring three points (exercise), 280–283
    types of, 39
    visualising, 272–274, 277
    working with in-time clients, 273, 274–275
    working with through-time clients,
        275–276
time perspective metaprograms, 172
Tip icon, 5

Tompkins, Penny (*Metaphors in Mind*), 40
tone of voice. *See also* non-verbal
    communication
    assessing a client's, 180–181
    chest voice, 180
    developing skills in, 179
    gut voice, 180
    head voice, 180
    heart voice, 180
    information conveyed by, 179–180
    matching and mirroring, 28
    recording and listening to, 180–181
    when asking questions, 74, 108
    when welcoming clients, 74
TOTE model, 187–188
toward metaprogram, 172, 175–176, 219
training programs, 351, 357
transitions. *See* change
traps to avoid in coaching, 343–349
triggers
    anchors as, 304
    finding for behaviours, 35
    memories as, 304
    for strategies, 186
trust
    being enough for the client, 54
    confidentiality for building, 49–53
    ethics and integrity for building, 54
    during panic attacks, 246
    principles of, 49
    qualities involved in, 49
truth, superficial versus deep, 35, 60
Try This icon, 5
trying hard
    flow defeated by, 155
    Pareto principle of effort, 155, 309
    questions to ask about, 157
Twain, Mark (*The Adventures of Tom
    Sawyer*), 215

• U •

unconscious competence, 43, 353
unconscious incompetence, 43, 353
unconscious mind, 110
unpacking strategies, 22, 188–190

unresolved grief, 238, 239
unresolved loss, 239

• *V* •

VAK or VAKOG senses. *See also*
    representational systems; *specific*
    *senses*
  described, 28
  developing familiarity with, 30
  experience as a result of, 286
  lead representational system clues, 107
  as modalities, 286
  notation system for eye accessing cues,
    191
  notation system for strategies, 189, 190
  sensory-specific words or phrases, 29
values
  assessing decisions based on, 146–147, 148
  beliefs and values level, 99
  core, establishing, 83, 142–143
  dream future based on, 148–149
  end values, 141–142
  establishing evidence for, 144
  establishing for teams, 223
  in everyday life, 148–149
  as guiding principles, 148–149
  importance of understanding, 139, 140
  list for intake pack, 83
  list of, 142–143
  in Logical Levels model, 99
  'Love for Family' example, 141
  meaning of work due to, 159–160
  means values, 141–142
  modal operators of necessity, 140
  must-haves versus shoulds, 140
  of parts of yourself, 318
  questions to ask about, 83, 142, 144, 148,
    149, 336–337
  setting priorities for, 143, 145, 146
  tension between, 145
  for transforming conflict into action, 256
  violated, responding to, 147–148
  in vision statements, 165–166
victim, Drama Triangle game position,
    235–236

vision statements
  of companies, 163
  creating, 165–166
visual sense. *See also* VAK or VAKOG
    senses
  depression's affect on, 289
  identifying submodalities of, 288
  as lead representational system, 107
  as a modality, 286
  with New Behaviour Generator, 134–135
  in NLP Communication model, 106
  for representing the future, 111
  submodality intervention using, 287
  words or phrases of, 29
voice. *See* tone of voice
*Voice of Influence* (Apps), 179, 180

• *W* •

well-formed conditions for goals
  context defined, 125
  ecological evaluation, 127–128
  evidence procedure described, 124–125
  first step identified, 128–129, 341–342
  necessary resources identified, 125–127
  overview, 122
  positive statement, 122–123
  questions to ask, 123, 124, 125, 126, 128
  self-initiated, self-maintained, and within
    control, 123–124
well-formed outcomes
  described, 21
  as goal-setting process, 122–129
Wheel of Life form, 81, 82
Whyte, David (*The Three Marriages*), 145
Williamson, Marianne (*A Return to Love*), 36
Wisdom of Mentors exercise, 198–199
The Work, 299
work
  career coaching, 12
  career recipe creation, 258–261
  communicating confidently about, 266
  economic and social contexts of, 257–258
  exploring types of, 258–261
  finding meaning in, 159–161
  getting feedback at, 263–264

making sense of tough times, 160–161
networking, 266–268
Plan B for job loss, 261–262
preparing for interviews, 264–266
reputation's importance for, 262–263, 264
success stories for, 264–266
traits of dream jobs, 258
vision statements of companies, 163
workshops, 352

Yes/No lists, 200–201
you cannot not communicate
    (presupposition), 222

# FOR DUMMIES®

## Making Everything Easier!™

# UK editions

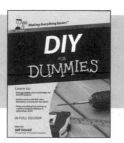

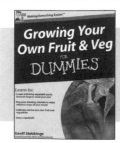

# FOR DUMMIES®

## A world of resources to help you grow

## UK editions

### SELF-HELP

978-0-470-66541-1

978-0-470-66543-5

978-0-470-66086-7

### STUDENTS

978-0-470-68820-5

978-0-470-74711-7

978-0-470-74290-7

### HISTORY

978-0-470-68792-5

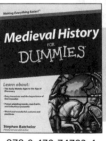

978-0-470-74783-4

978-0-470-97819-1

Origami Kit For Dummies
978-0-470-75857-1

Overcoming Depression For Dummies
978-0-470-69430-5

Positive Psychology For Dummies
978-0-470-72136-0

PRINCE2 For Dummies, 2009 Edition
978-0-470-71025-8

Psychometric Tests For Dummies
978-0-470-75366-8

Raising Happy Children
For Dummies
978-0-470-05978-4

Reading the Financial Pages
For Dummies
978-0-470-71432-4

Sage 50 Accounts For Dummies
978-0-470-71558-1

Self-Hypnosis For Dummies
978-0-470-66073-7

Starting a Business For Dummies,
2nd Edition
978-0-470-51806-9

Study Skills For Dummies
978-0-470-74047-7

Teaching English as a Foreign Language
For Dummies
978-0-470-74576-2

Teaching Skills For Dummies
978-0-470-74084-2

Time Management For Dummies
978-0-470-77765-7

Training Your Brain For Dummies
978-0-470-97449-0

Work-Life Balance For Dummies
978-0-470-71380-8

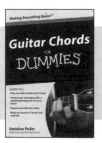

# FOR DUMMIES®

**Helping you expand your horizons and achieve your potential**

## COMPUTER BASICS

978-0-470-57829-2

978-0-470-46542-4

978-0-470-49743-2

## DIGITAL PHOTOGRAPHY

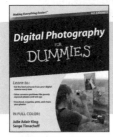
978-0-470-25074-7

978-0-470-76878-5

978-0-470-59591-6

## MICROSOFT OFFICE 2010

978-0-470-48998-7

978-0-470-58302-9

978-0-470-48953-6

Access 2010 For Dummies
978-0-470-49747-0

Android Application Development
For Dummies
978-0-470-77018-4

AutoCAD 2011 For Dummies
978-0-470-59539-8

C++ For Dummies, 6th Edition
978-0-470-31726-6

Computers For Seniors For Dummies,
2nd Edition
978-0-470-53483-0

Dreamweaver CS5 For Dummies
978-0-470-61076-3

Green IT For Dummies
978-0-470-38688-0

iPad All-in-One For Dummies
978-0-470-92867-7

Macs For Dummies, 11th Edition
978-0-470-87868-2

Mac OS X Snow Leopard For Dummies
978-0-470-43543-4

Photoshop CS5 For Dummies
978-0-470-61078-7

Photoshop Elements 9 For Dummies
978-0-470-87872-9

Search Engine Optimization
For Dummies, 4th Edition
978-0-470-88104-0

The Internet For Dummies,
12th Edition
978-0-470-56095-2

Visual Studio 2010 All-In-One
For Dummies
978-0-470-53943-9

Web Analytics For Dummies
978-0-470-09824-0

Word 2010 For Dummies
978-0-470-48772-3